About the Author

Up until joinin | John D. Rowbot-
tom, had not l
 His grandfa   received the Military Medal foi   e was temporarily
blinded. Fortu   1 wouldn't be here
to tell of it.
 John's fathe   the World War II
at one time as   wly formed R.A.F.
Regiment.
 Throughou   were subjected to
their father's a   ing the wars on an
almost daily b:
 So, it was p   s – first Martin, in
the R.H.A. (R   n himself into the
R.C.T. (Royal   Yeovil, Somerset.
(The camp is 1   . Football Club.)
 In those days   job, had to be able to
drive a Land Ro   ugh the military basic
training on a high but when it came to driver training, the army's philosophy
was: if you can drive a 4-tonner and pass your test, then it is easy to drive a
Land Rover. He was probably the only one on the course who had never been
behind a steering wheel in his life, and the first time sitting high up in the cab
looking down on all and sundry filled him with dread and fear! Thus, he was
never able to pass the driving test (though he did a few years later) because the
nerves got the better of him. So, he left after a year. But bitten by the military
bug, just had to join up again, so he joined the R.A.F. on 19 September 1967,
in which he served nine years – firstly as a steward and later to remuster to the
R.A.F. Regiment.
 His time up, he demobbed back to UK in August 1976. He was out about
2/3 years and had to do it all again but not full time now, but in the T.A.
(Territorial Army), but that's another story…
 'Come back, Capt. Mainwaring – all is forgiven!'

Dedication

To my darling wife, Viola.
This book is dedicated to you and I thank God for the day
He brought you into my life.
For being there for me during the good times and the bad.
For being my 'Rock' and always being by my side when
I needed you.

John D. Rowbottom

ADVENTURES OF A COLD-WAR WARRIOR!

AUSTIN MACAULEY PUBLISHERS™

LONDON • CAMBRIDGE • NEW YORK • SHARJAH

A CIP catalogue record for this title is available from the British Library.

ISBN 9781528926249 (Paperback)
ISBN 9781528926256 (Hardback)
ISBN 9781528964616 (ePub e-book)

www.austinmacauley.com

First Published (2021)
Austin Macauley Publishers Ltd
25 Canada Square
Canary Wharf
London
E14 5LQ

Acknowledgements

John Skuse
To my dear friend John – or is it Jack? Without your encouragement and belief in me to get this book in print, it would still be gathering dust on the shelf. For that, I will be eternally grateful.

Norman 'Geordie' Hall
For being my best friend, no matter what! Viola and I knew we could always rely and depend on your friendship – and so it has been proved. Right from when we first became friends until now all these years later.

For putting promotion at risk rather than betray a friend – a real 'brother in arms'!

Alex Goddard
I always look back at our time at Odiham as the best time and posting I had in the R.A.F.

You as my sergeant i/c section were always easy-going – no shouting, ranting and raving, just quietly getting on with the job and never giving me a hard time – or anyone else for that matter.

You always treated everybody as a person and not a number, thank you.

Contents

Foreword

The following adventures you are about to read were courtesy of H. M. Forces, from September 1966 to August 1976.

Throughout the book, I have endeavoured to emphasise the typical 'gritty' service humour and comradeship. They have made me the person I am today – for good, bad or otherwise.

Some of the language and terminology are of another age, some of it over 50 years ago. Some of it will be offensive to persons not used to 'Life in the raw', but it is of a time when it was normal and accepted. It was a man's life and not for the timid or easily offended.

Things are different now; some of the subjects mentioned and language used would not be allowed today and rightly so. For example, in my part of the country during the 1950s and '60s, when referring to someone from an ethnic background the term 'coloured people 'was used as a means of respectful expression. The term 'Black man or Black people' wasn't used; it was thought of as insulting and disrespectful.

I have taken the trouble to change names of those who might take offence at appearing in this book. Otherwise, the events are as I remember them, or as others told them to me, allowing for the passage and the mists of time that may cloud my memory – and my being tongue in cheek now and then.

When working in 'Civvy Street', there will be people who don't like you and with a daggers-drawn look for any opportunity to put you down.

In the forces, it's different; yes, there will be people who don't like you and you don't get along with them, as in all walks of life. But in military circles, it's different.

'Off duty', there may be extreme times when you come to blows with each other, but on duty – now that's a different matter.

'On duty', you are the consummate professional! And personal differences are put aside. Whether digging and sharing a trench together or on patrol, completing the mission/objective is all that counts. Even boring menial tasks are treated the same way. Whatever the job, your mate comes first, above and beyond your wants and needs.

On active service, you are ready – and prepared too! And WILL 'Take a bullet!' meant for the chap in front – or behind! Even if you don't like each other – professionalism – comradeship! Civilians can't understand why someone in the forces would be prepared to lay down his life gladly for another.

On a less dramatic note, you don't let your mate/others down even if it means you getting 'charged' or risking losing promotion. You do not let your mates down as you may need them to do the same for you one day. Just ask any service personnel!

The message I hope to convey through the service humour is one of who served his country and who was and still is part of a very special 'team/unit'. Something more unique, spiritual even. You become part of a 'brotherhood' that lasts a lifetime. One may have been out of the forces for many years but will find themselves subconsciously using the military discipline and reasoning to cope with life outside the military without realising it. It is a bond that binds us together – as long as we live. As the saying goes:

"You can take the man out of the military but you can't take the military out of the man!"

You may say goodbye to your friends, not knowing if you will ever see them again, but the bond will remain with you for all your days. And if you meet up, as I did with Geordie Hall after 40 years, and after a couple of beers you start going over old times – the years just drop away and you are still stuck in that muddy hole together, cold, wet, hungry and cussing the officers/sgts. You're back taking the 'mick', insulting each other.

Real friendship never dies. And I wouldn't want it any other way.

I hope you enjoy reading this book.

Regular Army

R.C.T. 1966-7

Aldershot, Queen Elizabeth barracks

How it all began

I had never been the sort who, through their youth, had wanted to join up; unlike my brother, Martin, who had thought of nothing else throughout our childhood.

I still remember my boss saying, when I told him I was leaving to join up, that he'd been expecting it for a few months now ever since hearing that my brother had already joined up.

I had been gainfully employed at the time as an apprentice plasterer.

My brother, Martin, had been the first to join the army a few months before; he had joined the R.A. (Royal Artillery), later joined the R.H.A (Royal Horse Artillery). Though I had pointed out to him it was a different regiment to which I was going, he told me that with me joining up, he had won a bet with his wife about it.

So came the big day; I was sworn in at the Scunthorpe C.I.O. (Career's Information) office on 17 October 1966.

About a week later, presuming that during that time my documents had been prepared, I proceeded to Queen Elizabeth barracks, Aldershot, to be inducted and kitted out. I arrived at Crookham near Aldershot, Queen Elizabeth barracks, R.C.T. (Royal Corps of Transport).

Induction

Once we had reported in, we were issued bedding and shown to our temporary accommodation for the night. That night in bed for the first time away from home, it felt very strange but I had made my mind up not to dwell on it as it was entirely of my own choosing; it was up to me to make the best of it for my own sake, and so I did.

The first morning, we reported in and were subjected to a series of briefings, lectures on various things such as military and regimental history, military law/discipline, the do's and don't's of service life, on and off duty, the code of comradeship towards your fellow servicemen, etc.

Then the form filling started, reams and reams of it, never-ending, day after day.

This was the first time I had left home and travelled anywhere on my own, so it was quite a scary adventure for me – and I suppose most, if not all, young men and women who leave home for the first time to start a new exciting adventure must feel the same trepidation, not knowing where it will take them. As you can imagine.

We then had the old army customary short back and sides haircut, or should I say a more like a quick head-shave; although I was the only one that got away with it, I still had to go and watch the others get theirs cut. However, I wasn't able to get out of it for long as I and all the others had to get another haircut the following week, and the week after that, and every week to come during our basics.

Stores: kit

Afterwards, we proceeded to the stores where we were presented with even more paperwork. The store man (a large burly sergeant), after sizing you up and taking your measurements just with his eyes, shouted, "Beret-medium, pullover-medium, trousers-medium, socks-medium, boots – what size boots do you take, laddie?" with a wry smile. Yes, you were allowed to speak.

At the end of the counter, you had, yes, you've guessed it, even more forms to fill in. If you had the misfortune to get an item that needed changing…and I had to complain about the boots I was given.

The conversation went as follows.

Sergeant: "What size boots do you take, laddie?"

"10."

"Can't be, laddie, I know you take a 9."

"But I do take a 10, Sgt." The look I got was enough to make the strongest person wilt; I had committed the unforgivable, cardinal sin of disagreeing with the Sgt, but 10 it was.

After making out all the paperwork, you were shuffled along to the next man, where all the kit you had accumulated was shoved into your arms in one great pile, which made your legs buckle under the weight; you shuffled along to someone else behind the counter and were given even more kit.

Eventually, you ended up at the bedding store and were loaded down with four blankets, two sheets, pillowcases, pillows, mattress, mattress cover and bedspread. On top of all the other kit you had acquired. It was enough to break the spirit of lesser men, but not me – I was lapping it up.

After taking our things back to the accommodation, we went for tea laced liberally with that old army standby, 'Bromide', to put paid to any fancy ideas that any would-be randy soldier may or may not have had for that evening in town or in the Naafi.

Afterwards, all but the strongest fell asleep on their beds where they fell, and that's where they lay until morning.

Jabs

In the morning, it was 'Jabs' time, with every one standing in a long line, in alphabetical order, of course; I was stuck somewhere towards the end as it was always to be during my time throughout the services.

The M.O. came along, giving everyone their Jab! By the time he got to me, the one and only needle by now was a very blunt needle.'

This was before the modern method of 'individual-disposable needles'. Though not given just one as we had hoped, but several in each arm, I thought, "This is not why I joined up – to be a human pin cushion." But this was one of those things you had to put up with when in the forces.

P.T.
Afterwards, we had a vigorous session of P.T., by the end of which our arms were aching, fit to drop off, or so we believed. This session was conducted immediately after the morning Naafi break, and naturally some of the chaps were unable to keep their meal down, all was revealed! Though I did OK.

This P.T. and training were, we found out later, to determine who were to train at Queen Elizabeth barracks, Aldershot, or go to Yeovil, Somerset, which was what I was hoping for.

Yeovil
Once we got the results after a week of training and tests, I found out to my delight that I was destined to transfer with most of the others to go to Yeovil.

After that first week, we were shipped off to Yeovil for training. Upon arrival, we had even more forms and papers to fill in and yet even more kit. Finally, we were led to our accommodation, which was to be home for the next few weeks.

I was assigned to 14I/6 Golden Troop, Houndstone Camp, Yeovil, Somerset.

Houndstone camp, Yeovil, Somerset

Best dress uniform, outside the accommodation huts.

Sgt Dredge

We were introduced to our head instructor for the six-week basic training, Sergeant Dredge, a giant of a man, all five foot four of him, also his Cpl assistants. Sergeant Dredge may have been small in build, but what he lacked in inches, he more than made up for in stature; in that he was a giant of a man, a hard but fair man, as we were to find out well before the end of the six weeks training prior to commencing our driver training.

A number of things were said to him and him to me that I will always remember. The first of these things was during the first days we had a parade/roll call. On this particular roll call, I had been offended at first as I and others had been addressed by the officer, Sgt Dredge no less, by our surnames only (as is normal in military circles). As I had been called as usual by my surname in front of the others in the squad, I took a half pace forward, raised my hand to get the attention of Sgt Dredge and spoke up, "John, Sergeant, you can call me John," much to the amusement of the other squad members and NCOs. All chuckled at that. Sergeant Dredge told me politely, straight-faced and without the hint of a smile, that Christian names were not used in the army. I felt a right prat. But how he refrained from laughing I'll never know; he was probably used to daft questions from raw recruits.

Throughout my time in the forces, Sergeant Dredge always remained my favourite NCO. My first, favourite and best D.I. (drill instructor). Whenever I think of Sgt Dredge, even after some 53 years later, I look back fondly on those six weeks in Somerset and I hope when my time comes and I report to that great parade square in the sky, there will be Sgt Dredge telling me, "Get on parade, laddie!"

Inspection

I shall never forget the first time I was inspected; it was in the room we were due to have ourselves, and kit, inspected for the first time. Naturally, most if it not all of us were worried if we'd done enough to get out of a rollicking as we didn't know what to expect or how the standard of the inspection was at the time.

Bum Fluff

I was about fourth from the door, each of the other chaps in turn had received a rollicking; by now, the rest of us were definitely a little unsteady on our feet, shaking a little with fear, dreading the time it would be our turn when Sergeant Dredge would verbally tear us to pieces.

Sergeant Dredge walked past me, stopped, turned around and came back, looking very closely at my chin as I towered above him – all of 5'9" of me.

He then pretended to pull something out of my chin. "What's this, laddie?" he said. Looking down from the corner of my eye and not daring to move, I saw a small grubby finger and thumb shoved up my nose.

"What's this, laddie?" he repeated.

"I don't know," I said.

"Bum fluff," said the worldly wise sergeant. "Its bloody bum fluff, isn't it, laddie? Have you got hair around your balls, laddie?"

Very nervously, I said, "Yes Sergeant!"

"I bet they're not bum fluff, eh laddie? You'd better stand closer to the razor next time, hadn't you?" And with a wink of his eye, he was gone.

So the seal was set for my favourite time during basic training – inspections and drill parades. Though very few would share my enthusiasm for them.

Drill sayings

I will always remember Sergeant Dredge's favourite sayings during drill sessions. "Raise those legs 12", drive them in 18, don't worry about the concrete, it'll give way if you crack your foot down hard enough." And daft as it may seem, we believed him.

Years later in the R.A.F. Regiment, I had the chance of taking a squad of R.A.F. Regiment for drill, I couldn't wait to try out Sergeant Dredge's saying: "Raise those feet 12 inches and drive them in 18"!" I allowed myself a big smile thinking Sgt Dredge would be proud of me if he could see me now.

Closely followed by his other quip when marching, "Open those legs; don't be afraid, you won't lose anything, you have a little bag to catch them in!"

(I always wondered what the Women's Royal Army Corps drill sergeants used to say to the girls drilling.)

Training

The majority of the military training consisted of square bashing, foot and arms drill, map reading, lectures, military law and discipline. Weapon training, and if you proved yourself safe and competent, it culminated in the live firing of weapons on the ranges, such as the S.L.R. rifle, S.M.G., L.M.G. or W.W.2 Bren, which the L.M.G. was developed from. Hand grenades – as one can imagine, once it came to weapon training, this sorted the men from the boys! And proved too much for some of the recruits, resulting in more people leaving/kicked out than any other part of the training. Some just couldn't handle it; they were either dangerous, scared or couldn't get a grip of the weapon training These were classed by the instructors as 'dead wood' starting with about 60/70 recruits, less than 10 passed out on parade.

The more I got a rollicking, the more I would laugh and the more I would get rollicked again, until the drill instructor would get fed up and walk away and pick on someone else, not quite as strong-willed.

I remember when I joined up, my father said to me, "Keep a sense of humour, especially when getting a rollicking, because if you don't, you will certainly be upset and they will pick on you all the more." He, of course, was right.

Can't cope

In the opposite vein, I have seen several of the lads reduced to blubbering hulks as they became victims of the NCO's cruel and vicious tongues.

They were in fits of uncontrollable sobbing and crying; of course, when this happened, the rest of the lads in the room would burst out laughing at them, making some cry all the more and some would even run out of the room. This was great fun for the rest of us; of course, it made it all the more difficult for these chaps to re-enter the room and face their mates who had been laughing at them.

As cruel as it may seem, there was a definite purpose behind these taunts by the staff, as the whole syllabus had been geared to not only teach them the various military skills but the staff also had to sort out the weaklings, the bad wood, they had to find out those who could stand the various and different kinds of pressures and see who would crack and who would remain strong; it was no good letting some pass their training only to find out at a crucial time in the future – say, in an emergency or under fire – when he may have been in charge for him to crack. When the going gets tough, better get rid of them now before it became too late.

More jabs

Whilst at Houndstone camp, we had more and more jabs, which proved my undoing on one occasion for many years to come. We had reported to the medical centre for a few more jabs – this was in the days there was only one needle for a whole squad of men, in alphabetical order. With my surname down towards the rear, the said needle by the time it got to me was, as you may well imagine, very blunt. All I remembered of the incident was waiting in line for my turn.

The M.O.

When the M.O. (Medical Officer), an ex-Indian Army officer and a stickler for discipline, was about three chaps from me, all I remembered was taking a look at that very large needle getting nearer and nearer and feeling a little unsteady on my feet, a hot flush and then nothing more until I came around a few minutes later in a side ward. The medic asked if I'd had breakfast. I told him I hadn't, he then instructed me to tell the M.O. when he came to see me that I had indeed had breakfast, as not only was the M.O. very keen on this point but it was also classed as an official parade, and to miss it was a chargeable offence.

The M.O. was a bit of a character and several stories sprang up about him. Ex-Indian army, and was known throughout the camp as the 'Codeine king' for no matter what you had wrong with you, he always prescribed 'Codeine', the standing joke was, you had a broken leg or an arm hanging off – he would give you Codeine and tell you to rest it.

It certainly had a deterrent effect on the recruits, as no one dared to report sick; it put me off Codeine for life. I've always dreaded being prescribed them by a medic, and only once have been, where I promptly threw them away.

The next most popular story about him was when he was given this job, he was already in retirement and asked if he could have permission to wear his old uniform. The request of course was refused and this was the reason why he was always so grumpy.

Naafi breaks

The Naafi breaks we had there were the best I'd ever come across; throughout my military career, they were never quite as good as at Houndstone camp. I think it must have been for a variety of reasons: the R.C.T. lads were the best I'd ever served with, up to that point. It was a very warm summer and a whole new experience for me. I think it was a combination of a number of reasons why it was the best. The tea, cheese and onion rolls, the jam/cream doughnuts, etc.; we always used to look forward to Naafi breaks. Not to mention it was the swinging sixties, great music, great times.

Great leveller

Basic training for most people was a great leveller – it generally made you or broke you, finishing up at the end of the six weeks or so with everybody having had to make some sacrifices on the way to a greater or lesser extent than your mates and in the end all thinking along the same lines.

Usually, the hard men, the barrack room lawyers, the barrack room comedians had been put in their places, but on the other hand, everyone's confidence had been boosted by anything from 100% plus.

When everybody first arrived on a military camp for the first time, the very great majority were non-smoking, non-drinking virgins, aka, boys!

By the end of their training prior to posting to units, almost everybody smoked, drank and were sampling the delights of the female form to some greater extent than what they had done previously, with almost no exception – including me.

The latter of the two nobody minded, but you were virtually forced into taking up smoking, simply because during the training periods, every 20 minutes or so, when the instructor felt like it, we were told, "Smoke break, those who don't smoke stay and look after the weapons/equipment, while the rest take it easy or go for an early Naafi break."

So after a few days of this, you were so fed up of being taken for a mug that you learned to either smoke like the rest of them and get out of these duties or pretend to smoke and go through the motions.

So by the end of the second week of training, virtually everyone was smoking or going through the motions, so setting the pattern of service life.

Lufton Camp

On the opposite side of the road to our camp was situated Lufton Camp, a training camp the same as ours but for the training of civvy girls into W.R.A.C.'s (Women's Royal Army Corps). We guys of course had our own version of what WRAC was supposed to stand for (Weekly Ration of Army?), Officers groundsheets, etc., etc.

We shared each other's Naafi facilities every other weekend, as the other one would always be closed.

Girl raped

Inevitably, with the camps being situated so close to one another, there was bound to be some trouble, and a WRAC girl was allegedly raped. The girl concerned did have a bit of reputation of a flirt, who liked playing with fire. When the word went around our camp, the general opinion round camp was, "Bet she enjoyed it really!" An uncaring and cruel thing to say, but it reflected the attitude of the times.

So the powers that be set out to find the culprit and every guy on Houndstone camp had to queue up in turn to be interrogated and then sit in front of a screen and read off a card the words the 'rapist' was supposed to have said to this girl.

"Get your knickers off, I'm going to f*** the a*** of you," etc. (If anyone was able to get a pair of the WRAC army issue knickers off, they deserved a medal, not arrest, as they were virtually impossible to remove – even with the girl's permission!) Though when I had to read the card, it took me all my time to try to refrain from laughing, it was written in such a vein. It must have taken me about five minutes to read through in front of a screen, and of course, the victim was on the other side of the screen and knowing this had the effect of making me a bit nervous reading it (we had to read it as if it was us actually going through the rape). On reflection, good try for 'Am Drams' though.

What made it so embarrassing for me was I would never even think of saying such a thing to a girl before, I'd never even seen a girl's 'lady parts' close up at that time (soon to be rectified though!) except in a glossy men's magazine.

In the end, they did catch the culprit, a chap in my room, and to see him and listen to him, you would have never thought it could have been him, which was the usual thing – the culprit was usually the one you least expected.

Financial benefit

Financially, Houndstone camp was very profitable for me: I smoked hardly any at all, got drunk on a couple of pints a night on Scrumpy – Cider @ 9d per pint. (Ah, the good old days!) The camp cinema was only about 1/3d = 6½ new pence to get in whereas civvy cinemas cost about 5/6p (25/30 new pence), unbelievable, wasn't it? A good night out cost about 4-5 shillings old money = £. s. p. Cinema = 1/3d (6½ new pence) + ice cream = 6d (2½ new pence) = 1/9d (14 n.p.) cider (3pts) = 2/3d (22 n.p.) Cheese board = 6d (2½ n.p.) total (in old pence) = 4/6 shillings per night out.

The same night out today would probably cost about £20 without the cinema.

Chippies

The 'local' we all used (it was to be my first local) was the 'Carpenter's Arms', very affectionately known as the 'Chippies' on the main road from Yeovil to the R.N.A.S. (Royal Naval Air Station) at Yeovilton.

Yes, Chippies holds fond memories for me as indeed it did for most of us there. It became the first thing that everybody said we'd buy if we won the football pools (as it was then), myself included, and for most people living within a few miles of it. It had the best atmosphere of any pub I've been in, great locals, plus the WRAC girls came down on their off-duty hours and the prices were the lowest in the area; at times it was so packed that you could barely move.

It just went to show how much business you could attract when you lowered your prices, the customers flocked in.

Over the years, I have been back to Chippies a couple of times since, but it's not the same. It's turned into a 'yuppies' restaurant. No atmosphere and the ultimate sin/crime – *no draught Scrumpy.*

Birthday

In fact, it wasn't long after I had been there that it was my birthday, my 19th.

What a birthday that turned out to be, my best ever. The best and most significant of my young life.

It was without doubt the best birthday I had up to the time, though at first during the day, I made the fatal error of letting the chaps know it was my birthday. This was not helped by the instructor making a comment to the effect the day before when they handed me my birthday cards from home.

My birthday happened to fall on a Saturday and that Saturday it was the turn of the WRAC's Naafi to be open.

The birthday celebrations started at the girls' Naafi. I was bought by the lads a beer, Newcastle Brown ale, and started supping.

My main friends were Fred, Alf and Fred, members of the F.A.F. They were a great bunch. Alf climbed onto a table, what an awe-inspiring sight, all 6'2" of him. He told everyone within earshot that it was my birthday and why don't the girls come over and wish me happy birthday, which the majority of the girls in the Naafi did and one after another, they came over and gave me long, lingering kisses.

It was the first time anything quite like this had happened to me and although I was a bit shocked and embarrassed, I soon got used to it and before long quite enjoyed it.

By the time I left, I wasn't quite the innocent I had been when I had first arrived. I was snogging multiple girls for the rest of the night, most enjoyable, trying to make up for lost time so to speak.

When I looked through the bottom of the glass, I would see another beer waiting for me; when I asked whose it was, I got the reply, "It's yours, shut up and get it down you!" This continued all night, who was I to argue.

We then finished the evening at Chippies, a short walk away from camp down some country lanes.

Bed goes 'walkies'

Needless to say, it was to be 'celebrated' in the traditional army manner, by the lads giving me bumps – 19 of them, plus one for the queen as was traditional – with the Saturday evening drinking session in the girls' Naafi. It was my first (though not to be my last) drunken night out. You can well imagine how I felt the following morning. Whilst in deep sleep from the beer/cider I had consumed, I sensed my bed was moving-rocking; I opened my eyes to see the lads carrying my bed and wardrobe and kit out on to the parade square and dumping me and them there! They all ran off laughing when they realised I was awake with me cussing them; I had the job of dragging my bed/wardrobe and kit back into the accommodation hut, all the time cussing them, and they were all 'tucked up' in bed pretending to be asleep but unable to contain their laughter. After a long struggle, I eventually got everything back in place and went back to bed – feeling horrible! I thought I was going to die, my first hangover, but not my last.

The Barn

The previous evening, I had somehow gotten off with a girl in the Naafi and arranged to spend the day in the way most Sundays were spent at the two camps; we went for a walk around the local country lanes if you were 'really well in' with a girl, if you get my meaning! The afternoons were spent in 'The Barn', which was to be found at the rear of the girls' camp, and it was here where serious couples finished their Sunday walks.

They would be found on a Monday morning by the local farmer/farm-hand, 6 concave depressions in the straw of human shapes, remnants of the previous day's actions such as Rubber French Letters, tattered knickers, stockings, etc. The poor old farmhand must have gotten a bit fed up of clearing the mess every Monday morning and having to clear the straw and replacing it. To the best of my knowledge, it was only ever reported to the camp once and we were subsequently banned from using it.

So thanks, farmer – whoever you were for turning a blind eye.

One girl I remember who I was taking out nearly put me off W.R.A.C. girls for good. Each time I was about to kiss her, she would burst out laughing even during the kiss, very annoying. I didn't know the reason, maybe it was the way I puckered up my lips, who knows, it must have been something I was probably doing, still being a 'learner'. In the end, I got so fed up and told her to p**s off, and I didn't see her again.

Guard duty

During my time there, I was collared for guard duty. I had to sleep on a solid oak bed/pillow in the cell of the guardroom. The first and only time I had been in a cell, fortunately the door was kept open and unlocked. The first time I had to be on guard duty, it was uneventful, we were armed and equipped to deal with anything or to deter any would-be raider or villain.

The army spared no expense to protect us, we were armed to the teeth with a pickaxe handle and one bicycle lamp for the whole guard (in all the times I did guard, the battery always seemed to be about to give out, providing virtually no light at all, and there never seemed to be a spare, if there was, you weren't allowed to use it. Yes, military cutbacks even then!)

What we lacked in weapons, we hoped to make up for in keenness and enthusiasm.

Call out

However, the second guard duty was more eventful. I had just finished my stint and had been relieved and still had my boots and gear on, the orderly officer for the night was my own troop commander Lt Golden – a real character and a gentleman.

First we knew anything was amiss was when he stormed in the guard-room and shouted, "Call out the guard!" We thought, "What the hell has happened?" For a moment, we even visualised a mass attack by the Russian 'Red' army. It was nothing quite as drastic as that. My mate and I being dressed ready were the first out; before we got to the accommodation hut we were heading for, I asked Lt Golden the reason for the call out. He told us that there was a report of a couple of poofs in bed together.

Poofs

We got to the accommodation hut and sure enough, there were two lads asleep together in one bed. One with his arm around the other, the rest of the squad stood around watching.

Without doubt, the guilty parties couldn't have had a harder or worst officer for discipline on Houndstone camp.

Lt. Golden burst into the room, shouted a few orders at some of the lads standing around, literally kicked the poofs out of the bed, threw the mattress on the floor, then while the poofs were still a bit drowsy, Lt Golden told them they had 30 seconds to get dressed and make their way to the guardroom.

Lt Golden counted 30 seconds off on his watch, by which time one lad had his underpants on and the other just had his socks on. So we did as Lt Golden promised, we frog-marched them to the guardroom as they were.

They were thrown in the cell for the rest of the night and first thing in the morning, when they went up in front of the C.O. – the camp Commanding Officer – they were thrown out of the army.

Sam Brown Belt

Whilst in the guardroom, I was asked to 'bull up' Lt Golden's 'Sam Brown Belt'. I quite enjoyed it; it came up a treat after all those 'magic circles'.

Homesick

It was after I'd been there about two weeks that I felt homesick for the first and the last time, the feeling lasted a couple of days only but once I'd gotten over it, I never looked back. I never did go back to live at home with my parents because when I had finished in the forces, I was married with a house of my own.

That weekend, I went to Yeovil and got drunk on spirits for the first time, which didn't help matters at all (vodka and lime).

Kit inspections

Just about the worst thing in any branch of the military – be it the Navy, Army or Royal Air Force – next to stealing one's kit/belongings was ruining one's kit.

This, of course, didn't count when it was your instructor who at times seemed to have a licence to run riot with your kit. After a three- or four-week period of a seven-day week, you had just about got your kit the way it should be, such as bulling your boots for about 3-4 hours a day.

Each day, along came the instructors and threw your kit/bedding from one end of the room to the other; the shirts, shorts, towels, etc. had to be pressed in just a certain way and size, it all took time, and you were expected to stand there and take it. I have seen men reduced to tears as they examined the remains of all those hours and weeks of hard work.

Many a night, we had to stay up until the early hours working on our kit to ensure it would pass inspection the following morning; it didn't take a mere 10 minutes to do it, even blancoeing your web belt – putting on a green type of paste – and cleaning the brasses took about one or two hours alone. Without the rest of your boots and uniform, etc.

You had to stay up until it was done, no matter how tired you were.

Basics was tough, the toughest thing most people had ever done, though when you've finished, you felt better for it, you really felt as though you'd accomplished something. It represented to me the most challenging and interesting time, a complete change from one kind of lifestyle for another.

Range

The very first time we went on the range to fire live ammunition after doing our T.O.E.T.(tests of elementary training) to find out if you were competent – safe enough to fire a weapon.

On the range, one young idiot got himself kicked off the range for being dangerous. I didn't know what exactly had happened but by the time we'd done a route march back to the accommodation block, his locker was empty, his bed stripped and he had left the army. We never found out why or ever saw him again.

Training methods

What I liked about the army's method of training was that you were shown how to do something once and once only, you had to pick it up immediately after watching an NCO or officer, or else get your mates to show you. If you couldn't get the hang of it – tough, you made sure you paid more attention the next time.

We were shown, for example, how to press our kit (uniform) as opposed to ironing it, we found out between us that some lads were better at bulling boots than others, some better at blancoing the webbing and doing the brasses and others. Far better than others at 'pressing' the uniforms than your mate (such as myself). I came up with the idea that why didn't we 'muck in' and help each other, such as I would do their uniforms and they would bull my boots, etc.; they all agreed to this and this was how we worked it throughout basics and it worked very well too.

When someone ended up on a charge, we all 'mucked in' and helped him do his kit, prior to the inspections, such was the comradeship.

Bull nights

Bull nights were another example of comradeship and teamwork; we had to clean out our accommodations once a week and a list was put up with each person set a specific 'room job' to do, i.e., window cleaning, toilets, dusting and cleaning the lampshades, polishing and bumpering the floor, etc. If, during the inspection, a particular job had not been done good enough to pass the inspection, the whole room suffered by being kept in or, worse still, getting another bull night – then woe betide anyone who had let his mates down, he suffered accordingly. I have seen the rest of the room give him the cold shoulder for days. Get beaten up or given a regimental bath. He didn't let the room down again.

Regimental baths

Regimental baths was the usual method of punishment. What used to happen was if someone had let the side down, the punishment was planned a day or two before execution, the only one not to know what was going on was the 'victim' himself.

About five minutes before 'H' hour, one or two would scout the area to make sure no one was coming and prepare the baths, one of freezing cold water and other full of scalding hot water; they would then give a nod to the lookout, pass it down the line until someone in the room saw it, people would work their way casually around the bed of the victim, then pounce and carry him kicking and screaming to the bathroom, where he would be politely asked if he wanted to go in with or without his clothes – quite often, they had no say in the matter.

He was then alternately thrown in the hot bath/cold bath about 3-4 times until it was considered he had learned his lesson.

If the 'victim' was to be punished because he was dirty, i.e., didn't wash or change his socks, wash his feet, etc., then the punishment would carry on from the baths. He would be stripped first, covered in Blanco (for cleaning/polishing webbing), scouring powder, Brasso (for cleaning brasses), boot polish, etc. He was then scrubbed with a large, stiff yard broom until his skin was red raw and then swilled down with a couple of buckets of cold water. It was a waste of time struggling as there were usually about 30 guys taking part. The punishment ranged from one cold bath to the full works, depending on the 'crime'.

Sometimes one got a cold bath because the lads were bored, and then it usually meant everybody in the room got 'done' one at a time. That was fun.

If the lads were a good bunch, the incident was generally forgotten in a few minutes and when you re-entered the room, they took you out to the Naafi and bought you a few beers and everyone had a good laugh about it.

Those lads who had had the misfortune to have a regimental bath made sure that they pulled their weight in future.

I have only once in 10 years, regular service, ever come across someone who had more than one regimental bath, and that was because he was a dirty lazy person and regimental baths didn't seem to bother him, and he had several.

The first one I saw started off by the lads going to Lt Golden and asking his advice how to punish a dirty person; they were told by Golden and the NCOs the traditional army method.

The lad complained the following day to Lt Golden. I overheard the conversation that followed with Lt Golden.

"The lads gave me a regimental bath, sir, what can I do about it?"

"F*****g tough! Laddie, you shouldn't be such a dirty bugger, deserved what you got. Next time, make sure you don't give them a chance to do it again!" and with that he was gone. Leaving this chap open-mouthed and shocked.

I found out at the end of basic training that I was well liked by Golden and the NCOs as I was always 'keen as mustard' in everything they asked me to do and always did my best, sometimes too much.

Baby sitting

The second bull night we were due to do, Lt Golden came to the hut and in front of my mates said, "Rowbottom, what are you doing tonight?"

I told him I was staying in to do my bull night then to the Naafi for a few beers before turning in for the night.

He said, "Wrong, you WERE doing bull night, you are now babysitting for me tonight and don't worry about missing out on a drink, I'll have a few beers in for you." (He did indeed!) "What are you doing tonight, Rowbottom?"

"Baby-sitting for you, sir!"

"I can see you will go far in the army, lad! Right, I'll see you at my house at 8 pm sharp!"

Then he swept out of the room, and some of the lads said, "You crafty bugger, how did you manage to swing that?" Others cursed me because that meant they had my jobs to share out between themselves, meaning extra work for them all.

I used to get back in the early hours of the morning when everybody was asleep (and when the officers' mess bar had shut).

As it turned out, I was the main 'baby sitter' whenever Lt Golden wanted one, not that I was complaining as it was nearly always on bull nights, but now and then on a Friday/Saturday too.

I got out of most bull nights this way.

It wasn't the skive that some thought, as I had to try and get my kit done before I left and if I couldn't get it done, I had to do it when I got back in during the early hours or, on the odd occasion, take it with me to the house, which wasn't exactly the 'done' thing – taking your kit to someone's house.

Up again at about 5:30 am and start helping out with the room jobs, then if you were lucky, you might have time for a bit of breakfast.

More often than not, you missed it as you had too much to do.

Inspections

On top of bull nights, the next headache was the inspection the following morning.

The first you knew was when the senior man/first chap to see the Officer/NCO approach would call the room to attention and, "Stand by your beds, with your (best) boots in your hand."

You used to think that your appearance was immaculate and there was nothing they could pick you up for. Wrong, they could always find something if they wanted, and they usually did. They would pull your appearance to pieces if they so wished.

You used to think prior to the inspection, "Well, they can't pick me up for such and such a thing as I've spent hours on it and it's immaculate, or for that matter, anything at all!"

They did pick you up and it was usually for the things you had spent most time on. For example, your boots.

"How long did you spend on those boots last night?" they would say.

"Three hours, sir."

"Lies, don't tell me lies, you only spent 10 minutes on it and then went out drinking, didn't you?" It was a waste of time arguing with them.

Then they would come out with, "You haven't even tried at all, have you?" This would upset most of us and then they would throw the boots from one end of the room to the other.

We felt angry as they thudded against the door, ruining the bulled toe cap, wasting all that hard work and the long hours you'd put into them. You felt a mixture of emotions, as only someone who has been in that position could understand, one of sadness and rising anger all at the same time that you would have to start all over again. You wanted to kill the NCO.

They still had to be immaculate for the morning. No excuses, this was what basics was all about, to teach you self-discipline and self-control. Yet the officer/NCO knew almost to the hour how much work you had put into it; after all, they had been through it all themselves when they had been doing their basics and it had probably been harder for them.

Ghosts

One evening in the Naafi, we were discussing various subjects towards the end of the evening and someone brought up the subject of ghosts and the supernatural.

Well, we set of for the hutted accommodation and ran across the parade square. Any old 'sweat' knows what happens if you are caught on the parade square.

We ran, there were three chaps in front of me and one behind, I overtook the three in front as we got to the other side of the parade square outside our accommodation. Five people overtook me at the accommodation, and as I came in, there were only four there. I told the others what had happened and they tried to change the subject. It sent a chill down our spines. So to this day, I can't say whether it actually happened or it was a result of the beer/talk.

Whatever, we never went across the parade square in the dark again; we took the long way around.

On the same subject, Houndstone camp (as all pre-war camps) was supposed to be haunted. The camp had been used by the Canadians during the war as a hospital; a patient with a wooden leg had supposedly died in our block. And was supposed to be heard now and then walking the corridors at night. Some of the lads had heard him, they said, though I didn't believe them.

An occurrence happened to me – had it been a joke by my friends or 'something else'?

During the early hours of one morning, I went to the toilets and as I walked down one of the parallel passages, I heard a scraping/shuffling sound followed by a scrape-tap, scrape-tap, like wood on the lino. Scrape-tap, scrape-tap it continued. Thinking it was Fred, my mate, fooling around, I ran as fast as I could to the other adjoining passage where the sound was coming from, which took me about three seconds. There was nothing there but immediately the same sound came from the passage I had just left, scrape-tap, scrape-tap; I ran back to the original passage I had come from, again the sound came from the other passage I had left only 3/4 seconds ago. I didn't know what it was but I certainly wasn't waiting to find out, I decided the toilet could wait until the morning, I ran back to my room – shaking.

When we all came back from the Christmas leave, there were stories about some of the guards skiving and laying on their beds instead of patrolling the camp as they should have. When one of these guards had been lying on his bed instead of patrolling, he awoke and said there had been a man dressed in a monk's habit standing by his bed.

Another awoke in the room another night by the lights being flashed on/off continuously, and every bed in the room turned over one by one including the one on either side of him but he was left untouched, as in both cases the room was empty save for the persons themselves, because their mates had gone home for Christmas. Creepy!

Wreath-laying

One of the highlights of my stay there happened to be that as the senior course, we had the honour of being the bearer party for the wreath of the Commanding Officer of the regiment who was to lay on behalf of the R.C.T. at the remembrance service ceremony at Yeovil town centre.

We were still on the buses and preparing to do our remembrance parade service in November. And ready to form up to march on.

Our officer Lt Golden came onto the bus and told everyone to be quiet and sit down. He then said there had been a slight change of plan; he wanted a good soldier who was smart and good at drill, etc. For a special job. "So," he said, "I want a volunteer to represent the army. Rowbottom, I'll have you! Put your cap on and come outside!" I was cheered, what an honour, most of the chaps were pleased I'd been chosen.

I was briefed and stood next to a WRAC girl, a Wren (Women's Royal Naval Services) and a sailor of the fleet air arm.

I was told that the colonel of the R.C.T. would approach me and take the wreath from me; he approached me and halted a few yards from me.

I thought, "Hello, I'm expected to use my initiative here," so I came smartly to attention, marched forward, halted (on the wrong foot, my mate told me later), saluted him, presented him with the wreath, he took it, I returned his smile. And he said, "Thank you, soldier," which made my day. I took one pace backwards, saluted, a smart right turn and marched away, all the time my heart pounding 20 to the dozen.

I was thanked by all concerned afterwards; they say that every dog has his day and I considered that I had mine that day.

Training exercise

We had all been dreading the end of training exercise, not quite knowing what to expect. It turned out interesting and exciting. The first few days we had adventure training.

Pot holing

Firstly came the pot holing; it was considered the most dangerous and I didn't like it. I was getting stuck quite often in these cracks and crevasses, no matter how cold it was down there, I was sweating profusely, though each time I got free with a bit of help from the chap behind.

I remember at one point, we had to swing across this black bottomless cavern where you couldn't see the bottom, only an inky blackness.

We had a paddy with us and he wasn't keen either, and neither would he go across until Lt Golden promised him a couple bottles of Guinness if he made it. He was across before you could say, 'Bejesus begorra'! We had a good laugh at that, which helped relieve the tension a bit.

Abseiling

This was the most exciting thing I'd done so far, very thrilling, and though at first a little scared, I soon overcame the fear.

When I looked down from top of that cliff at the near vertical drop we were expected to descend, I thought, "No way!"

Lt Golden went down first to show us how it was done; once he had done it, we knew we couldn't get out of it.

I was persuaded to be one of the first to go down, I was very, very nervous. The idea was to teach you confidence in yourself, the equipment and the officer and NCO eventually; I thought that the army was not going to put your life at risk unnecessarily so I had the confidence to try it.

By the time I got to the bottom, I wasn't scared any more, in fact quite pleased with myself. We all had another go and by this time I was raring to go again and tried to persuade Lt Golden to let me have another go, but it was time to pack up for the day; I was disappointed.

We did a map-reading exercise, de-bussing from a moving vehicle (anti-ambush drills) about 25/30 mph.

Route march

During a long hard route march with kit and weapons, I was exhausted. Without knowing what was about to happen, Lt Golden first took my rifle off me to help me, then after I had taken my turn with the 3.5 rocket launcher (anti-tank), he then took that off me too. So I did well but I was still aching all over.

Tank museum

We visited the Royal Armoured Corps museum at Bovington to see the 1st and 2nd W.W. armoured vehicles (mainly tanks) used by both sides during the wars.

Initiative test

On the initiative test, we had to set off from the Black Bull (a pub) to the White Swan (another pub) answering questions on the way and trying to avoid being captured by the enemy (the instructors).

We also passed about 7 or 8 other pubs on the way so by the time we got to the other destination, you could be (and some were) quite drunk.

At one point, we passed a Land Rover hidden in the bushes with the keys in it, but at that time none of us could drive; we found out later that had we been able to, we could have used it to save a lot of walking but I don't think the lads in my party would have taken it had someone been able to drive as that would have been too much like stealing. But that was part of the initiative test.

We were routed past a cottage that we found out later belonged to T. S. Shaw (*Lawrence of Arabia*). Later in his career to join 1 Sqn R.A.F. Regiment – as indeed was I.

Dartmoor prison

We also passed the infamous Dartmoor prison, very dark and foreboding in the late evening mist. We were told that we didn't have to worry about any escaped prisoners as that time of the year it was too cold and wet outside, the prisoners would not want to leave their nice warm prison cells. As it so happened, a prisoner did escape while we were there and we had to team up with some Royal Navy lads and wrens on exercise to search for him. We never heard any more about it, whether he had gotten away or was recaptured.

Final assault

We then had a few days practising our assault/defensive techniques, culminating in a final assault on a position, but during the early hours of darkness, it was decided that a recce (reconnaissance) patrol was to be mounted, made up of volunteers. So three others and myself were 'volunteered' by Lt Golden, no surprise there then; about an hour after setting out, we were ambushed – as I knew all along we would be – and taken prisoners.

The first thing we thought had happened was about a dozen machine guns had opened up on us but all that had happened was a couple of rifles and a light machine gun (L.M.G.) had opened up on us because of one of these brainless idiots on the patrol with us, who did nothing but shout his mouth off the whole time when we were trying to be 'tactical'; the enemy must have heard him coming a mile away, he set off the trip flare, which had us picked out in the darkness as easy targets, we panicked with a capital 'P' while we were being shot at.

We were taken to the enemy's position on the top of a large hill. The captors took away this idiot who thought he was a hard man. He was taken from our view to be interrogated, we found out later that he was asked questions, said he wouldn't answer so was made to strip to his underpants and a couple of buckets of cold water were thrown at him – he cracked straight away.

I was asked by the chief interrogator (Territorial Army), "I hear you like singing?" I saw one of our instructors in the background having a good laugh at this. I replied, "Sometimes!" So without further ado, he shoved an S.M.G. up my nose and said, "Sing! Sing louder!" Who was I to argue, though ironically enough the only songs I could think of at the time were "HELP, I need somebody, help!" and "Somebody help me!" (The Beatles and the Spencer Davis Group respectively). All were laughing at my choice of songs. Though I didn't find it funny at the time!

Eventually, our lads attacked and we watched it. Chanting "Ho-Ho-Ho Chi Min, we will fight and we will win!" (this was during the time of the Americans in Vietnam) constantly during the attack in between thunder flashes and flares going off, rifle and machine guns blasting away and people shouting. I was quite impressed. After the attack, we prisoners were quite lucky in that we didn't have to march another 8/10 miles back to camp as the others but were taken there in one of the enemy's L/Rs.

Upon reaching camp, I was really hungry and all there was to eat was soup and cheese; I had never had cheese up to then but I enjoyed it from that moment on.

After that, it was our turn to dig in, and one chap was partially blinded by a thunder flash; he had been in his trench during the attack and had just happened to look down at the bottom of his trench as the thunder flash exploded. Now whenever in daylight or strong artificial light, he has to wear sunglasses. It was very unfortunate but just one of those things.

During one of the map-reading marches, something happened to make Lt Golden go off his head and storm off and tell us to find our own way back (probably he did it deliberately to test us).

I did well in the first phase of training – military skills – but at one point, it looked as though I might be back-squadded, which meant you failed or struggled with a particular part of training and had to be 'back-squadded' to the next intake that started after yours – usually by two weeks. I was warned about it that I was trying too hard and things weren't going quite the way they should, so I had to re-train myself into thinking, "I don't give a damn whether I do any good or not." It was very hard for me to do but I managed it.

The next phase was driver training.

Driver training

I, unlike most of the men on my intake, had not sat behind a driving wheel of any description before. We were to be trained on Bedford R. L.'s three-tonners (later to be reclassified as four-tonners).

The army's thinking was that if you were trained and able to drive a three-tonner and pass the test, you could easily get into a smaller Land Rover and drive it.

Whereas it was for me more difficult to do it their way, I would have much preferred the Land Rover first. (At this time, the driving test for lorries was the same as a Land Rover; there was no H.G.V. as such.)

The first day behind the wheel was very nerve-wracking for me.

The first period was taken up with the paperwork side, applying for licences, etc. Then in the afternoon; we were shown how to D.I. (Daily Inspection) the wagon, how to check the levels of oil, water, tyres, etc., a skill I still use today. Then in the cab, I was shown how to change gears and so on, we then had a run on the nursery, a small marked-out manoeuvring area, to get the feel of driving.

We then had a turn in the countryside, with me watching how to drive, along a country lane to an abandoned airfield; the civilian instructor told me to get in the driver's seat and drive. I drove around the old abandoned airfield, where after a couple of circuits the instructor told me to stop, got out and said, "Take it around yourself, if you start to panic or don't know what to do next, stop, think about it and what I've told you and carry on!" Before I could complain or ask any questions, he was gone to some old outbuildings for a smoke, he needed it with me. Ha-Ha! I was very nervous at the thought, almost in shock and not ready for this, I didn't feel confident enough yet, but I couldn't argue.

First vehicle I ever drove. (Taken near R.N.A.S. Royal Navy Air Station – Yeovilton, Somerset.)

On reflection, I think it was the best thing he could have done for my confidence, but I couldn't get the hang of it and subsequently was on the carpet a couple of times with warnings. I think one of the bad things about it was the civilian instructors shouted and screamed at you, put me off my stride and made me very nervous; although I told the army guys in charge that I didn't like the civilian instructors, they would not give me a serviceman to train me.

Consequently, I was taken off driver training for a couple of weeks to see if the rest would do me any good – calm me down, Also there was quite a few of guys like this.

On resumption of training, I was better, though not up to the standard they said I should have been after so many hours of training, and was taken off the course and given further rest in a new troop (holding). This upset me a great deal as it meant I had left my friends and wouldn't be passing out with them to their units.

After a while, I tried again and for the last time didn't succeed. I think maybe the reason all along was that I was a bit scared of the immense power and size I was responsible for, and the death and destruction I could have caused had I had an accident. Yes, this was negative thinking but I couldn't get that part of it out my mind, maybe that's what prevented me doing well and passing the test, which had been comparatively easy at the time. Had I been trained on the Land Rover first, I would have probably done alright, but I guess I'll never know.

Although, I made my mind up that one day – no matter what it took or cost or how long – I would have a licence to drive these wagons. I did, some 12 years later, when the test was separate, harder, longer – 2½ hours instead of half an hour – for an H.G.V. licence. Trust me to succeed when it was more difficult; but I had had about 12 years driving experience by then.

A few weeks later, my mates, after finishing their training, were passing out on the parade square – without me. It upset me. Knowing I wouldn't be serving with such a great bunch of lads. I couldn't bear to watch them for long; they were the best bunch of guys one could serve with at the time.

Taken during a break in driving

Holding troop

The crowd I was now with weren't as good mates or close; most were strangers. We felt nothing in common with each other. However, I must not take anything away from the friends I made in the holding troop – Jackie Morrison, a Scot (the one who had his eyesight damaged by a thunder flash), Sam Starret (a paddy), Derrick Hodges (a Taff) and Ernie Combes.

We were good friends and went around together, but it wasn't the same.

Among the jobs we had to do prior to discharge, were further driver/ military training, re-badging to other regiments, etc. We helped out in the guardroom, mucking out the stables (where officers kept their horses, runners for different officers in their offices).

But my regular job was acting as a steward/waiter in the sergeants' mess.

Some of the memories of that place were that there was one of my brother Martin's pals from school, James, who had joined the R.C.T. as well and ended up at Houndstone camp just before I left. He eventually bought himself out as he couldn't stand the strain, such as making his own bed and cleaning the block's windows; he wasn't used to it.

I had bought some Scrumpy (real home-made cider) from a farmer for 6d (2 ½ new pence) per pint, I bought one gallon of 'medium', which tasted like vinegar, and one gallon of 'sweet', which still tasted rough though not as bad. I should have tasted it before I bought it. I decided I didn't like and couldn't stand the 'medium' so I tried to sell it but nobody was interested; eventually, Martin's friend from school, James, said he would buy it from me. So I sold it to him for 1/- (10p) per pint – not a bad little profit for something I didn't like.

We heard through the camp grapevine a few days later that James had drunk too much and it had gone straight to his head and he had gone berserk downtown, where the civvy police had picked him up, so the next thing we heard was he was finished with the army and was out.

It was very strong and potent stuff; in fact, one evening I drank a couple of pints or so in my room in the sergeants' mess and went to sleep, I awoke what I thought was the following morning but in fact it was more than 24 hours later, and when I didn't report to work that day, people were banging on my door and looking through the windows that I was fast asleep and nothing they could do could wake me due to the cider. Though, fortunately, they didn't take any action against me for not turning up for work.

During my deep sleep, I had not heard a thing.

Bank guards

One time I was called upon to be one of the four bank guards when the camp paymaster went to collect the camp's wages for the men/women serving on the two camps.

We were briefed and armed – just in case, with the good old army standby pickaxe handles, though what use they would have been against a band of armed robbers I don't know, we wouldn't have stood a chance.

The look of mock aggression on our faces couldn't have impressed or for that matter put anybody off.

R.S.M.

In the mess and the camp R.S.M., who on the parade square had been looked upon as a God-like figure, feared by all – officers and soldiers alike – was a completely different person, a quaint old father figure who went out of his way to help any lad in difficulties.

One lad for some personal reason had to get home quickly and was unable to due to lack of funds so in front of the rest of the whole camp on parade, the R.S.M. gave him a rollicking for not knocking on his door and telling him his problem as that was what he was there for.

Within an hour, the lad had been given some money by the R.S.M. and transport had been laid on to take him to the railway station and home.

In the mess, the R.S.M. was behind a W.R.A.C.'s NCO and had said to the cook she liked 'stuffing', to which the R.S.M. replied, "Stuffing, did you ask her if she wanted stuffing?" and giving her bottom a playful smack and a wink of his eye, said, "Stuffing, I like stuffing, it's my favourite pastime!" The poor old WRAC blushed even more.

There had been another WRAC sergeant, very young and attractive, about 23/24 years old, in fact she had just taken part in the annual beauty contest for WRAC girls and had come second. She had recently been caught 'having it off' with a male R.C.T. sergeant. She was getting some stick (if you pardon the pun) from some of the mess members including the R.S.M., though it didn't seem to bother her; in fact she seemed to be revelling in all the attention.

Y.M.C.A.
Our leisure time was sometimes spent in the Y.M.C.A. just down the road from both camps. We played darts, billiards, chess…I remember ordering one of the new 'Painting by Numbers', which was all the rage at the time, of the 'laughing cavalier'. I never did collect it once it arrived as I was short of money then. It was there that we heard about Donald Campbell being killed attempting to break the world water speed record in his craft, 'Bluebird', which took off, turned over and disintegrated, and all they had found had been a boot and his helmet.

Elvis
It was whilst at holding troop that my interest in Elvis Presley was born, though my brother had been a fan for years; years later, I went one better. (See 37 Sqn.)

Options
Eventually, I was given the option of leaving the army or transferring to another regiment, because in the R.C.T., everybody had to be able to drive trucks, even the clerks, and I was unable to manage to master the trucks so I chose to transfer to another regiment rather than leave the army.

Royal artillery
I went to the same regiment as my brother, the R.A. (Royal Artillery). I was based at 25 field regiment at Lark hill, Wiltshire. I trained on 25 pounder guns and 5.5 guns. It was very near Stonehenge.

Visits

After I'd been there a week or two, a trip out was organised to a chocolate factory (Fry's) and a brewery – the latter we didn't know about and was a surprise.

We arrived at the chocolate factory and were conducted around by a girl; some of the lads were trying to chat her up and she was not taking any notice of what was going on around her.

On each floor, they were making something different, i.e., chocolate cream, Turkish delight, Crunchies, etc.

We saw two or three coloured women. "Look," quipped one chap, "it looks like she has fallen in the chocolate vat," at which everyone laughed, but me! I felt a bit uncomfortable and it wasn't a nice thing to say, especially in their hearing. You couldn't get away with that remark now! And rightly so! This was over 50 years ago.

At the end of each of the production lines, we were given free samples of the goods made. I had too many free samples. Nothing was wasted on the production line. Everything was recycled again and again.

At the end, we were all given a box of free samples, most lads ate theirs but I saved mine and gave it to my mother. Afterwards, we had a typical army lunch in a pub and not knowing what was to come next, I had my fill.

Brewery

We set off for Wadsworth Brewery in Wiltshire. To be honest, the smell of fermenting hops smelt awful and it was quite boring, the only thing that was amusing was when a couple of 'comedians' in the party decided to take their shoes and socks off, they said they wanted to commit suicide in a vat full of thousands of gallons of beer, and whatever happens, they said, if we saw them going down for the third time, don't throw them a life belt to save them as they didn't want to be saved.

Even the brewery officials were laughing.

The end of the tour came as a relief to me and I think others too. The guide then opened a large oak door and we saw a bar c/w two barmen.

The guide then said, "Gentlemen, you have two hours, help yourself – it's free!"

He then quickly stood aside; just as well, otherwise he would have been trampled underfoot in the mad stampede for the bar that immediately followed. I then regretted having all those free samples in the chocolate factory as I was unable to drink very much.

I was only able to force down about 1½ pints, while everybody else got drunk. I must have been the only soldier to walk out of a brewery sober.

I wasn't very popular in a different regiment. I was never accepted as 'one of the lads'; I always felt left out.

Returned to Unit

Eventually, I was R.T.U.'d (Returned to Unit).

I was then discharged, as I was told it was my last chance to stay in the army when I went to the R.A. I then left for home, which was to be only a temporary stop, upset and swearing one day to return to Yeovil and Houndstone camp, which I did several years later with my wife to be.

My time in the army had been a time fraught with memories, both happy and sad, pride and regret. On the whole, I wouldn't have missed it for the world and overall, I enjoyed it. The memories will stay with me for the rest of my life.

In fact, I enjoyed it so much so that once bitten by the military/travel bug, I just had to join up again, and within a month, I had signed on in the R.A.F.

Royal Air Force

1967–76

R.A.F. Stn Swinderby (Recruit Training)

Travel bug

I had not been out of the army more than a few days before I realised that I had been bitten by the 'services'/travel bug. (Though up to that time, I had been out of country only once on a whistle-stop tour of the major European countries.)

It wasn't many days after that that I started getting the bus to Lincoln to make enquiries about joining the R.A.F. and on 17 October 1967, one month to the day since my official discharge from the army, I signed on in the R.A.F. as a steward. I asked myself a question before signing on the dotted line, "Was I prepared to kill or be killed for the Queen and country, even though that seems unlikely at this moment in time?" I answered, "Yes!" Had I not done so, I wouldn't have joined; I think everybody joining the forces should ask themselves that same question.

I joined for 3/9 (3 years on the colours full-time and 9 years on the reserve), making the statutory 12-year engagement. I later extended that service to 9/3.

I was sworn in at Lincoln by Flt Lt Farthing. I received my joining instructions by mail a short time afterwards.

I proceeded to my basic training camp at Swinderby near Lincoln, which at the time made it the nearest 'home' posting I had. (I was to be posted nearer to home in the coming years.)

Whilst there, a lot of the training was similar to what I'd been through in the army. It didn't seem as tough or was it that I knew what to expect now?

Bull nights and regimental baths

We got the usual do's & don't's of the service life, history of the service, etc. Haircuts fortunately weren't as often as in the army, only once a fortnight, but still far too short by my liking; as I said to my friends throughout my time, "If the navy is allowed to grow it longer and have beards, then why shouldn't the R.A.F. and the army?"

We had what was to prove to be the traditional part of service life, which I believed to be peculiar to the army alone, bull nights and regimental baths.

Although I tried to install the army method of 'mucking in' to help each other, these blokes (mostly Scotsmen) weren't interested. There were too many 'individuals' to make it a good atmosphere.

Overall, the basic training wasn't as tough as the army as far as I was concerned. With these Scotsmen, all that comes to mind, that I still recall, is when they weren't drinking themselves stupid or fighting, they would be homesick for their football team. Of course, they would be singing how great Scotland is at every opportunity.

One chap even went to the extreme of buying himself out and going back home for just such a reason, he missed his football team, Morton. I'll never forget it! I saw the officer by his bedside trying to calm this Scot.

My reply to them, which didn't make me many friends, was, "If Scotland is so bloody marvellous, why did they leave in the first place?" All I got from that was calling me all the rotten anti-Sassenach names they could think of, and that was quite a few. I didn't know.

Basic Recruit training. Aged nearly 20

Also on the course were the lads who were due to do their trade training with me as a steward at the R.A.F. school of catering.

Amongst them was Mike McFont (who would do sober what most of us wouldn't dream of doing drunk); he was quite a character. At Swinderby, he kept quiet and in the background, though he came out of his shell when we were on the other camp. (More about him later.)

Bubbly Stubley

Another most unusual character was David 'Bubbly' Stubley or some-times called just 'Stubs'. We became close friends over the years; he was a 'Geordie'.

He was the only 25 + years old 'self-confessed virgin' I'd come across.

Non-smoking, non-drinking, non-girl chasing. What a boring life he must have had. He used to lend money to people and forget not only how much he had lent out and when but also to whom. This led him into trouble on more than one occasion whilst together on the same camp. (Full stories later on.)

Our instructors for the military training were members of the R.A.F. Regiment, which, unknown to me at the time, I was to later join.

One of the instructors was an Indian c/w turban who, one day when marching us, came out with the most famous drill saying, and my father's all-time favourite. With a broad Indian accent and the now tradition-al shaking of the head side to side, "You may have broken your mother's heart, but you won't break mine, O goodness me. Yes!" It seemed so funny I thought I would never hear it as it was such an old saying from the war years, we as a whole squad having heard this old saying spontaneously burst out laughing, the Indian Cpl seemed shocked and surprised, then he must have realised what he had said and had a little laugh with us; to hear him go on was too much for a couple of others and myself, we ended up getting a rollicking for laughing on parade.

When he asked me what I was laughing at, eventually I had to tell him what my father had said and I had been waiting all this time for someone to say it. He allowed himself a wry smile and left it at that. Once we arrived, we had to send our civilian clothes home as they weren't allowed.

For the first two weeks, we had to march out, even around Lincoln, in uniform; of course, the locals, knowing we were servicemen, picked fights accordingly. It also had the effect of making you an outcast and this the lads resented most of all, as you had no chance to chat up the girls because they kept their distance. So the lads turned to drink on their nights off and this, when the girls saw the lads drunk, it put them off us all the more. An ever vicious circle.

The R.A.F. had an effective method for waking you in the mornings, and that was to book in at the guardroom, inform them of the block/room and location of your bed, and for the purpose of a real thickie who may have the duty of waking you, another method – you put a towel on the end of your bed just to be sure.

Yet some idiots were still confused, if there was more than one towel out that day.

Part of training involved what was called 'air experience training', which involved giving each intake a bit of experience of flying. On the way to the airstrip, everybody was obviously nervous and was trying to alleviate their apprehension by cracking jokes and such. It was an R.A.F. Hastings that we went up in, and as it happened, that particular type of aircraft didn't have many more years left before the R.A.F. withdrew it from service, the easiest way to describe it was our four-piston engine version of the U.S. D.C. 3 Dakota.

Once we were up, I kept looking at the wingtip at the starboard side, the wing was bouncing up and down too much for my liking, I was sure it was going to drop off. I felt a little uneasy to say the least, and felt a little airsick too.

So I spent almost a whole flight with my head buried in the airsickness bag, though fortunately I survived the trip unscathed. Just to deter anybody 'taking the mick' afterwards, I tried to make a big joke of it at the time. I was very glad to get down to 'mother earth' again; though in later years I was to fly thousands of miles and come to enjoy flying. I have since flown on a great range of aircraft, both civilian and military.

Amongst the tests we had to pass before passing out, were some practical/theory, also a physical training that included a run around the airfield. I didn't set the world of athletics alight, I came out 5th from last, which was a good result for me. I still got through and passed out.

On the passing out parade, it was very cold, cold enough for passing out in greatcoats (the first and last time I had worn a greatcoat). I never wore it again during my service, but I still had to carry it around with me for the rest of my service, and it was very heavy – even more so when wet.

I had my mother and father and another relative who had driven them to the camp for the passing out parade. It was a pretty ordinary parade compared to some that I did in later years, though at the time there was one part worth mentioning, an immaculate piece of timing.

Towards the end there came the climax. 'General salute – present arms'. As the movement was carried out, on the very last moment as the foot went in to complete the 'salute' while at the 'present', the flypast was directly overhead – perfect timing.

We had a Canberra Bomber/Recce aircraft. Other intakes had different aircraft.

I was so impressed that it took all of my willpower to refrain from making admiring noises or wanting to watch it as it flew overhead.

Afterwards, everybody, including parents, girlfriends etc., had a laid on lunch in the airmen's mess. After lunch, we went home.

We had about two weeks leave before reporting to our various camps for trade training. I myself went to R.A.F. Hereford School of Catering to train as a steward.

Visit

On 10 March 1981, I visited my old basic training camp R.A.F. Swinderby to look around and refresh my memory, to see if anything had changed and indeed it had.

I booked in at the guardroom and was introduced to my guide and escort on behalf of the station, S.A.C. Pearson, who showed me around and later had lunch in the mess.

In comparison to our sparse and bleak accommodation at the time, the present accommodation was to be classed as nothing less than luxurious – one telephone, washing machine, carpets and quilts on the bed. None of which we had in my day. Just to think – no more bumping and polishing of floors well into the early hours of the morning.

Gone was the panic and the worry of will we/wont we pass the inspection in the morning and dreading the consequences if we didn't. I believe it was the little things like this that bonded you together as team.

Now that's gone, what has replaced it?

They even had washing machines and fridges in the block. No more dobbying (washing) in an old sink in the middle of the night after having to wait hours for the queue to disappear. Bull has all but disappeared.

The Naafi had been split in two permanent staff and trainees.

The latter had everything a 'sprog' could need, a reading room for studying and about the best newsagent for choice I had never come across before.

With a large section of hard/soft back books covering all aspects of service life and aircraft flying.

The trainee club was called 'The Newcomers club'; not very original you must agree. Near the guardroom, I saw that my old accommodation, No 1 accommodation block, was still there and looking much the same from the outside, 'Mansion Block' it was now called.

They had a new reception system employed there: now a new recruit went through a 3-day selection system where they were shown all various aspects of R.A.F., e.g., what each job entailed to see if a recruit's first choice was the right one for him and the R.A.F Some, of course, changed their minds about their initial chosen trade. Some by choice, some without having much say in it. I believe it was an improvement on my time. Once decided, proper training then started.

I had a good look around camp and one of the places of call was the gym.

Very well kitted out, even more so than when I was there even though the R.A.F. had always been proud of its training/leisure activities; the gym was far better now than then.

We would always dread physical training sessions but with this gym, it was a pleasure to go. It was carpeted! There was a drinks dispenser. I was introduced to the P.E.O., Physical Education Officer, a very nice chap, and his NCO. The P.E.O., once he knew I was there to research my book, started to reminisce of his former basic training days. Once he started, I had a job to get him to change the subject.

In stores, I was shown a new 'fast feed through' system, a lot better than before when they would visually eye you up and down and throw something at you that vaguely resembled your size.

I was invited back later to see the system in action but I didn't bother as I wanted to get away.

Old habits die hard; I kept calling the W.O. 'Sir' but was told not to, it embarrassed him. That took quite a bit of getting used to, I can tell you.

One of the last places I visited was the station R.A.F. Regiment section, a couple of the chaps had just returned from a basic's selection course with the S.A.S. They both had injuries ranging from broken leg, twisted ankle, even an arm in plaster. A little tougher this S.A.S. basic training course was, compared to Swinderby, it seemed!

When I was alone in the ops centre, this R.A.F. Regiment lad, in typical rock-ape fashion, kept moaning about officers, penguins (non-R.A.F. Regiment trades) and other rock-apes.

I had to chuckle to myself; rock-apes never change, that much was clear.

As I was about to get in my car and leave, I saw an R.A.F. bus going past.

"Ah," said S.A.C. Pearson. "That's the recruits just back from the gas chamber on the airfield." (Less than half a mile away.)

In 1967, you were expected to run there in full N.B.C. kit, get your whiff of gas and run back, which, apart from keeping you fit, helped clear the gas out of your lungs and off your clothes.

You were expected and DID run everywhere.

We were not carried everywhere in a cosy warm bus. In previous years, your transport was – if you were very lucky to have transport – in the back of a cold and draughty 4-tonner.

You sat on the back, shivering, cold and very uncomfortable but thought yourself lucky because the alternate was marching/walking miles around the airfield in all kinds of weather. But to take raw recruits half a mile on a bus was really mollycoddling them, taking things too far.

When they had to rough it, they would find it hard to take.

Discipline – there seemed a definite lack of it these days, no wonder when they got things easy as they appeared to.

Overall, some things were easier, others the same, but too easy for my liking.

Discipline never did me any harm; on the contrary, I agreed with most of it – and enjoyed it.

R.A.F. Hereford (November 1967 to January 1968)

Steward training

The start, of course, began with introductions to each other and the training staff/instructors, course/station rules, etc.

I saw at the start of the course four chaps who were with me during basics at Swinderby: Mike McFont, Dave Stubley, Robert Beech and Ted McAndrews.

R.A.F. Hereford 1967/8. My second D.J. show. Taken during my trade training – steward

We also had a small number of WRAFs (Women's Royal Air Force), which helped make the course a bit more interesting; there was only one of them that I had a bit of interest in and that was Serena whom we all fancied.

Serena was a brunette and the best looking girl I'd seen for a long time, certainly in the WRAFs. Trouble was she knew it and acted accordingly, a bit big-headed and cocky, she would egg blokes on, give them a bit of encouragement by all her actions, then give the brush off; in short what we guys called a P.T. – more politely put – a big flirt.

I could see that she was that sort of girl so I never made a play for her; it would have been a waste of time and frustrating as well so I thought best to leave well alone. Even though, as I said, I fancied her.

What also added to her attraction was the perfume she used. 'Timeless', she once told me and it certainly turned the heads of the guys. The other WRAFs weren't bothered by the guys because of Serena; I think this left them feeling frustrated. They were so plain and ordinary that I don't remember much about them, least of all what they looked like.

Robert Beech

Robert was small and an Elvis fan, used to walk around with a swagger thinking to himself that he was indeed Elvis; he even had an Elvis 50's style haircut. He was an ex-bus driver from Plymouth.

We were posted together to Thorney Island and I spent a weekend at his house once, all we did during the weekend was put on bets – horse racing, drink at lunchtime, more bets, out drinking in the evening; not my ideal way of spending a weekend.

Dave Stubley

What I can say about 'Stubs'? As aforementioned, he was a self-confessed non-drinking non-smoking virgin, whose total excitement in life up to that point had been when a girl whom he thought had fancied him in civvy street had stolen a kiss from him when she was drunk.

He did have one interest and that was photography (not even nude photographs). What a very boring life it seemed to us, but with his other interest of military aircraft, he was very surprisingly quite happy with his lot.

Ted McAndrews

There's not much to tell about 'Mac'. The only thing that I recall about him was that he was a big mate of Robert Beech from their bus driver/conductor days at Plymouth. And at our first posting, he was having trouble with his marriage back home in Plymouth.

He got off with a barmaid working in the Naafi and had a long stormy affair with her, so we were led to believe. He was so smitten with her that he stopped going out with his mate Robert, drinking every night. This Robert didn't forgive her – or him for that.

Mike McFont

A real crazy case, he eventually got thrown out of the R.A.F. More on this later.

Training

The training of stewards was very interesting and varied; it involved training in all aspects of catering: book-keeping, stock taking, ordering, etc. Bar work – mixing various and exotic drinks; knowing your different wines and everything about them, the grapes, where they grew and any specific points of interest up to serving it in the correct manner, at the correct temperature and so on.

Reception: taking bookings, allocation of rooms, answering the telephone and making tannoy – internal messaging system and announcements. Waiting on tables: laying tables for a three- to seven-course meal and continental/silver service (served from a silver salver with spoon and fork), dining in and guest nights.

Valet: waking the officer/guest in the morning with a cup of tea/coffee. Preparing his kit – uniform and shoes – making the beds and cleaning the rooms.

Nut job

The nut job previously mentioned, Mike McFont, would do things while perfectly sober that none of us would dream of doing while drunk. Mike McFont would get great enjoyment out of embarrassing people (usually girls or weak chaps who wouldn't fight back for their own good) the more embarrassed the victim would be, the more pleasure he would get out of it.

The most major incident that I can recall is something that I don't think I, he or the victim would ever forget. It started during the first week of training, some of the WRAFs, in fact most of them, were believed to be virgins possibly with the exception of Serena (a crime in the services). I do believe that most of them were.

Mike McFont, for some reason or other we never found out why, singled out one girl for his 'play acting'; he set off with the intention to embarrass this young girl whenever the opportunity arose.

One of the most regular things he did was first thing in the morning in the classroom while we waited for the instructors to arrive. He would approach this girl, sat at her desk and commence his 'act'; she, quite rightly, tried to ignore him as much as possible. He then progressed further, approached the girl's desk (whom we shall call Jane), then promptly took 'it' out! Sometimes he would wave it in her face, other times he would put it on her shoulder in front of us all in class or other times would slap it down on her books. He would always accompany the action with some rude, suggestive remark. Quite naturally, she (and us too) was very embarrassed.

Although we all were embarrassed, us lads were supposed to take these things in our stride instead, we made out at first that we thought it was funny, we were prepared to let him get away with it once or twice, but after we'd seen him do it a few times and he had started making a habit of it, so much so that poor Jane must have dreaded coming to class each morning. Eventually, the rest of us guys thought enough was enough. MacAndrews was the first one to warn him, then me and a couple of others. He chose to ignore us and continued his vile tricks. He was warned once more, but again he ignored us; it was a big joke to him.

So we lads were left with no choice, we had to do something for Jane as she was too timid to help herself (we were later to be proved wrong). So Mike McFont was physically 'persuaded' into the error of his ways with the aid of our fists and boots. Still! He kept on; we were at a loss now what to do with him. He kept on for a couple of times a day, for a number of weeks.

The worm turns

Then a remarkable thing happened. Either a) she was talked into it by the other girls or b) she had had enough, but the worm turned. She must have realised that if beating him up wasn't going to cure him, then she had no other choice but to stop him herself.

Nobody had an inkling that something was going to happen, so one Monday we were in class as usual and he made his usual suggestive remarks.

Suddenly she said, "Oh all right then, but we'll have to be quick. Before the corporal instructor comes!" With that, she put her pen down and grabbed the offensive weapon.

Everybody was stunned into silence! Mike McFont was open-mouthed, agog; he wasn't the only one!

We were trying to behave as if nothing was happening, doing our revision on our notes, Jane then proceeded to do all what he had been suggesting these past weeks, he tried to get away, but she was having none of it. She wouldn't let go of 'it' or him.

He was now getting a taste of his own medicine, he was beginning to get a bit frightened, she wouldn't let go; I do believe she was enjoying it.

She even started to insult his manhood, his sexual prowess – or lack of it. He was so shocked he was silent for the first and last time. It was what he had been asking for, now he had gotten his just rewards.

They didn't have full-blown sex in front of us, but it was enough to teach him a lesson.

They had just finished and had got cleaned up and dressed when the Cpl walked in; he immediately started to rollick Mike McFont, saying, "Couldn't you wait until you've finished work? There's a time and place for that sort of thing, and this is not the time, nor the place, are you stupid or something, anyone could have walked in and caught you both at it!" How had he known what was going on, had he been watching? Or had he been told in advance that something was going to happen today? But he certainly sided with Jane.

Afterwards, we all congratulated her for what she'd done as it must have taken a lot of courage and she finally stopped him asking impertinent questions. And making suggestive gestures.

The next day he did half-heartedly ask again, but immediately Jane moved towards him and he backed off, scared! Then the other girls said they wanted to join in, as they wanted a piece of the action. He ran out of the classroom so fast he never asked again, they had cured him. Now it was our turn to laugh at him and laugh we did. He wasn't used to it.

The girls get their revenge

Just to make sure that he didn't pick on any other girls, the WRAF girls hatched a plan to 'get even' (as if they hadn't already). He was lured to the entrance to the WRAF block one night by a girl he was courting, then the girls who had been lying in wait pounced! He was dragged inside the block. (It was against military law for a male member of the forces or civilian to go inside the girls' block.)

One of the chaps on our course who happened to be passing at the time had seen what had happened and said that all he could hear outside the block was screams of terror coming from a male voice (Mike McFont) and loud laughter and giggles and screams of delight coming from the girls inside.

What they had done to Mike McFont we shall never know, for when we tried to quiz him, all we got was an embarrassed silence and he tried to change the subject. When we asked the girls, all we got were giggles and laughter and big beaming smiles.

Record

On the camp, there was a broadcasting station, so on the spur of the moment, I asked why they weren't playing Elvis Presley's latest record. They told me that they were told what records to buy unless a petition was raised requesting that particular record to be bought by H.B.S. (Hereford Broadcasting Station). So this was what I did. I got the girls on my course to ask around the other girls on the courses and in the WRAF block, I asked the chaps and in the Naafi.

It started as a half-hearted effort but it suddenly took off, everybody wanted to sign it and were queuing up to do so.

I even got the camp bike to sign it (so called because everybody liked to...I'll leave the reader to guess the rest). Crude I know, but that was service humour.

After less than two weeks, I presented my petition to H.B.S with two/three hundred signatures.

A few days later, the record was played over the air, preceded with an announcement by the DJ, "And now by very popular demand, in fact a petition was raised to ask us at Hereford Broadcasting Station to purchase the record, we hope you all enjoy it. Elvis (if I remember right, it was *If I can dream!*).

After this success, I thought I would try and fulfil a small ambition of mine; I would see if I could get my own show and play Elvis records. I saw the people concerned and before I knew it, I had my own show. In fact, I did three shows. I felt very nervous at the outset and had to have a large cigar to try and calm my nerves.

Memorising

Early in the course, we had to memorise various parts of the training. One evening in the block, I sat down and memorised the seven-course meal; e.g., 1 to 7 courses, and also all the various types of glasses in use in the messes, about nine of them.

The next day in class, I was asked to 'reel them off' and did so correctly, I wasn't asked any more as they thought I knew them, just as well, because with not having to remember them any more till the final exams, I promptly forgot most of them.

Foot and mouth

Whilst we were there, there was the national outbreak of foot and mouth disease in cattle, which all intakes at Hereford were put on standby or called out to help the local vet; we were lucky, we never did get called out as the disease was brought under control before we were needed.

I'm very glad as it was a terrible job, towing carcasses and preparing them for burning/burying, then washing and scrubbing down the sheds and such other dirty jobs.

New Year's Eve

New Year's Eve 1967/8 was spent in a local nearby pub with – unbeknown to me at that time I now understand – members of the S.A.S. I didn't know who the S.A.S were but I'd heard of them only once before at Houndstone camp (R.C.T.) in which an R.C.T. trainee had taken a S.A.S. man's girl-friend from him. The R.C.T. man, not knowing who this lad was, had told him in a not too polite way to 'Go away'. At this point, the S.A.S or trainee S.A.S. man jumped on his back, sunk his teeth in this R.C.T. chap's ear, bit a large lump off, spit it out and calmly walked away. None of us who had heard this story believed it, but a few days later, I saw this R.C.T. chap and got talking to him. He wouldn't state categorically whether it was true or not, but he did indeed have a large chunk out of his ear in the shape of a bite.

We had a great time that night, a good bunch of lads – whoever they were.

Serena and her troubles

One thing still amuses me even after all this time, concerning Serena. She loved attention, especially when she was the centre of attention. After we'd gotten settled in into a routine, she seemed to have a lot of personal problems or that was the impression we all had of her, also the other girls on our course.

The instructors seemed to be forever trying to help her. Eventually, the other girls ignored her funny habits and tricks she used to get up to.

Serena naked

One such trick got everybody a bit worried about her at first, until she made a habit of it; the other girls soon had her weighed up, then they would ignore her. For example, her most regular (and most popular with the male population) trick – or was it a call for attention? – was to do a bit of scene stealing in the WRAF block to attract the attention of any passing men, then she would take off all her clothes, open the window (when she was sure there was somebody in the room to try and persuade her to come back in and talk about it), jump on to the window sill naked and threaten to end it all as nobody wanted her any more.

This happened on a Thursday night (just as the men would be going past the girls' block to the Naafi dance) so she was assured of a good audience and a willing one. The male audience was getting bigger and bigger (excuse the pun).

It happened the following Thursday, and then each Thursday afterwards at a regular time. As you can well imagine, the word didn't take long to spread around camp; in fact, after the first Thursday, after the initial incident, there was a small crowd of men gathered – hoping for a repeat performance (including me); we were not disappointed. In fact, the crowd got bigger each Thursday with Serena crouched naked in the window and threatening to jump and end it all.

Of course, the lads watching made some wry comments like, "Come on then, love, jump and end it all on the end of this." (gesturing to their lower genital regions) or making other suggestions such as placing one arm over the bicep of the other and pumping vigorously up and down and other comments like, "Come on then, jump on this," "Go on then, love, do yourself a favour – impale yourself on the end of this! It'll make your eyes water." And so it went on. Had she been serious and called their bluff, I bet they would have probably run a mile (or gotten crushed in the rush).

How the R.A.F. police never came to stop it I don't know. (They were probably there watching in civvies and enjoying it.)

After a number of weeks, she didn't do it anymore because one of the girls told me that when she threatened to jump, the other girls in the room said, "Go on then, and shut the window after you, it's cold with it open." Then they would ignore her, and even the blokes got a bit bored with it as it was the same thing each week and after all the promises of a soft/hard landing – get my meaning? – she never did it and the guys gave up hope and realised it was all an act.

Henlow

During the course, towards the end, we had to spend a week at an officer cadet training unit at Henlow.

While walking around the camp one day, a young trainee approached me. I didn't know whether I had to salute him or not, I wasn't sure if he had been commissioned or not. The problem resolved itself; the 'Sprog Officer' came along, snapped up a smart salute and said, "Good morning, Sir." I was taken aback; he still had his head and eyes smartly towards me and his hand still up in the salute position. So I returned the salute, saying, "Carry on." I had heard trained airmen, regardless of rank, were senior to any officer cadets, but not so much that he was saluted. After I told him to carry on, he said, "Thank you, sir." So for some reason, he must have thought I was a fully commissioned officer.

Finals

We took our 'finals' consisting of a practical and theory test. I finished second overall.

WRAF W.O. humiliates Mike McFont

We were given our marks and results by the senior steward in charge of training, a WRAF Warrant Officer. She started by saying, "Congratulations, you have all passed, I will give you your marks and postings, but before I do, I want Mike McFont to come out here!" We were hushed, as we all had a very good idea what she was going to say – and we were right!

"I want you to tell the class exactly what it is you have done to your mattress and the reason behind it, I want the rest of the class to know just what sort of person you are." (Too late – everybody knew!)

He was made to explain to us. (He had already told us in private what he was about to tell publicly.)

He had cut a hole in the mattress, exposing one of the holes in the sponge mattress, then with a black marker pen had 'decorated' it accordingly with the outline of a woman. The WRAF Warrant Officer then said, "Go on, I'm waiting, tell the class what you did with this hole!" She needn't have, we were streets ahead of her by this time. The whole class, all with the exception of the Warrant Officer and the corporal instructor (who had just been told that he had gotten his sergeant up), broke out in fits of laughter at Mike McFont, even the WRAFs did when they got over the initial shock.

We all started to make jokes at him; he was still smiling through this. Then the WRAF Warrant Officer started to pull him to pieces and give him some stick. And finished by saying, "You have torn, stained that mattress, you will not leave here until you have bought a new one and replaced the one you've ruined!" I had to admire this WRAF warrant officer, she had guts and she wasn't embarrassed at what she had to say, just disgusted – as we all were. I believe he was also charged. She had a lot of experience of life, you could see that.

End of course 'do'!

The last night there, we had a course do at the instructor's house. We even got Bubbly Stubley to have a couple of drinks, and as you might have guessed, with him not used to alcohol, he was drunk in a few minutes. In fact, by the end of the evening, I would say he was paralytic.

It was very difficult to look after him when he was drunk as he was very strong. It took all us chaps to keep him under control, or so we thought.

We said good night to the girls outside the block. We set off for our block with Stubley in tow, he said something we missed and then broke free and turned and ran in to the WRAF block and disappeared inside; none of us dared to go in after him as we didn't want to get in the WRAF block.

But knowing the fearsome reputation of the girls, no one dared to venture in that land of the unknown. When a man came out, he was never the same again. And none of us were 'that' brave.

We thought it best to leave Stubs to his own chosen fate, when we heard such a commotion from inside; there was furniture being knocked over, girls screaming (not in delight this time), we even saw some of the girls running out of the block and coming out of the window of the ground floor to escape.

Whatever Stubs was doing, it was enough to break the spirit of the WRAF girls *en masse*. I have never known anything to unnerve the WRAFs on their own ground before.

Faced with their invincible reputation, we did the only thing that tough, well-trained and brave R.A.F. airmen could do in the circumstances – we ran back to our blocks. It was too bad about Stubs! He was on his own. In the morning, he had one almighty hangover and couldn't remember how he had gotten out of the block or even what he had done in the block. All we found out was the R.A.F. police had been called out to the girls' accommodation to try to restore order.

Some reports had two Land Rovers full of R.A.F. police.

Stubs would not talk about it even when at our next posting, only that he would not now under any circumstances ever drink again! I never did see him drink again.

To try and sum up Stubley, we all had photos on our lockers, such as their football team, family pet, girlfriend and family, but usually there would be photographs of women in various stages of undress on the lockers. Not Stubley; he was different – he had photos of aircraft on his.

Occasionally, on the odd inspection, we were told to take down the pictures of the girls in case the inspecting officer took offence to them. Through my experience, we learned that most of the young officers, NCOs, used to go locker to locker, comparing the girls in each locker to the next and these young officers clearly enjoyed examining the evidence; only natural.

Of course, Stubs and his aircraft were quite often quizzed as to "Why haven't you got pictures of naked girls on your locker, laddie? Are you batting for the other side? Are you a poof?" Actually, Stubs was not a Poofter, just a bit different, you might say by our standards, that's all. It takes all sorts when there are up to 14 men in a room. Not all are going to have the same interests.

The following day, we left Hereford for two weeks' leave before moving to our new posting. We said our goodbyes at the railway station.

I was sorry to see the back of most of them as they were a good bunch of people. All except, of course, the 'Nutter' Mike McFont who had been posted to a different camp to the rest of us. And who, we heard through Robert Beech who had been writing to him at his camp, was thrown out of the R.A.F. (as he was up to his old tricks again).

We all went our separate ways, then after another couple of weeks leave, arrived at our new postings. It was my first posting after training – the first of many.

R.A.F. Thorney Island (Jan 1968 to June 1969)

I arrived at my first posting, Thorney Island, and was instructed to report to the officers' mess, as that was to be my place of work.

I found out that there in the same officers' mess from my course at Hereford were Robert Beech, Ted MacAndrews and 'Lady Killer' Stubley.

I was rather pleased at this because I didn't fancy the sergeants' mess. At that time upon arrival at the mess, I was shown around and introduced to the civilians that we would be working with. I, along with the others from my course who had been posted with me, were the first R.A.F stewards to be posted to the officers' mess at Thorney Island, followed within the next few weeks by other R.A.F. stewards.

Ex-navy resentment

Thorney Island had been predominantly a Royal Navy base most of the time and the civilian staff who were mostly ex-Royal Navy or family of Royal Navy personnel resented the R.A.F. being there and they were not slow in letting us know it. We were to convert the mess from civilian to a mixture of both service and civilian. We servicemen were not popular nor wanted by the established civilian staff, they resented us from muscling in on their territory and felt their jobs were at risk, which was absolute nonsense.

Obstacles to our efficient running of the mess were put in our way all the time. After about a year, we were gradually accepted by most of the civilians with only a couple of them still harbouring a grudge against us.

The last time servicemen were in the mess was when the Royal Navy had the station and most of the male members of the staff had been ex-Royal Navy, including the mess manager who even as a civilian thought along the lines of a Royal Navy mess and not R.A.F. This was to cause a lot of resentment between the civilians/R.A.F., especially with me being at the forefront as the other R.A.F. stewards wanted a quiet life and skulked into the background; not me ! If I saw wrong, I tried to put it right. After all, that was the way we had been taught at Hereford.

Station history

The station had changed hands between the R.A.F. and the Royal Navy several times since it was found quite by accident after an R.A.F. aircraft had crashed and during the investigation that always followed, it was thought that it would make an ideal station for the maritime branch of the

R.A.F., which was to play a vital role during WWII. The R.A.F. now had a base right on the edge of the channel to enable it to keep an eye on the German Navy/Luftwaffe. It was attacked and bombed several times by the Germans.

Operational conversion unit

It was now an O.C.U. (operational conversion unit) for aircrew converting or learning to fly/operate the R.A.F.'s transport aircraft, which at that time were A) Beverly, which had just been taken out of service, b) Argosy, c) Andover, which did not have much longer to serve in the R.A.F. before being replaced and the presently in use though at that time just coming into service, the U.S. built c130 Hercules, which was being used by most of the world's free countries in their air forces.

Whenever I went to a new camp, I always made a point of keeping in with three of the most important departments – the cooks, stores and R.A.F. police. You never knew when you were going to need 'inside help'.

Officer's valet

I was shown what duties I was to perform, which started as a valet looking after three officers, whereas all the other stewards had about 12 officers to look after, so I was lucky. I found out I also had the toilets and bath-rooms to clean, which I hadn't been told in training. It wasn't too bad as the officers kept themselves and the toilet/bathroom reasonably clean. The worst time was if they had been on the ale the night before or had a dining in night, which happened about once a month.

Whilst doing the valet's job, I eventually got down to just one officer to look after. The civvies said I would never get any weekly perks from this officer as he was very tight with the money; he had never given anybody any money before. how wrong they were. I did get weekly perks from him, maybe he didn't like civilians or he must have liked me and appreciated the job I did for him. Just like the airmen, officers too were not allowed to bring girls/men into their rooms.

He had a photograph of one of his girlfriends on his bedside table; she was working as an Air Traffic Control officer in Gibraltar at the R.A.F. airfield there. She was a cracking bit of stuff. This officer wanted to bring his girlfriend of the moment to his room.

One Friday, he told me not to wake him up in the morning as he had something else in mind; he gave me a couple of pounds and a wink, the purpose of which at first I didn't catch the meaning. I soon found out though. 'Be discreet!' It was probably his way of saying, 'don't say anything about this'!

That following morning, I must have been on the beer the night before as I wasn't thinking, so as normal I knocked on the door, walked in with his coffee and saw out of the corner of my eye, my officer straining, moaning and giving the bed some hammer and underneath him, was his girlfriend from abroad.

"Good morning, sir!" says I, then I looked towards the bed and saw what had been making the grunting noises, it was 'Sir' banging his bird. "Good morning, ma'am!"

"What a lovely morning it is, the sun is shining and the birds are singing. I'll bring another cup in, sir!" Then I left the room.

I cleaned their shoes and in the privacy of my service room, I burst out laughing at such a funny incident.

It wasn't long before they came out of the room. I wished them both good morning as if nothing had happened; they smiled back and wished me good morning too. I must have put him off his stroke; not every day when you're on the job and your valet walks in and catches you at it.

I thought when I saw him again, I would get a big rollicking, but as soon as I caught him on his own, I approached him and apologised, he forgave me and said he understood that I'd simply forgotten.

El Adem

I had heard that at Thorney Island, you were expected to take your turn in going to R.A.F. station 'El Adem', Libya/North Africa, as part of relief crew for the personnel at El Adem but it was primarily a pilot/navigation exercise for the aircrew converting to the Hercules.

After a number of weeks to enable us to get settled down, we did indeed get told that we were to go El Adem. I was looking forward to this as an added bonus; my father had visited El Adem during the war in the desert. About one week or 10 days later, we set off on a Monday morning for El Adem. We flew in one of the station's Hercules, a very long, boring and uncomfortable flight. We sat on the 'Para' seats, which consisted of a hollow metal frame and nylon straps. They certainly were not made for comfort as a Para was not on board long before they jumped, so they are not bothered about comfort. Bum numbing was the word, and very loud engines, no wonder we were all a bit deaf. I was glad to get on the ground. If anyone out there has had the same sort of experience, after 8 hours, you will surely have sympathy for me.

All we did when we arrived at R.A.F. Luqa-Malta was collect our bedding, have a bit of tea and then I spent the first night in Malta in the Naafi watching a very inferior TV programme (in quality to British TV technology). I got drunk and was ill.

Next morning, we set off on the second and final leg of the journey to El Adem, Libya (pre-Col Gaddafi days).

Again we arrived after everyone had finished work for the day, so again, we collected our bedding and settled down for the night, again I spent the night in the Naafi as I didn't know how far the local town 'Tobruck' was; as it happened, it was a good few miles away across the Bondu (desert) by R.A.F. bus.

The next day, I reported for work in the airmen's mess. Officers' mess was fully staffed as it was a permanent camp. The water in the mess was nice and cold, but a little salty. I believe it had been salt water from the sea and treated to make it drinkable. We had very large air fans; the old sort you see in films of people abroad.

Cockroaches and flies

You will always find cockroaches where there is food, but these were the biggest I'd ever seen, they were huge. I had a sneaking suspicion that the cooks were breeding them for racing, and flies, they were everywhere, and squadrons of them.

The place I dreaded going to most was the toilet, even though it was primitive. You had to fight your way through a curtain of flies to get there, it was as if they were hovering around waiting for you and thinking, "Come on, come on, what are you waiting for, I'm hungry!"

You were in such a state that you were frightened to start; the flies were on you before you had a chance.

I didn't have an alarm clock there, I didn't need one, I had something better (or worse). At 5 am precisely every morning, a fly would hover above my face and then land on my nose and start to walk all over my face. I was up and out of bed like greased lightning to get a wash, paying particular attention to my nose and face.

Arab staff

The dustbins and worst of all, the swill bins were directly outside the back door of the mess, so you can imagine the thick swarm of flies there, and sat in the middle of these flies were the Arab Services; they seemed to live next to the bins, for no matter what time of day or night you would look, there they were.

The first evening off, I was waiting for a bus to Tobruck for the first time during dusk and got a rollicking by some sergeant passing by saying that I wasn't allowed out after dusk in shorts because of the mosquitoes. These shorts of mine came halfway down my calf, reminiscent of 1939-45 pictures of our lads in the western desert.

Martin

During the next day, I was confronted with the biggest coincidence of my life.

After finishing work in the mess one afternoon, I thought I would spend the afternoon in the camp swimming pool and while there, I saw one of the chaps who had come out with me from my mess in Thorney Island. I'd been there about an hour when I felt a tap on my shoulder, I turned and to my astonishment saw next to me my brother, whom I had thought was still with his army regiment in Germany. Though he had written to tell me the regiment was expected to fly to Libya sometime in the future for an exercise. We stood face to face together for a few seconds, not really believing our eyes.

In the end, I said, "Martin, is that you?"

He said, "Yes, is that you, John?" It turned out that he and his troop had been out on the Bondu (desert), miles from anywhere, live-firing their 25 pounder guns. They had run out of ammunition and had come to El Adem for some more whereupon the vehicle had 'conveniently' broken down; had it not done so, they would have been returning back to the desert straightaway and we would have not met.

Wasn't it convenient for the truck to break down on camp and not in the middle of anywhere? Of all the hundreds of miles it could have broken down, it broke down at camp where there were all these facilities including a bar selling alcohol!

We all ended up that night in the Naafi; they had not been paid before leaving the army camp and were to be paid upon their return, though I couldn't for the life of me think what they could spend it on in the desert. I believe that it was to be done this way so as not to encourage them to stop at El Adem had they been paid. Needless to say, Martin and his chums had very little money among them. So I bought them as much beer as I could and then to enable them to pay their share of drinks, they started to sell their personal possessions to an Arab cleaner in the Naafi; they were selling pens, watches, rings, etc.

The Arab in the Naafi was the main dealer; all the other Arabs came to him for advice on goods to buy. I think he was trying to corner the market in watches; he had several dozen up both arms and legs too.

At the end of the evening, we were surprisingly all drunk; I asked Martin if he knew where he was sleeping. All he knew was that the sleeping bags were in a Nissan hut and he didn't know where the hut was.

We set off for the hut, not knowing where it might be, and started walking. Before long, we suddenly realised something was wrong, it was getting darker. We were walking into the desert away from the camp and civilisation.

We did an abrupt about-turn and headed fast for the welcoming lights of the Naafi; eventually, we did find his bed – it was on the same road and directly opposite my Nissan hut.

I gave him a few presents before we parted, such as an Elvis magazine and five cans of fly spray (which was most appreciated). One day in the Bondu, Martin and a friend stood by the latrines and emptied the five cans of fly killer into the flies; afterwards, there were still lots of flies not killed!

When he saw my sheets and blankets, pillows, etc., he said it was sheer luxury as they had to make do with sleeping bags, made really to keep you warm in a cold climate, and bedsprings, not even a mattress.

I had one more day to work before R.T.U.'d back to UK. Martin was to leave first thing that morning to the army camp in the desert.

Return to UK

On the return trip, again via Malta, there was an Indian corporal with us and he, a couple of others and I went to a local bar in Luqa village.

The landlady and the Indian corporal seemed to know each other well, he then introduced everybody to each other and we started to drink.

During which, we were all a little peckish so the Indian corporal asked his landlady friend to make him a 'special', which she promptly did – it was a large (about 12-14") French-style loaf full of everything you could imagine, cheese, tomatoes, onions, lettuce, liver sausage, etc. – it was great! In fact, it was so big that even I found it a struggle to get down. It was washed down with lots of the local wine, very cheap.

About 1/- 'one shilling' per bottle (10p) and the speciality of the house, tasting a bit like port, costing a lot more – 2/6 (12½ p).

I wasn't used to wine, sweet wine at that, so as you may imagine I was ill, I thought I was going to die, swearing, "Never again, never again," but of course, there always was another time.

The homeward flight to England the following day was hell, I thought my head was fit to burst.

Bar work

This was my favourite part of the job; it was certainly the most rewarding financially as well as for satisfaction. The only part I didn't like was the early shift, we came in to find the place in shambles and it stank to high heaven of stale tobacco smoke and beer.

Making money in the bar was quite easy, there were that many officers who could authorise the late opening in the officers' mess bar and there were, for example, Orderly Officers, Station Duty Officers, Mess Manager and Squadron Leader or above, any member of the mess committee, and of course, the Station Commander. If they wanted the bar opened after time, then the official method was put the book around (I only did this two or three times). Nobody liked this method as you had to wait a long time for the money due to you as the Mess waited until the end of the month when they sent out the mess bills before you got the money (the officers were charged a set percentage of the Mess bill for us) but it wasn't much.

During my first such late opening, I was about to put the bar attendance books around for the officers to sign when the officers who told me to keep the bar open said, "No, don't put the book around, put the pot around." (Beer mug) He then started a collection from all the officers and guests present and filled the mug with money; I'd shared it 50/50 with the chap on duty with me and we had about £5-6 each, a lot of money in those days. Each time after that, when the Orderly Officer or Station Duty Officer was on duty, we always put the pot around, if it was the committee, then they wanted the book put around, we weren't keen but it was better than nothing.

This wasn't part of the training; we were to find out by ourselves once 'on the job'.

Late nights

As a bar steward, late nights were often and frequent but it had its compensations such as putting the pot around. This went on until the officers were too drunk to care or their money ran out.

Linda Masters

Not long after getting posted to Thorney Island and settling in, I had been home for a weekend and was standing on the platform of Doncaster railway station waiting for the London train. I had noticed on the Scunthorpe to Doncaster train from Scunthorpe that there had been a great-looking girl who had stood out from all the other girls on the train as a bit special.

I was tempted to chat her up but as with most good-looking girls in this country, experience showed that they usually became a bit particular in who they went out with and very choosy, even known to be sarcastic towards the would-be suitors instead of taking it as a compliment that several people fancied them. The would-be suitor normally found his efforts 'shot down in flames' (unless of course, he had the 'spiel' or plenty of money).

Added to this, her mother, who happened to be travelling with her, was looking my way and so I thought, "No way am I going to attempt to chat her up if her mother's there." Though I did notice her mother sneaking more than a casual glance my way.

They were also both talking quietly about me. It was obvious (I found out later my suspicions were correct), though whilst waiting for my train, I was still keeping my eye on her hoping just half-heartedly that her mother would disappear and then I just might get the chance to chat her up; even though I risked a rebuke, I thought her attractive enough to risk it.

Imagine then to my great surprise, delight and good fortune when suddenly, unexpectedly this girl approached me and started talking to me.

She introduced herself as Linda Masters and her excuse for approaching me was that had she seen me in a local disco in Scunthorpe over the last few months?

Yes, I told her she had and she wondered if I remembered seeing her there. I couldn't but didn't want to seem like a twit so I told her yes, and that I'd had my eye on her for a while.

We continued chatting for a while longer and I plucked up courage to ask her for her address; very surprisingly, she agreed and even seemed pleased. I'd asked her and I discovered that she was a nurse at Hull, living normally in Scunthorpe. The journey back to Thorney Island seemed endless and I was full of impatience and couldn't get back to camp quick enough where I immediately started to write to her.

That was the biggest morale/confidence booster I had had in the short time I'd been chatting up girls. After that, I was never in doubt as to whether I ought to chat up a nice, beautiful girl in the future, and for that I was/will be grateful.

This was in the days that the man who was traditionally the one to start the chatting up, though it was after the swinging sixties that the girls became more and more in the open and to the fore.

It was one of those things that all men would like to happen to them – to be approached and chatted up by a pretty girl.

She had everything a guy looked for in a girlfriend – 'the girl next door' appeal, classy, natural beauty, intelligence and very sexy – not put on.

I was quite excited about a quick and prompt reply, which I didn't honestly expect, but received within a week of my first letter to Linda.

Several letters passed between us during the next few weeks and I arranged to meet her on my next visit home, which couldn't come quick enough.

After what seemed an eternity, the fateful weekend arrived. I met her as arranged and a very enjoyable weekend I had too; we went to the previously mentioned disco.

We went from strength to strength and became very close. Linda became something special to me. I experienced very great 'highs' and one or two 'lows'. Linda became my first real serious experience with girls and the then love of my young life so far, they were some of the happiest days of my life.

The only thing that seemed to put the kibosh on things was her father, he seemed quite a stuck-up middle-class snob. He had a fairly good job c/w company car, trouble was that Linda was/or seemed scared of him, which spoiled our fun. For example, he would tell her what time he wanted her back home although she was about 22/23 years old. Though I did deliberately try and keep her out longer, just to spite her father, I told her many times, "You're above the age of consent. He has no legal right to demand anything like that; you're over 21. Stand up for yourself!" But she wouldn't. I don't think her father liked servicemen; I don't think he trusted me. Was he worried I might 'defile' his little girl? Or was it that in his mind, I came from the wrong side of the tracks! Not of the same social standing as him, to quote an Americanism?

Normally, he would have just reason to be worried but not on this occasion with me. I suppose it was only natural he was worried about his precious little daughter (his daughter though wasn't as innocent as he thought).

Her mother though was completely different. She was smashing. I got on very well with her. She was straightforward and very friendly. It was thanks to Linda that I got my first real regular contact with the most interesting parts of girls – mentally and physically.

I was wary of going too far too soon for fear of offending her; unbeknownst to me, I had nothing to fear as far as that went. It was with Linda I was emotionally and physically committed. After a while, we seemed to drift apart and be less and less keen on each other. Trouble was I respected her too much; as far as I believed, she wasn't the sort to 'go all the way', yet! So I didn't try to push it at first.

Being wise now with afterthought and being told in so many words months later, that's partially why she went off me, she wanted 'it' and thought she wasn't going to get it on a regular basis from me and I had not noticed the 'signs' and she became more and more frustrated. Plus, I was disappointed after my proposal been turned down and that put me off.

Months later, a casual remark by a chap in the block made me write and contact her again, and I started to go out with her but this was a new more determined, self-assured me. Linda also seemed to have changed, a bit more distant, different, but that didn't bother me.

This time, I wasn't going out for love or for the sake of a platonic relationship – it was purely lust! This time, I approached her with a different attitude, I was out to get as much as I could (sexually speaking) from her and no longer respect her virtue. "Stuff her virtue," thought I, quite literally – so to speak!

I was out to seduce her as much and as often as possible, until she had – or I had, enough, nothing more, nothing less.

On my first attempt in the back row of the cinema in Hull, I immediately commenced the way I intended to go. I was surprised at how keen she was and how quickly I was able to get down to the nitty-gritty in the cinema.

This was a new non-shy, sexually aggressive John.

At one point, in my parents' house, my father actually caught us 'in the act'; he never mentioned it to me – just gave me a knowingly broad smile.

What seemed to amaze me was that Linda seemed to enjoy the new me. From that day on, I left my shyness behind and started the new John that many girls in the future were to get to know. I then went out with girls for one thing and one thing only. The new debaucher of women was born.

Good old Linda. I learnt things about her (and girls in general) and just what I was capable of with a little practice; from then on, I have never looked back.

After a few months of 'serving my sexual apprenticeship' with Linda, I got bored with her, dumped her and consequently set off for pastures anew, realising we could go no further together. Linda would always be remembered with love and affection as she (and the army) made a man out of me.

Sqn Ldr Daddy Owen

Doing bar work, I met some characters, the most prominent and popular with the other pilots and aircrew being Flt Lt 'Daddy' Owen, a Scotsman but hardly any trace of an accent.

He had been a Sgt Spitfire Fighter pilot during the war. He had been forced, he said, against his wishes to take a commission though he tried all he knew to get out of it.

He was a real character and gentleman! He would talk to us lowly stewards and the Mess staff in the same manner as he would talk to his officer friends. Quite often, he would be feeling low and pour out his troubles to us lowly stewards or ask our advice. Most nights he relived, for the benefit of the very young pilots who had just started their career in the R.A.F., 'The Battle of Britain' on an almost nightly basis. He hardly ever bought himself a drink as the young lads were more than happy to keep him in drinks just for the pleasure of hearing of his exploits against the Luftwaffe circa 1939-45. He drank pure malt whiskey, Glenfiddich drunk neat, it was strong enough to take the lining off your throat if you weren't used to it – he was.

"My mother didn't wean me on milk," he often used to say. "She weaned me on this!" gesturing to a half-full glass of his favourite tipple. "Better than mother's milk!" he would say, though I don't think he was right there.

"Much purer than mother's milk, I cut my first teeth on a bottle of Glenfiddich!" His favourite stories to these future Hercules pilots of the R.A.F. were: "My mate and I, when we were sergeant pilots, would be flying on patrol with my mate as my wingman, or we would wait for the klaxon (warning siren) to go off, and the order to 'scramble' if 'Jerry' had been spotted. We would be in the air having a jolly, on patrol or about to intercept and we used to say over the intercom to each other and to our flight under us, 'Will we fight, will we f**k, will the krauts win? Will they f**k?'

After I'd been there in the bar for a few months, we saw 'Daddy' Owen come in the bar and sit by himself for a couple of days. He would look all sad and dejected. When people tried to cheer him up, he wasn't interested. It didn't seem like the old, regular 'Daddy' Owen that everybody had come to know and love, he was the life and soul of the party, the very spirit of the mess and of the R.A.F. itself! He was what every civilian imagines an R.A.F. fighter pilot to be – happy, carefree, couldn't care less, just living for today as if there was no tomorrow. Sadly, for a lot of our fighter pilots, there was indeed no tomorrow!

Here was a sad and dejected man. I realised it must be something serious.

As soon as I got the chance, I took him aside and asked what the matter was and could we (behind the bar) help. He thanked me for my concern and help and said that no one could help, he then poured out his troubles to me. It had seemed that he had been taken in front of his Commanding Officer and told that because he had reached the age set down by the R.A.F. for pilots to be grounded (safety rule as one's reflexes were not what they once were) because of age and with modern sophisticated aircraft, to allow someone of the age where their best years of flying were over, it could be dangerous, therefore it was with great regret that the squadron had to remove him from flying duties.

He could however stay on in the R.A.F. for a few more years if he would take a ground/desk job. He had told them that they could stick the desk job; if he couldn't fly, he wasn't going to stay in the R.A.F. grounded, he couldn't do it, his heart was in flying and if there was no job in the R.A.F. for him flying, then there was no job in the R.A.F. for him.

He was heartbroken and flying was his whole life and love and now it had been taken from him. He had resigned his commission and was now waiting for a date to leave. I and the other members of staff, especially me, felt so very sorry for him, he was heartbroken, a sad and broken man.

The R.A.F. had taken him off flying. It was as if they had taken his heart too.

He said he was going to buy a small farm in Wales and settle down, I bet he wouldn't be happy or able to settle down.

He was such a pitiful sight and he was never the same again, the old happy-go-lucky 'Daddy' Owen we once knew; it was as if he was dead and gone. He just faded from the mess life and was seen less and less until he left, he didn't even have the heart to come in and say goodbye to his friends in the bar, and it was too hard for him to do. It was such a sad case, I felt so sorry for him.

The evenings were quiet, never the same again. It was a different mess since he left.

Second detachment to Libya

I had a second detachment to El Adem a few weeks later. This time, we stopped off at Malta again on the way out in the Hercules.

The first evening we had off, a chap who had come with me from Thorney Island said he would show me around Tobruck as he had been posted here before. I told him I did know my way around pretty well as on all my previous days at El Adem, I had wandered around and gotten to know the area of the main square and main road; he said he would show me a few places anyway, starting at the Nuffield Yacht club for British servicemen in quarters at Tobruck.

In the club, we had a drink or two, he then saw an old girlfriend of his he used to go out with on another camp and she was in the WRAFs and single. Sabrina was her name and now she was married to an R.A.F. Regiment fireman.

Her husband was as drunk as the proverbial newt when we were introduced to him. Sabrina, I suspected, was a natural redhead (my favourite type); she was gorgeous c/w a marvellous figure too. Her husband was Phil Davy.

We all had a few drinks that night and then my friend and I were invited back to their flat for coffee before catching the last bus back to camp that evening.

After coffee, Sabrina's husband staggered out of the flat with my pal to show him the best place to catch the bus back to camp. I was alone in the flat with Sabrina and after a little while of small talk, she asked me to excuse her for a little while as she wanted to go to the bedroom to change into 'something more comfortable'. Where have I heard that before? She then left the room and I suddenly felt nervous; it was the way she had said the oldest line in the book. For the first few seconds, I never realised the importance of her words until it suddenly came home to me and then I felt strangely uneasy.

I had a gut feeling that something was about to happen but I tried to put it out of my mind as vivid imagination. Even when I thought back to the Nuffield club, she had sat opposite me and gave me an almost uninterrupted view of her legs, suspender belt, stockings and more than a polite, friendly smile.

She left the bedroom door ajar so I could see her shadow on the wall from my seat as she changed and undressed.

If she was trying to 'turn me on/get me going', it was working. I didn't know what to do. "Do I make a play for her? What if she rejects my advances? Will she inform her husband? Is it worth the risk? What if she makes a play for me? What should I do? Is it worth the risk of being caught 'at it' by her husband?" I quickly came to the conclusion it wasn't worth it, the odds were stacked too much against me; however, if the opportunity arose in the future with things a bit different, then maybe!

I must have nodded off because I was woken by a loud high-pitched scream coming from her bedroom. It sounded like she was in trouble so instantly I leapt to my feet and raced to the bedroom door. She screamed again and again; I asked from outside the bedroom door if she was all right.

In a (so it seemed) frightened voice, she replied that no, she wasn't all right and could I come into the bedroom and help her?

So, being the Sir Galahad-knight errant that I was, I rushed into the bedroom. Upon my entry, I was greeted with the most wonderful sight I had seen in a very long time, certainly since coming to North Africa. There was Sabrina stood on her bed, semi-naked save for a very short, transparent, 'baby doll style' nightdress, which did nothing in hiding her curves or covering her most interesting parts of her fantastic figure. It was so short, it was only as long as to 'just' cover her most intimate part but being short and see-through, it did not cover 'it' as she had her hands clasped to her mouth, which caused the nightdress to ride up, revealing all.

She was indeed a natural redhead as I had thought, and with her long hair, what a sight she made. She smiled a naughty smile as I stood rooted to the spot in a (very pleasurable) state of shock, not believing the sight that my eyes told me I saw. I stood staring at Sabrina's semi-naked body for what seemed like ages.

Sabrina broke the silence and snapped me out of my trance. "Look, over there," said she, pointing to the biggest cockroach I'd seen in my life. (I think she must have been breeding them for just such a purpose.) "Please kill it for me," she pleaded with a wicked smile.

It must have been the great-granddaddy of them all, she must have kept it as a pet and been fattening it up...

So like a silly bugger, I started to chase it around the bedroom for a few minutes until eventually, I caught and killed it. She jumped off the bed and threw her arms around me and started to kiss me and thank me for 'saving her life'.

She then (as expected) tried to get me on the bed and said that she would show me 'just how grateful' she was for what I'd done for her! I told her not to be daft, if we were to do as she suggested, her husband would walk in and catch us. She told me not to be silly as he wouldn't be back for ages! (Sounds familiar, doesn't it?) Besides, she wanted to show as a mark of her appreciation for what I'd done for her, how corny! It took me nearly10 minutes to fight my way to the door, I was pulling one way, she the other, and she was trying to undress me all the while.

I had just managed to get to the bedroom door in a dishevelled state, when – yes, you've guessed it – in walked her husband and my friend.

Now it was his turn to stand rooted to the spot. It must have been quite a shock to see a stranger you had only known about two/three hours with his clothes in disarray, in your bedroom, with your wife almost naked.

He must have thought the worst.

I took advantage of the shocked silence and made some excuses and left. My pal from Thorney Island came with me.

All the way back to camp, he kept asking me if we'd done 'it' and if we had, then why? And was it all right? Was she good in bed? I must have had some nerve to 'screw a bloke's wife' after knowing her such a short time and in his bedroom at that, when the husband was expected back at any moment, did I really have it off with her, did I, did I? I said nothing; I just smiled and let him form his own opinion.

The next day, a stranger approached me and asked if I was J. R. I said, "Why, who wants to know?" He said, "If you are, I have got a message for you from Phil Davy, if not, pass it on to the person concerned." (Last time I let any strange girl know my full name!) I asked what the message was; he then relayed it to me.

"If Phil Davy sees you again, he's going to kill you; he will put a knife through your ribs for having it off with his wife!"

"Is that all?" I asked. So I gave him my reply, "Tell your mate if he's got something to say, then why doesn't he come and tell me to my face instead of sending a messenger boy, and you can also tell him that if he believes I did 'make it' with his wife, that's contrary to what happed, I did not 'have it off' with her, but I wish I had now, after I've been accused of it and blamed for doing it, I wish I had bonked her now and will do so next time if I get the chance!"

From then on, I kept watching over my shoulder expecting him to come in person and 'sort me out' but he didn't come. Coward!

Return to UK

The next day, we left for UK. I was relieved to say the least. On the plane, I had plenty of time to sit and think about that 'adventure'. Though this

73

Sabrina had made her intentions absolutely clear! She had come onto me strongly and she was clearly up for it, but I had not been interested. Even if the circumstances had been different and the opportunity there to 'capitalise' and seize the moment and the husband had been unaware of his wife's dalliances, when it came down to it; I still wouldn't have. It would have gone against my own set of rules. 'Never get involved with a married or separated woman; it only brought trouble. Stick with the single girls!' And I stuck to that rule rigidly.

She must have been desperate to go to these lengths for sex with a complete stranger. I'm not naïve enough to think that she had found it impossible to resist my manly charms; poor lass, there must have been something wrong with her marriage, maybe she was not getting any at home. Maybe her husband wasn't 'keeping her topped up' and she had to go outside the marriage bed for a bit more excitement. I know that had I been married to her, she wouldn't have had to go looking for more; I would have been more than pleased to oblige her! Still, we don't know the circumstances.

Wrong aircraft

We heard that we were to fly back on the same Hercules that had brought us out here but it had gone to u/s so we flew back on one of the station's Argosy.

I was glad about this as the Argosy had proper seats in it; they were nice and comfortable and we came home a different way this time via Gibraltar. I liked Gibraltar, there were Union Jacks everywhere and pro-British slogans and anti-Spanish slogans; the people couldn't do enough for you when they found out you were a British serviceman.

It was the sort of place that you couldn't spend more than a week in as it was too small a place to spend more time than this. We returned to Thorney Island the following day, about lunchtime. I was one of the first to get cleared by customs and away home with my duty free; it wasn't long before Christmas so the duty free came in handy.

When I returned on the Sunday evening, one of the other chaps with us in Libya said that a couple of things had happened since I had been able to get away early.

First was that customs were about to give the all clear to the aircraft when one of the custom's men leaned against the inside of the aircraft and felt some lumps in his back, he looked around and decided to pull away the packing/cushioning and found thousands and thousands of cigarettes, dozens and dozens of bottles of spirits, i.e., vodka, rum, brandy, etc., and no one owned up to it.

So everybody was held behind for a long time before being allowed out.

We didn't find out if the culprits were found though nearly everyone felt that they were the air/ground crew. Nothing was ever said and it was all hushed up. The air/ground crew probably brought it back for the mess or were 'flogging it' and making a tidy profit.

The second point was that we shouldn't have returned on the Argosy but waited for the Hercules to be repaired. The person who had instructed us to fly back by Argosy via Gibraltar had been wrong and was in trouble.

"So what is going to happen?" I asked this chap. "Why, we're going back tomorrow to Libya!" he said. I didn't believe him but once I had reported back at the officers' mess for duty, I was told to go back to the block and pack my bags ready to fly out to Libya in a couple of hours and he explained to me the reason that the other chap had told me the night before, about the wrong aircraft.

So we flew out and, as was by now usual, had an overnight stop in Malta, then onto Libya the following day. I spent the night in Tobruck buying presents and in the 'pool' during the day. I did, however, avoid the Nuffield Yachting club. There was no point inviting trouble after the last time.

After one day's work (about 6 hours), we set off the following day back to UK on the original plane that we were supposed to have come back on. It still left an unsolved question as to what would happen to the aircraft that we'd come out in. Either way, that still left one aircraft to fly back empty, so was it worth it? So they thought it best to split up the passengers in each aircraft, which still meant that there only was about a dozen or so in each aircraft; not that I was complaining. I was still bringing some large bottles of spirits home and it was better than working a week in the mess; it made a pleasant change.

One whole week away for just one day's work, that was the R.A.F.

Dining in nights

When we used to do bar work on 'dining in nights', we were working in the bar and that generally meant from about 6 pm until about 7/8 am the next morning.

This particular night, we had been given strict instructions that once the bar was shut, under NO circumstances were we to sell any more from the barrel or bottles. (It was an officers/sergeants' games night.)

We had cleaned up and were about to go back to the block, our job finished. We heard a knock on the back door; it was a sergeant who was begging us to sell him some beer. We told him we couldn't, strict orders. He kept begging. He got so worked up that he started to get nasty. He even offered us 10/- shillings (50p) for a pint (nearly 10 times the price); eventually, he offered us £2 (about £6+ today) for a pint of dregs out of the slops tray. We couldn't refuse such a good offer, so we gave him just that! The slops! He thought it was from the pumps, but he asked for dregs, and dregs were what he got. (We kept the money.) So we still obeyed orders, no beer from the pumps or bottles was sold. This happened with various people 2-3 times during my time in the bar.

If they only knew how the stewards looked down on them. The word soon got around. They must have been very desperate to sink to such levels. In all the time I'd been drinking, I'd never stooped to such levels and they were sergeants (and officers) and they were supposed to be our superiors!

I believe I made one big mistake with one officer in the bar; I always liked to call last orders early, a couple of minutes before I should have because there was always someone who said they hadn't heard them being called.

I was just about to pull down the shutters and pack up for the night when this officer said to me that I hadn't called last orders. He was rather nasty about it, I heard him shouting about it, all the others in the bar could hear him condemning me.

For years, when I thought about it, I was still mad at him, whether I was right or wrong, there was no need for his 'holier than thou' attitude, whether he had a case or not.

In a way, we were lucky as stewards in that we didn't have any guard or fire piquet duty to do, because we were committed to at least one function per month. We were unlucky in as much that often in a busy mess, you may have 2/3 functions per month, whereas on guard, you probably only do maybe one or two duties per year.

The first one I had to do was the annual summer ball, which was very memorable. There was this young cocky sprog, Rimmons, who thought he knew everything. A few others and I were working in the dining room on various jobs. I was detailed by the senior steward to go and pick up the top table centrepiece from the V & A store (valuable and attractive) – such as mess silver/gold trophies/cups, etc. I informed him I was already busy having been detailed for another job I was working on.

He then instructed the sprog to collect it and to be very careful as it was very delicate and valuable (insured for about £5,000). A week's wages were only about £15-20 per week in those days.

He collected a three-tier centrepiece trophy from the V & A store, carried it as one piece across the centre of the dining room.

When about halfway across, the senior steward saw him and gave him a rollicking; then told him he should have carried the trophy in three separate pieces and reassembled it on the table. As he was going to break it carrying it like that, there was a definite sense of panic in the corporal's voice.

Rimmons replied, "Don't worry, I know what I'm doing, I won't drop it!" I sensed the atmosphere in the room change; I had a feeling something was going to happen, so I and everybody in the room stopped what we were doing and watched.

He went to the table and put the trophy only halfway on, turned around and walked away; inevitably, the trophy fell on to the floor, I cringed as it seemed to be in slow motion, and it hit the floor with a sickening bang; what wasn't broken off was bent or dented. It was soft brittle silver.

The senior steward was watching the whole thing, he said quietly to this lad, "Get out of here before I lose my temper!" He did just that; he didn't need telling twice.

The senior steward walked over to the smashed trophy and put it on the table slowly, piece by broken piece. He stood and looked at it and wept silently, the tears rolling down his cheeks. I suppose to replace the same item today would probably cost about £25-30,000.

I turned and almost ran out of the room. I was about to burst out laughing, which I didn't think the senior steward would have appreciated.

After that, Rimmons was never trusted with anything as important or with anything valuable again; you couldn't really blame the senior steward, could you? He had probably been told by the mess committee not to trust him again.

Just before my first 'do', which was a summer ball, I was told that the officers and their wives got carried away when they were drunk, so much so that one year, they had a fountain as a centrepiece in the foyer and also a small pond as well, and 'anything goes', starting with their clothes. Quite a few people of both sexes stripped off and frolicked in the pool by the fountain, naked! They had a rare old time that year.

How true that was, I didn't know, but I didn't believe that they had stripped off. Had a wild time? Yes, because I had seen it for myself since, but not to the extent that this civilian told me; not naked!

Once I recall the partygoers had managed to get a mini car into the foyer and were most disappointed that they could not get it down the passages from one end of the mess to the other.

I had also seen them 'relax' by drinking several free 'champagne cocktails' as many as the officers and their guests wanted; of course, it went to their heads.

After the formal dinner, some officers were making animals out of fruit with match/cocktail sticks, then throwing them at each other. This led to pitched battles, throwing fruit at each other across the table until all officers and guests were involved.

'Zulu warriors' was performed at these do's by the young officers, including one time in front of a very high ranking WRAF officer. She was asked if she would like to leave the room while it was going on. But she wanted to stay and watch the fun and she wasn't in the least embarrassed; on the contrary, she enjoyed it.

Now, a Zulu warrior was usually done by drunken servicemen (we didn't realise that officers also did it), undressing on a table to the cheers of their friends and bystanders chanting, "Get them down, you Zulu warrior, get them down, you Zulu chief, chief, chief!" Continually until either the guy was naked or collapsed due to being too drunk, then in some circles they were doused with beer from all who were watching. There was, of course, another further version of this but I won't go into it here.

Eventually, the participants, after doing their Zulu, were split into two teams in various stages of undress and had a tug of war in the dining room.

During the night, a crate of champagne disappeared. The cooks had taken it to their accommodation block and were drunk.

Loyal toast

During our training, we were taught that in preparation for the loyal toast (to the Queen), if an officer didn't drink and didn't want port or sherry or madeira, then they were offered water, as the toast must be drunk in some form.

That was fair enough and it was bearing this in mind when I saw that the civilian mess manager (ex-navy) didn't take into account the people who might have turned down alcohol, they were given nothing but expected to go through the motions with an empty glass, and this annoyed me. I was determined to impose the correct method one way or another even though I had no rank or power to enforce my wishes. But I didn't let a little thing like that bother me.

So the second dining in night, I placed out on a table a water jug for the officers' use as and when required. It was used as it should be with the non-drinkers using it for the loyal toast.

When the mess manager saw this, he went mad, he took me aside and tried to give me a rollicking, but I wasn't going to have any of it. He asked me if it was me who had put out the water and why. Someone must have seen me do it and reported me to him. And in front of the other lads, he tried to show me up and snarled, "You never do that, we don't do such things in my mess, not here!" I calmly informed him that it was the correct way.

He then started to get very nasty with me and I was determined not to be bullied or put down in front of all the staff, so I very firmly but politely informed him that he was wrong in not doing it this way, that was the way it was taught in the R.A.F. steward training.

"We don't do that in the navy!" he snarled. "And we have never done it here!"

This really got me mad, something snapped and now I was angry! I was determined to have it done right.

So I retaliated with what I'd been tempted to say for a very long time, but had kept quiet. "Well, Sir! You're not in the navy now, you are a civilian!" (That hurt him, but he had asked for it.)

"And this is an R.A.F. camp and we'll do it the R.A.F.'s way!" Then I walked away. I must have sounded very cheeky and cocky, only a couple of months or so out of basics, he must have thought I was trying to challenge his authority as boss, I hadn't intended it to sound that way, but that was how it must have come across. He was fuming; mind you, so was I.

There were a few officers watching all this and afterwards, a couple of officers came to me and said they backed me all the way and was glad it was finally brought out in the open. That really made my day. And prior to the next couple or so dining in nights, this matter was mentioned again to me by these officers who had backed my stand. I therefore respectively asked and requested that they mention it to this mess manager, to inform him that I was right and had a point.

I don't know that if they did, but would you believe that I won my point! From then on, there was always water provided for the officers/guests during functions.

The mess manager never forgave me for that. We both avoided each other wherever possible; I sometimes caught him glaring at me when he thought I wasn't looking.

That is the sort of person I am and will always be; if I believe I am right, I will fight, and fight against all the odds if need be, and continue to this day even if it looks like a lost cause, as long as I believe I am right. Some people nowadays will not fight for what they believe in if they think they a) might have trouble from it, or b) they don't stand any chance of winning – they don't even try. But if I am proved wrong, I will apologise or admit it.

To get an insight of this mess manager character, as was normal in the R.A.F upon posting to a new camp, you find out a) the places where servicemen were banned, and b) the bars of a 'shady reputation' frequented by 'girls of ill repute'. The poof bars to avoid. Bars where the civilians didn't like servicemen.

We found out that the mess manager frequented the most infamous poof bar in Portsmouth, the Albany. He said he hadn't seen anything out of the ordinary there or even any poofs.

During my first summer at Thorney Island, a few friends and I thought we would spend a bright and sunny Sunday down by the beach on the airfield by the Nuffield centre where, for a nominal fee, you could join the sailing club and learn to sail. My mother thought I should take advantage of this and learn to sail, but I had no interest whatsoever in sailing and I still haven't.

We got it all organised, some of us would bring the beer, others the music and so on. We found ourselves at first on a grassy area leading to the beach; we thought we would have something to eat there and then onto the beach later.

During the afternoon, two attractive long-haired girls came and sat opposite us about 25-30 yards away. I, of course, had my eye on them all afternoon. Before long and before we realised what had happened, they had changed into their bikinis and were laying out, getting a tan with the top of their bikinis undone to get a nice even tan on their backs.

None of the others were paying them any attention, all they were interested in was drinking and listening to the records on a Battery record player we had brought with us.

Eventually, I noticed one of these girls acting suspiciously; she must have been aware of our presence though I doubt she cared as we weren't in hiding, we were all in the open. And we weren't exactly quiet. Suddenly, she got up, walked over to the bushes behind them and looking around to see that no one was looking, but I was! – she pulled down the pants of her bikini and bent down and stuck her backside out and believe she answered nature's call. Then still thinking no one was watching, she made herself decent and rejoined her friend. I was flabbergasted. Some of the lads asked what was so funny to have me laughing so much. By the time I had gotten my breath back enough to tell them, she had already joined her friend and the lads didn't believe me. But before I could try and persuade them I was right, her friend got up and went through the same motions, but by the time she got to the bushes, had looked around and her pants came down, we were all watching. As all was revealed and she had crouched down, we all spontaneously let out a great cheer. This surprised her and she hurriedly pulled her pants back up and looked around to see where all the cheering was coming from, but she couldn't see; she must have been blind or was she aware and was giving us all a quick flash? We were right in front of her! She then ran back to her mate who, when the cheer had gone up, had sat up in surprise wondering where the cheering was coming from and consequently left behind her bikini top and we saw her nice, large breasts swinging free.

This raised yet another cheer.

They promptly packed their bags and within seconds, they were gone.

I wonder if they had been there with the intention of giving us a flash, just to titivate us perhaps. Some girls were like that, they were about 20+ years old so they must have known what they were doing and aware that servicemen came there on weekends.

We'll never know; were they civilians on the camp (allowed in for the sailing club or the beach) or were they the daughters of camp personnel?

One chap with us during the lowering of the girls' pants episode was 'Bubbly' Stubley; he was the only one who had been embarrassed and hadn't bothered about watching them. He got some stick about that, as lads do, he was called poof, virgin, etc., it didn't seem to bother him though.

Whilst in the block, once someone made a harmless comment while trying on his crash helmet for his motorbike. "Why don't 'Stubby' wear it in bed!" So the draft prat did!

The look on the orderly corporal's face that following morning was worth a thousand words; all he saw sticking out of Stubs' bed was a head in a crash helmet, still wearing his glasses.

I came back to the block one Sunday after a weekend at home and found, when I walked in the room, everybody stood by their beds and the R.A.F. police were searching people's lockers, suitcases, etc.

I was asked by the R.A.F. police if I knew anything about some money Stubley had. I said I didn't!

Stubley had reported some missing and didn't know if it had been taken from his locker or not.

R.A.F. Thorney Island 1968/9 . Author (aged 21) and my best friend – Dave Stubley.

After an hour or so, another chap who had been home for the weekend came in and was also asked if he knew anything about this money. He said yes, he did know what had happened!"

"Stubley lent me the money to go home with and said I could pay him back as soon as I wish!"

The policemen looked at each other, then looked at Stubley, we looked at each other, then at Stubley. A policeman said to Stubs, "Get outside and wait for us!"

Stubbs confessed to me later that now he did remember lending the money but at the time, he had forgotten all about it.

At Thorney Island, apart from the O.C.U., we also had 'B' Flight 22 Squadron, a S.A.R (search and rescue) helicopter squadron, flying 'Westland Whirlwind' helicopters.

I was told by one of the lads that he had never been in a helicopter before and he rang up the squadron and asked if he could have a flight, which he did. It was Easter and I was on camp because I was due over the Easter week to do a rare guard duty, my only one while there; so I rang the squadron and arranged for a flight in a day or two. On the phone I was asked if I could swim. I asked why and he said, "Oh, it's nothing really, we just need to know for insurance purposes!"

But first, I had my duty to do.

I had rung up from the barrier post as that where I was stationed, checking the identity of people wanting to come into the camp. I was alone so if anyone wanted to get in, they wouldn't have come in by the main road and my post.

Or if there would have been any trouble, I could have been overpowered; there wasn't even any R.A.F. policemen in the area to help me out.

After checking the validity and identity of a truck driver who wanted to come in, I raised the barrier and he started to come forwards. I started to lower the barrier slowly, then the wind caught it and brought it crashing down on the truck – inevitably, the barrier pole snapped.

So, I had to report it to the main guardroom and write out a report on how it happened. I was to blame a bit – I think that I should have let it go higher and I probably brought it down a bit too quick.

In my report, I put the civvy driver entirely to blame, and with just a query about the wind, my report was accepted.

I reported the following day to 22 Sqn for my first flight on a helicopter. 22 were at that time flying Westland Whirlwind helicopters. It was still a means of flying I'd never tried but always wanted to.

I was told that they were very busy rehearsing for the forthcoming International (Search and Rescue) Helicopter meet; it was UK's turn to host the event this year, in which all the NATO countries sent their best search and rescue teams to compete for a trophy.

With them being busy, could I help them practice? Otherwise, they couldn't fit me in. I agreed readily; I was rather looking forward to it.

The sergeant winch man asked if I was the one who had rung up; I said I was. "Oh you can swim, can't you?" I was getting a bit concerned now. Why did they keep asking if I could swim?

We took off straight up; it was a weird sensation going up vertical instead of rolling down a runway first. We flew over the sand dunes and mud flats; at about 10-15 feet, the winch man on my helicopter shouted over to me as I sat in the hatchway looking out and dangling my feet over the edge of the helicopter.

"You can swim, can't you?" Now I was definitely getting worried about being able to swim, I said yes then looked out at the people below, waving as we flew low and fast at near wave top height.

Next thing I knew, I felt a shove at my back and I was thrown out of the helicopter. I was so surprised that I didn't have time to scream before I hit the shallows. Fortunately, the sea was going out and was only about 2/3 feet deep but the mud was about 6-8 inches deep. I cursed and shook my fist at them as they circled overhead then came in low and hovered, ready for the 'rescue'; even from a good distance away, I could see the crewmen, especially the winch man, laughing as though he was fit to burst. The winch man came down on the winch and metal strop still laughing, so now I knew why they wanted to know if I could swim – crafty buggers.

I had the life belt/jacket on and with the aid of the winch man holding me, I was slowly winched aboard; as I was raised up, the helicopter at the same time came lower so you were never far from the ground in case the strop/winch broke. A most unnerving experience nevertheless.

As I came aboard, I cursed him, he was still laughing.

I couldn't stay mad at them for long, they knew what they were doing and hadn't taken any unnecessary, uncalculated risks.

For the rest of the afternoon, I was 'dropped off' and picked up a few times. A couple of times, which was the most unnerving part, I was told to lay out on the airfield as if I was unconscious and the chopper came over and the winch man came down with a stretcher into which he strapped me, then I was winched on board – it was a bit frightening. On the airfield, the wind was blowing and the stretcher with me on board started to swing about and if anything would have happened, there was nothing I could have done, being strapped in as if in a straitjacket, very unnerving.

When we had landed, the crew went out of their way to make me relax and apologise for their 'planned bit of fun'. I was bought a pint in their mess as a way of saying thank you for my help and no bad feelings for throwing me out. I accepted their apology.

Overall, I enjoyed the experience. One thing I did tell my friends that if they wanted to fly, make sure they could swim first.

S.A.R. meet

The Search and Rescue meet was interesting, seeing all these different types of helicopters from all the different NATO countries taking part.

I believe that the two R.A.F. teams taking part, 22 Squadron and 202 Squadron, came in the first four places but I can't say for sure as we were never told who did win.

One impressive display I saw was by a specially rigged out CI30 Hercules as a Search and Rescue aircraft with two prongs on its nose and flying low, it picked up a balloon/wire strop to which the person to be rescued was attached. And the person to be picked up was gradually winched into the open and waiting large door at the rear, all in one swift non-stop movement, very impressive.

It was the same type of rescue done in a James Bond film and John Wayne in the *Green Berets*, which proved it wasn't all fiction. And it does work.

Complaints from farmers and nudists

Some weeks later, there was a rumour going around camp that complaints were being made by angry local farmers about a large military helicopter poaching game from their fields. They were supposedly shooting the game, such as rabbits, pheasants, etc. Landing, picking up the kill and taking off again.

When approached, the Royal Navy asked what colour these helicopters were and were told by the Farmers, yellow! "Ah!" said the Royal Navy. "They can't be ours as Royal Navy helicopters are coloured blue and orange, not yellow. Try the R.A.F.!"

What the outcome was we didn't know as we heard nothing more at the time.

We heard from the same source that complaints were received from the local nudist colony that large yellow helicopters were coming in low, making a draft with the down-wash of their rotor blades and the crew making suggestive gestures at the nudists below and taking photographs. I did read sometime later in the papers that R.A.F. S&R helicopters from our part of the country had been on the carpet for the nudist story. That was in keeping with the military sense of humour, all on camp thought it a great weeze; not, I fear, the nudists though!

R.A.F. police dogs

One day during Easter, one of my friends who had friends in the R.A.F. police, suggested we spend the day with them as it could prove interesting, and so we got in with a couple of R.A.F. police dog handlers.

During our chat to these policeman, I was asked if I wanted to earn myself a pint, all I had to do was put on this special protective gear worn for training purposes, 'shoot at the dog', then try and run away and let the dog attack you and bring you down. "No, thank you," I said. "If any police dog is going to attack me, I want more than one paltry pint, I would want nearer a barrel for me!"

What put me off was that the police had said each dog had a favourite part of the body it went for when bringing you down, and one of them loved going for the lower genital regions. I didn't fancy that as I couldn't remember which one it was that liked these parts, so I wasn't going to risk it.

I graciously declined the offer, but for the rest of the Easter weekend, we hung around with them and it was quite interesting.

Naafi credit

During the evenings in the Naafi, if we were a bit hard up until payday, we used to get a bit of unofficial credit from the manageress who was from New Zealand and a widow; she had a soft spot for R.A.F. servicemen as her husband had served with the R.A.F. during the war.

Credit was strictly not allowed in the Naafi establishments, but this lady allowed it. And as far as I know, she was paid back by everyone come payday; as expected, one or two might have been a bit slow in paying back or not paying back at all. It didn't happen as she had so many friends there that she had plenty of support or 'muscle' if she needed to use it to get the 'culprit' to pay up, and as far as I know during my time there – 18 months – it never happened once because she was well liked and respected by everyone.

S.A.C. crook

At Thorney Island we had an S.A.C. steward in the mess who was always in debt; though he always seemed to have a brand-new car that he seemed to change every 6-9 months. We wondered how he did it as he was on the same money as ourselves and even spending our money wisely, we couldn't afford a new car so often. We found out how he did it, he was court-martialled as he was getting credit from various places and giving the names of his neighbours, friends and such.

It came to light when I was summoned by the S.I.B. to report to the Naafi manager, present alongside them was one of the staff. I was asked if I'd bought an expensive item, which I obviously denied. I was asked to give an example of my signature, which didn't match the one given by this other guy for the said item that had been taken out on hire purchase and none of the repayments made. The member of staff when asked said, 'No! I wasn't the one who made the purchase!' Why didn't they ask her first? Fortunately, they didn't actually accuse me at any time, just asked questions; had they done so! Well, I think the reader has gained sufficient knowledge by now as to how I would react in such an event. The guilty party was eventually summoned in front of the station commander after the Naafi brought charges against him for a very large unpaid bill (of several items). He was court-martialled and sent away to the military 'Nick' at Colchester.

He had always told us it was his ambition to have a brand-new Rolls Royce within 5 years. And a new one cost then about £100,000 +. Should have suspected something when he was only on the same wages as the rest of us, but I just put it down to idle bragging. I didn't think I would see him again but I did some time later, he had been promoted to Cpl. So much for keeping your nose clean to get promoted.

We used to go drinking at the local bars usually in Emsworth and the local nearby pubs. We would catch the old 'Thorney Island flyer', an old pre-war vintage bus that was still being used by a private firm each and every day. And in about 18 months, it only broke down once, not bad going, but even when it did, it would be plying its normal route the following day.

Many a drunken night I spent at Emsworth, and I got to know some of the pubs pretty well. After being paid on Thursday, I would sometimes not go out until Friday night where I would catch the Thorney Island flyer to town where I would catch another bus or a train to Portsmouth for the weekend.

I would usually, though not always, sleep overnight at the Servicemen/Sailors' club where for a small fee you could have a small room with a bed for the night. Saturday daytime was spent sightseeing, sometimes at the seaside resort of South-sea or looking around the Royal Navy dockyard finishing up Lord Nelson's flagship H.M.S. Victory, where at the battle of Trafalgar in 1805, the British fleet under his command achieved probably our greatest naval victory in our history. Putting paid to the invasion of England by Napoleon.

The ship has been preserved and restored to its former glory in Portsmouth, where you can now walk around it and see it close up. I fully recommend it for anyone who hasn't seen it, well worth a visit.

In the evening, I would spend the rest of the night touring the bars, checking out the local females or trying to find out what other activities there were.

Most Saturday evenings would be spent in the 'Top Rank' dance hall in Portsmouth. We R.A.F. were not very successful with the women. In fact, it was as if we had some terrible disease or something. Then one evening, I found out why. I was chatting up a girl and she didn't seem to want to know me, tried to ignore me, then I told her, "I am not in the navy, you know!" Her attitude changed instantly for the better, I was finally getting somewhere.

She was amazed that I wasn't navy and rather pleased too. She told me, "The girls in Portsmouth are fed up with Royal Navy lads, they all seem to be interested in two things only, drinking and you-know-what. I bet the R.A.F. lads don't think the same, do they?" I didn't have the heart to tell her that yes, we did! I allowed myself a sly grin, no point in shattering her illusions!

I still didn't get anything though that night, unfortunately.

Knowing now why you couldn't get anywhere, I changed my method of approach when chatting the girls up in Portsmouth. I was quick to get in, "Don't worry, love, I am not in the navy!"

The funny thing was that things improved but not for long as I was posted before I had perfected my new 'line in patter'.

Once I had found good places to go, I thought what good my bike, Honda 50, was doing at home; I might as well have it here on camp with me so I could get the fun out of it. I had only used it 2/3 times per weekend when I went home and that was only about once every six weeks or so; meanwhile, I had it taxed and insured – a waste of money.

So the next time I went home, I came back to camp with my bike via Kings Cross railway station in the luggage van.

Getting across London proved a quite harrowing experience as I had never been through London except in a taxi/tube before.

After checking maps from the local library on the London roads through to Waterloo station, I had decided on my route but when I got there, I found there was a lot of one-way streets that hadn't been marked on my map in Scunthorpe, so I had to play it by ear and somehow I eventually managed to find my way to Waterloo.

I did it so quick, about half the time it took the London taxi drivers to get you there, which only goes to prove that they do take you the long way around.

At the local railway station near camp, I rode into camp feeling rather chuffed with myself. At first, I kept the bike outside the block until it was pointed out that it was a fire risk. I applied for a garage and a few weeks later, I was allocated a communal garage where all the motorbikes were kept by the lads in the various block accommodation. After a while, I couldn't be bothered to put it away, especially if it was raining as the garage was some distance from the block.

Then I thought, "Why pay rent if I'm not going to use it?" So I handed my keys in and kept the bike outside the block from then on. After a while, things started to go wrong with the bike, then the problems started to multiply, and eventually, I took it to a shop to repair, but they presented me with a huge bill. I was sure they were trying to 'do' me. I couldn't afford to pay it; it was equivalent to about two weeks' pay.

So after some advice and thought, I told them to stick the bike where it would hurt the most to try to cut my losses.

One weekend, I wanted to go home and couldn't afford the rail fare, so a chap in the mess offered to take me on the back of his scooter. I asked if he had passed his test and was legally able to take me on the back of his scooter. He said he had.

I didn't really comprehend until that weekend just how far home was; we rode through all weathers – rain, snow, sunshine and moonlight/sunrise.

I was so tired and bored on the back that 2/3 times I nearly fell asleep and fell off the scooter. When I woke on one such occasion, I found ourselves on the motorway. I shouted to him, "Are you sure that you have passed your test in case we get stopped by the police?" I got no reply.

Before long, the inevitable happened, we were stopped by a police patrol car and when they examined his driving licence, the police man said to this chap, "Bloody hell, lad, do you collect provisional licences for a hobby, there is a lot of them!"

He was not qualified to ride a bike on a motorway or with a pillion passenger; fortunately, I was qualified to ride with a pillion passenger so we were able to continue our journey, otherwise we couldn't have gotten any further.

Eventually, we ended up on country roads again, it took longer but we never saw another policeman all trip. After about 14+ long, endless hours, we got home. We had only a few hours' sleep and by then, it was time to think of heading back to camp.

This idiot spent his time sleeping on the settee, then without speaking, he set off back to camp on his own. He had been told that I was going back on the train, no matter what it cost; I had learned my lesson. That was the last time I went on the back of his scooter.

When I got back to camp, I laid into him and told him what a bum he was and left him in no doubt how it had felt. Even all the civilian staff agreed with me and gave him some stick. He avoided me after that and kept out of my way.

I had learned that bikes were OK for getting from A to B on short journeys, but really no good for long trips home or a social life, so I thought I would try and pass my driving test, then get a car.

I got myself fixed up with a one-man driving school that used his duel control Vauxhall Viva saloon for his and his wife's use when not training anybody. He was a bit of a nutter, a Pakistani. He had some weird and wonderful ways, but there was no taking anything from him, he was a good instructor who, if nothing else, introduced me to Chinese food, so at least I have that to thank him for. I eventually got him fixed up with another three pupils from my block.

I did have a go at my driving test but failed miserably on two accounts: a) I was far too nervous, I was shaking so much I couldn't control the pedals and was a bit frightened of making a mistake, b) I was taken around the back streets of Portsmouth, which I didn't know as I had not been down these streets before.

I thought it better to stop for a while and have a rest before starting again, I got talking to an R.A.F. policeman and he told me that the instructor was banned from entering the camp, but he wouldn't tell me why, only that if people wanted to use him, they had to arrange to see him at the barrier and that was far enough to put people of.

Most people who had him as an instructor didn't have much to say in his favour, though I thought he was quite good.

During my stay at Thorney Island, I spent two weekends with lads at their places. One was with Robert Beech, the ex-bus conductor previously mentioned.

The other one was at a chap's wedding. I was invited just before I was posted though I think he only invited me thinking that I wouldn't turn up. I told him if he invited me, I would come and so I did.

He had confessed to us all that he had made his girlfriend pregnant, but asked us not to let on. When I turned up at his house, both he and his mother were very surprised to see me. The house was a bit crowded with guests but I was still offered a bed.

At the reception, the part arrived where the best man read out the telegrams and he came to one. "And now here's one from Steve's mates on his camp at Thorney Island. 'Today's the day, tonight's the night, already the stork's begun its flight!' Signed: the lads in the mess!"

There was an uneasy shocked silence in the room; you could cut it with a knife! The best man, realising what he had said, was embarrassed, the new bride was shocked, mothers/fathers, in-laws were mad. I saw them drag the poor old groom aside and give him hell for telling the lads on camp that his 'new bride' was 'up the stick' when they didn't even know.

He pulled me aside later and angrily wanted to know if I had anything to do with it. I replied, "How could I? I am on another camp so I don't know what is going on now at Thorney Island!"

He asked if I knew who was responsible, had I heard anything being planned, I told him categorically no on both counts, though I did have a very good idea who it could have been.

From then on, I felt the atmosphere change against me, as if I had been the one responsible, probably it was handy blaming me as I was the only one from Thorney Island there and it was convenient to blame me, even though I had now been posted and had nothing more to do with Thorney.

The bridegroom in the pub later asked if I could lend him a fiver as he was a bit short, he promised to pay me back by the morning.

When he didn't, I left it as long as I could, then I just had to ask him as £5 was a lot of money then and I needed it to get back to camp with. He didn't seem very happy to pay me back. "Tough!" I thought.

His family also seemed embarrassed in front of their friends, I wouldn't have asked for it back had I not been so hard up and if he had offered to pay me back without me asking for it, I may have given it for his wedding present.

Bowling

Another town I visited frequently was Waterlooville, primarily for the ten-pin bowling alley, which was still all the rage at the time. After talking to some of the guys in the mess, I found out that there were several people in the mess who said they could play and play well (or so they led me to believe).

So making further inquiries, I found out there was enough interest to form a ten-pin bowling team.

We played only a couple of games, losing both in a league. It was most frustrating after all the work I'd put in to get it organised. I think the team broke up because a) the team was not good enough, and b) most of them never turned up half the time.

Before watching them play, they had all talked as if they were so very good and made it sound as if I was going to be the worst player in the team; as it turned out, I was the best player. The rest of them were pathetic, and I am only average.

I was led to believe I had the making of a good team. I made the mistake in taking part in a league before I'd seen them play and had a chance to improve everybody's game before making fools of ourselves in public in a game.

I really didn't think any of them had rolled a ball before, let alone played a game.

Chichester

Of all my favourite nearby towns I liked to visit was Chichester. Although historically and entertainment-wise it wasn't as good as Portsmouth, it didn't have as much going for it; but it did have more character, especially the old part of town.

One day a new chap who had just been posted wanted to know what Chichester was like for the 'essentials', such as beer, bars and girls.

So I offered to show him around. That evening, we set off in his car to see what we could find. At the age of 20/21, I thought I was just doing fine. I had yet to see a real pro in action and see how it was really done!

We called in several pubs until we finally arrived at one where he went into action. He was a little older than me, but a real expert at his craft, made my attempts look very amateurish. We, or should I say he, pulled a couple of classy looking girls, they were Danish or Norwegian, we never did find out just which.

I would certainly not have stood a chance on my own. He offered to take them back to the country cottage they were staying at. I was in the backseat with one of them, but I couldn't seem to get anywhere 'at the time'. So we took them to their cottage!

Drugs

Towards the end, I got depressed and a casual friend offered me 'pep pills'; he said they were great for lifting depression and afterwards, I would feel great! I didn't take any. They were, I believe, drugs he was trying to push but no matter how bad I felt, I would never be bad enough to sink to such levels as those. He was trying very hard to push these so-called pep pills. That was what gave me some idea that they might be something they weren't. The only way I would get high was by getting drunk, and I have done that often enough.

One such occasion was my 21st birthday at Thorney Island. It started at work, there was a request for my birthday over the radio on the 'Jimmy Young show'; my mum and dad had requested Elvis Presley but they played something else instead.

My party was held at the Nuffield centre and a cake was made for me by one of the civvy women in the mess. I had organised everything including the food and bar extension myself, and the surprising thing was that when I left, I was the only one sober.

After it was all over, about 7-8 of us piled into a very small car and drove along the beach and the sand dunes and surrounding roads. At one point, the driver said, "What's happened, we've run out of road!" And sure enough, we had. We had driven straight into the sea!

We had to pile out and push it out onto the beach and firm sand, word must have somehow gotten to the R.A.F. police as they appeared and gave chase, we piled into the car and shot off towards the main camp, chased by the 'fuzz' in R.A.F. terms. They were nicknamed Snowdrops because of their white hats. Their driver couldn't have been very experienced as we gave them the slip quite easily; mind you, when your driver was drunk, you took risks that you might not otherwise have taken, which helped us escape.

We managed to get to the carpark near the Naafi and we all piled out and ran in about seven different directions upon the hastily shouted, "Run".

The R.A.F. police screeched to a halt after us but with there being only two of them and with us not really breaking any laws (as then), who do they chase first?

Upon reaching the block, I stripped off and was in bed in record time, making out I was asleep. That was where the matter ended; we heard no more about it.

Nuffield centre

The Nuffield centre was a very nice place; it had large glass windows that overlooked the sea and a small beach. The décor, service and drinks were of a higher standard than the Naafi and it was the place where the officers/ wives and the NCOs went for a social evening when not in their own mess.

The drinks were cheaper too, which was a good attraction. They also catered for most water sports including sailing, water skiing, etc. I spent a few nights there.

Whilst there, my mother and father came down to camp to see me. They stayed in a bed and breakfast place near the railway station in Emsworth and had most of their meals in the airmen's mess.

One such meal they had was a curry that my father enjoys and for years my mother had strived to get it just right, similar to what my father had had in India during the Second World War. But to no avail. He enjoyed it so much that he wanted to tell the cooks how good it was as it was the best curry he had tasted in years and just like he remembered in India.

I said (knowing the mentality of the cooks), "Don't be daft; they'll not only think that you're crazy or sarcastic but where did they go wrong!" He insisted and the cooks stood open-mouthed, leaning on their spoons.

As we left, they stood in silence, as I said they would be, wondering what they had done to warrant a compliment. This worried them no end!

Once my folks had gone home, a couple of the cooks approached me and asked if he had really enjoyed it or was he being sarcastic? I assured them he wasn't and he did enjoy it. They walked away muttering to themselves and scratching their heads, they still couldn't believe it; they were only used to insults and complaints, and for them to have a compliment was a completely new experience.

Before joining up, I had been a keen gardener and in the R.A.F. at Thorney, I thought I would brighten the block up so I put some flowers in the room. I was called all the poofs/ponces under the sun for doing this so I learned that no matter how dull the room is, under no circumstances do you try and brighten it up with flowers. Not on a military base anyway.

Another thing that you never do in the R.A.F. as well as civvy street is stealing! And the biggest crime of all is to steal from your mates or comrades.

For a number of weeks, we had noticed that things were going missing from the block and the mess. One chap was suspected and we all kept an eye on him, though as yet, we couldn't prove a thing, until suddenly, he made a mistake and was found out. We were about to send for the police when one of the civvy cooks in the mess said, "Don't tell the police, leave him to us and we'll deal with him as we used to deal with his sort in the Navy, just keep watch and let us know if anybody comes!" This we duly did.

The next thing that happened, this lad was lured into the kitchen where the cooks were waiting for him. We heard a scuffle, shouting, then silence, then a series of very loud screams from the lad concerned.

A few minutes later, we heard an ambulance come screaming up to the back door of the kitchen. He was taken to the medical centre and was never seen again.

What had happened was that the cooks had grabbed him by the hands and dragged him over to the oven hot plate, which had been on since about 5-5:30 am. It was now about 10:30 am and with several of the cooks holding him, they had put and held his hands on the hot plate.

No one in the mess or block ever stole again!

And when the guilty party had been questioned by the relevant R.A.F. departments, i.e. Doctors, R.A.F. police and S.I.B. as to why had he been subjected to this ordeal by the grass roots justice, they discovered just why it had happened and he was given a medical discharge. It had transpired that the M.O. had asked how and why this happened and was told. The M.O. was then reputed to have said to this lad, "Well then, serves you bloody well right!" I couldn't verify this but my source was reliable.

A few weeks after we'd arrived in the mess, a corporal was posted to take charge of us; he wasn't very well liked by the servicemen or civilians. He was stubborn, short-tempered and wouldn't give anybody a fair crack of the whip. He would listen to one side of a dispute and make his mind up there and then, without the other person being allowed a say in his/her defence.

I think the reason for this was that he must have had a lot of pressure and couldn't take it in his stride; maybe he had just been 'made up' and was panicking? So he unfairly took it out on all of us.

One Friday night, he invited the R.A.F. stewards to his house for a bit of a do at his quarters. I was going out with a girl from Chichester at the time (Mandy) and she was quite attractive and had a very nice figure with curves and bumps in all the right places, she was very sexy.

At the end of the evening, after everybody had left, there was only the Cpl and his wife, Mandy and I left.

Eventually, they went to bed and left Mandy and I alone downstairs – with their permission. Talk about outstaying your welcome! Mandy let me do anything I wanted with her until I tried to get her knickers off, she didn't want to know about that.

She threatened to scream rape if I constantly persisted in trying to remove her knickers. There she was laid out on the carpet with her naked breasts – large but soft and firm with a pert cherry red nipple crowning her glory; but she had a so very hard look on her face that I lost all interest in her.

I think if I would have insisted in trying to get her knickers off, she would have – as she so very firmly insisted, screamed rape so I couldn't be bothered anymore and I gave up all further attempts to seduce her.

So I took her to catch her bus home, unsuccessful in trying to have 'my wicked way' with her that night. On reflection later, it was probably because she didn't feel at ease in a strange house when the owners would hear what was going on; she might have been a bit of a screamer. However, she never suggested any other time or place, so she probably wouldn't have gone all the way, no matter what I did or the circumstances. Some girls I found were like that, you could have a 'nibble' but you couldn't have the whole cake!

I only saw her once more then I packed her in. She was getting a bit too big for her boots, a bit cocky.

I didn't mind them putting up a bit of a half-hearted fight (so they don't give the impression they are 'easy'), but just the same I didn't like them to give in too easily. Of those that refused all advances and insisted that they were not that kind of a girl, fair enough, I tried no more.

Of those girls that agreed to 'participate', it was really amazing in my experience, the same story/excuse they would come out with no matter whether you were in the North, South, Scotland, Wales…they nearly always came out with the same excuse. "I'm not a virgin, it's not my first time, you know, I had a boyfriend, and he got me drunk and took advantage of me!" These excuses seemed so commonplace that I knew them by heart and the story would start, "It's not my first time, you know?" and I would try to look surprised and sympathetic. And if I was in 'that' sort of mood, I would interrupt and say, "Oh, isn't it? Don't tell me, you had a boyfriend and he got you drunk and took advantage of you!"

"Yes! But how did you know?" It took me all my time and effort not to laugh and very hard to keep a straight face. These excuses were so commonplace that only the 'scene of the crime' and the girl's name would be different; amazing really as if pre-arranged.

However, forgetting the lame excuses they came out with, they all seemed to be quite experienced in their sexual expertise and not beginners as they should be if their excuses were true. After a while, when I'd gotten a feel of the situation, I devised a plan, a sort of personal guidelines, which I used to work to and it proved very effective.

I got very choosy at times; I would finish with a girl for a number of varied and different reasons, great fun.

Talking of s-e-x, it was arranged at one time for me to take out one of the civvies' daughter when I first arrived at camp. I turned up, the girl didn't; I heard nothing for a day or two, then the girl's mother approached me and informed me that her daughter didn't want to go out with me any more due to the fact that I had insisted on groping her when she had told me she wasn't interested.

"Not bad going," I told the mother. "I am accused of groping a girl I have never even met!" Fortunately, her mother understood and was quite amused, and so was the rest of the mess, it became a standing joke for some time in the mess, about me groping girls whose mothers worked in the mess.

I never heard any more from the mother. I believe she had words with the girl concerned, probably she had been out with someone else that night, thinking it was me and that person was responsible for groping her, and for some reason I got the blame.

All in all, I wasn't happy any more at Thorney Island and I was ready for a move – a posting if I got the chance. I did get the chance not long after, when the R.A.F. was re-organised and those who wished for a posting nearer home could apply, so I did.

I shall always remember that a few days before I had a chance of a posting, I overheard the mess manager talking to Rimmons (who had smashed that trophy) and a couple of others. They too didn't like Thorney Island anymore and wanted a move.

The mess manager said to them, "You're typical of all these young lads, you do a lot of moaning, but if you really wanted to move, you would do something about it!" (I must agree with the mess manager on that count.) "You're all talk!" How wrong he was on my count. I thought, "You wait and see if I get a chance to move, I'll jump at it!"

My chance did come and I grabbed it with both hands. I applied for 1st choice: Scampton, 2nd Cranwell and 3rd Finningley (near Doncaster); all were only about 30-40 miles away from Scunthorpe.

My posting came through; I was to move to Cranwell (the main top flying station in the R.A.F. and only the very best trainee pilots with the very best qualifications and background went).

The next time I heard the mess manager talking to the young lads was, "If you don't like it here, why don't you do as J. R. did, and do something about it instead of just moaning around!"

I was glad to leave and was looking forward to my new posting; it was only a few miles from home.

I never did see my mate Dave Stubley again once I had left Thorney Island; we had become the best of pals. I have always wondered what happened to Stubs and where he is; despite many attempts to find and contact him, I have drawn a blank. The last I heard he may have passed away; I do hope that isn't true.

One evening, a few days before I left on my new posting, I was on late turn at the mess and it was my turn to stay behind and prepare things for breakfast. There was just me and the duty cook and by about 9 pm, we were just about to finish for the night when a young officer came through in the dining room and asked me if I could get him something to eat. I told him I would see if the cook could rustle up something for him.

The young officer then came into the kitchen and asked the cook if he could have something to eat as he had just been asked to cover another officer's duty and this was his first time. The cook (a New Zealander) replied, "It's too late now, Sir!" Leaning on his serving spoon, I noticed this seemed to be most cooks' normal position. "The cookers are switched off and all that's left is what's in the bin!" The officer laughed nervously and said, "Oh, that will be all right then, as long as it's warm!" He was assured that it was.

Now here came 'crossed wires', the officer thought the word 'bins' meant the trays that the food was placed in, in the kitchen and then placed on the servery for the stewards to put on the plate and serve. But what the cook meant was the slop bins that all the waste, rubbish and unwanted food went in at the end of the day. Without further ado, the cook rolled his sleeves up, started to fish around in the bins: a sausage here, an egg there (wiping them on his dirty cook's whites). He found some baked beans and threw a handful of them on the plate, a tomato, a bit of bacon there, he would get his dirty serviettes and wipe the remnants of yesterday's breakfast, lunch and today's dinner off it.

I couldn't believe my eyes. "You're not serious, are you? You're not going to offer him that, are you?" said I.

"Yes, of course!" he said indignantly. "I offered him the dregs and the slops and he said that it was OK!" He pushed the plate at me and said, "Here you are then – serve him!"

I turned and went into the dining room where he sat patiently on his own waiting for his meal. And laid it in front of him, I turned to walk away and saw out the corner of my eye he was tucking into the meal with gusto. "Rather you than me, pal, it's your stomach!" I mumbled to myself. I couldn't get out of the dining room quick enough, I felt ill.

The cook asked if he was eating it. When I told him that he was, we both burst out laughing, I am sure that the officer heard us.

We then got ready for home and just before leaving, the officer came into the servery and actually complimented us on a 'most enjoyable meal';

we were struck dumb and couldn't get out of the mess quick enough, laughing as we went. There was always the chance that he'd find out that when the slop bins were full, they were collected by local farmers and fed to their pigs. Yes, it was pig swill that this officer had enjoyed so much. He never did come back.

The time eventually came for me to leave Thorney Island and my 'adventures' behind; I was looking forward to Cranwell, wondering what lay in store for me there.

R.A.F. Cranwell: College and Flying School, June 1969 to 1970

Settling in

I was looking forward to Cranwell with a bit of apprehension as, a) a new camp and not knowing what to expect, b) with it being Cranwell, things were bound to be 100% on the ball more so than any of my previous camps.

My fears though were mostly unfounded that discipline and general conduct was higher, and it was! But not to the extent that it got on top of you.

As before, I tried to get my belongings sorted out ASAP and into a regular routine, I didn't like being moved from bed space to bed space and barrack block to barrack block as what happened occasionally. I liked to get my cases unpacked and my locker laid out then I could relax.

Passing the driving test

At Cranwell, I was able to go home a lot more as I was only based about 50 miles from home, especially if I'd finished my shift and I wasn't due for another day or two, so taking advantage of this, I had a few more driving lessons, took my test in uniform and passed.

Buying my first car

A week or two later, I bought my first car, a Morris 1100, which was to make life a bit more bearable. I was able for the first time to come and go as I pleased without being tied to buses, trains, etc. An added bonus was that it improved my 'courting and sex life', such as it was at the time.

Introduction tour of the camp

We were shown around the various areas and sections that made up the camp. You had an insight on how the other sections worked/performed that otherwise you would only have heard about. I never had this tour before on any other camp I was stationed at. It was very interesting, seeing how all the different departments worked independently, only coming together in the last stages to enable the training of the aircrew of the R.A.F. and ultimately how it all finally turned into an efficient fighting, operational unit.

It had the effect of making you a little more proud of being British, if that were possible.

We were also shown the R.A.F. Cranwell museum where we saw the first jet engine invented by an ex-Cranwellian, Group Captain Whittle, also a mock-up of the first jet aircraft.

'Student officers' mess

I was assigned to the Student Officers' Mess where the officers of different countries were trained as engineers and on the technical side of flying and operating an air force.

I noticed that some of the countries represented were Barbados, Canada, Jamaica, Singapore, Malaya, Hong Kong, Fiji, Samoa, New Zealand, even U.S.A. and lots of African countries, including Kenya.

And two countries that went to war with each other while I was there: Nigeria and Biafra.

Before the war, they had been reasonably friendly with each other, but on the outbreak of hostilities, whenever the opportunity arose – that usually happened at mealtimes as they were kept apart during working hours, they had a go at each other, fighting, throwing things at each other and swearing, at least I think it was swearing in their own tongues and dialect.

The R.A.F. officers got a bit fed up of separating them, so a compromise was reached to restore peace and order. One of these 'gentlemen' would have his meals during the first half of mealtimes and the other at the second half. This succeeded in restoring calm to the mess. Except after the evening meal was finished, they couldn't be kept apart. There were one or two fights but eventually they saw sense and avoided each other at every opportunity, we had no more trouble after that.

Snow

This same and other foreign officers hadn't seen any snow before. So when the snow came, all these young officers, especially those from Africa, were out playing in the snow, throwing snowballs, building snowmen and giggling like schoolboys at play time. A couple of senior R.A.F. officers went by and I overheard the conversation that ensued (African officers), "How lucky you are to have this snow, it's wonderful. Do you like it as well?"

To which the R.A.F. officer replied, "No, and you can keep the bugger. Take it back home with you if you want – bloody silly foreigners!"

Snapping fingers

This was the first and only mess where I heard someone snap his fingers for service, and expect us to come running.

There was only one, a large burly African. R.A.F. officers – as in the Army and Royal Navy – were educated as part of their basic officer training on matters of etiquette and the correct manner in which to behave in public that would stand them in good stead no matter in whose company or where in the world they were.

So, the R.A.F./British officers did not ever snap their fingers.

This African tried it for two or three days and as per unwritten law, he was ignored and everybody was served first before him. And he sat all through the mealtime before he was finally served. We stuck to this then someone reported it to the senior steward, a Warrant Officer – not me this time!

So the Warrant Officer waited in the dining room for it to happen, and when the African started to snap his fingers, he moved in. The whole dining room came to a stop and an uneasy silence fell over the room; everybody looked towards this African and the W.O.

"And who the hell do you think you are – SIR? Snapping your fingers at my staff – SIR! Maybe you do it where you come from but you do not do it in an R.A.F. mess, especially in MY mess! My men are airmen in the Royal Air Force. They are not dogs you order around with a snap of the fingers, maybe you do it in your mess back in Africa, but not here. If you do it once more, I shall instruct my stewards/stewardesses and cooks not to serve you at all and you shall go hungry, do I make myself understood? SIR? Report to my office after lunch where I shall endeavour to show you what to do and not do in an R.A.F. mess!" And with that he walked away, with the admiration of all R.A.F. personnel in that dining room, be it airman or officer! Both the officers and the stewards had beaming smiles for the rest of the lunch.

The R.A.F. officers were quite amused and thought it good that the person concerned had been put in his place. After all, as they said, someone had to instruct him in the errors of his ways and educated as to the correct manner of the mess! They were lapping it up; the other overseas officers were, however, cowed into silence and looked a bit worried as if the W.O. was going to start on them next; they ate their lunch in silence and tried to keep a low profile.

He never did snap his fingers again; he had been cured by the W.O..

Elvis fan from Kenya (officer)

For a little while, before I went to work in the bar, I had brought a record player and amplifier and played Elvis records while working in the dining room (between sittings/mealtimes). One Sunday, while getting ready for high tea and dinner, an officer from Kenya, a real nice chap, came in with a friend of his and asked if I liked Elvis (that was all I was playing, just Elvis).

He had heard me playing Elvis before, I told him that indeed I was a fan and he said that he too was a fan, and at the moment Elvis had just become very popular in his country. At this moment in time, Elvis was still at the height of his 'rock-n-roll' phase, that phase in England had passed many years before.

He was having some friends up with some girls from London next week, he asked if I would like to come along and play my Elvis records for them at a party he was throwing at the mess, I told him I would love to but I wasn't allowed to mix with officers. He was disappointed and couldn't understand why; I tried to explain the situation. I suppose if I had or he had made enquiries and tried to get official permission, it may have been possible, but I was still reasonably new to this R.A.F. lark and I didn't want to cause any unnecessary trouble for myself.

I let the matter drop there, but we did come to a compromise. I was due to work that weekend he was talking about and said that as normal I shall be working in the mess and I would have the record player going. If he was walking past the dining room with his friends and they wanted to dance, unofficially, in the dining room then there was nothing I could do and I would change the records as I would anyway. If anyone questioned them why they were dancing in the dining room with his friends, then it was nothing to do with me.

Kenyan officer and friends dancing to Rock-n-Roll

This was what happened though no one questioned them dancing in the dining room. It was funny to see them trying to perform rock-n-roll! You could just imagine them in their native dress dancing in front of a fire in the centre of the village; what was certain was that they couldn't do rock-n-roll.

Who knows what it could have led to if I'd have kept in with them. Probably in a year or two, they would have led a rebellion and made me head of the air force, married to about a dozen big buxom native girls (it had happened in the past to others). On second thoughts, I was probably well out of it after all.

I moved into the bar, most of the officers using the bar were R.A.F. and NATO countries, as the others didn't come in due to various reasons such as religion.

I think that most must have liked the records I was playing as there were no complaints. I did hear a couple of officers taking about Elvis Presley and trying to figure out why he was still so popular.

King Dick

At the Student Officers' mess (one of four officers' messes), we had working there a civilian who, for want of a better name, we shall call 'King Dick'; all will be revealed as to why.

He was said to have been 'excused the wearing of shorts' in the desert during WW2 due to 'an abnormally long penis'! Said to be about 14/15 inches long. Let's just say we were prepared to take his word for it. As neither I nor anyone else were willing to take a tape measure and see for ourselves. I didn't believe this until he showed me the doctor's note he had kept all these years. It was true!

One of the famous mess stories was a year or two prior to my coming to the mess, there was a WRAF girl who bragged she could take any size; she was told that she could not take this one!

She still was adamant! So the civilian, King Dick, took it out, put it in her hands and said to her, "Can you take this then?" When she saw what he had put in her hands, she promptly fainted! She was cured of bragging and did not brag anymore. I was assured that this story was true by several people but not being there I couldn't say for sure.

He had a well-known party trick, which again neither I nor any of us newcomers believed. I and some other new postings were told that he could line up 12 half-crowns (pre-decimal days = two shillings and sixpence, now 12½ new pence) on the table and knock them off in one movement with no hands. Of course, I and the other lads laughed and said we didn't believe it.

So a demonstration was promptly laid on for us 'unbelievers' during the period between meals, and the coins were laid out in line on the officer's dining table. The coins we'd be talking about end to end were about 14/15 inches and sure enough, they were removed in next to no time in one swift movement and no one used their hands. What some girls might call these days a W.O.M.D. – a weapon of mass delight!

Senior college

Apart from normal dining in nights, we also had to help out when they had a 'passing out wings dinner' at the senior college, prior to leave and posting to their first squadron or O.C.U.

I was working on one such function – the wings graduation and passing out dining-in night – the culmination of 5 years of training. This function coincided with the first manned landing on the moon.

There was a life-size mock-up of the moon vehicle set up in the foyer of the mess, very cleverly made.

During serving of the main course, there was a bit of a commotion at the servery door, with several stewards and cooks surrounding King Dick in a huddle. I didn't pay much attention as I was busy. Unbeknownst to me, King Dick had been given an order for braised sausage, he had come back to the kitchen, popped 'it' on an oval silver salver and decorated it with water cress, tomatoes, mashed potatoes, etc. The cook had then covered it with cool-ish gravy and then covered it with a white serviette. He walked out to the dining room and every cook and steward stopped what they were doing to watch the fun and games, trying to stifle their laughter. I was now intrigued and positioned myself close to the officer he was serving. Bending down with the silver salver, he presented the contents to his officer. The officer was busy chatting to another officer. "Sir, your braised sausage!" said Dick, he then whipped the serviette away, the officer was just about to spear the offending article on the salver's contents all nicely decorated with Dick's 'White Snake' peering up at him. He just stopped himself in time. He burst out laughing and his girlfriend did too. Dick stood there with the biggest grin on his face. When everybody on the table realised what had happened, all the wives/girlfriends including all the staff burst out with the loudest laughter; he even got some applause from others on the table.

When I asked him why he did it, he said that this young trainee officer (at the time) had given him some cheek and a hard time and this had been his last chance to get his own back. Ever since, when I hear the term 'Trouser Snake', my mind goes back to those days in Cranwell – that truly WAS a trouser snake!

Copulating couples

A few hours into the function, after the meal had been served, most of the guests were worse the wear for drink, in fact most were 'Blotto'.

Some of the couples were feeling randy and couldn't wait to get it on and then proceeded to get down and get with it wherever they happened to be at the time. Tables, large easy chairs, throughout the mess or even on the floor, all were used for their carnal pleasures. All inhibitions and clothes were thrown to the wind.

I was a bit embarrassed to be constantly stepping over copulating couples having a go. Whilst serving or collecting glasses, I was forever tripping over people; looking down, I would see a girl with her attention on other things, the same with the chap, in a state of undress. "Excuse me, Sir, whoops! Sorry madam!" Nobody seemed to care anymore, they were getting close to the 'point of no return'.

As the evening wore on, I got so used to it that it didn't bother me anymore and I didn't bat an eyelid and became a little blasé about it all.

Over the next couple of days, we heard from various sources, including the radio, that five people had been killed going home from the Wings parade and dinner that night: one couple on a motorbike, one in a car and two others in another car. How tragic that after all those years in college to get the necessary qualifications, joining the R.A.F., starting and finishing a five-year course, only to be killed on the day your efforts came to fruition and you finally were awarded your 'Wings' and given your 'Queen's commission' – so sad, so very, very sad!

Another amusing incident that happened that night was that most of the girls that had been escorted to the do by the young new officers had donned dresses that had low necklines and revealed quite a bit of cleavage, some girls more than others, depending on their build.

We stewards found it quite difficult to concentrate on our jobs with all these lovely distractions, the vast majority of us were able to keep control but, of course, there had to be one or two who couldn't.

Spilling gravy in officer's lap

A young sprog when serving his officer couldn't keep his eyes off his girl-friend's cleavage and while trying to pour gravy onto the officer's meal, wasn't watching what he was doing and instead – being distracted by this young officer's girlfriend's magnificent cleavage – poured the gravy all over his lap.

Much to the amusement of everyone in the immediate vicinity, including the girl, only her boyfriend wasn't happy.

Leching his girlfriend's boobs

Another young chap, L.A.C. Brown, did almost the same, the only difference being he slapped mashed potato on the officer's lap while looking at the officer's girlfriend's boobs. When he realised what he had done, he tried to wipe it off his uniform, which had the effect of making it more and more ingrained and spread. He was told off for not concentrating and for 'glaring at my girlfriend's boobs'! Again, the officers were not amused but their girlfriends certainly were!

We enjoyed watching the goings on, I too got a good eyeful of these girls' low necklines but I and everybody else was able to manage it. Silver service was difficult at the best of times but especially when rushed off your feet and distracted.

1st world aerobatic championships, Hullavington

A few months later, I was sent with L.A.C. Brown to help out in a mess at R.A.F. station Hullavington, which was looking after the competitors in the first 'World Aerobatic championships' including most countries such as France, Italy, Canada, USA, UK, Russia and others at R.A.F. Hullavington, June 1970. It had been organised by the Royal Aero Club.

About halfway through, L.A.C. Brown was R.T.U.'d back to Cranwell in disgrace, he was not only playing cards with the A.T.C. (Air Training Corps) for school boys hoping to join the R.A.F. and taking their money off them, but he was showing off, making himself out to be a 'big hard man'. He was also beating them up and climbing into bed with them. So were the rumours we heard. He told me himself he was playing cards with them and beating them up.

Whenever any of us saw him with the A.T.C. lads, he would start to show off that he was not much bigger than the boys themselves. Upon my return to Cranwell, I was told to report to the catering officer. I couldn't think what it was at first but then in his office he asked me if I knew the reason Brown had been R.T.U.'d and what he had been up to. I told him that I had only heard rumours and didn't know the official reason why. I was ordered to tell him what I knew and of the rumours I had heard, so I told him what I knew. Brown eventually was charged and got 14 days 'Jankers'.

The British team (civilians) had the help of R.A.F. pilots for training and planning their manoeuvres. Bit unfair on the others though, they defiantly had the advantage of some of the Retired Red Arrows pilots. They took the team prize and the second place for individual flying; a Russian took first place.

Russians want "Bread!"

Whilst there, I made up my mind that I was not going to serve the Russians! Things went well until towards the end of the last week, I was walking past the Russians' table, one called to me, "Bread!" I ignored him and served others, eventually going past his table again, he said, "Bread, I want bread!"

I thought, "F*** you, mate!" and ignored him again.

A few minutes later, a Cpl told me to serve him. I told him where to get off; I wasn't serving him and that was that! In the end, I was ordered that if I didn't do it, I would be charged, so I said, "Bread he wants, you say? I'll give him f*****g bread!" I placed a bread roll in the bread basket and promptly 'doctored' it.

When a couple of the lads saw this, they too wanted to doctor it themselves. I noticed that until I did it first, nobody else did anything; I let them do their bit. It had the unwanted contents of a cook's nose, regurgitated spittle, urine – not mine – cigarette ash all rubbed in. The Cpl said, "You're not going to serve that up after all that, are you?" I replied, "You think not? Just watch me!" As I went into the dining room, the Cpl ordered me to come back, I ignored him and marched boldly out, watched by all the cooks and stewards. There was a hushed silence from the staff. I walked up to the said Russian and said, "Bread, you want bread? Sir!" with all the sarcasm I could muster.

He just said, "Yes." I turned and walked casually away with a large grin on my face.

I noticed that he ate every scrap of the bread. UGH! And I got away with it scot-free.

Air display

On the last day, after all the competition phase was over, the public was invited for an international air display.

The individual winners gave displays and then the teams, followed by the professional display teams from the NATO countries in order to impress the Russians, I'm sure. First due were the Italians, they got lost and only three out of nine turned up. Don't know how they did it really, they took off together and flew to England in formation. So their display didn't have much impact with only three aircraft.

Next were the French; they didn't turn up for another two hours due to their aircraft going U/S before take-off.

After everybody had done their bit, it was the turn of the 'stars of the show', the Red Arrows. I was especially interested to see how the Russians would react to the Red Arrows. All was quiet and everyone was watching the airfield runway in anticipation of the arrival of the Red Arrows in their 'Gnats' aircraft.

Then suddenly one zoomed over the Air Traffic Control Tower just low enough to clear it and came at us from behind; nobody expected it (not allowed now).

Then just cleared the heads of the audience and climbed into a near vertical climb into the sun. While everybody was watching it climb, the sound of the engine came and hit our ears and nearly deafened us; the public cheered loudly followed by the smell of aviation fuel; that's how low it was. We were all still looking towards the sun after this first aircraft and before we knew what was to happen next, the entire team, including the first to show, zoomed in and started their display from the least expected direction. The public really cheered every manoeuvre; they were without doubt the most popular display. It was the usual high standard we have come to expect from the Red Arrows.

When it came to the part where two aircraft fly towards each other at a combined speed of 800 mph, eventually missing each other by inches, even the Russians cheered louder than anybody. Towards the end, I even heard the Russians say that they thought the Red Arrows were the best. Indeed, we all knew this already and have for years.

The winner of the individual event was announced – a Russian, over the tannoy, it was said that he was a quiet modest chap, but he was climbing out of his plane waving his hands above his hands and grinning as if to say, "Look at me, I'm the greatest!" Big-headed swine. Thankfully, he wasn't the one who had wanted bread!

Saying goodbye to the great gang
On the last night, we were there, all the stewards/stewardesses had a night out together in the Naafi and the 6-8 girls were escorted to the block by about 25 stewards, then all the lads without warning burst out spontaneously into song, *We'll meet again*; of course, we never did!

The R.A.F. police were called out to this 'noisy carry on'! They stood aside, smiled at us and left us to it as we weren't causing any trouble. It was a very enjoyable detachment (with the exception of the Russians), they were a great bunch and I was sorry to say goodbye, I had enjoyed their company.

I had a few days at home before having to report for duty at Cranwell.

Night out (inc. Spitalgate)
I didn't visit the Naafi at Cranwell more than a couple of times. I had my car now and was somewhere different each night, usually R.A.F. Spitalgate near Grantham on dance nights about three nights per week (more about Spitalgate in my next posting).

Great pub (unable to find)
One bright and warm summer evening, I had a run out along some country roads. I found a great country pub somewhere near Ancaster, Lincolnshire. It had everything – low oak beams, horse brasses, cheese board, beer served from the wooden casks, hand pumps, women and that musky smell

particular to country pubs; I enjoyed it, great atmosphere. I have since, on several occasions, tried to find it again and failed. It was a mystery!

Whilst there, we saw a film on an officer's initiative test between being dropped off in the middle of nowhere and facing many difficulties on the way back to the college. A film crew filmed one man and saw him peering through bushes 100 yards from the finish and within sight of the end. There was a tap on his shoulder, an instructor from the R.A.F. Regiment sent him back, all the way to the beginning – 40 miles away.

Their basic course was tougher than ours; I found a new admiration for these officers.

Throughout my time as a steward, I had heard lots of stories from cooks/ stewards being 'propositioned' for sex by officers' and sergeants' wives at special functions, so many, there must be some truth in this.

Barrack room hard man

During my stay at Cranwell in the block, the so-called 'barrack room hard man' approached me. (He was well built, as broad as he was tall, and he was tall.)

I was on talking terms but not really pally as was the norm, everybody pals up with someone and you didn't bother very much with others. He came to my bed space and commenced to beat me up with his mate alongside, laughing. It caught me completely off guard.

I tried to ask why he was doing it. He just said, "You know." I didn't! About 2-3 weeks later, he came to my bed space again but this time I was ready for him. I thought, "Hello, he's going to try it again, but I'm ready for him this time." He surprised me by trying to stumble out an apology. I was shocked! He told me that he had heard that I'd told stories to his girlfriend about him and talked about him behind his back to her. It was only now he realised that not only did I not know her, but that I'd never even met her. I asked him how this story had come about. I was told that it was his mate who had seen his girlfriend and told her.

That infuriated me. "As I told you before, I had not had anything to do with your girlfriend, don't know her, never met her! It was your so-called mate who is trying to cause the trouble!" He reluctantly agreed that I was right. "Besides," I told him, "I don't do that sort of trick to anyone!"

I asked where his 'friend' was who had caused the trouble; he wouldn't tell me and I told him to "Pass a message that if I ever saw him again, I was going to have the b*****d and smash his face in. So he had better stay out of my way!"

He apologised again and told me, "Not to worry about it, leave my mate to me, I'll deal with him my way." I never did see his 'mate' again. The 'hard man' tried a bit harder to be friends but I wasn't interested.

Flu and Christmas

Just before Christmas 1969, I had a dose of the flu and was admitted to the medical centre to prevent it spreading prior to Christmas. There were about six of us in that ward for the same complaint, about a dozen in the medical centre.

They discharged me on the 23rd thinking they were doing me a favour. I told them to keep me in as I wasn't fully recovered, they didn't listen to me, I said, "Then don't be surprised if on my first day back, I have to be readmitted!" They thought I was joking, I wasn't and I was readmitted on my return to camp.

I was due to work with L.A.C. Brown over the Christmas break, just he and I working shifts in the mess to cover any emergency, unexpected visitors to the mess. We were to handle the reception desk, tannoy and telephone exchange. I reported sick upon my return to camp and was readmitted within 12 hours. I told Brown that I wasn't going to take him off the following morning as I would be in the medical centre. He went mad and said, "I forbid you to go; after all, you're not ill! You're only imagining it, you were told by the W.O. that you had to work over Christmas and so you shall!" I just laughed at him to his face and said, "Want to bet?" and walked off, I didn't even bring up the small matter of rank as I outranked him and so he couldn't tell me what to do. It wasn't too bad inside the ward; we all got on well together and had a good laugh. It was the only Christmas that I'd spent with so little to drink (the next worse was on active service). I only had two glasses of sherry and one small can of beer.

I don't know how Brown coped on his own, I don't think he had the brains to contact someone in charge and arrange for a replacement for me, he worked continuously for about three days, just grabbing what sleep when he could, ruddy fool. Had it been me, I would have sorted something out immediately.

Catering officer gives me a rollicking

One day, I was told I had to see the catering officer. So in I marched, smiling and wished him greetings of the day. As it turned out, I was in for a rollicking; I had no idea what I was called in for.

The O.C. said it had come to his notice that I was 'leading the young lads astray'! I was shocked into silence; after a while I spoke up and asked just what did he mean by that.

Leading others astray

He said that he had been told I was telling stories to the impressionable youngsters and leading them astray, and giving them the wrong sort of encouragement. I was fuming. I really hadn't gotten a clue as to what he was talking about. And I let him know that too.

No matter how much I tried to persuade him to tell me who it was. (Could it have been Brown?) Or another? I never did find out. He wouldn't tell me. I demanded to no avail, I said, "If I am condemned without a fair chance to defend myself, at least give me the satisfaction of knowing who has condemned me?" I told him that the idea of me 'leading the others astray' was preposterous, as I was a loner and didn't care about the others, didn't bother with them at work and when off duty, I was usually on my own. He wouldn't listen to me, I was already 'tried and found guilty' and condemned out of hand.

I demanded a posting; I wasn't going to stay under these circumstances. He refused me a posting, I told him that I would do all I could to obtain a posting ASAP and I 'will' get a posting! He (the O.C.) would not stop me. I believe that this incident changed me, no longer was I the 'do anything to help' person. I was now bitter and from then on angry and wouldn't help anyone; I withdrew further into my 'loner' persona, fighting my corner with renewed aggression if I thought I had been done an injustice.

Nocton Hall dances

One Saturday, after hearing about the great dances to be had with the service nurses at the R.A.F. Hospital Nocton Hall, near Lincoln, I, along with a friend, went there in my car.

Yes, it was a great time but I didn't 'dip my wick' that night. I did, however, meet a girl, a nurse, who wasn't a ravishing beauty and, throughout my time in the R.A.F., kept sending me the occasional letter and Christmas cards, B/card, etc. She must have thought more of me than I did of her; to me she was only a one night stand. I got inevitably drunk that night on cider, but refused to sway to my mate's request and drive back as this was the year that the dreaded 'breathalyser' was brought in.

I knew I wasn't capable and if I'd been picked up by the police and breathalysed, I could have lost my driving licence and I'd been through too much for me to risk that. I wasn't having any of it, so I gave him an ultimatum! He could walk back on his own down the dark, mist-shrouded country lanes, about 6-8 miles, or he could sleep in my car until the morning when I'd sobered up and then I would drive back. This he very reluctantly agreed to, but he was most put out when I claimed the comfortable backseat for myself, he had wanted it. Still what did he expect, it was my car, did he think I had to give it up for him, no way, I'm not daft.

In the morning, I drove back, still worried that I may get stopped as the alcohol was still in my blood though by now greatly thinned out.

I saw no other vehicles on the road on the return trip, though I was on tenterhooks throughout the drive back. We got back about 6-6:30 am and I went straight to bed to sleep the rest of it off.

Posting

Shortly after, the opportunity arose for me to apply for a posting and I lost no time in doing so.

The R.A.F. was reorganising the pay/personal system and they said that for ease of costs such as travel warrants, meals, etc., anybody who wanted a posting near their home, the R.A.F. would try and comply as it would also help people settle in more easily. So I applied for Waddington, Scampton and Finningley.

Waddington was only about 5 miles or so nearer home but at least I would be away from those two-faced, back-stabbing bar stewards in Cranwell's Student Officers' mess. I told the catering officer I would get a posting and despite his refusal I did!

I got my posting to R.A.F. Scampton, home of 617 'Dam-busters' Sqn. About 30 miles from home and the nearest R.A.F. camp to home. It was the posting I wanted. It was at Scampton that my father had been stationed here during and after the war, and when he had met my mother.

I had a few days at home, then moved to my new posting – officers' mess, R.A.F., Scampton.

Shortly before I'd left Cranwell, H.R.H. Prince Charles joined the R.A.F. and commenced his flying training, eventually going on to fly helicopters and command his own ship, H.M.S. Bronington, a minesweeper, in the Royal Navy.

So once again, I packed my bags, ready to start a new adventure.

On a recent trip back home in the summer of 2019, I called in at Cranwell to see if it was still as I remembered all those years ago. As it is, Cranwell is based either side of a public road so I was able to drive through.

They say never go back; it has changed dramatically from my time, though this was the view from the road only. I barely recognised it. From the viewpoint from the road, it seemed – save a couple of buildings that I remember, it is all changed; there have been many changes since my time there.

But thankfully, the main college is still there.

R.A.F. Scampton (1970 to November 1971)

Lancaster: outside the main gate

I was posted in 1970 assigned to the officers' mess at first in the dining room. Then the bar for most of the time I was there.

Outside the main guardroom, there was a wartime Lancaster bomber astride an array of weapons it used to carry on its raids nightly into Germany. Including the Barnes Wallis 'Bouncing bomb' used in the attack and breaching the Mohne, Eider and Sorpe dams in the industrial Ruhr of Germany.

Also on show was the 10,000lb tallboy used on the raids destroying the German pocket battleship, Tirpitz! It had a good clean out while I was there and in its flaps, they found 37 birds' nests. It was decided that if something wasn't done soon, it would be too rotten to be stood outside in the elements.

Conveniently, the R.A.F. museum had just opened and was on the lookout for a Lancaster for display, so Scampton offered the Lancaster and was accepted by the museum. Ironically, it was the Lancaster that had flown more missions than any other of its type, so quite appropriate.

Airmen's mess: wartime ops room

A surprise was awaiting me when I went for my first meal in the airmen's mess. We only ate in our own mess when not working. I discovered that the upstairs grill and lounge was the wartime ops room where the aircrew was briefed before setting off on their bombing missions (from which some 55,000 men of Bomber command were never to return).

There were photos of wartime briefings, raids and the aftermath of raids, and mock-ups of the missions including 617 Sqn Dam busters raids on the dams. The one I was particularly interested in was the scale model of the Mohne dam, with the surrounding hills and countryside. The very model that was used to brief the crews before 617 squadron's famous raid on the three dams (really impressive). It gave you an understanding of how difficult it was for the crew to fly the 'dog leg' between the hills and lakes. Level off to the right height and speed giving the bomb aimer only a few seconds to line up the sights and drop the 'Bouncing bomb' in just the right spot. Even part of the room was left as it was during the war years.

Good food

The standard of the food was the best I'd come across in an airmen's mess. It was superb.

One day at random, I thought as a matter of interest I would count how many main/meat courses there were and counting eggs, sausages as two, I counted 17 main courses to choose from one lunch time.

In charge of my room

I was put in charge of my room and make sure it was kept clean and tidy at all times, by detailing the others to do their bit and allocation of daily room jobs. For several months, all went well until one week not long before the annual A.O.C.'s inspection. I had given everybody their room jobs for the week and as normal, detailed one lad to go around each morning and check all the jobs were done, and if necessary put it right before leaving the block and going to work.

Charged, proceed to Finningley

One morning I was informed that I was to be charged for 'failing to ensure the room was kept up to standard'. It wasn't my first charge nor was it my last.

I was informed that the room had a pre-A.O.C. inspection and had failed to come up to standard. (The actual A.O.C. inspection didn't happen for another six months.) The floor, I was told, had not been swept and bumped up.

I confronted the lad concerned and he said he hadn't done the room because he was late out of bed. At the first opportunity, I checked the room to see what was supposed to be wrong. I had to look very hard to find something wrong. After a long search, I found the cause of the inspecting officer's anguish.

There was one piece of fluff under two beds.

I think they were overreacting and panicking too soon, six months before the inspection.

This I soon found out was an old trick in the R.A.F. It had me fooled a couple of times in the beginning, but from this incident, I wasn't fooled any more.

They tried and made you panic and work that much harder by telling you somebody important was coming. It didn't bother me who was to inspect, I did my best each bull night, no matter who was due. I was satisfied that I'd dome my best and couldn't do more; if they didn't like it, 'fecking tough'!

I was given seven days (Jankers) restrictions, I only did one day before being told that one of the Vulcan bomber Sqns was to be detached on an exercise and some of the catering staff had to go along to provide a service. I volunteered to be one.

We were to proceed to R.A.F. Finningley near Doncaster Yorkshire. One NCO made his own way up and I took three others in my newly acquired car. We got about halfway between Scampton and Finningley when one of my tyres shredded; it was a new remould I had bought only a couple of weeks before.

Eventually, after a real struggle, I got the wheel off, put on the spare, reloaded the baggage and continued the journey. Consequently, this delay made us late in arriving at Finningley; it was well after 6 pm and I should have been doing my time working in the guardroom. However, my section officer excused me for the night because I was late. That was the second day of my seven days.

As I booked in the guardroom on arrival, I was greeted with a surprise. The Orderly Cpl on duty was the same S.A.C. I had worked with at Thorney Island who had been court-martialled trying to get these new cars and was on the fiddle. Now here he was with his two tapes up – promoted! I was disgusted, what incentive was there to work hard and do your best, might as well be on the fiddle.

During the first day there, I was approached by the senior steward who suggested that if I was willing, they would inform the guardroom that I was working late nights, which meant I was finishing about 9 pm each evening and that I would be excused 'Jankers' and wouldn't have to go on parade each night or report to the guardroom. I agreed and was quite happy about this as it got me off these duties; I did no more jankers.

Green Dragon: take girl's matches

One evening back at Scampton, a friend and I went for a night out in Lincoln and we finished up at the 'Green Dragon'; we started to chat up some girls who we found out were students at the local teachers' training college. Things were going OK, then for no apparent reason, their attitude changed and they seemed to be more distant, very cold. We wondered why and tried to figure it out. We couldn't get any further with them; it wasn't until I got to the block later that night that it came to me I had asked for a light for my cigarette. I had used her matches, then without realising, I had put the matches in my pocket. So that explained their sudden coldness. I felt really bad about it and for the next couple of nights, I went down to the Green Dragon to try and find the girl concerned and try and give her matches back but I never saw her again so some woman somewhere has a bad and false impression of airmen and me!

One lunchtime at 2 pm, after I'd finished 6/2 shift, I set off for home as I wasn't due back at work until 2 pm the following day.

Report chap for taking photographs of the Vulcans

At the main gate, I turned right instead of the usual left and set off a different way home for a change; this route took me around the back of the airfield. On public roads, when I saw a civvy at the perimeter fence taking photographs of the aircraft – the Vulcan Nuclear bombers. I did a fast about turn and headed at full speed for the guardroom. I reported the facts to the R.A.F. police who contacted the mobile patrol to intercept. I then set off back for home again the same way through Scampton village instead of the more direct A18.

By the time I got to the same place along the fence, the civvy and his car had gone; had he been intercepted by the R.A.F. police or left before they had got there? I never found out but whenever I drove past that area again, there was always a visible police presence. Why had it taken me to show them the chink in their security? Surely some officer must have done an assessment of likely spots for breaches in security? It was all too easy for someone to get over the fence unseen for a closer look or something more sinister. It beggared belief! I had also spotted a security breach that the R.A.F. police had missed sometime later on another camp. (See Odiham.)

A story doing the rounds while there told of a pilot of a Vulcan getting drunk in the bar, taking his aircraft up and doing aerobatics over the city of Lincoln. The aircraft was not designed for such flying, and not over cities. When he landed, the station commander, civvy and R.A.F. police were waiting for him.

I personally have doubts as to whether the story had any truth as the aircrew was not only highly disciplined but several things had to be done – set procedures to follow before you could get anywhere near the aircraft and that excluded the R.A.F. policeman and his dog on duty at the aircraft's dispersal. If he would have seen the pilot drunk and about to climb into the aircraft, he would surely have had authority to restrain him from taking the plane up. So this must have been some sort of local gossip without foundation.

Off-duty; Linda Masters

I went home during my off-duty hours usually for a 'fun' time and usually with a very sexy nurse, Linda Masters, who meant more to me at the time than any of my previous girlfriends – or since, excluding meeting my future wife.

Spitalgate: spoilt for choice

I also spent some of my off-duty evenings at R.A.F. Spitalgate, the afore-mentioned training camp for girls that joined the WRAFs. (See Cranwell.)

They held dances and discos about 3-4 times a week – Thursday, Friday, Saturday and Sunday. They were marvellous. You could always guarantee a new intake of between 50-70 girls each fortnight. So there was always plenty of scope and chances, in fact there were so many girls to choose from that you were never bored, only spoilt for choice!

With all these girls to choose from, it was sometimes difficult to decide which girl you would go after first, and what where the 2nd and 3rd choices. It was nice to have several options.

Display for the lads

This problem was overcome by the girls themselves. In the 'sticky bun bar' downstairs in the Naafi, one girl would put on the jukebox one or two of

Neil Sedaka's records, usually *Breaking up is hard to do!* or maybe *Oh Carol* or even *Calendar Girl.*

At this time, the record was about 8-10 years old. The girls would then *en masse* place the tables around the edge of the room and at 8 pm, the record was put on and all the girls that were available would form a long line, Conga fashion, and dance around the floor in time to the music, all doing the same dance someone had devised. No doubt some years earlier.

At first, you would wonder what it was all in aid of. The simple answer was they were displaying for all to see just who was available and what they looked like in the light as it was far too dark upstairs to make out any details.

Type of girls

Meanwhile, the visitors, usually airmen from all over Lincolnshire bases such as me, eyed them up and made our choices and plans for chatting them up. Talk about a meat market! I bet it would upset these women's liberation people but it was the girls' idea so these women's libbers can't complain. Minutes later, upstairs in the dance/disco, you had a good idea whether they were pretty or ugly! And if not shy, such as me, you moved in on them and bombarded them with your line of patter.

From then on in, it was 'every man for himself', and your luck with the girls was 'in the lap of the gods', as my old dad used to say, and dependent on your tongue and line of 'patter'. They ranged from ugly, plain to some who were really good-looking. Of the latter, there was no shortage of suitors and occasionally, you would have to wait your turn to chat them up.

Country types

There was always one or two who appeared not used to this 'market' and appeared to be wearing home-made dresses and probably came from farming communities or not very well-off; they looked and probably felt very conspicuous but some lads used to chat them up. I liked to concentrate on these 'innocent' girls' as they seemed nicer. And were more genuine, you could get more out of them, especially if you treated them well and had a good line in patter so they didn't know if you were having them on or telling them the truth, they were easy 'prey'!

Lesbians in the WRAF

They used to nearly all be fixed up with someone by the end of the evening. There were three particular girls and what they did and said that stuck in my mind. First, when I was talking to her, I asked if the rumour was true doing the rounds about WRAFs that there were a lot of lesbians in it, especially in basics.

She said that from what she'd seen of it, yes, there was and it was quite revolting at times, but she didn't think it was any different from any girl's/ men's military unit anywhere in the world; there were bound to be some until dealt with by the others serving in the same room or the military authorities heard of it and dealt with it swiftly as they did! (It was not tolerated in the services during my time, and I saw very little of it.) The guilty were always severely dealt with, usually a dishonourable discharge when I was serving. Things have changed now!

Get pregnant

Number two: When discussing the R.A.F. and WRAFs and comparing the two, I said, "Is it true what we hear that some girls in the WRAFs are prepared to get pregnant to get a free discharge from the services?" I was surprised to hear her reply.

"Yes!"

I said, "I think they must be mad to do so, just to get out of the WRAF!"

"You think so?" said she.

"Yes, definitely, that's a bit drastic, isn't it?" I replied. "By the sound of it, you don't disagree with the principle. Would you be prepared to get pregnant just to get out?"

She said, "Yes, I would!"

"Ah, Ah!" I thought things were looking good here for a bit, a 'nookie' tonight. "Why, don't you like it in the WRAF?" I asked, knowing the right answer could get me my carnal pleasures for the night; I was hoping dearly for a 'No' answer.

Which would put her in an awkward position where she would be tongue-tied and unable to refuse my verbal and physical advances.

She answered, "Yes, I do like the WRAFs!" My heart sank.

"Just my luck," I said. Even she had to laugh at this reply of mine.

Start my car for me

Number three: I seemed to be getting somewhere with her; she was responding to my attentions. I even was able to have a grope under her clothes on the dance floor. We came to a mutual agreement that it would be better to find somewhere more comfortable and private; we agreed to go to the bedding store near the airfield, which surprisingly always seemed to be 'open' on dance nights.

We drove up to it in my second-hand car, we thought it better to stay in the car; at least we wouldn't be seen so we had to be content with the backseat of my car, as we had been beaten to the bedding store by several others.

Unfortunately, by this time, she had cooled off and wasn't in the mood (or frightened of a full commitment). "Damn," I thought. She then asked me to take her back to the girls' accommodation block: "Typical of my luck," I thought.

I tried to start the car but it just wouldn't start. I was beginning to sweat and panic, I had visions of having to leave it there and walk back to

Scampton – a very long way! Also not to mention all the probing questions I would be asked – what was it doing in an 'out of bounds area'?

I felt so embarrassed by now.

Eventually, she got fed up of waiting and got out of the car, then told me to lift the bonnet. I asked what for and she said she would have a look at the engine for me, she messed around under the bonnet for a minute or two, then told me to try the engine now, lo and behold, it started the first time.

I had never felt such a fool in all my life, having the engine started by someone who had refused my advances and not knowing how to fix my own car.

I then had to take her to the block; I breathed a sigh of relief when she'd gone inside, I was glad to see the back of her. Though I must say I didn't feel put out too much, I went straight back to the dance and picked up another girl.

Spitalgate: look back fondly to Spitalgate

I have had several weekends at home where I have set off for camp hours earlier than normal just to meet a WRAF that I'd met up with during the week and arranged to meet her on Sunday.

They were the best dances I have ever been to as a single man; I shall always look back very fondly on Spitalgate dances, happy-happy memories.

"You'll always have friends with a car!"

I well remember my grandfather telling me, my parents too, "As long as you've got a car, you will never be short of friends. They will always want a lift in the car but when there is a repair bill to pay, they won't be able to be found and won't help you by lending you the money." How true! How very true.

Guys have to pay me for petrol

Whilst at Cranwell/Scampton, there were always lots of lads who wanted to go to Spitalgate and wanted me to give them a lift, even if I wasn't going myself. So, to make sure I wasn't going to be taken for a mug and taken advantage of, I said "OK. If I'm planning on going, I'll charge you 5/- each for helping me with petrol, tyres, running costs, etc." (5/- = 25 new pence) Then due to inflation, I increased it to £1 per car full – three passengers. They moaned and said they wouldn't pay so I said, "Fair enough, get a taxi, that will cost you more if you can get one and don't forget, a taxi won't wait for you if you're late whereas I am prepared to do so, within reason."

Nobody would use my car that week, but by the following week, they came around and agreed to pay, so I got a nice little sideline going.

I also said that if I hadn't planned on going that particular night and my car wouldn't be used, if you insisted on being taken, then it would cost you more, for unplanned wear and tear on the engine, tyres, etc., then I won't take it out for less than £1:10s (£1:50 new pence) + drinks.

I got even more moans and insults. But I was adamant and stuck by my decision, unpopular though it was; in the end, the chaps realised that I wasn't going to budge and they had no choice but to pay.

Spitalgate, including on compassionate grounds

I even took a chap home to Doncaster on what he claimed was compassionate grounds; he said he would pay me when he got back but I didn't trust him, if he got back, he would have probably forgotten to pay me or make out he'd forgotten, and if there was one thing I hated, it was chasing people for money they owed me.

I made sure I got the money first, he wasn't happy but as I pointed out, "You pay up first or you don't get the lift!" Tough! Whilst at Cranwell, S.A.C. Brown asked if I would take him to Spitalgate to one of the dances when I was there. I told him I hadn't planned on going that night so it would cost him; he was hard up, couldn't afford it. But eventually, I took him to Spitalgate for £1:10s. I didn't mind as I had a good time myself and as part of the deal, the passengers I gave a lift to had to buy me my beer for the night and anyone knowing me knew that wasn't cheap as I liked my beer and in later years, drank an awful lot more in the evening, though not now.

I had to prevent people thinking that with persuasion/browbeating, I would lower my prices; each time I would be no better off.

When I took lads to the dances, I would wait for them for a little while, then of course, there was always one or two who had to be told to hurry up although most turned up on time.

Accident in Grantham town centre

One time, I had more than the safe limit of alcohol (three beers); we went through a police roadblock set up in Grantham town centre. I thought, "Oh hell, I've had it. I'm bound to be breathalysed and get done!" The lads panicked too. I was stopped by one of the policemen who told me there had been an accident involving some lads in the R.A.F. from Swinderby, he asked where I had come from and where was I heading. I told him and he said, "Be careful!" And I continued my journey, breathing a great sigh of relief. The chaps said how well I'd done in keeping calm. I told them if they kept calm, we would be all right, I was right. He must have smelt the beer on my breath, but didn't pursue it – thank goodness.

A couple of days later, at the guardroom at Spitalgate at the next disco, I found out what had happened. A mini car had been seen arriving at the main gate with eight people (which was only built for four). The Orderly Sergeant had told them that he didn't care how the others got back to camp but the car was not going to leave the camp with more than four in.

At the end of the dance, the lads from Swinderby, all eight, tried to get out of camp in the car but the Orderly Sergeant was waiting for them and after much complaining, four were made to get out and walk back.

In the town, that same car ran into the back of an articulated truck, slicing off the roof of the mini – decapitating the four inside. It would have been 8 had it not been for the vigilance of the Orderly Sergeant. So there are four men alive today thanks to the Orderly Sgt on duty that night. I hope they appreciate it.

I will always look back with affection to my days at Spitalgate.

Bar steward

While working in the bar, there was one chap, a steward, whom I couldn't make my mind up whether he was brave, stupid, greedy or just plain ignorant.

Most evenings, when the officers wanted a bar extension, he as tradition goes, put the pot around, when he got it back, he took the money out, counted it, if he thought it sufficient, he allowed the bar to remain open.

If there was insufficient money in the pot, he told the officer requesting an extension, "There's not enough in here, put it around again!" Anybody else on duty would stay open as long as necessary and not dare to put the pot around again. But this chap would put the pot around every hour they wanted to stay open – cheeky bum!

617 Sqn standard

One day prior to a 'dining in night', as we were putting the Sqn standards into place on display, I got chatting to an officer who, when had I first gone to Scampton had been on 617 Sqn and then was posted to 27 Sqn, still based at Scampton. I asked him which Sqn he preferred, cheeky me. He said he wasn't really bothered, but when we were handling 617 Sqn standard, he panicked and was so frightened that we might damage it, it showed that he still had a preference for 617 Sqn. I had a chuckle to myself and pointed out to him what I had observed; even he allowed himself a little chuckle. I have always preferred R.A.F. aircrew; you can talk straight to them. They will listen to your point of view and what you have to say and treat you with equal respect. Unlike most ground trade officers, Respect!

Entertainment

There was more entertainment at Scampton for the other ranks than on any other camp I had been in to date (or compared to all the rest during my service) – theatre, cinema, another club (with a bar), most hobbies catered for and even a ten-pin bowling alley c/w bar.

All told, on the camp there were about 6-7 bars, which could be used, normally, you only had the choice of two at the most.

Show, old-time music hall

Once a month, the Naafi put on a show of some description. The best show I had seen for a while was the 'Ken Goodwin's Old-Time Music Hall', a really good night out. There was an attractive girl singer on the show and throughout her act, there were repeated calls from the nearly all male audience to "Get 'em' off". She was wearing the old-fashioned Victorian/Edwardian style long dress with a bustle at the back. Most lads weren't interested in her singing/dancing, she must have been a bit fed up of the catcalls so in mid-song, she stopped singing and addressed the male audience, "What's the matter with you all? Do you want me to take my clothes off?" This was greeted with a great and tumultuous cheering and applause. So she said, "OK, if that's what you want!" and without further ado or ceremony, she did just that – she took her clothes off and stood there in her underwear, bra, suspender belt, stockings, frilly knickers and high heels. This had the effect of stunning the audience into total silence, first and last time I had ever seen it.

She went on with her routine and at the end was cheered wildly, in fact at curtain call, she got the most and loudest cheers of all and a standing ovation. Funny how a bit of female flesh could have that effect on men! She must have done shows on service camps before and come to expect such comments and reactions; why else would she wear something provocative and enticing for the male members of the audience?

Stag night

There were also the usual stag nights with so-called blue comedians, strippers and female impersonators who I have always found quite vulgar.

During the first half of this particular show, the three girl strippers stripped all off but left intact their G-strings; there was a lot of displeasure voiced at this and the male audience seemed to get more and more restless and agitated. Eventually, the Master of Ceremonies had to announce to us all that he had had words with the girls and had been reassured that in the second half of the programme, the girls would remove their G-strings. "Please keep calm and let's not have a riot!" (As a riot was indeed brewing.) When they came out, the girls looked very nervous and they did indeed dispose of their flimsy G-strings, much to the delight of the audience and the relief of the MC. When they had finished, they got off the stage ASAP.

Raving Rupert

There was also a show by my friend who lived not far from me: Malcolm Hassle, stage name: 'Raving Rupert', an Elvis impersonator. For some reason, he seemed a little nervous this night. When I went up to him for a chat after the first half of his show, he seemed surprised and pleased to see me and we got chatting. He seemed more at ease during his second set.

Unsettled: want an active life

It was after I'd been at Scampton about 9 months or so, I felt unhappy and unsettled so I thought I had better do something about it, and it was here that fate took a hold of my life and changed my life in a more dramatic way than I could ever have guessed. Because of the treatment I had received;

and also at Cranwell I realised and felt I had gone as far as I could as a steward. It was pointless to go on. My career was at a dead end and going nowhere. It was time for something new – a new adventure.

It was a decision that was to change my whole life and future forever! It led me to meet my future wife. I had become fed up of being an officer's skivvy and I had always missed the active military life such as I had experienced in the army.

I then felt if in the forces, you ought to do a proper military job, though I realise you need the other supportive trades. I enquired about what trades I was eligible to go for and was told I was qualified to re-muster to any R.A.F. ground trades, technical or non-technical! And for a while, I considered trying for Air Traffic Control. But then hearing that it involved some work with figures and mathematical problems, I thought better of it as maths has never been a strong point with me; it was a shame really as it was a well-paid and very important job with a lot of potential and the chances of a well-paid job in civvy street.

But I was fed up of these civvies and no way to retaliate or get even; I felt that even though I didn't like fighting, I would like to join the R.A.F. Regiment as it should toughen me up, which was what I wanted (it did!) and I would get the chance of some active service. So I came to the conclusion that the R.A.F. Regiment was the best thing for me. Besides, my father had done service in the R.A.F. Regiment during the war. So I applied to join and had several interviews. The catering officer said, "Of all the trades available in the R.A.F. and you could choose any trade you wanted, what on earth makes you want to join the R.A.F. Regiment? You're better than that, you're better than them! They are the lowest of the low, scum of the earth, animals, the dregs of society!"

At that point, I was only 80-90% sure I wanted to join the R.A.F. Regiment.

But after this officer's ranting, I was now 100% sure it was the right choice for me! After all, they couldn't be *that* bad, could they?

Interview with R.A.F. Regiment officer

I had an interview with the R.A.F. Regiment officer and some of the regiment guys at Scampton to determine why I wanted to transfer to the regiment.

I was asked questions as to why I wanted the regiment. Could I hack the discipline of the regiment as it was a world away from stewarding in a nice warm mess with plenty of good, hot food?

My re-muster took about a month to come through.

Meanwhile, I waited for confirmation that I was accepted for training.

Picked on by the mess manager and W.O.

Once the mess manager and Warrant Officer found out I had applied for a re-muster, their attitude changed, they became even more awkward, nasty and belligerent towards me, they picked on the state of my uniform, my appearance, everything! I was probably one of the smartest; I always had a pride in my appearance. And there were others a lot scruffier than me in the mess who were never spoken to. I was criticised on my appearance, punctuality, etc., I was given a taste of what was to come if I joined the regiment to see if I could take it.

I couldn't change my uniform; I had already tried it. They were just being bloody-minded, I believe; who knows...maybe the regiment officer had told then to behave this way to test me? I didn't know. I certainly got more harassment during my last month as steward than ever before and I was glad to get away when the time came and I was really looking forward to the R.A.F. Regiment.

Measured for new uniform

I was sent and measured up for a new uniform as the other, although it appeared all right, was badly made and didn't fit me properly. I had pointed this out to the so-called tailor at the time but was made to accept it as it was. Now with the passage of time, it looked even worse so another was ordered for me but wasn't ready for me by the time I left for the R.A.F. Regiment depot at Catterick in Yorkshire.

This was approximately in November 1971 and I didn't get it until about April 1974. It was amusing really when asked several times why I was wearing such a scruffy uniform by regiment standards, but acceptable as a 'penguin' trade. And then having to tell them that it was on order and I had been waiting for it for years, they must have thought I was another 'Sergeant Ernie Bilko' (from the 1950s TV series) with a readymade excuse but the ironic part was that it was true and it did take three years to catch me up.

Scampton also had its own broadcasting station similar to Hereford; again, I volunteered and had another go at being a DJ. I only lasted three shows as I would only play Elvis Presley and my favourite old records from the 60s.

I was asked by one of the officials to play some more modern records; I told him I wasn't interested; I didn't like most of the records as they were rubbish. I think there was a bit of 'back room talking' going on after that; as I wasn't given any encouragement, I didn't bother going back.

Maybe a comment I made on my last show might have upset the person my comment was aimed at. It went thus, "And now a dedication from me to the mess manager, the message is in the words of the song by Dean Martin! *There are too many Chiefs and not enough Indians!*"

I believe although he was a civvy living off the camp, the message somehow got to him via the grapevine, though I was determined to leave and had my date, I didn't like the bloke and it was my way of 'getting at him' legally. I was past caring; I knew I hadn't got long to go before leaving for the regiment.

Leave for R.A.F. Regiment depot: Catterick

So in November 1971, I left the steward's job forever and set off for the R.A.F. Regiment basic training depot. Even though I'd passed out years before in the R.A.F. basic training, I still (along with over 70 others) had to prove I was tough enough to be trained in tactics, weapons training, map reading, navigation, etc. If I was to fail, then I would be posted to another camp as a steward. That was incentive enough to ensure I wouldn't fail.

I had been very nervous and sometimes during training wondered what the hell had I let myself in for! I needn't have worried; although not everything went right all the time (Nothing ever does, does it?), I still didn't regret making the decision to re-muster. In fact, when I look back, I am very glad I did change jobs, it was the best thing to happen to me and because of it, I have seen more of the world (America and the Far East, which I have always wanted to see) and met my future wife and also, the 'King' Elvis.

R.A.F. Regiment Basic Training Course
R.A.F. Regiment Depot: Catterick
(October to November 1971)

Move to Catterick

Finally, the big day arrived and I was posted to Catterick, home of the R.A.F. Regiment. I was full of anticipation and nerves; I had an idea that it would be tough but I didn't know how tough it would turn out to be.

The course was held during an autumn of 6 weeks so it got cold at times, especially on the final phase, the four days 'all in' exercise.

There were about 70+ of us to start the course; all bar about three of us were straight from basics so they had all their kit including boots bulled up to a high standard. Most were young about 17-19, I was one of the eldest, if not the eldest, at 24 years old. I certainly had had the most service in than anybody else.

Disadvantages

A big disadvantage for me was with most being straight from basic training at Swinderby, they were very fit and I wasn't, having all the years behind me of drinking and eating too much in the messes and very little or no exercise at all. I knew I had a struggle on my hands, and so right I was. I was nearly always last, finishing on road/cross country runs and P.T.

I would be aching and hurting all over but I kept up with them, it was a case of gritting your teeth, getting your head down and getting on with it.

Extra boots

Once I commenced training, I was issued with a further two pairs of boots.

The normal kit issue was R.A.F. Regiment two boots and one pair of shoes whereas the other trades were given two shoes and one pair of boots. The Depot must have thought that as a steward, I must have not been issued with any boots so was given two pairs, actually making me three pairs + two pairs of shoes to everybody's two + one. It was to save me not only rollickings during the training but to enable me to have clean, dry boots on when everybody else had to make do with wet soaking ones and of course, on inspections, the instructors would praise me highly on having clean, dry and highly polished pair of (bulled) boots compared to the others dull, wet ones. The instructors would tell the others in the room, "See, it can be done; why aren't yours as highly polished compared to Rowbottom's?" The lads would ask me, but then it was my little secret, 10 bonus points for creeping.

Training's quaint little things I'd missed

On the course, we were reintroduced to the 'quality' little things that we'd not been associated with since our very first days in the R.A.F. on basics at Swinderby such as bulling, regimental baths, kit inspections, bull nights (not half as easy as I had gotten used to on a normal camp) and bed packs.

Also blancoing and brasses (our webbing), an awful lot more than at Swinderby, so again the guys newly passed out from basics had an easy job just keeping on top of the webbing as it was already up to scratch.

The NCO instructors told us we ought to be grateful that we only had these few to do each night and not like the poor old sweats before us in years gone by who had a lot more to do each night, who had in the region 47 brasses to do as well as the rest of their kit.

As modern warfare developed and techniques changed, the 'average soldier' had an awful lot more to learn and something had to go to give him time to do it and study so it was to be unnecessary bull that was to go out of the window.

Talking of 'going out the window', many lunch times we were only given about 30 minutes for lunch, but in that time, you also had to get back to the block, change uniforms, assemble webbing, bull the boots, etc.

On top of this, when you had just got your kit absolutely perfect, the contents of all the lockers would be thrown all over the room and out the window. It took ages to sort out who had what and where, your hearts sank, all that work wasted (this was just the response they were after).

It brought some of the lads near to the edge of tears/anger. This was to see who had the discipline, self-control and so on.

Throwing kit around

If you were unfortunate as I and some others were and lived in one of the upstairs rooms, we looked out of already opened windows and found out that before the instructors had thrown the boots and kit out the windows, they had banged the toe cap against the wall first, then thrown them outside. You then had your kit to wash and iron on top of the usual boots, webbing, brasses, best uniform and so on. Looking out, we could see our shirts, pyjamas, u/pants, etc. lying in the mud of the flower border, scattered on the concrete and grass verges. And others were blowing down the road.

Find kit, make time

The usual thing was that we found our kit like "Whose last three are 365?", "Who's D.H.?" Someone would call out that they were theirs and I would get my kit back the same way. It sounds impossible that we could get all these things done and lunch in 30 minutes but it's funny what you can do when you are under pressure and panicking; we learned that we were better off missing lunch altogether to help yourself get finished in time.

Of course, the instructors knew this would happen, they had it calculated to a very fine art to the minute just what we should be doing and where we should be.

That night, you had so much more work to do – wash, iron all your kit to a certain size and bull your boots until about 1-2 am before going to bed and getting up again at about 5-6 am.

More training, less messing about

After the first few weeks, the 'buggeration factor' got less and less, as the NCO instructors called it, and we began to concentrate more and more on the training side of it and less on inspection, marching, P.T. and fitness training.

Of course, we all enjoyed this phase a lot better for this was what it was all about, what we'd joined the R.A.F. Regiment for. As the course progressed and at the end of each stage, we had oral, written and practical tests to pass before being allowed on to the next stage. At the end of each stage, we would lose more and more people off the course; it was known as getting rid of the dead wood! These T.O.E.Ts – tests of elementary training – and discipline were devised just for such reasons.

The dirty baker's dozen

Down and down came the numbers, sometimes one or two then 8 or 9 at once, we lost a dozen at one go. At the point in the course, when we had only about two weeks to go, we had eventually got down to only 13 left. What was popularly known as 'the dirty baker's dozen', this number then remained intact until the end of the course, I felt proud of myself that from the huge 70 + number at the start, I was one of the last to survive.

Can't hack it

What made it all that much sweeter was that at the beginning of the course, a lot of people had approached me after learning my age and previous job. Nobody thought I would be able to hack it and it was a different world away from an easy cushy job. I would fall at the first fence and be the first to pack it in (including the NCOs). How I had the last laugh on them, as most of those who had pulled me down and written me off had already been thrown out having failed; it was my turn to laugh at them now.

Mock final

At the pre-final point, about a week or 10 days before passing out, we had a mock final. We were told those that had failed would not have their names read out, but the Flight Commander would see them in his office later, where some would be leaving the course.

The people who had passed just with the lowest mark were called out first, the next highest mark and so on; after several minutes, my name had not been called out and I was getting very worried. At the end, the Sergeant came to the final position. I was paying him no attention as I was convinced I'd had failed and foresaw myself marching into the flight commander's office and being told to pull my socks up or else – or worse! The winner's name was then read out, S.A.C. Rowbottom! It was me, I couldn't believe it, I was shocked. I had come out top!

So the NCOs kept saying, "Just to think, he was a steward, so it shows just what can be done if you get your head down and try!"

Boots, cry-baby

To give you an idea on how hard we worked on our boots.

One inspection in the room one morning, the first lad the sergeant approached was inspected and asked the lad how long had he been working on his boots the night before. He told the sergeant, to which the sergeant replied, "No, you haven't, lad, you hardly touched them at all, work on them a bit more tonight and make sure they pass the inspection in the morning!" With that, he walked away.

The sergeant then walked to the next lad to inspect him. All of a sudden, the first lad burst out crying and blubbering, we were all trying not to laugh, thinking, "The silly bloody kid can't take it!"

Though fair was fair, we did try not to laugh at him though we couldn't resist it. A few seconds was all we could manage before the whole room erupted in fits of laughter and the instructors immediately got hold of the situation and told us in not so quiet and polite terms to "Shut your effing mouths and be effing quiet! And you (the one crying), get out of the room and wait in the corridor and stop blubbering like a bloody silly schoolgirl and act like a man, I'll speak to you later!" He gave the lad several minutes to compose himself and quickly finished the inspection, then went out to see him in the corridor.

Once all the instructors had left the room, discipline went to pot, we all fell on our beds laughing at this lad. We were not aware of the reason why he had cracked up.

Poor lad must have heard us all laughing at him. We heard from outside the sergeant saying to him at the end, "You have got to face the lads in the room sometime so I suggest you go in now and get the worst part over!" So he quietly sneaked into the room and started to get his kit ready, hoping no one would notice – some hope there! Nobody dared to speak to him for a couple of hours for fear of laughing again. The poor lad looked so embarrassed and down.

After a few days, we found out that his widowed mother had been trying to pressurise him into coming out of the R.A.F. but he hadn't wanted to, he had wanted to stay. He was in a quandary: he wanted to help his mother but didn't want to fail the course (she wanted him to run the shop she had). We think allowances were made for him, the pressure seemed to be off him slightly and I think a special effort was made to get him through his final exam. He was incidentally one of the few of the course to pass out of training and get posted to a Sqn. The word was, he stuck the regiment for about a couple of years and finally bought himself out.

Cute sayings of the DIs

What I remember with most affection was some of the cute little sayings I had missed that the instructors used to come out with. Especially at Catterick basic training, such as:

"What have you got between your legs, laddie? Then don't be afraid to open your legs when you march, you won't lose anything: you have a little bag to catch them in!"

"Am I hurting you boy?"
    "No, Sergeant/Cpl."
    "Well, I effing well should be, I'm standing on your effing hair, get it cut!"

"What did you do in Civvy Street, laddie? I bet you played in a band/
orchestra, didn't you? You must have done, you look like a bloody violinist
with all that effing hair! Get it effing cut before tomorrow."

"Did you have a fight this morning, boy?
    "No Sgt/Cpl."
    "I think you did, you had a fight with your razor, and the razor won!"

"Did you shave this morning, lad?"
    "Yes Sergeant."
    "Then tomorrow I suggest you stand a bit closer to the razor blade, it
might just take off your whiskers."

(The language used was a bit stronger than that.)

Those were the days, the best of times and the worst of times. Those who
have been through it will remember those days.

Pick on one man
One method all military units used was that they picked on one man all the
time to try to break him; it was usually the one the NCOs thought would
weaken and crack first.
    The R/Regiment was no different to the R.C.T. in this respect. They
tried to pick on me at first as I was a scruffy ex-steward with grease all over
his boots/shoes and uniforms – their words! Until I looked them in the eye
and had a big beaming smile, for which they would give me a 'rocket' or I
started to laugh at them straight to their faces, and again as in the R.C.T.,
they left me alone and went to pick on someone else, who was weak-willed,
such as the lad who cried.
    Whatever they said to me, I just laughed at their little quirks and threats.
They soon gave up.

Pin ups on lockers
During the inspections of the accommodation of the stewards, the inspecting officers would frown at pictures of naked women on the lockers and
make you take them down, but not in the Regiment! The officers/NCOs
always used to take their time going through a person's kit/locker. In the
R.A.F. Regiment, you were positively 'encouraged' to show you're a 'real
man' by having loads of photos of naked/semi-naked women on your
locker door. "The R.A.F. Regiment gunner is a 'man's man', not a Nancy
boy or a poof!" to have anything but masculine things on their lockers.
Otherwise, once seen by the staff, they had 'the urine extracted' as it was
'sissy-pansy and queer' not to have women on show, not soft poofy things
like football teams.

Man's man
You were expected to be a hard fighting, hard drinking, beer swilling, rough-tough sort of man; if not, then you just weren't one of the guys and had to take all the knocks coming your way.

What would an R.A.F. Regiment Sgt have had to say if he saw Stubley's locker with aircraft and no naked women? He would have been instantly branded weird, a poof! Of course, he wasn't, but he wouldn't have lasted a week in this man's world.

Naked girlfriend on the locker
One chap even had a photos of his girlfriend (one of those instant Polaroid types); she was of course naked and in several poses, some indecent.

His bed space was a very popular meeting place for lads in the room to have a chat in while having another look at his 'girlfriend', thing was we eventually found out from his friend that it wasn't really his girlfriend at all but a girl 'on the game' he had picked up one weekend when his friend had been present, that's why they had near pornographic pictures of this girl. So we came to the conclusion that if he had 'paid for it', then the photographs were probably all he had gotten for his money, just to try to impress the lads. Cue lots of 'micky-taking'.

Had to remove picture prior to an inspection
On the very, very odd occasions, we were made to take down our pictures prior to an inspection, 'in case it offended the eyes of the inspecting officer!' what a load of clap trap!

This ensured a lot of protests and it was our turn to accuse the inspecting officer of being a poof, queer and/or Nancy boy. And not real regiment material. I know most of the officers enjoyed looking at the pictures as much as anyone else; after all, they were servicemen and must have enjoyed the delight of females in various stages of undress as much as anyone else.

River crossing
Part of the training involved crossing the Swale, the river in North Yorkshire that happened to run through the camp. Part of the training was to learn to cross fast flowing rivers with all your weapons. A bit more difficult; you had to do it in full kit, fully clothed with rifle, ammo and such.

The Swale was a fast moving and rocky bottomed river, which made it very difficult to keep your feet when it came up to chest high on me; I was more than a little worried, I can tell you, I felt sorry for the small lads on our squad. If it came up to my chest, it was nearly over the heads of some, how they got across without falling in or drowning, I'll never know.

Losing my rifle
Then it came to my turn to cross this fast flowing river. I got about halfway across. Suddenly, my worst fears were realised, I fell in, and when I had

surfaced, the NCO asked where my rifle was! I had dropped it in the river and I didn't have a clue where it was now as I figured the current must have taken it downstream. I felt panic in the pit of my stomach slowly start to rise, I felt sick as the proverbial parrot.

"Retrieve that rifle or you will stay in the river until you do find it!" bellowed the NCO. I didn't need telling twice. Only trouble was my arms didn't reach the bottom so reluctantly I knew there was only one thing I could do! Holding my breath, I went underwater to try and find it by groping about on the riverbed – several times I came up for air without my rifle and by now I was getting worried. I began thinking I was going to finish my days court-martialled and doing time in the military 'nick' in Colchester followed by a dishonourable discharge.

By this time, all the lads and the NCO had made it to the other side and each time I came up for air, they were laughing their heads off at me.

I felt so embarrassed and panicked each time I came up; I felt less confident of ever finding it. The lads then made their way back across the river towards me; I assumed it was to help me find the missing rifle. I was still looking for my rifle and beginning to really panic now!

I was told to have one more look for it then come out, with or without it. Then suddenly, I felt the familiar shape of the trigger guard. I allowed myself a bit of a smile under water as I got a firm grip and surfaced holding the rifle aloft in triumph. Boy, was I happy! The lads cheered as they saw me surface holding the rifle aloft.

I had then to make my way to the far bank on my own and then back to join the others.

No rest for me as we set off across the river again trying to be more realistic as if advancing on a position. This time, I was one of the first across and two others got into trouble so it was my time to laugh at them. One of the lads who was small couldn't hold his footing and was struggling, another also lost his rifle. (He also found it later.)

Towards the end of the training, we had to mount attacks on 'enemy' positions with thunder flashes, rifle/machine guns firing blanks, going off everywhere, great fun and realistic, under fire and trying to cross the fast-moving Swale whilst being fired at. And hoping I wouldn't lose my rifle again. I was not looking forward to cleaning the rifle as it would be full of cordite and rubbish from the bottom of the river, yet it still worked perfectly. I had to give it a better than ever clean and oil to prevent the whole thing rusting.

Swale, in PT kit

Another time we had to cross the Swale during a P.T. period. Only after we'd crossed in P.T. kit, the sadistic P.T.I. thought it would be great idea and fun if we gave each other 'piggyback rides' across the Swale; what an event that turned out to be!

Of course, the small ones were terrified at the thought, it took them all their time to try to remain in the upright position or their heads above water and not drown without having to carry anybody on their shoulders. As you may have guessed, they didn't keep their feet for long before their 'passengers' were sent flying over their shoulders headfirst into the water.

I got lumbered with the P.T.I. himself, as was my luck. Who loved hitting me with a stick and laughing, as if I was a mule. I thought, "Right, you b*****d, just you wait, I'll make you pay!"

Stinging nettles

I didn't have to wait long; as we came out of the water, we were made to do various exercises and running about, carrying a partner. I deliberately picked the P.T.I. I had spied a clump of stinging nettles and I headed straight for them.

He kept whipping me and laughing. I warned him to stop whipping me – or else! He laughed and whipped me all the more. I gave him one more final warning; still he laughed and kept whipping me. Suddenly, the P.T.I. must have realised what was in my mind; he saw the stinging nettles that I was heading straight for. And starting to panic, he screamed at me to stop and threatened to charge me; all the others stopped what they were doing and watched as they too had spotted my intentions. They didn't think I would do it. And stood and watched as I ignored him and said, "Oh dear, whoops – I've tripped!" Then threw him headfirst into the stinging nettles, he cursed me something rotten. "That'll teach you, you bar-steward," I said to him. And it did, but afterwards he smiled and shook my hand and had respect for me. He was OK with me after that.

The lads thought it hilarious when he 'fell' in the nettles and let out a big cheer, and they heard him come up saying, "Oh, you are naughty – you shouldn't have done that!" Well, words to that effect. The language was much more colourful than that, I can assure you! This was great fun for me, and sweet revenge!

A/Tank range

On the range during basics, we had to fire live ammunition on a new anti-tank weapon we had just trained on; it was the modern equivalent of the infantry anti-tank weapon. The instructors picked the five best shots to fire the H.E.A.T. (high explosive anti-tank) rounds as they were expensive, and that 5 was our allocation. The rest fired the T.P.T.P. (Target Practice Target Projectile) round as it was cheaper, similar in cost to an ordinary rifle round. I was one of the lucky ones who were chosen to fire a H.E.A.T. round, I unfortunately missed the target and the round failed to explode and the officer had to go out to find the unexploded projectile and destroy it.

He wasn't very happy about it, I could tell.

For the next couple of days or so, whenever I came back to my bed space, a person or persons started leaving notes on my bed saying things like 'J.R.,

Tank killer'! I was mad and they knew it but when I demanded to know who it was, nobody had the guts to own up as they knew I would smack them.

Funny thing was we had also fired another anti-tank weapon that was much more difficult to aim and use yet I did well with it and hit the target.

One evening, I was woken in bed by one of the guys who was looking for a fight. I told him, "Go to bed, you're drunk, if you really want a fight, I will fight you in the morning when we are both sober and an even match! If we fought and I won, you would say it was because you were drunk."

I didn't want to fight but I couldn't let it be seen that I had refused. The next morning, I woke early and approached his bed; I was feeling nervous but it had to be done!

I kicked him and pulled the bedsheets off him and said, "OK. You wanna fight? Let's fight now!" He didn't! Or made out he didn't know what I was talking about. And tried to dissuade me but his mates reminded him of the previous night, he still kept making excuses and said he didn't want to fight me.

I had no more trouble with him after that.

Digging in

Towards the end of the course came the climax to which we had been working with all the different aspects of training. It was the practical phase, the digging in exercise. As I started the course late autumn, it was near wintertime so it was starting to get cold. So, knowing how cold it could be on the Yorkshire moors, I took a few precautions.

On the day we were to leave, I was out of bed about half an hour earlier than usual. I commenced to get dressed, starting as follows – underwear, vest, pyjamas, shirt, olive green trousers, two pullovers, overalls and combat suit. I was not going to be cold!

I had so much on I could barely move, I even needed help to climb into the back of the wagon, but I was warm. The dirty baker's dozen had arrived and started the exercise doing several patrols, putting all we'd learned into practical experience.

We started to dig into our position to be defended halfway up the side of a large hill. By the time we had started to dig in, we were all soaking wet through from our patrols in the rain, it didn't stop raining the whole time we were in the field. I'm sure the instructors had called on 'the big guy upstairs' to send rain on us the whole time, how else would they know it would be raining for the duration? I am sure the instructors knew every pond, stream and river on the moors, and we had to go through each and every one. I felt more like a sailor than a soldier.

I was wet, but couldn't make my mind up if it was the water we'd gone through or was it just sweat because of all the clothes I had on. I found out later it was both.

In each trench, everybody had a problem of some sort when digging in, i.e., solid hard clay, rocks, sand with the sides of the trench falling in or like me, unfortunately sited in the path of an underground stream. It was a case of you dug down 12 inches and there was 6 inches of water. And we had to dig a trench about 4-5 feet deep.

I complained to a Cpl and he said, "Count your blessings, look at it this way, you can have a bath or a shower already installed and on hand!" Sarcastic swine! He walked away laughing. He must have thought it funny, I didn't.

When another instructor was sent to have a look, he said, "Now you know how important it is to have proper drainage!" With this, he too walked away laughing his head off.

By this time, there must have been about two feet of water in a three-foot trench. As we threw out a couple of inches of mud, the water level got higher and higher. Eventually, by the time the trench was the regulation depth, there was nearly 4 feet of water.

Stand to

When we got 'stand to' ready for the first attack in our new positions, I and my partner were told to jump in the trench. We told him in quaint old English language, "Not on your Nelly! Would you jump into 4 feet of water?" He laughed and said, "I don't have too," and said it wasn't that deep! This was greeted by us with, "Take a running jump!" or not so polite words such as these.Nevertheless, we still had to get in; we made a slow move towards the trench, not in it, but we lay behind the trench.

By the time we'd got our kit together and sorted out, we found everything, including our change of clean dry clothing, soaking wet through.

I wouldn't give in

By the time evening came, there were only four of us left at our posts, my mate, me and two others in two other trenches, others were going down with 'supposed' exposure, the NCOs saw that if you collapsed, you were taken into a nice warm tent for a couple of hours or so to bring your temperature up, then out again. All the others had gone down one by one of exposure; it started with a couple of lads, one who fancied himself as one of the S.A.S. I would have done better than him, it was proven so, and I stuck it out! Neither of us would have passed the rigorous selection process based on this exercise.

We all suspected, with some justification, that Andy Rowe, along with others, was not really suffering at all but he just wanted a warm up in the instructor's tent, just as others couldn't hack it. As welcoming as that seemed, it would have been worse to, then go out back to your trench, so we thought better of it. I didn't want to mess up my chance of passing the course, even if it meant a warm, hot meal and a sleeping bag for a couple of hours. All told, about 10 from 13 did go down with suspected exposure.

Needless to say, we three remaining tough nuts who could stick it and wouldn't give up gave some stick to the ones we thought were skiving, all in good fun.

"Can't hack it?"

"Go back to Mummy!"

"Bloody effeminate nancies!" And so on.

We were cold, wet, hungry, shivering, miserable but glad we had stuck it out in the end.

At about 3 am, we were all at a low-ebb, one of the Cpls approached me and said, "I bet you wish you were back as a steward in a nice warm bed right now, don't you?" "No!" I said through chattering teeth. "No way. This is why I put in for the R.A.F. Regiment. I love every minute of it!" This wasn't completely true, for I was beginning to think, "What the hell have I let myself in for this time. I must be off my head!"

To say I was looking forward to the end was an understatement.

However, there was no way that I was going to admit defeat, I wasn't going to give them that pleasure of saying, "Well, we were right, he can't take it!"

I was determined to prove not to them but to myself that I 'can take it', no matter what they threw at me and I did.

Enemy attack

At dawn, we were attacked by the enemy (the intake behind us), there were only about five of us to defend the site by then. They walked around our site holding lights, quite eerie, they then went around our position chanting. Quite an unnerving experience as it got louder and louder, they got nearer and nearer then all fell silent, nothing was heard for about 45 minutes.

We wished that they would attack and get it over with so we could get some sleep. Of course, that was the whole idea.

Suddenly, when we least expected it, all hell broke loose, explosions behind and at each side of us, it woke us with a start from our drowsy state. There were thunder flashes to simulate mortar and grenade explosions illuminated flares that bathed the entire area with white light; it looked almost like daylight. Finally, screaming like banshees they charged, firing blanks and throwing thunder flashes, we fired back, though five against 40-50 seemed a bit uneven, we soon got in the swing of things, swearing at them and taking careful aim as if it was the real thing.

Later, we were told that the enemy would have taken the position but we could have accurately accounted for about 50% of their numbers, dead or wounded, at odds of 10 to 1, not bad for us.

They overran us in no time and the whole engagement took less than 10 minutes, though they didn't play fair – when we had shot them, they wouldn't lay down and play dead; most annoying, we were so mad we all threatened to punch them in the face.

End Ex

After three days, the exercise was called off early (it was supposed to last a week).

The NCOs finally convinced the Flt Commander that if he didn't call it off, he could well have real casualties and maybe a fatality or two as we hadn't come fully prepared for the severe weather conditions. It was a test to see if you could 'hack it' and test us on all the training we had. We hadn't expected non-stop torrential rain or snow either, but we got snow too.

The officer took some convincing, we were told. In fact, an NCO said that they had told the Flt Commander on the first day to take us back for a change of clothing and collect the rest of the stuff that we needed for a 7-day stay, but it took three days to finally talk him into it.

We were told 'End Ex' – the most beautiful words in the English language! A great spontaneous cheer from all of us rang out and amazingly enough, the lads down with exposure and the skivers suddenly found new life and energy. I wonder where they found those reserves of energy from.

When it came to filling in my trench, the shovelfuls of earth just disappeared into the murky depths and it seemed a futile job and a complete waste of time filling it in. So faced with a trench 5 feet deep with 4 feet of water, we decided to get rid of the water another way; we lobbed our remaining thunder flashes into it.

There were great torrents of water shooting up skywards as they exploded quite spectacularly; we soon got rid of the water that way. Though when the water came back down again, we got drenched but we didn't care, we were already wet through. As we were told, "You can't get any wetter!"; we were past caring a long time ago.

It took less than an hour to break camp, a lot less time than it had taken to set up. On the road back to camp, we were all so glad to be going back to the relative comfort of the block that we sang all the way there, the journey seemed to end in no time and as we came within sight of the block and our cars, another spontaneous cheer rang out.

We couldn't get the kit unloaded and back to the block fast enough. We then went home for the weekend immediately afterwards and after three days without sleep, I fell asleep at the wheel and just woke up in time to stop myself going over a bridge and certain death.

Final exams

Upon our return to camp, we took our finals, written tests, practical phase and tests on the 17 weapons we had trained on. I didn't do any revision immediately before the tests as was my norm, but when the final results came through, I came second overall.

I was quite pleased with myself but disappointed that I hadn't revised again and come top.

Passing out parade

We didn't have enough people for the passing out parade as there were only six of us left out of the original 70 or so. The numbers were made up with the intake behind us who had played the enemy on our exercise. The reviewing officer stopped at one of these lads and asked him some questions; he couldn't understand the answers he got until our Flt Commander explained that they were really not with us and they weren't passing out all.

During the end-of-course do, a Cpl instructor confessed to me that none of the staff had thought I would be good enough to go all the way and pass out. In fact, they had a bet, as they usually did at the start of training a new intake, that I would be the first to fail and pack it in.

He also confessed that the instructors had gotten great fun out of throwing our kit out of the upstairs windows and making our work all that much harder – damned sadists.

We had been tested on the Monday, a week off at home and then arrived at the respective Sqns. I had then been successful in joining the R.A.F. Regiment and leaving the steward trade behind for good and getting the chance of active service.

Postings

On passing out, one went to 2 'Para' field Sqn. One to 'Queens Colour display' Sqn, his ambition all along. Three to 37 LLAD Sqn, including myself, to 'C' flight, Andy Rowe and one other. And the cry baby went to 48 Sqn. The chap who went to Q.C.S., John Todd, we believe he later took his commission and became an Officer!

Historical Interlude:
"It must be different now"

This description of the R.A.F. during the Second World War was written by 'EX 1577434' – Peter Rowbottom, my father.

Part 1

The very first time I saw the R.A.F. Regiment was at a dusty crossroads between SFAX and GABS during the Tunisian campaign (early 1943). We were moving forwards in a convoy and were held up at the crossroads as the area was coming under artillery fire due to an enemy counterattack. There were the usual rumours. To sum up, we were likely to be pushed right back to Suez. Near where we had lingered was a small group with a 15 cwt truck, a sergeant and four or five men identified as R.A.F. Regiment merely by shoulder flashes. They did, I'm afraid, look rather lost and forlorn.

We were talking in groups, not knowing if we were going back or making a detour when an army colonel came flying up in a jeep and enthusiastically yelled at the sergeant, loud enough for us to hear, "I'll have to throw your men in to hold them!" Or words to that effect. I did not hear the sergeant's reply, but to us the idea of the small frail band stemming an attack by the 'Afrika Korps', Panzers and all, was to quote an expression of the time, 'sheer Fred Karno'. We moved south-west in a wide sweep so what happened I knew not. I like to think they were not needed as on our way we saw long-range desert groups and a free French column moving up, not that the latter impressed us a great deal. Moreover, we suspected the French of not moving forward much from the time of Louis XV and true to expectations, most had beards about a foot long, Foreign Legion-type kepis and two or three field guns of at least the Crimean War period.

At the end of the Tunisian campaign, I had a static period at El Biar near Algiers. The next move was the invasion of Sicily and Italy and I re-mustered to the regiment, I suppose basically because I thought there would be more chance to travel, which was what I wanted. So it was about March or April that I was transferred eastwards again to Sétif on the road to Constantine and at a mammoth airfield, I joined number 2870 Sqn LAA R.A.F. Regiment. The number intrigued me then and though no doubt there was some simple explanation, it still does. Did the R.A.F. really have almost 3000 squadrons or more? Did we miss a thousand or two somewhere to confuse and/or impress the axis powers? Now and again, I see a Peter Seller's film on TV where he is the head of a tiny European state and to impress visiting delegates of the Soviet Union and USA, he refers to his half a dozen motley uniformed Ruritanians as the 'three hundred and eighty' something or other mountain infantry regiment. 2870 Sqn always comes into my mind at this point. We shared airfield defence with an American unit and our total armament, as far as I could see, consisted of two twin .303 Brownings on Stork Mountings. If there was a second mounting, I never saw it, and you could not hide much as we were under canvas and short of that as well. One of the Brownings was almost always in pieces for instruction, cleaning or repair, so it was as well that enemy aircraft were not likely to penetrate that far south at this stage. For the rest of our weaponry, we relied on a few dozen ancient rifles, Lee-Enfield (or were they Lee-Metfords?) picked up, the wags said, after the battle of Mon's. (The biggest moaner said it was after Mafeking!) When not on airfield guard duties, training in the mornings usually amounted to stripping the weapon and assembling the Browning for cleaning (we never actually fired) and a five-minute lecture on grenades. This nearly always was simply explaining what the keyword STRAW stood for – short range, high trajectory, etc.

Evidently, if you remembered STRAW, you were fit to have served as a grenadier under Napoleon's Imperial Eagles; we never actually threw live grenades. The idea of not using ammunition in training was supposed to be due to shortage, but everywhere I had been in North Africa, there seemed to be mountains of it.

Afternoon sessions were filled in with drill, foot, rifle and bayonet fighting; this was the part I liked the most. We would charge around slashing and stabbing with those great long bayonets and screaming and yelling "Yah Ah" – stomach, heart, throat, left groin, right groin, "Yah Ah". It was one thing everybody was enthusiastic about and it appeared to me at least there was something in the old German tale about the British always being at home with cold steel. This must be where the now famous quote of Lance Corporal Jones of *Dad's Army* fame had its origins when he came up with the saying, 'They don't like the taste of cold steel, and they don't like it 'up em!' Night guards on the dispersed airfield entailed two hours on and four off for 12 hours operating from a lonely tent; hard biscuits, hard cheese and cocoa without milk and sugar were the rations. And Africa or not, the nights were the coldest I have ever known. The job was mainly to stop the local Arabs from pinching pieces of aircraft or anything else that was lying about; seeing that our chaps always got the better of them in trading deals during the day, I suppose you couldn't really blame them for trying to even things up at night. Now and again, we fired shots over their heads or over shadows to clear them off but it reached the stage where we thought the hanging about in what should have been time off, to explain incidents, was the lesser evil to having a couple of aeroplanes pinched and there was always plenty of action down Sétif.

Part 2

For relaxation, if that was the right word, we went down to Sétif. In uniform, in a group, and a long way from home, former quiet shop assistants and clerks of civvy street become passionate Casanovas and dashing Don Juans. The escapades were legion. Sometimes the liberty garnys took us to town but hardly ever back to camp. It was usually a long walk, sometimes arriving in the early hours, and some never got back that night at all. One party, in an ingenious and successful attempt to enter an area 'off limits' to us but open to the French and their colonial forces, exchanged uniforms with a group of our Allies in a local hostelry, arranging for the lesser paid soldiers in arms to drink in a back room while the airman carried out their operations. When our chaps returned, hours later, they found that the soldiers had been taken away by one of their own patrols. Our boys arrived back in full and in Arab burnouses, which they had bought, begged or otherwise acquired, having made a timely escape across the flat rooftops from an upstairs room. One even returned with virtually no clothes at all after a similar escape. I am convinced the reason most houses in near, middle and far east are built close together with flat roofs is for the very purpose of quick getaways.

One affair in which I was involved was in retrospect both alarming and amusing. My great friend of the time was a John Stenner of Cardiff John, a daring spirit, liaised well with local Arab labour on the base. He arranged for a night's entertainment for four of us with drink, music and girls laid on, for a sum, of course, and after dark we were led through a back courtyard and a small door into a single room, barely furnished, but containing four Arab girls. They were not bad looking but eyes dark with kohl, liberally coated with henna dye and laden down with garish jewellery of the slave bracelet type, exact age and looks were difficult to ascertain. We drank, danced, etc. and had one of our better times. We could not converse much, they spoke no English, each party only odd words of French, and we no Arabic except for the Bedouin battle cry I had learned from the Hot spur or wizard boys Mags, 'La Illaha Ilallah Mohammedan Rasul Allah', which was not much use under the circumstances, but the girls did laugh all the time at everything, continuous shrieking, almost uncontrollable laughter. They were the happiest, gayest (in the 1940 context) ladies I had ever known and with a fairish record of adventure. Later, we found out why. Our contact, with admirable business acumen and no doubt a little bribery and corruption, had taken us to the local women's asylum, and we were not the only ones to be taken there and let out either.

Returning to more serious things, we had a spell of duty in Bone on the coast and during this time, there was an enemy night air attack. I would think about this last belated attempt at this stage as they were operating a long way from their bases now and the defences were much too strong for them. There was a flak ship in the port, in action an amazing sight to behold, bristling with guns and ablaze with light from bow to stern – white, orange, yellow, green tracers, balls of fire, flaming onions from Oerlikens, Bofors, multiple Pom poms and many other and heavier armament. Every ship in the port was firing plus batteries on shore and the attack was beaten off with losses to them and without causing much damage.

We returned to Sétif and some of us spent a few days with the American unit who held gun emplacements around the airfield perimeter. They had five water-cooled Brownings and we trained with them. We were issued with their rations, chicken brought hot in containers and ice cream among other things. Strangely, our people did not like their food – messed up, sloppy, not substantial were the complaints – and anyway, it was sissy, ridiculous food; after all, there was a war on. Discipline among the Americans was hard to define, they had much longer duty hours than us, were rarely allowed off camp and for being a few minutes late for any task, they received severe punishment. On the other hand, officers, NCOs and men seemed to be yelling and arguing with each other all the time and the stars and bars of the confederacy fluttered proudly from more than one emplacement.

Between duties, we held football knockout competitions and once, a camel race. I think out of the score of entrants, only two or three managed to stay on and only one finished correctly but it caused great amusement. Cultural visits were also arranged in the area to the finely preserved site of the Roman city of Djemila, a marvellous day, and a smaller party this time to the town of Borj Bou Arreridj near Constantine; this was another marvellous day for our transport broke down and we had to spend the evening there. John Stenner and I in the company of two Spanish ladies, I didn't know what señoritas were doing out there but we left them having arranged to return for them after the war, of course. Funny how one always remembers the good times and there must have been a lot of bad ones, a sign of the great resilience of the human race.

A lull had now entered the war and we were ordered to Fort de l'Eau near Algiers for a week before embarking for the UK. During this time, we came to know the Casbah like the back of our hands. Here, inter-service and inter-Allied Forces rivalry reached fantastic proportions. I have always maintained that if we had all fought the enemy as hard as we fought each other, the war would have been over in half the time. Then on board HMT Strathnaver and back to Southampton and then on to Morecambe where the squadron broke up, some to be re-mustered and some to be transferred to other regiment squadrons.

37 Squadron R.A.F. Regiment, Catterick

Northern Ireland, 1st detachment

We were told by W.O. Taylor upon arriving at the Sqn for the first time: "The Sqn is on two detachments abroad; there is very few left on camp, one detachment is in Hong Kong and the other is in Northern Ireland. Sorry lads, but you're going to have to join the Sqn on active service in Northern Ireland on Monday as we're so short of men!" Half the Sqn was abroad in Hong Kong, which I would have loved to have gone to as it had always been my ambition to get posted to Hong Kong, but unfortunately it was not to be.

Though I didn't mind going to N. Ireland. That was one of the reasons I wanted to leave the stewarding job, I wanted to see some action.

Preparing to leave

After a few days at home, I joined the Sqn proper.

My mother was naturally upset at the thought of me going to N. Ireland, which I could tell, though my father I believe was rather proud that I had volunteered for some action and was going to do my bit, as we were from a very military-minded family. My grandfather had been in Ireland when they had sent British troops during the Easter rising. Nobody ever thought one of the family would ever go back, 'full circle' and all that.

Moving out

Once we had been kitted out, briefed and prepared the supplies we were to take with us, we moved off on the first stage of our move to reinforce the Sqn.

There were about twenty of us in the packet. I noticed that most of the lads were quiet and seemed a bit worried about what may or may not happen out there and would they be coming back in one piece – if at all.

Lads were worried; I was not worried

To be perfectly honest, I wasn't at all bothered; whilst looking forward to it, I too also wondered what lie ahead off us and if I saw action, how would I fare, that was my biggest worry, would I panic, put myself or the section at risk, do anything daft/brave, I had nothing to worry about.

Last will and testament

Before I left England, I made the necessary emergency arrangements. I made out a last will and testament with the praise and blessing of the W.O.

Dad's advice

I got some fine words of advice from my father before leaving.

"When the bullets start flying, keep your head down, never mind what you're told what to do, if you disagree with the section commander in action and think he is about to put your lives at an unnecessary risk, do what you feel is right, never mind what the others say!" I did keep this advice at the back of my mind but fortunately, the situation never developed to do as he advised. Besides, this was not 'all-out war', this was different, this was a lot of civilians between us and the gunmen, not to mention cameras everywhere.

New disruptive pattern combat kit

We were kitted out with the brand-new issue Disruptive Pattern camouflage combat kit not seen in public before. We were probably the first unit to be equipped with them, certainly in the R/Regiment. Up until then, we had been using the old-fashioned plain green style.

Docks in Belfast

We had a bus to Liverpool then a short ferry ride across the Irish Sea to a dock in Belfast in N. Ireland. The active service started from the moment we disembarked at the dock to the camp. Upon arrival in Belfast, I and some of the others had to hand in our weapons while we helped unload the kit from the ferry.

Meanwhile, the others were standing guard, along with another R.A.F. Regiment section. The Army Regiment sent to escort us was too casual for my liking; they didn't seem to be very alert. It had me worried for the first time since coming to N. Ireland. A sniper could have so easily picked us off – and he would have gotten away as the army weren't observing the likely sniper positions.

I took my weapon off a young officer who had been looking after it, I checked it over (safety precautions), saluted him, turned and marched smartly away. He and the other officers complimented me on it as the other lads had not done it. I thought, "That's a good start to a tour!"

Loading live ammo
We were then given the order to load the weapons with a magazine of live rounds. I felt the excitement rise in me as the last time I had loaded live ammunition on a weapon was on a firing range in the safety of the UK. This time it could be for real.

Escorted to camp
We were escorted back to the camp that was to be home for three months. (The army had a slightly longer tour than us, four months – but they also had a period of R and R halfway through. The R.A.F. Regiment didn't, we worked straight through.)

Truck guards
On each truck we were on, we had several chaps who weren't allowed to put their weapons down and were on the alert, watching for any trouble; they also had smoke grenades to affect our escape and other weapons in case of attack. It brought home to you that you had to be extra careful from then on in, not taking anything for granted and checking everything out. This was for real.

Settling in & briefing
At our camp, R.A.F. Aldergrove, we started to settle in. After a couple of hours, we went for a briefing. (The officers had already had theirs.) Whereupon we were told of the up-to-date situation on the province and the area of our jurisdiction. We were also told what sections we would be working in, our tasks and individual tasks. I was pretty lucky, of the three sections, I.R. (Immediate Readiness), stand-by and stand down section, I was on the stand down section and had about 20 hours off before starting work.

Hector's house
Our immediate duties were to guard the R.A.F. airfield aircraft and auxiliary buildings from intruders, terrorists, bombers, snipers, etc. We were

based in a fortified house in the middle of the airfield (which had been nicknamed by some wag as 'Hector's house' after a children's puppet programme, don't ask me why, I hadn't a clue!). From which we could reach any part of the airfield within a couple of minutes in our Land Rovers, whose engines were kept constantly warmed up to enable us to get a quick, reliable getaway when we got a 'call out'.

Radio room
We had the radio room rigged out so as soon as a message came through, we would be getting ready while the chap on the radio would get the details; when the broadcast was finished, most of us were ready and the radioman got ready as he ran outside, we had our berets on, weapons loaded and our webbing with our reserve magazines of ammunition and a water bottle.

2 i/c
In command of my section was a sergeant, all the others had a corporal. I was made to my surprise and delight 2 i/c of the section and when the sergeant wasn't there (it happened quite a bit) on briefings, sick parade etc., I had the command of the section. Not bad for someone who less than two weeks before had been classed as a steward and had been on basic training for the regiment.

Bayonet
Although the lads thought me crazy and would laugh, for when we were called out into action, I would let out a whoop of joy, leap over the back of the chairs/settees and be ready with my kit on before any of them, with my bayonet fixed. I would have the bayonet on in a flash saying, "They don't like cold steel, Mr Mainwaring, they don't like it up 'em!" (From the popular TV series, *Dad's Army*.) It was as one of them would say, "You'll never get the chance to get near them and use it!"

I said, "I know this (the terrorists would shoot and scoot as the popular saying goes) but if ever I do – they won't like it up 'em!" I may not get the chance or time to fix bayonets so it was best to be ready for them, no sirree – they didn't like it up 'em! Quite amusing, I thought, they must have thought me stark staring bonkers!

Watching TV
We used to watch the TV all day and night while waiting for a call out. When someone would start transmitting, it would interfere with the picture and sound, obliterating both simultaneously. The person responsible would be cursed something rotten, even more so if there happened to be an attractive-looking girl or a cartoon on the TV at the time. They were also cursed if it meant a call out as we didn't want to miss the programme on at the time.

Call out

At Hector's House, we had to be ready to react to a call out immediately. That meant all we could remove was our berets, webbing and jackets. When the call out came, we were expected to be ready, weapons loaded and in the vehicle with the engines running before the message finished, less than two minutes.

While waiting for my first call out on I.R. section, it was going through my mind what would happen on my first call out. I was making myself nervous by dwelling on the subject. I eventually thought, "Whatever fate has in store for me, there is nothing I can do about it, what will be will be!"

I didn't give it any more thought from there on in.

My first call out wasn't long in coming. As we rushed to the Land Rovers, I felt a bit of queasiness in the pit of my stomach, but at the same time the adrenaline kicked in. The message we had received was from the R.A.F. policeman at the station pump house, he had said he was being shot at and had returned fire. "This is it!" I thought, "this is the action I've volunteered for." I then felt elated and excited and nervous at the same time. I couldn't wait to get there.

The driver wasn't wasting any time getting there either, it was foot hard down all the way and if anybody got in the way or fell out – tough!

At the site, we saw that some sodium lights were trained on the building from all directions. The section commander – the sergeant, took his half of the section around the back of the sodium lights and told me to take mine in front of them. I didn't like the idea of this as we would be silhouetted in bright light against a dark background; an easy target. Still, I thought I'd better do as I was told as this was the first call out, so nervously I signalled my half of the section to follow me. A couple of them felt as I did, very nervous and said they wouldn't go in front but I told them to do as they were told and follow me in, this they reluctantly did.

With hindsight, I now know why the sergeant had done this, it was to draw the unknown enemy's attention, and fire if necessary locate and deal with them at our expense! I felt very relieved to get to the other side, but the problem was now that our night vision, what was left of it, was useless in trying to see through the inky blackness.

I had never felt more vulnerable before in my life, and such an easy target. We circled around in a pincer movement, with me and my section arriving a few seconds after the sergeant at the location.

The sergeant already had the three prisoners neutralised; they were lying face-down in the boggy area, hands above their heads, that surrounded a large lake full of ducks or that's what we thought we had heard in the background.

We escorted the prisoners to the pump house where the sergeant took one of them inside to check out his identity. The other two we kept outside under guard, with me and the rest of the section. The section removed their magazines and lit up their cigarettes, I went mad as they hadn't been told to remove them so I ordered them to reload. These two hadn't been cleared yet, so most of them reluctantly reloaded.

Once their identity had been established and cleared, we returned to Hector's House. The prisoners, we found out, were not terrorists after all but two army officers and a sergeant who had been brought along to reload their guns while they thought they would have a spot of duck shooting. They didn't realise they would cause such a commotion. (Hadn't they heard of what happened to people caught carrying, or worse still, firing guns off in the province?) They could have so easily been shot by our section. Thick or what? And these were officers!

After finishing my second stint on I.R. section, we were dismissed at 8 am after a 24-hour duty. And I and just about everybody else went straight to bed. I was woken up by Ben Holingson and his mate, 'Paddy'. They asked if I would drive them to Paddy's hometown, Dungannon, where we would be fixed up with a bit of certain nookie. We got a short wheelbase L/R and had to travel in civvies; we also had to travel armed with S.M.G and full magazines. It took ages to get there; we got lost a couple of times and had to ask our way. We eventually got there about 10:35 after the pubs had shut (which was a good thing for us, as it turned out).

Accident: Dungannon

We met five girls and offered them a lift on our way out as they said they would show us the way out of town; we actually gave a lift to only three of them.

Before this meeting with the girls, we first arrived in town and headed straight for the local police station where we booked in and deposited our weapons in their armoury. (This again turned out very good for us.)

I appeared to be tired so Ben Holingson offered to drive; he said he had not got a full licence but it was better he drove than me falling asleep at the wheel. I agreed. His pal Paddy was in the front along with two of the girls and I in the back with the third.

The next thing that happened was that I was asking this girl what her name was while at the same time I was trying to get acquainted with her lower regions. She didn't have time to reply as from the front the two girls screamed and Paddy shouted at Ben Holingson who was heading straight for a long-articulated truck with his foot hard down; he hit it smack on.

I was thrown forward with the force and sideways into the large radio set, which stopped me going all the way to the windscreen, the girl on my lap was thrown into the front seats.

We were either unconscious or dazed for a while. I got out and went around the front to see if everyone was OK. Ben Holingson was in a state of shock, still behind the wheel upright and staring straight ahead; he had cracked open his head at the hairline from hitting the windscreen and had a broken leg, his mate had concussion and a broken arm. I got two cracked ribs. (I still feel a twinge of pain with now and then.) Two of the girls had broken legs, concussion and a broken arm.

Hospital

I remember chatting to one of the girls in the ambulance that seemed to be there in seconds but must have been several minutes. And was asking her out the following night, the nurse gave me a reassuring smile as if to approve my taking the girl's mind off her injuries.

I remember upon our admission that the first thing they did was not find out what was wrong with us but what our religion was! This in a society dominated by Protestants where the answer meant at best a good job or at worse a sectarian killing, just because of a person's religion. I laughed and said, "Neither!" They seemed to relax once this was established and became friendly towards me.

After about 2-3 days, an R.U.C. (Royal Ulster Constabulary) policeman came to see us in the hospital.

He asked what had happened before and during the accident. He said that not only did the girls claim they saw weapons on the floor of our vehicle but said we were showing off with them and threatening them with these weapons. (She/they must have been referring to my loaded finger – it's very dangerous when cocked.)

I laughed and told him it was untrue, he said could I prove it?

I said, "Sure, just check with your armoury and you will see that not only did we book them in but they are still there!"

He went away and the next I heard was that they were not bringing any charges against me; I heard no more from them.

Though Ben Holingson was done for: driving without a licence, dangerous driving and driving without due care and attention!

Tests were done on us to see if we'd been drinking and how much alcohol we had in our system, again this helped us. The policeman said that the girls (two Catholics and one Protestant) said we were drunk and that is what had caused the vehicle to crash.

I told him what a load of rubbish that was; all he had to do was consult the accident report made out by the doctor who had treated us and find out that we had no drinks at all. (He did this.) What a nasty piece of work those girls turned out to be. Were they put up to it?

I quite enjoyed my stay in hospital; I had quite a rapport going with the nurses.

Aftermath

I was dreading when I had to return to the Sqn as we were told that the Sqn had been confined to camp after the accident and we in the hospital weren't very popular with the lads, and all liberty runs had been cancelled. Everyone thought it was me who had been driving at the time so most of the bad feeling was directed against me, until I told them all that it was not me but Ben Holingson. That seemed to satisfy them.

The R.A.F. held an enquiry into the accident in which I was blamed for allowing Ben Holingson to drive but the R.A.F. really threw the book at him. After all, the L/R was a write off.

We were told that the day after the accident, the remains of the vehicle were taken by the police to the nearest army garrison. Ironically enough, it was the same regiment/battery as Martin who was still in Germany at that time.

Apparently, the first thing the Orderly Sergeant said to the policeman upon seeing the wreckage was, "Where's the bodies?" And found it hard to believe that we had all walked out of the wreckage with relatively minor injuries.

The police said if it had been a civvie car, the whole thing would have been completely smashed in and no one at all would have gotten out alive, it was entirely because the L/R was so well built and strong that saved our lives.

To finish off about the accident, I must thank the R.A.F., for the first day back on duty, they had me driving so I wouldn't lose my nerve.

Reinforcements

One of the first call outs I had upon returning to the Sqn was at the announcement of the internment of terrorist suspects. Trouble was expected and reinforcements were sent in to increase the army's strength on the ground.

I had just finished a shift on I.R. and was in bed. When the whole block was woken and the rest of the Sqn dragged out of the bar in various states of drunkenness, some in uniform, a lot in civvies. We were all issued with rifles and ammunition and told to ring the airfield and runaway, there was an alert on.

We didn't know what it was for at first but before long we saw the landing lights and heard the engines of several R.A.F. Hercules transport aircraft coming in to land. Before they were fully stopped, the rear hatch was opened and army men were running out to take their positions with us to guard the unloading of the rest of the men, supplies, equipment and vehicles, then dispersed to take up their positions around Ulster ready for any trouble that might come.

We were then allowed to stand down after about 2-3 hrs. I went back to bed, the others carried on drinking where they had left off. In the morning, the entire Sqn was on parade to try and establish who was the blithering idiot (stronger words were used than that) who opened fire with live ammunition on one of our aircraft! The R.A.F. police on patrol afterwards had found an empty bullet case where the Sqn had been located. Yes, some idiot had actually opened fire on one of the planes and it had been one of those unbelievable things that no one was hurt. It was possible that if the pilot had been hit, the aircraft would certainly have crashed, killing good-ness knows how many, including us lads on the ground. Some of the guys claimed they knew who it was but most of us didn't know. We had an idea who it was but we weren't certain. It was almost certain that it was one of the men who had been dragged out of the Naafi bar drunk and given a rifle and live ammunition, what had the officers expected? No one said anything though; you did not rat on your comrades.

Eventually, after 2-3 days, the matter was dropped. The officers must have realised they were not going to find out.

The Red Arrows

Another call out we had involved putting a ring of defence around a dispersal pan, then the Red Arrows landed. Once they had left the aircraft, one of them approached me and we got to chatting. He asked what (army) regiment I was from, I told him the R.A.F. Regiment. (Hadn't he noticed the cap, badge and beret then?) He looked shocked and said, "I didn't know the R.A.F. Regiment were out here." Hadn't he known that was the main purpose the regiment had been formed in the first place? I told him I was enjoying my detachment and I still had most of my three months detach-ment to go. Again, he was surprised as he didn't know that we had that long a detachment.

Half Mile House: whisky

One of the recreations for the lads was at Half Mile House just outside the camp boundary, the landlord enjoyed servicemen coming as we were the mainstay of his finances. He even had a pop group on most nights. I won my first ever raffle there, half a bottle of whiskey; I thought I'd save it for when I got back to the block. However, inevitably, we all got drunk before leaving and in the morning, I realised that I hadn't drunk it. I couldn't even recall getting it back to the block the night before. What had happened to it I didn't know, maybe I had left it on the table at the pub or more likely it had been nicked by one of the blokes on our table and drunk by him and his mates.

Cigarette factory near Londonderry

During our tour, it was arranged for us to have a day out as a break from the pressures of active service. All of us (except I.R., standby and HQ personnel) set off to visit a nearby cigarette factory – Gallagher's, near Londonderry. Quite an experience. I was usually first through the door to each section. A cheer went up from the girls within accompanied with rude ribald comments thrown my/our way. I was, for one of the few times in my life, embarrassed by women. At the end of the tour, we were given some packets of free cigarettes; the difference of fresh cigarettes from old stock in the shops was amazing.

Range, now Long Kesh Prison

While in the area, we called at the camp of the Coldstream Guards; we were to use their firing range for a spot of live firing and to re-zero our rifles – just in case!

The camp also turned out to be later the military-run prison for internees arrested during the troubles, 'Long Kesh'.

Throwing berets out the back of the truck

On the way back, the blokes were fooling about in the back of the wagon and throwing mine and others' berets out of the back of the truck, and I and the others were constantly jumping out the back to retrieve them.

Even the civvies following in their cars would stop to pick the berets for us. Now, when I look back, I realise how ruddy dangerous that could have been.

Dispersal, dismiss

At the end of my first three-month detachment, we were – as expected – very pleased to be getting ready to go home; we'd been looking forward to it for so long. As we flew out of Aldergrove airfield, the moment the wheels left the ground, the whole Sqn spontaneously let out a great cheer; we all broke into laughter when we realised what a coincidence that we were all thinking the same thing at the same time.

Upon arrival at the Sqn hangar, we got off the trucks and were faced with a well-organised advanced party that had come home a few days before us to get things ready for our arrival.

We stepped off the trucks, handed our weapons and equipment to one group of lads, our service kit, which was not going to be needed or wanted washing, to another. The cases/holdalls and kit bags that were taken off us were kept under lock and key until we were due back, then taken and put on our beds/bed spaces. That's what I call organised! I only wish my future postings had been half as well organised.

We formed up and were addressed by the Sqn Commander, Sqn leader, Hawkins – a real gent. He thanked us for a job well done and said that the higher ups (i.e., the senior army commander and A.O.C., N. Ireland) had lavished praise on the Sqn. We then got from Sqn leader Hawkins, "Again, thank you lads for a job very well done!" A few years later, he became the Commandant General of the R.A.F. Regiment.

We had our names called out on the roll call roster and then, "We'll see you in two weeks' time, dismiss!" Again, we let out another cheer, louder than the last one. This was the moment we'd all been waiting for the official end of the detachment. Two unofficial weeks leave. We didn't have to lose two weeks of our annual entailment.

We all ran out of that hangar and some were outside the camp gates in their cars in two minutes flat, it took me a little longer – five minutes, as I had to walk to the A.I. and thumb a lift home, and was I glad to be heading home.

So ended my longest and most enjoyable detachment, I had enjoyed the locals' company; they themselves had said they had all gotten on well with each other and couldn't understand why the boundary lines between Catholics/Protestant in the cities were there.

Girl didn't wait for me

While on my first detachment to N. Ireland, back home, an ex-girlfriend (I was going out with several girls) Delphine had promised to wait for me but I suspected that she wouldn't keep her word, I was right! Before I went away, she said I could only have sex if I got engaged to her and give her an engagement ring. 'Gun to my head' – I don't think so! I had not told her I'd dumped her prior to leaving UK.

I came home a couple of weeks earlier than what she had believed and in the corner of the local dance hall saw her with another man, she didn't even know I was there. I watched her all night.

I had meanwhile got myself fixed up with another. Another Saturday (whilst with this new girl), I waited to catch Delphine alone and sided up to her and asked how she was; the look on her face was a treat, shocked and embarrassed. I pretended at first nothing was wrong, then said, "I see you didn't wait for me. I didn't think for a minute you would, notice you've got an engagement ring on, that sums you up, doesn't it? (Or words to that effect.)

I then picked up my pint and walked slowly and deliberately away. I noticed that she was talking about me to her 'fiancé' and all night they kept looking my way, so I made sure that they saw me enjoying myself with this new girl. Many years later, I found out that Delphine's fiancé had been killed in a motorbike accident. Maybe this was the same guy? And she remained single for many years; in the 90s, I came across her again and completely ignoring my wife, she grabbed my arm and behaved as if nothing had happened, as if we were still going out together. She introduced me to her parents as 'John, *my* John'! Both the wife and I were embarrassed and you can imagine the effect on the wife. We both felt sorry for her. Eventually, she did get married and when she saw us, she completely ignored us.

Commencing training on the 40/70 A.A. guns

Upon returning to the Sqn after our leave at home, we were told that our anti-aircraft training was to take full priority as our next detachment was live firing of the A.A. guns in Manorbier (South Wales).

Before we were good enough to fire live ammo, we practised on the airfield on rare and convenient passing low-flying aircraft; we had been trained up on static targets on the airfield. It was decided quite rightly, that we now had to get used to moving targets, we had to settle for the next best thing: train the guns on a vehicle going around the airfield perimeter track. Once that was mastered, we happily switched our attention to the cars travelling past the camp down the A.I. We would leave the gun pointing at a point on the airfield and on the command, 'Gun Action!', we would run to and mount the gun, swing around when given the directions of the target and follow the car/van/lorry all the way past camp and before he disappeared completely, give it simulated burst of shots on automatic fire. This was very good practice as we had only about 5-7 seconds to spot, give the orders, lay on the target and fire.

It was very funny really when about 6-7 A.A. guns, each about 5 tons+ and all the accompanying equipment, had the effect of making the traffic suddenly speed up and get out of range and sight as soon as possible, quite amazing. And funny, though I bet the drivers didn't think it was funny! Looking through a pair of binoculars, we had a good laugh at the expressions on their faces, it was hilarious to watch the driver's driving past, quite blissfully unaware that they were been tracked, then he/she would usually turn around and see themselves in the sights of several guns tracking every move and being followed. Sometimes the missile Sqn armed with Tiger Cat ground to air missiles would join in the fun too. (Though we were assured that they would only have drill rockets mounted on the launcher unable to fire or explode.) The poor old civvies didn't know that. The look on the faces of the drivers was pure magic, some had a look of shock and terror on their faces and others were convinced that they were about to be blown clear off the face of the earth at any second. Their expressions were worth a thousand words, followed by a sudden rapid acceleration of speed.

There would be some, though not many, probably ex-service who realising what we were doing would allow themselves a smile or be so fascinated that they didn't watch where they were going and nearly crash.

The Zoo
The first week back on the Sqn, I was told the 'in place' to be was the dance on a Thursday night in the Naafi, nicknamed (very appropriately) 'the Zoo'! As it was full on dance night of nothing but 'animals' (the hairless Homo Sapiens type), so-called because of the lack of moral standards there. And just how some penguins/officers thought all 'rock-apes' – our nickname, were like.

The Black Widow
We, new to the Sqn were also warned to be on our guard against the highly dangerous 'Black Widow'. No, not the spider variety, but the more dangerous variety – the human type; a woman who, like her namesake, preyed on young innocent soldiers.

The Zoo had only about five females who were brave enough to go to the dances. Three who were daughters of servicemen living in married quarters and the infamous Black Widow (she always wore black hence one reason for her nickname) and her daughter.

Animals

There would also be usually about 300 sex-starved drunken rock-apes! And a few very brave 'penguins' (other trades in the R.A.F.). That was our nickname for them; the shiney being clerks or the like.

If anybody was brave enough – or foolish enough to ask one of the girls for a dance, they would find a few beer glasses thrown at them or beer poured over them (I know from experience), they might even get themselves beaten up for a laugh by a couple of the blokes saying, "Fecking sprog, that's my bird you asked to dance!" Then they would go back to leaning up against the bar for the rest of the night and get drunker and drunker, and that's all they would do; they wouldn't talk to the girl or ask her for a dance, they were happy talking to their mates.

Army lads get beaten up

If any army lads from the army Catterick garrison 5 miles down the road were daft enough to come to the Zoo, they never left without a few bruisers, cuts, black eyes as a semi-permanent reminder of their night with the rock-apes! Of course, they were always very heavily outnumbered, something like 40:1. Fights were frequent, and often, and usually furniture got broken in the disorganised melee.

Smashing up the Naafi

On parade the following morning, we were usually on our best behaviour as if 'butter wouldn't melt'; the Naafi manager/staff would come around and try to identify the culprits who had smashed up the place the night before.

Initiated

In fact, the first night I went to the Zoo, I was initiated into the Sqn by this walking muscle bag. I had made the fateful mistake of approaching the Black Widow and asking her for a dance.

Before I knew what was happening, I had beer poured over me and this gorilla hit me saying, "You've been chatting up my bird and I don't like sprogs!" I was told that it was a way of been 'welcomed' to the Sqn. I was lucky really as the other two who had come on the Sqn with me from basics were not so lucky. I was expected to stay there with the beer dripping off me and the lads told me not to go but I said, "Bugger this, you might be used to hanging around dripping beer but I'm not, I'm going back to shower and wash my clothes!" I was also told that it just wasn't done and you were expected to stay until the dance finished and they didn't like anybody leaving and tried to persuade me to stay! I left as soon as I could! I went back after I'd gotten cleaned up and changed.

Apologies

This gorilla approached me on the Sqn next day and said he had been told by his mates what he did last night, he couldn't remember, and he was sorry as he had been drunk and didn't know what he was doing. "You're telling me!" I told him.

More on the Black Widow

About this Black Widow, she was the camp bike (if you get my meaning) and she had been married twice, once divorced and once widowed.

She was always to be found around camp and had a reputation for not been able to find a man who could satisfy her (doesn't say a lot for the male population of Catterick, does it?), though not for the want of trying. And had a reputation for doing anything to get as much as possible and there was a lot of men on that camp, an almost unending supply of new blood, so to speak. As I have also said, she always wore black. A pretty formidable character to come up against was the Black Widow.

Thumbing a lift home

When I used to go home for the weekend, I used to nearly always thumb a lift home as the nearest railway station was at Darlington and that was about 17 miles. You then had to change trains at Doncaster, which could have you waiting for a connection for anything from half an hour to several hours, depending on your luck. It was far quicker (not to mention cheaper) to thumb it. By train, I would be only halfway to Doncaster. Providing you were lucky in catching your connections – about three hours, usually longer. Thumbing it, I would be at the pub near my house. On the way home, it took about 1½-2 hours in uniform…well, part uniform.

If I did as you were supposed to do and put on my best uniform for thumbing it, that would be another half an hour longer while I got changed, and when you called into pubs, people would be staring at you all the time. Most important of all, the girls would avoid you like the plague for various reasons known only to them-selves. It was that most of all that I didn't like.

So, I had a good idea; I would put on my civvies, then on top of that my R.A.F. raincoat and beret. It still helped me get a lift, but as soon as I walked in a pub, off would come the coat and beret so I was stood in my civvies and nobody would stare at me but most important of all, I was able to chat up the girls. This was strictly illegal in military law but I was only caught and given a rollicking twice in three years; not bad going for wearing mixed dress as it was called.

Sports car

As soon as I got back to Scunthorpe, I would fancy a pint occasionally on the way too. Sometimes the trip would be quite uneventful. One week at the usual Friday teatime, I was picked up by a chap who was very lucky for me to be heading for Grimsby via Scunthorpe. We did the trip in his sports car in half the time it took 45-50 minutes and that was a trip of about 90 miles – it was some going, foot hard down all the way.

Old couple going slow

On the other hand, an old couple gave me a lift to the end of the A1. Took about two hours; when I got out, I then had to make it to home from Doncaster. They explained that their only son had been in the forces and loved it but he had been killed in the war and they only gave lifts to servicemen. There were times that I thought we were never going to get there, they went so slow.

Lorry driver hits my thumb

Another time, just a few miles from home, I was thumbing it back and a lorry came close to the side of the road, too close, so I took a step back to make sure that I was clear. He went past me as I was thumbing a lift and part of the trailer hit my hand as it went past and caused my thumb to start bleeding. I was so shocked and stunned that by the time I had my senses about me and thought about getting his number, he was gone, long gone.

Could imagine the b*****d laughing away to himself in his cab. He was deliberately trying to get me; probably a commie or terrorist supporter.

I was picked up shortly after by another lorry driver, he asked what was the matter when he saw me holding my thumb with blood pouring out; I told him and he apologised for this bum and tried to convince me that not all lorry drivers were like that. But he also told me that things had an amazing way of getting around. Lorry drivers had a code of conduct, he would leave word when he stopped and if somebody else found out who it was, he would be 'dealt with' as most of the drivers were ex-servicemen and liked to give lifts to servicemen when they were thumbing a lift. I thanked him for that.

Thumbing up the A1: taxi

Most of the time, I used to return to camp by train, though on occasions I thumbed it back up the A1. It used to be easier to come back by train.

After clearing Doncaster one Sunday, I was on the A1 by the roundabout waiting for my first lift. I remember thinking at the time, "Wouldn't it be funny if I was to get a lift back in a taxi, arriving back in style!"

Whatever made me think that I don't know. Five minutes later, incredibly, around the corner came a taxi. I allowed myself a little smile; I paid no more attention to it as it went by. I heard a horn sounding behind me and glanced backwards. I saw the taxi driver stopped at the side of the road and beckoning me towards him. I approached him slowly, thinking he was going to offer me a lift and I would have to pay. He said, "Where you heading?" I told him, he then said, "Hop in, I'll give you a lift, I'm going past there!" I hesitated for a moment, he laughed and said, "Don't worry; you don't have to pay. I'll be grateful for someone to talk to!" He had taken some people from Newcastle to London Heathrow airport, a long journey. I couldn't believe my luck and I rode back in style. In the back just as I wanted to. It was a treat to see the expressions on the faces of some of my Sqn personnel as they had just gotten off the bus. Here was I, getting out of a taxi, walking away and not even paying.

Taking Welsh girl for a drink

Another weekend at the same spot, I was picked up by a young Welsh girl in her car, I thanked her for the lift and politely asked her if she fancied a drink; she accepted graciously. I thought it would be a good opportunity to chat her up, you never knew what contacts you might make. We pulled up at a plush roadside licenced restaurant; I thought, "Oh hell, it'll cost a fortune here!" (It did turn out expensive.) I asked her what she wanted to drink and thought, "Here it comes, a large expensive spirit!"

Meeting my match in drinking

She asked what was I having, she'd have the same if I liked! I breathed a sigh of relief and told her beer. She settled for the same. I have always considered myself a fast drinker, but that day I met my match and to my shame, it was a woman.

By the time I'd drunk about one-third to half of my pint, I glanced over and she had already finished hers, two swigs and it was gone. I bought her another and again, she finished it at about the same time. I finished my first.

I bought her another and myself too; she had finished hers when I had got about halfway down mine. I thought, "Bugger this, I'm not going to buy her another, she'll have to sit with an empty glass!"

It was all credit to her for she then insisted on buying me a drink. I think I'd embarrassed her into getting me a drink.

She gets very friendly

I left her with a kiss and a fondle. After all, I'd almost paid for it, that beer had been expensive, nearly twice the normal price.

I was convinced that had we travelled down some country roads, I would have gotten a lot more out of her, in fact confident that we'd have gone all the way; that's the impression she left me with, she was becoming definitely more and more friendly; the alcohol was beginning to have its effect.

I will give her credit for one thing, even with the alcohol, she was a very good driver.

Coming back through Darlington

Most weekends, I came back on the train through Darlington. I always used to time it so that I could get to camp just before the bar closed and it also gave me a bit of time to play with in case I missed a train/bus and for any breakdown/emergency.

A lot of the chaps seemed to have the same idea too; however, it also coincided with the pubs closing and the throwing out with the drunken rock-apes who then had to make their way back to camp after a weekend pub-crawling around Darlington.

The civvies used to sit at the front of the bus bringing us back to camp, as they didn't want to associate with us. (Who could really blame them?)

The servicemen were banished to the back of the bus out of harm's way.

Bus

One particular occasion on a Sunday night, there was a bit more noise and rowdiness than normal and several times, the driver stopped the bus and threatened to throw us all off; of course, this had the opposite desired effect, it made the drunkards carry on much more, they were loving it, having lots of fun to the consternation of their fellow passengers.

One of the rowdy ones was a chap recently posted to us from basics and his name was Harry Grey, aka 'the Nutter/Jankers king', who was used to making a home from home for himself in the guardroom. As he spent as much time in close arrest as he spent out of it.

So if for that reason only, he was popular with the old hands.

Nature calls

It had been a heavy night's drinking for Harry and his pals and inevitably, he kept asking the driver to stop for him to go and 'water his horse'! The driver got fed up of stopping for this reason and in the end, he ignored the pleas from Harry and his mates, thinking that were just messing him about.

The pleas to stop got more and more desperate and fell on deaf ears. It was a long bus ride from Darlington, down mainly country lanes about 17 miles. You could see the pain on their faces and of course, this made the rest of us laugh all the more and again the driver thought we were up to something. Eventually, the driver was told bluntly by Harry that if he didn't stop immediately, something would happen. The driver chose to ignore the plea though he could have stopped as we were in the middle of the country at the time, about two-thirds of the way there. This had the effect of Harry doing what he had to do where he sat, in empty beer bottles, in fact anything that came to hand, this was after he had first tried to wind the window down and stick 'it' out the window.

The driver didn't see what was going on, he only heard us all whispering and laughing, eventually, Harry and his mates, encouraged by his getting away with it, ran out of receptacles as the bottles and beer glasses they had pinched were full, so Harry did the only thing left to do – he finished off by being covered by his mates and availed himself of the use of the floor of the bus.

Even we were all shocked that he could go as far as this, even his fellow cronies. We all for the first time sat in silence; the driver then kept looking back to see why it was so quiet at the back, of course, he couldn't see anything as it was too late.

What he didn't see was the results of his misdemeanour. Harry's urine started too slowly, ever so slowly at first, snaked its way forward down the centre aisle of the bus towards the driver and past the other passengers, inch by inch. It got to within a couple of feet from some old ladies minding their own business. We were chuckling like daft school kids under our breaths; as it drew level, we all fell silent! Holding our breaths as it trickled past them and we slowly let out our breath.

A few moments later, one of the old ladies started to sniff the air and didn't like what she thought she could smell, she looked down and saw what was responsible for the assault on her nostrils. She was (quite rightly) shocked by what she saw; she couldn't believe it. She kept nudging her friend and pointed to the reason for her discomfort. They became edgy, fidgety and couldn't wait to get off. As they got off, the first one to see 'it' told the bus driver, he went mad, he promptly threw us all of the bus. The army lads weren't pleased as they still had several miles to go to their camp.

We were thrown off by the driver about five miles from camp and had to walk the rest of the way; we weren't very happy and informed Harry Grey accordingly in our not so subtle way. From then on, we all tried to catch a different bus to him on a Sunday.

It wasn't the only time we were thrown off the 'Darlington flyer', though we never had as far to walk again, just a few stops from the camp gates.

Harry tries to work his ticket

I don't think Harry Grey was really suited to the life and decided that he was going to get out but as he couldn't afford to buy himself out, he thought he would try and 'work his ticket'.

So, reminiscent of the film *Virgin Soldiers*, which also features a chap trying to work his ticket by making himself deaf and failing every time.

Harry started his 'operation out'!

Working your ticket for a free discharge before your service (contract) was up was a ruse quite often used but very rarely successful as the NCOs/officers were wise on all the tricks, especially the senior NCOs who had many, many years of experience under their belt.

His opportunity came one morning when he had been told to dig and weed the garden outside the C.O.'s office. Just before Naafi break at 10 am, he came into the hangar trailing a piece of string behind him and talking to it.

Harry finds a new pet, 'Fred'

We thought he really had flipped this time, not knowing what he had planned. At the end of the string, he had tied a worm, a common or garden earthworm. He was – we discovered, taking his newly acquired pet called 'Fred' for a walk.

Tries to train his new pet

He was also trying to 'train' it by commanding it to 'sit, stay and walkies'! Even how to 'beg'. He even smacked it and said, "Naughty Fred, you've just peed yourself. Walkies!"

When all this failed to have any response, he said to the worm, "What you really need is a bit of military discipline!" (Ironic really, it was Harry who needed military discipline and not the worm.) So he commenced to drill the worm. "Worm, worm shun! Quick march!" When the worm failed to respond, it was threatened with a spell in the guardroom.

With all this coming from the 'Jankers King' himself, we were in stitches; nobody was doing any work as this was far too amusing and we didn't want to miss whatever Harry had planned next.

Just watching him trying to drill this dirty, withered, half-dead worm was hilarious, he even took it to Naafi/YMCA breaks with him. The officers would walk by, see what was the cause of all the commotion and say, "Grey, you bloody idiot, you're trying to work your ticket or something?" They used to just shake their heads in disbelief and walk away, chuckling under their breaths.

Most of the lads knowing Harry or what he was up to would think, "He's a ruddy nutter! But he's good fun!"

Pet dies

He kept up the act whenever he had the chance. Eventually, Fred became all dry and shrivelled up and died. So Harry decided that he had to be buried with full military honours, and with half the Sqn present, hymns were sung and we held a requiem mass for this damn silly worm.

"He was a noble worm, truly a worm amongst worms," said Harry. He had even invited some 'guests' from the other Sqns in the hangar for the 'funeral'. Probably the only worm in the world that has had a military funeral, such as it was.

Fun

We used any excuse we could think of for a bit of fun, some civvies would be convinced that everyone in the forces was mad! Such was our sense of humour, anyone not doing time in the 'mob' wouldn't understand, but ex-servicemen will.

Fred II and beetles

Harry was grief-stricken (or so he told us) for about 24 hours, then he found something else to take his mind off Fred's death, another worm! This was, we were assured, Fred's brother so it was called 'Fred II'. When bored with that, he trained beetles, which he would race and we would bet on.

No bull nights

These attempts to get out failed as we all knew they would. So he then told us he didn't like bull nights and would find a way of getting out of them, so he got married, thinking that would get him out of bull nights. It did, but what he didn't realise was that in married quarters, you had to keep them spotless and that was harder than a block bull night; if the inspection (on marching out) failed, it would hit you in the pocket.

The girl was, needless to say, in the family way before they got married. The things some people did before doing as they should.

Harry is posted

Harry was posted a few months later and we heard that the new Sqn wasn't going to stand for his stupid ways and he was kicked out. He had gotten his wish to get out before his time, but probably with a dishonourable discharge, so his prospects for a job in civvy street weren't very good. His new posting, we heard, was to a helicopter Sqn. So did he beat the system or did it beat him?

Scotland

First thing on a Monday, we found that we were to fly out to a military base at one hour's notice, at which the US Navy/Air Force were operating, in Scotland. This was the second of many detachments that I did on 37 Sqn. We flew out to R.A.F.?

We saw that the Yanks were pretty dominant and the only R.A.F. personnel we saw were cooks and an awful lot of R.A.F. police; it was the R.A.F. police that we were working with mostly.

We were not supposed to know where we were but we found out, too easily, I think, we asked an R.A.F. policeman where we were and some of the Yanks told us, but before that was confirmed, some of the lads were sent on a familiarisation patrol to get used to the area. The patrol hadn't gone more than a couple of miles before they found the nearest road sign that showed them just where we were. In the West of Scotland, and exactly where!

We were with the R.A.F. police encircling, defending and escorting 'things'! Which I'm not at liberty to disclose as simply we weren't told exactly or officially just what we were guarding, but we all knew; it was pretty obvious. They might as well have made it official and told us.

US navy man

At one point, I went into a building to use the toilet facilities and on the way out, I got chatting to a US Navy serviceman about the States, especially Elvis Presley. He said he said seen Elvis so we got chatting.

Ben Holingson and his mate, Paddy, kept taking the mick out of the Yanks' accent. They wanted to approach him and ask the time as they were fascinated by the accent and no one had the courage to do so, so I walked up to this Yank, asked him and he said, "Sure Mack, it's 25 after!" I was admired for this and had a reputation of having the nerve to do things others wouldn't.

S. Wales
The next major detachment was, as expected, to Manorbier in S. Wales; it took us a couple of days to get there. We were to fire live rounds with the 40/70 and the 40/60 anti-aircraft guns.

They were worried
I was the only one on my gun team that hadn't fired them before so the lads were worried how I would fare and were frightened that I might 'cock it up' with the live ammunition. I turned on them and informed them in a not too polite way, "Don't worry about me, you a***h***s, I can look after myself and I won't let you down! Just make sure you do your jobs right and don't let *me* down or else!"

I don't think they realised (until I informed them) that I had been on live firing detail with the Royal Artillery on Salisbury Plain.

I think they realised that I didn't like these A.A. guns, but I was good at my job; in fact, it was some of them that got a rollicking during the detachment – but not I!

Travelling to R.A.F. Stafford
Most of us travelled down there in the back of the four-tonners; it was a long boring journey and we were glad to get to our overnight stop destination. We stopped at R.A.F. Stafford, a supply and maintenance camp and started to refuel. My flight commander approached me and took me aside and said, "Rowbottom, I have just come from the communications room and I have some bad news for you!"

I wondered what it could be. I had a suspicion at the back of my mind what it was about; as it turned out, I was right.

Granddad 'R' dies
"There's a telegram for you, shall I read it out, it was forwarded on from Catterick. 'Granddad Rowbottom has died, funeral Monday at 2pm stop'."

The officer agreed to try and get me off when we got to the other end but as we were the advanced party, we would have to wait for the Sqn C.O. to arrive first.

Getting very drunk
That night in Stafford's Naafi, I got very, very drunk. I was understandably upset and mixed my drinks, not caring really what happened. I was drinking beer, cider and spirits, that night I was as sick as I was upset, very sick and ill.

I was sure the lads knew something was wrong but never said anything;

they were very diplomatic about it. They certainly knew I wasn't my usual jovial self and something was afoot so later I thanked them for that. They told me afterwards that they did know but they weren't quite sure if, or how, they ought to approach me and so thought better of it.

Arriving in South Wales

The next day, we arrived at our accommodation at Penally camp about five miles from the range at Manorbier. The day after when the Sqn arrived *en masse*, the C.O. was briefed as S.O.P. (standard operational procedure).

He then authorised a vehicle and the duty driver to take me to the nearest railway station, there I caught a train home.

Train home

I unfortunately missed the right connection for Scunthorpe. (The first and last time I have ever done this.) I ended up miles off the beaten track at Goole, I didn't check whether it was the right platform; I took it for granted as the Scunthorpe train had been leaving that platform for many years; it just happened that that day it had left from a different platform, so unfortunately, I missed the funeral; I guess it just wasn't to be!

Even my other grandfather had been waiting for me at the railway station of Scunthorpe. When I didn't turn up, they figured what had happened and had to go ahead without me even though they had held the funeral up for as long as possible.

Penally Camp

The following day, I had to set off for the camp in Wales. Penally camp, at which we were accommodated, was generally used for TV units and other military units such as ours on temporary attachment.

Range

At the range itself at Manorbier, the guns were placed facing out to sea with the whole Sqn's guns on the range at one time, the only exception was the two guns we kept for spare in case of a breakdown.

Not every gun would fire at once but we did occasionally, and when that happened, it was deafening to hear them and very impressive – 12 guns firing on automatic at one target. 54 rounds per second.

Guns radius: punch clear

We (I) was to see just how deadly and accurate these guns could be sometime later. Surprisingly, within the 'live area', anything within that area could be within the range of the guns. Within the range was a monastery in which monks were said to still live. That's what I call living dangerously, but we had a method in which anything that was not M.O.D. property or publicly/privately owned could be very safely avoided by punching into the gun the relevant details and if the gun was firing once it got to that set position, it would automatically jam; as soon as it was clear of the restricted area, it would carry on firing automatically. And the gunner could keep his finger on the trigger all the time if he wished (and generally did), then the second it was free of its restrictions, the rounds were fired again.

Bofors gun (author second left)

Queen's flight

One day whilst firing, we were suddenly told to make the guns safe and withdraw behind the firing point as there was an aircraft of the Queen's flight passing nearby and an officer said, "We don't want to shoot it down, do we!" Some officer somewhere was going to get an almighty rocket for not making out the relevant flight plan so we could be informed and not fire that afternoon.

It may even be at R/Regiment level and not informing the Sqn/Range Safety Officer but what came of it we don't know; nothing was ever said to us at the sharp end! We had an easy afternoon sunbathing and having a good laugh at someone's stupidity. I could foresee the daily papers the day after, if we'd shot it down!

'R.A.F. Regiment shoots down Queen's plane!' The Russians would have laughed their socks off and we would probably have been dispersed to other jobs in the R.A.F. or transferred to the army after the R.A.F. Regiment had been disbanded.

Sqn misfit: idiot

We had our share (as all units did) of misfits and nutcases, 37 Sqn was no exception. We had on our Flt a chap who fancied himself as a bit of a hard man, his name was 'Taff' Kitchson – a Welshman and a bit 'slower' than most. Every time he went out, if by the time he got to bed he hadn't had a couple of fights that night, he hadn't had a good night out, he used to say.

At first, before the rest of the lads got to know him, if they saw him in a fight downtown, as in all close regiments/corps, you helped your mates out even if you didn't like the bloke, with him being on your Sqn that would be enough reason to wade in and help him out, they did this, then eventually got wise to 'Taff' Kitchson. They realised he was always fighting probably because he liked to, so the word went around the Sqn, and the next time he was seen by Sqn personnel fighting in the street/pub, they just walked on by and Kitchson got beaten up by civilians. Kitchson got beaten up on more than one occasion but it didn't seem to deter him any.

Trying for promotion

One afternoon during a lull between firing, Kitchson must have been in a funny mood, for he approached the gun controller, Sergeant (Tug) Wilson, and shocked us all within earshot to the core by saying to Tug Wilson, "Sarge, I have been thinking, I'm getting a bit fed up of fighting, it's a mug's game and I think I should start trying for my promotion exams!"

We couldn't believe it. Tug Wilson said, "OK lad, let me start with some easy general knowledge questions. We'll start with the very easy basic level for school kids and then we'll make them harder!" This Kitchson agreed to.

"Right lad, what's the capital of France?"

"Umm, just a minute, err…" (five minutes later) "Don't tell me, it's on the tip of my tongue!" Meanwhile, we were all sniggering and trying our best not to burst out laughing and of course, passing comments to each other as to the…shall we say, 'lack of general knowledge', to be kind!

Ten minutes later and he still hadn't come up with the answer to this simple question. "You haven't a hope of answering the question, have you?" said Tug. So Tug had to tell him the answer in the end.

"Of course, it is," said Kitchson. "I knew it all along, it was on the tip of my tongue all the time!"

"You don't have a hope, laddie, if you want to pass any exams, why don't you go back to fighting, at least you're good at that, you might as well stick to doing what you know best!" said Tug. We could hold it in no longer so we all burst out laughing.

Natural shot

The Bofor's A.A. gun was no different than any other weapon controlled by man. You will have good shots and bad shots, of the aforementioned. On the second detachment I did to Manorbier, there was an exited buzz going around the Sqn that there was to be posted to us a lad from an R.A.F. Regiment Sqn in Cyprus who was reputed to be the best Bofor's gunshot in the R.A.F. Regiment – if not in the whole anti-aircraft guns, Sqns/regiments in the UK forces.

Of course, all the officers were trying to get him on their flights and each gun controller (senior NCO) trying to get him on their particular gun as that would be the Top gun on the Sqn.

His reputation certainly preceded him; generally, when things like this happened, they didn't usually turn out the way they were expected to.

Now with a Bofor's 40/70 gun, you could fire a single shot/automatic or radar-controlled. On auto, it fired *4½ rounds per second.* Of the first two, when aiming at a target flying at you, taking evasive action and probably firing its guns/cannons, not forgetting the missiles and bombs, it could be pretty difficult to hit it, not to mention near impossible. So if you could get close, that was as much as you could expect and hope the shrapnel from the exploding round would do enough damage to bring the aircraft down. Well, 'Dead-eye Dick' we'll call him, as I don't recall his name, joined us on live practice straight on the range. Don't forget, he had never seen the other members of his crew before so he didn't know their ways or peculiarities. He was posted to 'B' Flt – not my 'C' Flt.

So 'B' Flight (equivalent to an army platoon) from then on thought themselves 'the' superior flight. He was a small quiet chap, not cocky or pushy, then came the day for him to show us on the range what he could do.

He sat in the firer's chair and the rest of the Sqn were 'stood to'! Loaded up with live ammunition but were excused firing on this particular run. 'Dead-eye's gun was the only one authorised to fire.

We all waited for the target towing aircraft to bring the target within range. It was as a matter of interest that a Canberra Jet bomber was used. The drogue was a large windsock similar to what was used on British airfields. The drogue came within range and we were all quiet, holding our breaths. I heard the sergeant on Dead-eye's gun say to him, "So, you're the big shot we've heard so much about, just how good are you really?" "Reasonable," came the modest reply. "Well, laddie, how many shots do you think you need to hit it with?"

"How many shots do you want me to hit it with?" came the confident reply. "What do you want me to do, hit it or bring the target down?"

With this, the sergeant burst out laughing and replied, "Are you trying to come the funny bugger with me or are you bragging? I will be satisfied if you can just hit the fecking target, neither you nor anyone else could possibly bring the target down." "Two rounds?" said Dead-eye Dick. The Sgt just laughed at him. With the whole Sqn watching, the target came over and the sergeant yelled, "Aircraft Action!" The crew ran to and mounted the gun. He laughed as he commanded the number 6, 4/5. "With one clip of four rounds, load and single shot!" It was normal practice to load with at least 12 rounds. The crew stared at the sergeant and he said, "This not only makes it a bit more difficult for you but it ensures you can't cheat by firing more rounds than you claim!"

The order was given – "Fire!" Bang! The first shot hit the target mid-way along its length. Bang! The second shot hit and snapped the wire to which the target was attached to the towing aircraft and the target fluttered and spiralled slowly downwards. (The target and towing aircraft were flying at about 1,500/2,000 feet at the time; the wire was about half an inch thick.)

The whole Sqn all stared for a few seconds, stunned into silence that he had done it. Then as one, the whole Sqn including the officers, range/camp personnel, let out an almighty cheer. So it was true, he was the best shot ever with a 5-ton Bofor's gun.

Even the pilot of the towing aircraft called down on the ground to air radio to say, "What the hell happened down there? I think I've lost the drogue!" It was confirmed and even the pilot offered his congratulations to the young gunner.

His gun participated in the competition shoot to find the best gun crew and inevitably he won it so from then on in, his crew wasn't allowed to participate in any competition as it was considered (quite rightly) that they had an unfair advantage. Any team having him was bound to win – hands down.

Thought my number was up

I thought at one time on the range that my number was up and I was about to be blown to pieces. During a shoot, suddenly everyone on the range disappeared. I wondered what on earth had happened. I looked around then the tannoy blared out, "Hot Barrel, clear the range, clear the range immediately!"

I didn't delay any longer; in fact I was the last to set off – but not the last to clear the range. I wasted no time.

There was the chance that a gun was about to blow up as it had a live detonated round jammed up the breach and the gun was very hot from firing on automatic. Added to that, it was still loaded up with nearly fifty primed rounds. A senior NCO then realised that all the other guns were loaded up with live primed rounds and if all of them blew up, the camp and that part of South Wales would disappear off the face of the map and no longer exist. So 'volunteers' were pressed into service to try and unload the ammunition from the other guns. I was caught and pressed into service; needless to say, I was more than a little worried.

Gingerly, I crept forward with two other lads and Lanky Benson driving the four-tonner.

One by one, we unloaded the guns and put – threw them, call it what you will, on to the back of the wagon, which had its tailboard down and was slowly driving from one end of the firing range to another.

On one such occasion, we were working pretty fast as we were getting nearer the gun that had caused all the bother. I threw a round onto the back of the truck then turned to go back for more, I saw out of the corner of my eye, the round starting to roll back towards the end of the truck as it was climbing a slight gradient. I turned to run back to try and catch it before it rolled off the back and exploded, setting off a possible chain reaction. I got there too late, the round dropped through my fingers and my heart stopped beating for a moment. As the round travelled from the back of the vehicle through my fingers on to the ground, I really thought for a second or two that was it. I started to say goodbye to the world/relatives, then it hit the ground. It didn't explode though, why I don't know, there was no reason why it should have failed to go off. It was my lucky day. In fact, once we recommenced firing, that round fired and exploded along with all the others.

I think one of two things must have been the answer. It would have exploded only when its timer automatically detonated it or someone up there was watching over me that day! You still have to add the fact that, however, the timer was set; if the round was unstable, it would have still been set off. I think that fate had not written my name on that round that day! Thank goodness.

Tenby

The evenings out I had, I mostly spent in the nearest seaside resort of Tenby, a very nice place. We were there at the end of the season so not only was everything open but the weather was nice and sunny, add to that the holiday makers were still coming and that included lots and lots of attractive girls. Whilst the lads went out drinking, you can imagine what I was doing? Having a walk around and getting to know the place and 'girl hunting'. I liked Tenby as it was a very pleasant place and well set out, clean and very friendly.

Golf course

We hardly ever walked in by the main road as we thought it too far; instead, we used to take a shortcut across the local golf course, much to the consternation of the golfers (including some of our Sqn officers and senior NCOs).

We then found ourselves on an old abandoned railway line, it was a good job that it was abandoned considering the state we were in after a night out in the town.

If the Sqn golfers saw some of us fooling around on the golf course, we were all blamed for spoiling their game or damaging the turf, the latter was certainly untrue. As for spoiling their game, they couldn't have been much good at the game to let a temporary (a few seconds) distraction spoil the whole game.

Pub crawling

As was our wont, we would move from bar to bar in a typical forces pub-crawl. As soon as we got bored with one, we'd move on and cause havoc elsewhere. Most of the landlords were prepared to put up with our noisy high jinks as the profits made it worthwhile to grit their teeth and put up with us for a while.

Young officers drunk

One evening, while standing outside a dance hall and debating whether to go in or not, we heard a lot of noise from across the road and saw some of our young (subaltern) officers being thrown out of this bar. They were drunk and very rowdy. They were, as they would say, under the influence of the grape.

On getting outside, they thought it 'a jolly good wheeze' to drill each other in the street, with all civilians looking on and like us, having a good laugh at them, they could hardly stand up, and were showing themselves up.

It was fun to watch them. As this was generally the state we got into, it was amusing to see them acting daft.

'Sqn stud'

On 37 Sqn, it was confirmed that I was 'deadly' when it came to chatting up the girls. I even had the dubious honour in some circles of being known at some time the 'Sqn stud'! What single man wouldn't like to be called that? While it wasn't 100% true, who was I to argue? It came about, I believe, when we went for a night out. Most of the guys would drink half the night to get up the courage to chat up the girls, I didn't, I had a drink or two with them to be sociable then 'moved in for the kill'. I did have quite a knack with the girls in comparison to most of the guys, purely I because I was sober when I moved on the girls! The guys were more interested in drinking themselves into a stupor and only had the courage to try and pick up a girl when they were 'tanked' up, but by this time, the girls (generally) didn't fancy some drunken Squaddie slobbering all over them and trying to have a grope on the dance floor.

I used to try and plan out my moves. This simply meant having a walk (generally on my own), getting the lay of the land, watching them for a while, trying and weighing the most likely to go for. I would then move in on the unsuspecting female. If I had taken a girl outside for a bit of fresh air, we came back and I would tip the wink to the guys and they would assume I had done the dirty deed. Actually, this was my way of having a bit of a laugh at the guys because when I did this, I hadn't! But they thought I had.

There was one on the Sqn, wherever he served, who truly deserved that honour. I was a mere sprog – a learner! My efforts paled into insignificance in comparison to his sexual prowess and adventures. (See Sqn/regiment folklore.) Jack (John) Skuse. He had the good looks and the patter. Some would say he was the spitting image of the Hollywood icon James Dean. No wonder the girls fell for him.

Spot the grot

We went into this dance hall I've mentioned and because we felt in the mood, we thought we'd have a laugh and have a game of 'spot the grot', which I shall explain to the unknowing.

Several chaps would go around and survey the talent available, or in this case, the lack of it! And if the girls weren't much to get excited about – plain/ugly – we would play 'spot the grot'

Certain girls were chosen as the 'victims' and a chap had to pick her up and take her outside (to be confirmed by others watching nearby), whereupon he had to get so far sexually, whatever had been decided on the outset. When it was agreed who was the 'Queen Grot' of all in the dance hall/pub, then he was declared 'King-spot the grot'! For the night, he didn't have to need for a thing, everything was bought for him – beer, cigarettes, crisps, nuts, etc. and his entrance fee if they all went somewhere after.

So competition was fierce though we all had to have a few beers before we could tackle some of the girls, they were so grotty and rough sometimes. I have won 'spot the grot' myself and on more than one occasion, I have been declared 'King'.

It was best to start as soon as possible because as soon as the winner was declared, the longer he had to drink free drinks. It may sound very cruel but it was not; the girls we used to go after were unattractive, haggard, smelly, scruffy girls, that nobody was paying any attention to. No one was asking them for a dance or offering to buy them a drink. So they were being ignored and always looked unhappy, we made their night, we made them believe that they were attractive. We were doing them a favour and cheering them up, that couldn't be bad!

On a few occasions, some of the girls were brought to the table and introduced to the others; she thought her new 'boyfriend' was proud to show her off to his friends. But if it got to a tie-breaker situation, the 'committee' had to see the finalists up close to see who was the grottiest and who had won the competition.

There were other times that the girls heard the expression 'S.T.G.' being used and asked what it meant, it took us all our energy to refrain from laughing and had to make up some excuse and was of course greeted with guffaws of laughter.

Hunting the **nt

On the opposite scale, we also used to play 'hunt the **nt' contest, which was similar to S.T.G., only this time you had to find the prettiest and most attractive girl in the room. And the one who pulled her was declared the winner. Again – same rules. All his beer bought for him, along with the honour for the night – 'King Hunt the **nt'! I have won both of these competitions, which helped enhance my reputation. Though not only was a bit of luck involved, but contrary to belief, I didn't get my 'end away' each and every time, very rarely in fact! But I wasn't going to tell them this.

Meeting Gillian

At Tenby, on the second Saturday we were there, I won the 'hunt the **nt' competition when I met an attractive girl called Gillian who was there with her parents on holiday.

I kept up correspondence with her for two or three years and I even visited her at her college in Leicester where she was studying, a little while later. It surprised me how easy-going student life was, they had a weekly programme of subjects they were studying and not one person I met said they attended each lecture. I was told that if they didn't feel like going to a lecture then there was no pressure or encouragement at all to try and make them attend! And even take a month off if they liked, nothing was said to them. I thought it disgusting; after all, if you were at college to study, then study. It was obvious that some of them were not even interested in studying for their exams. Surely if they got into a routine, they would not only pass the exams with ease, but unlike most, they would not have to lock themselves up for weeks on end and try and cram all the studying in a short space of time. With just a few hours a week given over to studying/revision, they would not only do well but also have a social life.

So now I knew why some of the students passed their exams with such ease. It wasn't because they were more intelligent but they obviously had a routine where they were able to study at a steady, organised rate and passed with ease.

Medal presentation

Not long after we'd returned to camp and had our 'Buckshee'-free two weeks off, we were in the middle of servicing the guns after their firing, the orders were published re-awarding of decorations earned in Northern Ireland.

The parade was called and we were all standing there in our entire finery (best blues). One by one, we were called forward to receive our awards (mostly G.S.M. N/I but some had other medals presented).

Eventually, my name was called out and I marched forward, halted, saluted the C.O./Sqn standard, then the S.W.O. Taylor, who smiled, shook my hand and said, "It's a good job we're not in the French Army, Rowbottom, I would have to kiss you and I don't fancy you that much!" I laughed and said, "I don't fancy you much either, Sir!" So laughingly, we parted and I went back into the ranks.

Naafi breaks

The Sqn used to have their Naafi breaks in the YMCA at Catterick because the sprogs used the Naafi itself.

TV programme

At one time, there used to be two programmes on TV, one was cartoons and if you fancied committing suicide then you made a noise or interrupted the programme; it was a crime to disturb the 'hard rock-apes' while they were watching *Tom and Jerry, Popeye, Mighty Mouse* and the like.

The other was 'sex education for schools'.

Amongst other things that it showed was the different male/female sex organs. If anyone dared to speak (as it did happen once), he was bombarded from all quarters with cans of soft drinks, bits of bread rolls, cigarettes, 'dog ends', ash trays, not to mention abuse!

One particular time, it showed the male organ getting larger and larger as it was supposed to be getting sexually aroused; you can imagine it was greeted with howls of derogatory remarks and ribald comments. Even the couple who ran the YMCA was laughing. Then when it showed the female reproductive organs, internal and external, in full colour and minute detail, every airman and rock-ape made some sort of remark/comment, with some chaps trying to make suggestive movements, telling us all what they were going to do to their girlfriends this weekend and a great cheer went up. You would have thought, if passing outside, that they had just declared the surrender of the Japanese and the end of World War 2 rather than just seeing a women's 'forbidden' parts.

If truth be known, it probably was educational to some of the lads, but they were sure as heck not to let on that they were still virgins – the worst crime of all! And they would never hear the end of it for 'extracting the urine'!

Great fun was had by all and we all left laughing and in a great mood for the rest of the day.

Camp cinema, sex

Just about every camp I've been on has had a camp cinema. They all had three things in common with each other and that was:

1. They were very cheap, far cheaper than the local flicks in the town

2. The programme was changed about three/four times a week so there was always a good new film on and you never got bored

When I first started to go to the camp cinemas, it only cost about 1/3d to get in equivalent to 6 ½ new pence. Now it costs not much less than the local one in town, about £1:80, that's inflation.

Sexually speaking, you could get away with a lot more than you could in the local flicks. The back of the cinema was pitch-black (kept that way deliberately for the lads) so you could not be seen by the usherettes, when there were some; they were usually doing what you were and didn't want to be disturbed. Mostly, you didn't have anyone at all running around with torches shining on you.

I know that to be a fact because I was a regular visitor to the cinema. I had heard of more than one case where a courting couple have gone into the back rows and stripped off completely and got 'stuck in'. I myself have had a few girls (usually WRAFs) but not got them quite to that level.

'Give her what for!'

The third thing was it was only advisable to go and watch all action films for if the scene shifted to a soppy love scene, the ribald comments came flowing forth. About how a male member of the audience could not only perform a lot better than the hero on the screen but the said member would 'do it better and longer' and he wouldn't be wasting all this time talking, he would get 'stuck in' ASAP and give the heroine 'what for' and make her eyes water and beg for more! "Go on," someone would shout out from the audience, "stop buggering about, go on – give her one, you know she's gagging for it!" This would go on throughout the film.

Usually, the ones who would make the most noise were the ones that would run a mile if a girl approached them and called their bluff. Those who were 'giving her one' were busy doing just that in the back seats. Additionally, once out of the cinema, you wouldn't hear them utter a word, it was as if the darkness would keep their identity secret and give them courage to shout out for a couple of hours.

These 'rude' comments would embarrass some girls, though not others. So it was a waste of time going to see anything but a western or a war film. You certainly couldn't follow the plot for all the noise. There were some films that were so funny and provoked audience comments that you couldn't hear a word that was said for maybe half an hour or more, still it didn't matter much as you were laughing too much to take any notice. Woe betide any American war film; you never heard a word, all we would hear was laughter at the way Hollywood portrayed soldiers and how different we did things in comparison.

One of the best films for provoking the audience to comment was *The Virgin Soldiers* about British troops, national servicemen in Malaya during the Emergency. They suddenly realise that they are on active service and virgins, and could end up getting killed before they have sampled the delights of the flesh. So they all set out trying to find a girl who will oblige them. I had seen the film in a civvy cinema and it was quite good but when I saw it in a camp cinema with a servicemen audience, it really made the film so much better. (I saw it about 3-4 times.)

Though I must confess I also used to enjoy shouting out witty comments as much as the rest, it used to be a good night out at the camp cinema, great fun, I miss those days.

S.A.S. lecture

One Monday morning, we were sent as usual to the YMCA for a long Naafi break then told at a certain time to report to the camp cinema and under no circumstances were we to bring a camera with us. The last bit we took no notice of and presumed that it was another boring training film; at least it would be a chance to catch up on a bit of sleep during the film.

After our Naafi break, we all made our way to the cinema. We noticed that guys from the other two Sqns at Catterick were also going to the cinema. "Ey up," someone said, "something's up!" and all went inside. Upon our entry to the auditorium, we were all stopped and searched for hidden cameras. All the lights were off and you couldn't see a thing, it was total darkness; a few sarcastic comments started to flow forth, such as: "Bloody defence cuts, trying to save a few pennies again!"

"What's up, what's going on, is this supposed to be part of a bloody effing test or something!" Once our eyes started to become accustomed to the dark, we could see that not only were all three R.A.F. Regiment Sqns inside, including officers, senior NCOs, junior NCOs and 'erks – airmen. I suddenly put one and one together and thought, "Hello hello, something important is up, I wonder what's going on?" It wasn't long before everyone's suspicions were proven correct! Suddenly, a single spotlight lit the stage and a few moments later, a man walked on stage, he was half dressed in combat kit and half in black.

On his head, he wore a mask that covered his face so only the eyes were visible. The whispers started circulating; he then introduced himself as a captain and a recruiting officer for the S.A.S. – Special Air Service.

Special Air Service

He was here, he told us, on a recruitment drive for volunteers for the S.A.S. basic course, then hopefully, if/when they passed out, to join the elite regiment proper. He told us that he couldn't show us any films or slides or even documents as 95% of what the S.A.S. did was secret. Top secret. In fact, he couldn't even stand here and tell us what they did, all he could do was answer questions, though with most questions his reply was, "I'm sorry, I can't answer that question!" Or "I am unable to comment on that!"

He told us that secrecy was all important in their operations and that usually meant the difference of whether they would be successful or fail. "So you (us) understand why we have to be very, very careful, especially in some 'jobs' that are very delicate – National and International. And we can't afford any publicity!" To the best of my knowledge, no one from our Sqn was put forward for training, though we think there was at least one who asked to be put forward – Harry Grey – and was refused because the C.O. knew he wouldn't be good enough.

In fact, we heard – didn't know if it was true or not – that he went from one extreme to another. In frustration, he left 37 to join a Chopper Sqn.

I can't say if the other Sqns sent anybody as I didn't really know anyone on there. In fact, all of us were very impressed by the S.A.S. but that was as close to them as anyone got.

Ashes

One weekend after a particular hard week's training, I was invited down for the weekend by one of the lads who had come from regiment basics to 37 Sqn. Ron Helgar was his name and he lived in High Wycombe to the east and outskirts of London. I was introduced to his mother and then wondered to myself where his father was! He said he had noticed I was looking at a jar on the mantelpiece above the fireplace. "I forgot to introduce you," he said. "John, meet my father, or at least his remains." Yes, we were looking at his father's cremated ashes in an urn sitting on the shelf over the fireplace. I felt a little uneasy about that, rather weird and unnerving to my way of thinking, though not obviously to them. It takes all sorts, I suppose.

Weird characters on the Sqn

We had some right weird and not so wonderful characters on 37. Some of which I'll tell you about.

Ben Holingson and his mate Paddy (already mentioned in N. Ireland detachment). These two I had the impression were envious of my reputation with the fairer sex; however, I wasn't quite the sex machine what they and others thought.

They really dropped me in it one night, as in most cases when I went looking for a decent girl, I liked to work on my own and not have the loud-mouthed idiots of the Sqn/flight around me and spoiling my chances. This night, I jumped in my car and drove around until I found somewhere to spend the evening; I ended up about five miles away at 'Scotch Corner' whereupon, after enquiring, I discovered that there was a special annual dinner/dance for the local farmers' union. I was able to get in as I had come out reasonably smart with a suit and tie on. I gave a bit of waffle to the chap on the door. You could see and feel the money here; it was posh do with bow ties and the girls wearing long evening dresses.

Farmer's daughter and B.H./Paddy

I started to dance with some of the girls and eventually got off with this friendly, attractive girl who I got the impression wasn't short of a few pounds, and seeing her family seemed to confirm this.

She was well educated too; I felt I was well in here and to be prepared for what a drive home through dark country lanes might bring, and thought that I was in with more than a fair chance of a long-term relationship.

I was convinced that she was being more than polite and really friendly towards me! I was going great guns then I saw a sight that made my heart sink, Ben Holingson and his mate Paddy had somehow 'conned' their way into the dance.

They saw me and I saw them smile, point my way and start whispering to each other. I could read their minds, they were going to try and spoil my chances but I was so confident that I was well enough in with this girl that they wouldn't put her off, she was too friendly and well educated to be put off with a bit of gossip. How wrong could you be!

I held off as long as I could before having to go to the loo, as I figured that would be the moment they were waiting for. Eventually, needs must and I had to go, I went to the toilet and when I came back, her ardour had cooled off a considerable amount, I tried to find out what was the matter and at first she told me there was nothing but in the end I managed to wheedle it out of her. She said, "How's your wife and three kids, or is it three and one on the way?"

I just laughed at her and told her I honestly didn't know what she was talking about. She eventually told me that my 'friends' over there had told her that I was married with children, was it true? I told her of course it wasn't. I then asked her if she believed them. She seemed too embarrassed to answer, so even though I really fancied her and wanted to go out with her on a regular basis, I replied, "I'm telling you it isn't true, I'm not married, I haven't one child, let alone three or four, now do you want to believe me or do you want to believe them? You have given them the satisfaction; they have put a stumbling block between us!" She thought that there must be some truth in the tale or why else would they say it, so I wasn't going to waste my time any more on a lost cause so I ignored her for the rest of the evening, it was pointless trying to convince her. Though she did seem a bit miserable after that; was it because she didn't want to finish or that she was disappointed to hear I was married?

I was gutted; I then had a go at these 'bar-stewards' – to put it politely, amongst some of the things I told them was, "If they can't get their own women, then don't try and queer anybody else's patch!" To a lot of the blokes on the Sqn, this was considered good, viable entertainment and fair sport; if you didn't like it – tough!

That was one tradition I never did or still like, it was stupid and childish. Who knows what that evening could have led to, she could have been the daughter of a rich farmer and I could have been set up for life.

Boxers (37-16 Sqns)

We had a boxer on the Sqn who we hardly ever saw as he was always away either training for or participating in bouts representing the Sqn or the R.A.F. When we were on detachment or firing on the range, he always found another job as we couldn't have him on the A.A. gun-live firing, or foot/mobile patrol, though he was above average when we fired the Sqn small arms, including the anti-tank gun. He never got anywhere in his boxing as he was quite keen to brag that women were always asking him to oblige them (entirely due to his being known as a boxer) and he claimed that even if he had a fight the next couple of days, he would still 'do it' if he got the chance. (That's obviously why he didn't get anywhere in his boxing.) He also smoked!

I tried boxing

If he had made an effort by cutting out the smoking and the women, he just might have gotten somewhere as he was reputed to have a good punch in his right hand; that is, if he had enough energy during the bout to throw it. He tried to get me interested in boxing, but I wasn't and never have been much good, but compared to me he was very good. I got an idea just how tiring a bout could be. I used to go help him sparring in the accommodation block, the regulation three two-minute rounds sometimes three five-minute rounds, I have never felt more tired or knackered in my life, every muscle in my body was aching (and I was reasonably fit at the time).

Coloured boxer

However, on one of the other Sqns, 16 Sqn – there was a coloured lad with muscles on muscles, a quiet and decent chap who did train as he should, non-smoker, no women before a bout and he became the heavyweight champion of the R.A.F. and heavyweight champion of the A.B.A.(Amateur boxing Association). He was a real nice chap and really deserved his success, though I should think he spent less time on his Sqn than even our chap did.

Their levels of skill were as far apart as were their respective weights, middle to heavy. This champion really made our chap look daft at the game. The champion had appeared on TV on several occasions and was well known in the 'fight game'.

Kitchson doing it 'a lot of times' in one weekend

Kitchson (See South Wales, Manorbier) once gave the Sqn its biggest and best laugh for a long time. I asked him on a Monday morning if he had had a good time over the weekend. He came out with a classic line: "Had a good time, you're kidding? I've just had the best weekend ever, I met this bird on Saturday night and I got my leg over!"

"Did you?" I said, trying not to laugh. (His next will be his first!)

"Yeah," said he, "I had it 37 times!" "What!" I said. I was really having a job trying not to laugh. "Over the weekend?" "Oh no," he said, "just Saturday night!" Unable to contain myself any longer, I laughingly said to him (holding out my hand), "Then let me shake you by the hand, this is a great honour!" He asked why. "I've always wanted to shake the hand of Superman!" He stared at me blankly as he didn't know if I was being sarcastic or I meant it. What a silly man.

On top of this, he claimed that he had an orgasm each and every time. I said to him in the end (not mincing my words), "Bollocks! If you had it half as many times as you reckon on Saturday, you would be half dead by now!" He still didn't understand what I was trying to say.

Within an hour, thanks to me and the other lads who had been within earshot, it was all around the Sqn and even the officers came out and 'took the mick'. Within a couple of hours, it was all around Catterick thanks to the grapevine! People who didn't even know him approached him and made fun of him.

Lanky Benson

Another weirdo we had was S.A.C. Lanky Benton. He was our gun detachment 4-tonner driver/generator operator.

When I first joined the Sqn, I noticed that he always sat on his own and people would mostly ignore him, I was to find out why later. I thought the blokes were being unfair to him, until I found out why, then I understood and in most cases agreed with the majority. At mealtimes, he sat on his own, I didn't want to have people think I was unfriendly, so at first, I would sit with him and have a chat. I then noticed one of the reasons he was not popular. His face was covered in large unsightly boils (which were popularly referred to as 'plukes' in Sqn terminology), which had a habit of bursting and oozing matter at the most awkward moment, usually as you were eating your meal. He smelt horrible; he stank. When I mentioned this to a mate, he said, "Oh, didn't you know? That's because he's a junkie, and queer to boot!"

From then on, not really believing the gossip, I observed from a distance for myself to see if it was true. I then avoided him as everyone else did. Now I knew the background story, just why he acted in such a way.

One time during a mineworkers' strike, I was assigned to accompany a 4-tonner driver to take a generator we normally used for the guns to a local OAP hospital so that they would have a source of electricity during an emergency; in fact, all the generators on our and 16 Sqn were temporarily dispersed in such a fashion.

I was unfortunate in getting assigned to accompany Lanky. I was dreading it, it was a long drive and made all the more unpleasant having to sit next to him in the cab and putting up with that revolting smell, the rest of the lads were very relieved they hadn't got him.

We left the 'Jennies' there and didn't pick them up for months. So long in fact that it occurred to me that the Sqn just might have forgotten all about them, especially as 16 Sqn had already collected theirs months ago.

The reason Lanky didn't actually go on the gun became evident, an 'addict' couldn't be trusted with live ammunition. Dread the thought that if he had secretly had a fix just before going on the gun range as a shooter, he would probably go off his head and try to shoot people he didn't like, not even counting the damage he would cause blowing things up. It was just as well, and with him having his lorry driving licence, it was the perfect job to keep him out of the way.

First thing every Monday morning, we all had to go and start the 'Jennies' to keep them in good working order and the water out.

Lanky would always disappear and when next seen would have had a fix and be high or else he would still be high from the night before.

The 'Jennie' would have three different speeds (rpm) going up to 18,000 rpm. At each speed, Lanky would be trying – unsuccessfully to dance, move in time to the revs; it was impossible but so funny to watch, he didn't see us peeking around the corner and watching him and laughing at him, he was too far gone. We would hear him saying to himself, "Oh man, that's real way out, I really dig it. It's real Hendricks, man!" (Jimi Hendrix was his hero, who had died from a drug overdose.) The officers knew he was a junkie but he was able to do his job and never tried to approach anyone on the Sqn to try and get them involved so that was the general consensus of opinion of why he wasn't reported. He went AWOL some weekends and the general unwritten law on the Sqn was that you were given (time varied from Sqn to Sqn) usually two to three days to turn up before being reported AWOL so if your train/car broke down or you were unavoidably delayed, you had time to get to camp or get a message to the camp.

One weekend, Lanky was AWOL and it had to be reported. The civvy police had allegedly picked him up at a known drug addict's den and reported this to the military police, who were sent to pick him up. He was thrown immediately into the military prison then the next we heard, he had been thrown out with a dishonourable discharge.

As a footnote to the Lanky saga, when we were flying to Germany for a re-enforcement exercise, Lanky had been sitting in his seat and the cabin area began to pressurise and his 'plukes' began to burst one by one. The puss oozed out, hilarious, as I was sat a good distance from him but not a very pleasant experience for this poor sprog, who happened to be sitting next to him at the time.

Chap didn't want commission

One day there was posted on the Sqn a chap from R/Regt basic's course. A nice quiet chap, he was on one of the other flights. What made him stick in my mind more than the usual sprog coming on the Sqn, who were of the usual loud-mouthed variety, was that he was quiet.

It came to pass that we heard that the aforementioned chap was very highly qualified; more so than even the Sqn officers, he had something like 8 'A' levels and about 2 'O' levels. (Some of the officers had only scraped in for a commission with the minimum 5 'O' levels.) He was the sort that didn't brag about it; in fact, he seemed almost embarrassed about it.

Trouble was that once the Sqn officers found out, they nagged and tried to persuade him to take his commission. They pressurised him at every chance they got, even in the middle of a training session, they never let up. He was just not interested, no matter what they tried. He said to me once during a quiet moment that his original idea was to join the R.A.F. Regiment as 'one of the lads' to enable him to learn the job from our level first, then apply for his officer course and commission at a later date, about 2/3 years time. The C.O. and officers kept up the pressure until suddenly this chap said, "Enough!" They had nagged once too often and pushed him a bit too far; he then bought himself out, he'd had enough, so the R.A.F. not only lost an airman but a potentially excellent regiment/aircrew/pilot officer. Serves them right.

I have since read in a service newspaper that the 37 Sqn C.O., Leader

Hawkins, was now a high-ranking (air rank) officer. Excellent officer. (Eventually to be Commandant General of the R.A.F. Regiment, fully deserved.)

Sports
Most sports were catered for at Catterick, some more than others because of its sheer size and turnover in manpower. There was a model (flying) aircraft club, chess, theatre, wood/metalwork, swimming pool, not to mention all the usual sports such as football, rugby, tennis, hockey, rock climbing, etc.

Race course
Although Catterick is the home of a quite famous race course, in all the time I was there, I never once went to the races, which was only half a mile from camp gates. I never participated in any of these activities.

Thing was we were either: a) away on detachment/exercise, b) too busy to go or as was the case mostly, c) once I got back from a detachment, I was only too glad to be heading home for a rest or meeting the girlfriend of the moment.

Another place I never visited but would have liked to was the R.A.F. Regiment Museum on camp. Though it was arranged for us to go on two or three occasions, something always turned up to prevent it, such as the caretaker couldn't be found or the keys were lost. Shame as I would have liked to look around.

Dentist
The new station dentist we had there wasn't very popular (are they ever?) for in the mornings, his breath would smell of garlic as he leaned over you, and in the afternoons, of beer. Unlike his predecessor who would ask you what sort of music you liked and tried to put you at ease before he started to drill away merrily.

There was a young chap whom I'd seen around camp a few times, he was in the intake behind us on the regiment basics course. He was, I found out, always in trouble and like Harry Grey, made his second home in the guardroom.

He was on, I believe, 16 Sqn. The last time I saw him, he had been in close arrest in the guardroom and being escorted by two burly R.A.F. policemen when going for his meals. This time, he was waiting for his court martial for being AWOL.

The night before his case was due to be heard, he was let out unaccompanied, possibly to get his best uniform cleaned and pressed, it was certainly most unusual and unheard of. (We had heard that the officer on duty that night had been his officer from his Sqn and had trusted him.)

The burning of S.H.Q.

That night, the Fire Piquet was called out to a fire reported in the S.H.Q. building (station headquarters). By the time the civvy fire brigade got there and got the blaze under control, the station commander's office was gutted, though fortunately the most important – the pay accounts, were untouched.

The fire had been started and contained in the station commander's office. The culprit had not taken any precautions to hide his presence or fingerprints. So when the S.I.B. of the services came in to investigate, they found without any trouble fingerprints belonging to this lad due for his court martial that morning. He had left the guardroom and gone immediately to S.H.Q., broke in and set fire to it.

He had his court martial all right; he was sentenced to two years for his AWOL charge. For burning S.H.Q., another 6 years and as he was about to be marched away to commence his sentence, the civvy police were waiting for him and charged him with arson (he got 10 years for that); however, the general thing, on a dual charge relating to civil and military law, was that the prisoner had to serve his civvy sentence first, then on his release the military police would take him into custody and charge him for being AWOL for the number of years he was away in the civvy nick and add the sentence on to what he had already gotten so our friend could have gotten about a total of 20+ years. Depending on the charge, it was sometimes arranged for convenience sake for all concerned that the sentence would be served in either the civvy prison or the military one, always followed by a dishonourable discharge.

The military was governed by two laws of the land, civil and military – unlike civilians who had one law to worry about.

A.O.C.'s inspection

Once a year in the R.A.F., we had an annual A.O.C.'s inspection – air officer commanding's annual inspection of the camp – personal and equipment.

This inspection frankly was a pain in the rear as we always had several months' notice of his arrival and he knew that everything was going to be spruced up and immaculate; he would not see the real camp, only what the permanent staff wanted him to see and he knew it, so it defeated the whole object of an inspection in my opinion.

I always said that he should come on an hour's notice and then he could see the camp and personnel as they really were and how well they were/ were not doing their jobs. Of course, the other lads said that was wrong as he wouldn't have the formality of an official parade, etc. I said, "What is the purpose of the visit – a parade or an inspection. A parade can always be arranged!" It always meant lots and lots of cleaning and scrubbing/polishing; that was the only good thing about an inspection in as much as things such as hangar floors got cleaned once a year.

The Sqn decided gladly so, that it would be best for us all to be out on training and not on camp having to clean everything from brass handles to toilets, gardens and kerb stones, etc.

The C.O. said, as an excuse, if the A.O.C. picked anything up: "I consider training more important than cleaning toilets and sweeping floors!" (I wished more officers thought like him.)

So it was all arranged that on the day petrol, rations, road maps, etc. would be drawn and prepared, we would have one of the flights give a demo on the airfield of our primary and secondary roles. The rest of us set off as soon as we knew the A.O.C. was on camp.

Lake District

We couldn't believe where the Sqn had planned to spend the day at the Lake District: big, touristy, climbing, walking area.

We set off for Lake Windermere at about 10 am. And a great time was had by all. One of the most interesting and funny events happened on our way there.

Suggestive comments to girls from the back of the wagon

As usual, whenever a wagon full of soldiers/airmen in the back passed young attractive females, there were always things shouted at them, rude and ribald suggestions and comments as to what the guys would do if they got their hands on these passing females. But as always, if the vehicle was stuck at traffic lights or a road junction and a girl walks by, the lads sat all quiet and embarrassed and they daren't look at the girl, let alone say anything to her.

If they were given a wave or a smile in return from the girl, there would then result in an argument as to who she was smiling/waving at. "Cor, see that, I got a smile from her!"

"No, you didn't; she was smiling at me!"

"You're all wrong; it was me, she was waving to me!"

"Liar, it was me, and if you say different, I'll knock your fecking teeth out! And kick your fecking head in!"

"Don't threaten me, you ***t; I'll fecking swing for you!"

This would go on for a few minutes until another pretty girl smiled at someone, then it would start all over again, great fun. I wonder if these girls knew the trouble they caused by a simple wave or a smile?

This day, I was to witness something I'd not forget and I don't think the lads would either; they finally got their comeuppance! Upon passing this particularly attractive and very pregnant girl, who was also pushing a pram with a baby in, the usual comments came flooding forth from their mouths aimed in her direction, accompanied by the placing of the left/right hand over their other arm/biceps and pumping vigorously up and down. They would say things like, "Come here and I'll give you something to take your mind off your worries!"

"If you come here, I'll give you another baby to keep the other in the pram company!" A few seconds later, we had pulled up at some traffic lights, and this time the suggestions came forth.

One girl retaliated

She came up to the back of the wagon and stunned us all by being the first and only girl to answer us back. Pointing to her large abdominal swelling, she said, "How the fecking hell do you think I got this, it was a bloody Squaddie who did this to me and he's buggered off and left me!"

This had the effect of shutting all the lads up immediately.

This was the first time I had seen the lads put in their place, she had succeeded where many others had failed. I was the first one to break the silence as I burst out laughing followed by the others. The rest of the trip was done in comparative embarrassed silence, amazing really.

Lake Windermere

The local populace must have wondered what on earth had hit them when 40 combated suited rock-apes descended on them without notice. About 15-16 of us hired rowing boats and were practising our naval manoeuvres and we all headed for an island in the centre of the large lake in Windermere. Upon making land-fall, we did a typical Royal Marine-type beach landing, screaming and shouting at an imaginary would-be 'enemy position'. Only, at Lake Windermere at this time of year, the only defenders of that 'foreign shore' were bird watchers, ramblers and lovers busy canoodling alone in the bushes, but they hadn't reckoned with H.M. Forces spoiling their fun, and spoil their fun we did. After the beach was 'secure', we raced each other in the boats, only in our haste to get back, we went around and around in circles and one boat overturned and sank, we couldn't go to their aid immediately as we were unable to do anything but collapse in fits of laughter watching their boat sink. And of their 'self-imposed' misfortune, by the time we'd recovered our breath enough to go to their side, some of the others had rescued them first; good job as they were really in danger of drowning! Some may think this was a callous and uncaring attitude to have, but such was the serviceman's dark sense of humour, as only one who has served will understand.

It didn't help that we were worse the wear for drink. We must have been quite a sight, we had taken over the town much to the dismay of the holiday makers, and the place was packed with them.

Whips

We had two or three who didn't take anything back (apart from hangovers), except for large 10 feet bull whips, they were walking around town cracking these bull whips, especially when they saw an attractive young girl. I think that most of them got the message and not all were offended either, even though the sexual overtones were obvious.

Standby-R.T.U.

Back at camp, we found our Sqn was due to be on immediate stand-by, ready to be called out at a moment's notice for any spot of trouble anywhere in the world that British Forces or interests may dictate military intervention.

Your location at any time over the weekend had to be given to the Sqn so that if the need arose, they would be able to get hold of you through the local police at a moment's notice. One particular Friday night, I went home for the weekend as normal. Upon getting home, I changed and went out to my favourite pub as was my normal routine, it so happened I had no particular girlfriend at the time as I had just finished with my latest flame the weekend before. I'd gotten bored with her. This particular night, after about an hour, I left that pub and went to another for a change.

When I got home in the evening, I was asked by my parents where I'd been, I told them that as always I'd been to the 'Sherpa'. They asked hadn't I heard the announcement or seen the policeman? "What policeman?" I asked.

It turned out that about 10 minutes after I'd left the 'Sherpa' for the 'Queen Bess', the police had come in looking for me and had announced my name over the mike. I had to report home immediately to receive some important news from my parents concerning the Sqn. I rolled in that night later than normal about midnight, and drunk-singing.

The Sqn had affected an emergency R.T.U. immediately.

It was far too late to thumb it back to camp up the A1 and I didn't think there was a train yet so I said I would get the first train in the morning to camp. At that time, I didn't have a car anymore as I had sold it prior to going to N. Ireland. So in the morning, I got the first train to Darlington.

Both my father and I had a good idea what it was for – N. Ireland. We figured that we'd have to go out there to back up the other Sqns who were already there.

I arrived early in the morning at the Sqn and reported to the orderly room. I was given a rollicking by our Flt Sergeant (Tug) Wilson who tried to tell me I should have been there earlier; I informed him that I had got the first train and what more could I have done! He reluctantly had to accept this.

I felt sorry for the 'jocks' and the 'taffs' for they had no sooner arrived home from a long and tiring journey than they had to turn around and come straight back to camp.

We had a roll call and parade; the C.O. thanked us for our prompt reaction and overcoming difficulties in getting back so soon.

He then said, "OK lads, enjoy the rest of the weekend, that's all, I just wanted to see how fast you could all get back to camp if and when really needed!"

We were all fuming mad at this, he had ruined our weekend for nothing so without a word being said, we all moved forward together towards the

C.O. and in a second he was gone, he didn't wait around to see what we were about to do – he knew! We were about to mutiny. Such was the anger.

By then it was too late to go home. So most of us decided to spend the rest of the weekend in camp.

Specialist's training

We were told that our second detachment to N. Ireland was due and we were to be tasked differently this time, patrolling the streets.

So, we commenced various specialist courses. This started with anti-riot training.

A/riot training

The Sqn was split in two with one half acting as security forces and the other half as rioters; the latter started a 'riot', which involved throwing at us grass sods and then later when they really got into the swing of things, bricks! The rioters started being realistic.

We had two chaps on our Sqn, one on my 'C' Flt, Ron Helgar, and his best pal on 'B' Flt. 'B' Flt were the villains of the piece and we on 'C' Flt were the 'goodies'. Ron Helgar on our flank was getting a bit fed up of being bombarded with bricks and having to hide behind his riot shield; he then volunteered to be one of the 'snatch squads' who would go out and arrest the ring leaders. He ran out, grabbed his best mate and started to beat him senseless with his baton; he really got carried away and started calling him names such as Paddy Bas***d, Irish ***t and other sweet colonial expressions.

We had to physically drag him off as he was really starting to hurt his friend and his friend had blood running down his face. "Good," we thought, "if this is how he carries on with his best friend then what will he do to the real villains!" Ron Helgar was talked to by his Flt OC about causing actual bodily harm to his mate, we became very thankful for the riot shields in front of us. They certainly stopped anything from hitting us. After we changed with my Flt dressed in civvies and 'rioting', I must confess that I enjoyed 'creating a riot'! I would have no doubt have felt different if it had been the real thing. The authenticity was ruined by the simple fact that everyone was having a most enjoyable time laughing and beating your best mate up. We saw the troops in full riot kit coming towards us and they looked very impressive behind their shields and very menacing.

We also went 'somewhere in Yorkshire'; we were taken to a special purpose-built street, whereupon we were instructed in the art of searching houses.

Booby-trapped house

We also had to learn to clear a booby-trapped house. The idea was to enable you to search a booby-trapped house for explosives, weapons, drugs, etc. without blowing yourselves up.

All went quite well at first and the half section I'd been put in charge of was doing quite well. That was until the very last room. Upon entering the empty room, one round wooden table in the centre of the room, upon the table, there was a small wooden box.

One of the chaps made a move towards the box, I told him to leave it alone as it was bound to be booby-trapped. He told me to 'Foxtrot, Oscar!' (Or words to that effect.)

He opened the lid and took out a piece of paper and read it out loud to us. "BANG, YOU SILLY **NT, YOU HAVE JUST BLOWN YOURSELF UP AND YOUR SECTION!" Upon coming out of the house, the instructor asked if any stupid daft twit had opened the box upstairs.

He said it was so ruddy obvious that he didn't think anyone would be stupid enough to be tempted, but as he said, "There's always one, isn't there?"

Other courses

Some others went for training as drivers of 'pigs' (armoured personnel carriers) derived from the body of an armoured car.

Some others went to train as dog handlers – trained to sniff out weapons, explosives and some dogs who could sniff out drugs. Others as snipers and a couple of men left for a course we were unable to find out what it was. Some officers went on interrogation courses, liaison and policing methods with the R.U.C.

Sniper alley

As part of our training, we were sent down 'sniper alley'. It was a live authentic firing range that was specially rigged out as an ideal sniping country, two at a time set off down the narrow valley with an officer/senior NCO behind.

Their job was to pick the right moment and trigger off the target, which would pop up at various positions – from behind a tree, a rock, a building, in fact anything that you could possibly think of. There was also an officer walking between us to ensure safety with live rounds in a small confined area.

We had to fire two snap shots within three seconds of the target starting to appear. If you took too long to get off your shots or you missed, you had penalty points awarded and we worked it until we got down to the winner. I got into the last 5.

Sprog wants to marry the 'black widow'

Just before leaving for our second detachment in N. Ireland, some young sprogs were posted to the Sqn prior to leaving, as I had been. Upon joining his 'C and R' (command and recce) flight, one approached his OC to ask for permission to get married, Flying Officer McLennan, a great guy (who had been the officer on duty and had signed the authorisation for the L/R that I had been in N. Ireland first detachment and had got smashed up). We heard he had got two years loss of seniority, though an officer, he was considered 'one of the lads'! He had put his neck and career on the line for us, respect! We were led to believe other officers had shunned him to some degree as he always looked out for the rest of the guys. The only officer on the Sqn that all the guys would gladly follow anywhere and back, no matter how dangerous or suicidal!

The sprog was asked by Mac, "Who is the young lady, what's her name, do I know her?" The sprog told him her name, to which Mac replied – we were informed later, "What! F**k me lad, you can't be serious; you can't want to marry her! She's the Black Widow! Think again lad, it can't work – it won't work. She'll leave you as soon as she gets bored with you or she fancies someone else who's got a bigger dick than you – or more money!" But the lad was adamant and went ahead with the marriage anyway.

Mac was proved right after about only 6-7 weeks of marriage; she left him for another.

Taking guns to NI with us

Just prior to leaving for our next detachment in N. Ireland, the C.O. in his infinite wisdom told us that we were to take with us two of our 5-ton anti-aircraft guns so that if we had a bit of time to spare between shifts, we could practice our drills and keep fully trained and ready for the live firing detachment upon our return (four months hence after a three-month detachment to N. Ireland).

We never did touch them once all the time we were there, thank goodness, but I'll never forget the look on the faces of the local population as we drove off the ferry in Belfast and towed these formidable-looking guns through all the districts of the city where there was trouble. They looked very worried, as the British Government of the day had enough of the bombings, killings and riots. They must have thought we were about to open fire on their houses, as if we'd do such a thing!

My jobs

We never did get to do street patrolling as we were expected or trained for; we were located back at the airfield at Aldergrove. On this second detachment of mine, my job this time was working in the G.D.O.C. (Ground Defence Operation Cell) along with two others. We operated a shift system while our specific job was manning the radio set and acting as control over the Sqn radio net. Only on occasions such as a specific call out or incident did the duty officer in charge take over with specific instructions to the section commander on site actually dealing with the situation. However, the rest of the time, it was myself and the other two who had responsibility for the operation of the net and controlling the two sections on duty at that precise time, the I.R (Immediate Readiness) and standby sections.

While the work was interesting, I'd have rather have been 'in the field'.

Some of the others with us would have given their right arm to have a comparatively cushy and safe job for the duration, like mine. Not me; I wanted action, after all that was one of the main reasons that I had left catering and come into the R.A.F. Regiment.

R.A.F. Regiment (2nd) Northern Island detachment. Taken in G.D.O.C. – about to go on personnel protection duties.

Other tasks

Amongst other jobs we did was a general message boy going from G.D.O.C. to other sections/departments with messages that were too important to be disclosed over the phone/radio, assisting the M.O.D. police on the main station barrier and other duties.

Cinema guard

One of the main regular jobs we had to perform was cinema guard. Usually alone, sometimes with a mate or if we suspected any attack then the section on I.R. would be with us, this duty was a bit dodgy and the only one to cause me any worry during all my detachments to N. Ireland. You were so vulnerable, alone and exposed. You had an A41 radio man-pack strapped to your back and did a foot patrol in and around the cinema, although the radio slowed you down if you had to run fast from A to B. I felt comfortable knowing it was on my back as it still afforded some protection against small calibre bullets and shrapnel inflicted wounds if a bomb exploded.

Before the film started, we would check out the building inside and out, starting with my particular method, which was by checking the man operating the projector, then I would check on him again and escort him to wherever he had to go to take the money.

Meanwhile, we had to check out the buildings for bombs, suspicious parcels, etc. One major problem I learnt to overcome was that to do your job correctly, you were not only exposed but in the full glare of the sodium floodlights trained on the buildings for security reasons; fine, only that not only were you fully exposed but you were blinded and if there was anybody out there, you couldn't see further than about 5 yards into the dark; after that it was just a very bright orange glare blinding you. After a short while, I learned to take full advantage of this problem. I stood 'behind' the sodium lights and I could see a long way into the dark and see if anybody was approaching the cinema and crossing the field but it also had the effect of making me invisible to anyone standing within the glare of the lights. I could almost reach out and touch them. All you had to do was not stand/ walk in the obvious places but re-adjust your position in relation to the lights. By the time I had finished my tour, I had gotten this off to a fine art.

Except if there was a real good film on, then I altered my schedule of my foot patrolling and went inside and watched the film.

Most of the others who did this duty would watch the film all night and only carry out a couple of patrols in the entire night. I wasn't prepared to take that risk.

I never did the same thing each night at the same time – each and every time, I altered my timings and specific tasks that for all I know may have prevented me being attacked. Who knows, but it certainly seemed the best thing to do. Don't do the same thing twice in successive nights.

Stn commander bodyguard

Another time, or three, I had to act as a personal escort/bodyguard to the station commander. We would set off and try to be as inconspicuous as possible with the specifically rigged out escort vehicle c/w anti/landmine skirt, anti-garrotting stake, A/Riot protective screens, etc.

I was armed the first time with an S.L.R. rifle (which we found inconvenient and cumbersome getting in and out of his car).

I and the station commander travelled to and from his house/station in civvies. The staff car would pull up in front of his house off the camp and we noticed that there was several R.A.F. police with dogs walking around the grounds. The station commander in his civvies and I got in the car; we were supposed to be inconspicuous but we had escort vehicles in front and behind us and the station commander's uniform hat in the back shelf, talk about obvious.

It was a bit ridiculous, if we'd have been ambushed, with my large rifle I wouldn't have been able to get out very quickly, the delay could mean the difference between life and death.

The station commander suggested I get a small S.M.G. the next time. I agreed with him and saw about it ready for the next time I escorted him.

I also persuaded the duty officer to allow me to carry a 9mm automatic handgun, which he agreed to. Physiologically speaking, it worked wonders on my confidence.

'Mac' plays a joke on me

One morning, the duty officer woke me, asleep on my camp bed, and he told me to go and escort the station commander! Flying officer Mac shoved an S.M.G. in my hands and the 9mm pistol, and pushed me out of the door of the G.D.O.C. I saw straight away that there was a magazine on the weapon as I was still half asleep and Mac seemed to be pushing me outside. As soon as the fresh air hit me, I started to think straight and immediately took off the magazine and checked it. It was empty; no wonder he wouldn't let me check my weapon inside.

I stormed inside and gave Mac a piece of my mind and called him a few names. I had passed the point when you had to remember he was an officer; I couldn't care less, though I'll say this for Mac, he could take a joke, he was one of the lads, so much so the other officers didn't like him. He thought this a good laugh; he probably knew I would check the weapon. Had I not, then sods law, that would be the day I would have come under fire and not been able to defend myself with obvious outcome.

Anyway, I put on a full magazine of live ammo on the weapon after telling him off and went out and did the task.

R.R.B. Belfast (secret site)

After we'd been there about a month or so, we three in the guardroom were given a further task, with a difference! We had to set up and maintain an R.R.B. 'radio re-broadcast' facility to connect two units together, which normally were out of range with each other. This allowed Aldergrove to talk and communicate with another unit of ours out of normal radio range and stay in touch with the escort section on task.

It was a secret location, I did the second stint there (a week at a time). It happened to be too dangerous to go on foot or by mobile patrol so we were taken to the location by one of Aldergrove's helicopters at dawn/dusk.

I was dropped about 30 yards from the top of the large hill and told which way to go and not to worry, they were expecting me. They must have contacted the location once we were airborne. I ran a little way and as I crested the hill and rounded a rock, there it was! I was confronted with a large 15ft high fence and enclosed compound, topped with barbed wire and electronic cameras, amongst other things. The gates automatically opened for me to enter then closed behind me and locked.

I made my way to a large brick building that doubled as sleeping quarters and rest area, the radio room and other equipment was in another room. One other room was the charging room for the batteries. There were several people there, all from different regiments.

I introduced myself and they said they had been expecting me for the last few days. All regiments in Ulster were represented in this location (except the S.A.S.).

They were quite calm and didn't want to get up from their chairs to greet me or check my identity and relaxed. Nobody seemed to be bothered about security, which annoyed and puzzled me; they were too interested in watching TV.

I was to find later that they weren't bothered about security as the place was so secure nobody/nothing could get in or out unless expected. Yet surprisingly enough, during my two separate stints there, I never saw a TV monitor for the outer perimeter fence. It must have been kept very secluded as I never stumbled on the monitoring equipment, only authorised personnel would have been permitted to see it. Yet there was no one else, but no doubt there must have been someone watching somewhere!

At first, it made you nervous knowing there were only about 6-8 of you on the location, it made you feel vulnerable against any possible sneak attack, I thought we wouldn't stand much chance, but later I consoled myself with the fact that the army wouldn't have such a valuable and expensive and possible politically explosive site without adequate protection and emergency cover.

I then mentally relaxed. Even though during my entire time there, no one did any guard duties. I left the same way I had arrived, I walked out the main gates about 30 yards and an R.A.F. Wessex helicopter came in low and fast around the rocks, pulled up almost standing on its tail and at a hover just above the ground while I scrambled in (this was to enable it to turn on full power and make a quick getaway in an emergency such as an attack).

From the safety of the compound, you could see most of Belfast and most of the streets c/w riots; you could even see the petrol/nail and home-made bombs exploding. So if needed, we could direct the security forces straight to the scene, although that wasn't our purpose of being there.

Darts with R.U.C.

On my return to Aldergrove after my second stint, the Sqn had arranged a social evening playing games such as dominoes/darts with the local R.U.C. and M.O.D. policemen. I was chosen to play darts against an R.U.C. policeman. I lost and bought him a pint.

One day when it was my turn to be duty runner, I was doing a few jobs for the S.W.O. – W.O. Taylor.

Durex

One of the first jobs I had to do was pick up a parcel from the medical centre and return it to the S.W.O.

This was what I did, without knowing what it was, and paid no more attention to it. After lunch, I went into his office ready for another job and noticed that the parcel I had delivered had been opened and it contained a box of hundreds and hundreds of Durex, 'French letters' condoms.

Now normally, when British forces were abroad/overseas, they have issued to them as prescribed (if you can call it that) a number of Durex per week to prevent their 'associations' with the local populace (female type) from getting out of hand. In tropical climes, it was for the same reasons but also to prevent 'medical disorders' of a more tender nature and in tropical jungle, they were invaluable as a life saver with all the insects, leeches and such around.

After a few days, I made enquires and no one had seen them; they had not been issued to anyone; they had disappeared. I think I know where they finished up! They must have been sold to the local populace as 'French letters' were illegal in Ireland, especially in the south. (Catholics were forbidden to buy or use them.) So, there was money to be made on the black market if you had the right contacts.

Whilst there, I felt the need of a dentist so I reported sick. At the medical centre, I found out to my dismay that there was no facility for dentistry on the camp.

It was arranged that I and a few others would go collectively to a civilian dentist. When it was my turn, he examined me and unbeknownst to me (though I suspected it), he drilled my teeth that were perfectly OK and replaced all the fillings that were there already.

The first I knew anything was wrong was back at Catterick. I had been given so many injections and he had hurt me so my whole mouth was numb for about 24 hours and sore for a week The duty officer and the rest of the people in the G.D.O.C. thought it really funny that if I wanted to speak/answer a question, I had to write it down, I just couldn't speak. Of course, I couldn't operate the radio, so I helped out with other jobs.

Losing money, call in the S.I.B.

With the internal situation getting worse, I spent more and more time on camp so naturally I was able to save a bit of money. Once I had saved up a lump sum, I changed it into postal orders. After a while I thought I needed a bit of money so I decided to cash one of my postal orders; the problem was that I couldn't find them, I searched high and low but to no avail.

When I was convinced they had been nicked, I thought I'd better call in the S.I.B. The highly trained detectives searched my belongings, the locker, in and outside the block (including the dust bins), made enquires, asked questions to the lads in the room and the block (I wasn't very popular after that and each and every one in the block felt they were under suspicion of stealing; of course, this was ridiculous as I hadn't accused anyone in particular). The amount missing was equal to about two week's wages at the time.

I was wiser after the event. (Well, you always are, aren't you?) I should have put it straight in the post office or made a note of the serial numbers. As expected, nothing was ever found and no one accused or found guilty.

Then, one day 8 years later in 1978, after my de-mob, when I'd left the R.A.F. and was in civvy street, I was going through some old books at home, when suddenly the postal orders fell out on the floor from between the pages.

They were in mint condition and as new as the day I'd put them in the book all those years ago. I was able to cash them – no problem as they still even had the counter foils attached. They certainly came in handy for my holiday to the Philippines later in the year. What I couldn't understand was that I myself had checked through the books about three times and the S.I.B. another twice, to no avail.

Decimalisation

Talking of money, the day UK changed from £:s:d to decimalisation, I was in N. Ireland. And the day before, I had been on 24-hour duty and this day of change-over I had spent the first part in bed sleeping after knocking off at 8 am. The first I saw of the new currency was at lunchtime when I went to the Naafi for a drink and to watch the TV news.

I and a few others looked at the prices; we converted them all back to £:s:d and saw that every price had been converted wrongly; each and every item was a lot dearer than the night before. We were angry, disgusted and let our feelings be known to the Naafi manager, some guys even made a noisy scene.

In the evening, when the hard drinkers saw how much the price of beer had gone up, they went mad and there was a riot; in fact some of them got drunk and caused a riot by smashing the Naafi up.

Mind you, the Naafi got their just desserts.

Man steals TV from Naafi

One evening, I and lots of others were in the TV room watching TV, the room was packed. Suddenly, a chap in a white coat walked in and said, "Sorry lads, I'm going to have to turn the telly off as it has to go back to the shop. The Naafi hasn't kept the payments up!" This was met with a load cheer at first so this chap unplugged the TV and took it away, then he had the beer cans and bread rolls thrown at him. Neither he nor the TV was ever seen again, it had been stolen. How had he gotten into the camp, unchallenged? If he had been a terrorist, he could have killed everyone in the TV room.

There was an enquiry about it. (The R.A.F. liked holding enquiries.) To no avail; if anybody did know anything, they wouldn't have told, as we were still mad about the price of beer going up.

It was the sort of situation you thought would never happen but on occasions did. Nobody thought of asking for his identification, after all the training to drill it into us about checking a person out, nobody thought of doing it in the privacy of our off-duty time, and away from potential trouble, we had 'switched off' once in the Naafi, being so tired.

Various ways we had of relaxing

As you can imagine, in a hostile environment on active service, tension builds up and people get on edge, so the lads do anything to relax mentally and physically; here are several examples of how we tried to keep our sanity.

Dances in the gym

We had a dance once a week, which was held in the gym, and just in case, we had the escort section within seconds call from the dance.

The dances were attended by mainly nurses from the local hospitals and girls from the nearby village. Talk about rough, no 'sweet Irish Colleens' these; they were as tough as old boots, and tougher than most blokes in attendance. Some of the lads were rough and ready and it seemed that the rougher the girls were treated, the more they liked it. The toughest of these seemed to make the play and it was they who went in and picked up the lads they fancied, they gave out as much as they received. The toughest bunches were all given nicknames accordingly and the hardest, roughest and toughest were befitting the nurses, 'The Carrickfergus Commandos'!

Next were the 'Muckamore Marauders'! They were like a bunch of New York mafia and accordingly, most of us avoided them for fear of getting a kick, a punch or a twist where it hurts the most, we thought it better to leave it to the very brave – or stupid. The vast majority of us tried the not-so-tough girls and consequently, each of the 'normal girls' had about 20-30 blokes after them and of course, the inevitable fights broke out.

It was amusing or sad, call it what you will, but each and every time I made a play for a girl, they all seemed to have the same idea in mind no matter what part of N. Ireland they were from! Marriage and getting them out of the province before they became possible victims.

R.A.F. turns a blind eye

The R.A.F. turned a blind eye to the lads if they took these girls to the accommodation block to get 'better acquainted', you might say, even though officially it was banned and frowned upon. In N. Ireland, the rules were relaxed for obvious reasons to prevent the lads being invited and tempted by the girls to their flats in civvy street whereupon there might be an ambush set up for them. (This had happened to army lads.) Better, thought the R.A.F., 'do it' in the comparative safety of our camp, and so they did. This proved successful as the lads 'enjoyed themselves' and were in the minimum danger.

Plastic models

Some of the lads took to building model aircraft/ships and such to help while away the off-duty hours, including myself.

Only, I started a new craze. As I was building my model of a Hawker p1127 (prototype to the Harrier), I packed it full of an explosive substance I had devised out of an everyday match-heads – not much, just enough!

When I got bored with it, I lit the fuse and stood back and watched it blow up and burn; quite realistic it was too. Some chaps came around and asked what was that smell (burning plastic). As I explained, there were a couple of small explosions as the aircraft slowly disintegrated and melted and burned from nose to tail.

This appealed to the warped sense of fun to most of the model makers.

From then on, several guys, when they got bored with their models, rigged them up to explode. Some days, the barrack block would echo to the sound of models exploding and blowing themselves to pieces and burning merrily plus the strong smell of burning plastic that would creep around the block. As they say, a violent environment breeds violence.

Tepol

When we had somebody who, for medical reasons, was taken off task and put on light duties, they usually had to help out in the G.D.O.C. doing odd jobs, such as cleaning up and spelling us off on the radio set, etc.

One such lad with us was approached by the duty officer and asked to make him a fry up, the usual things such as fried eggs, sausages, bacon, beans and so on. After a while, the aromatic smell of the food cooking came wafting into the Ops room from the kitchen. "Umm," we thought, "that smells good!" We were in two minds as to whether we ought to ask this young lad to make us a fry up too. The officer complimented the lad on his cooking ability. Not for long though, after about half an hour, the duty officer went to the toilet.

He'd no sooner come out than felt the need to go again; this happened a few times, eventually it got to the stage where he couldn't leave the toilet for fear of being caught short. He called the lad to come outside the toilet and asked him from inside the cubicle, "What on earth have you done to the food, what have you cooked it in!"

"Nothing, Sir," came the reply, "I've just cooked it in cooking oil!"

"Cooking oil, cooking oil?" replied the officer. "We don't have any cooking oil in the guardroom, lad!"

"Oh yes, we do, sir," said he, and he promptly brought the can to the toilet and said, "Look Sir, this is it!"

The officer let out a loud scream. "TEPOL, f***ing Tepol, you've cooked it in f***ing Tepol? No wonder I've got the f***ing runs! Tepol is a very strong aircraft cleaning solution. And you've used Tepol to cook my meal. Wait till I get hold of you. I'm going to f***ing kill you! No bloody wonder I've got the shits!" With that, the officer gave chase to the lad around and around the G.D.O.C. with one hand holding up his trousers and shaking his fist at the lad with the other. "Wait till I get hold of you, I'm going to bloody kill you!" (In between bouts of having to go back to the toilet.)

This poor lad was running as though his very life depended on it, which it probably did! It took the officer 48 hours or more to recover.

By the time he had finished duty, he was so sore that he could hardly walk or sit down, and he cursed this lad something awful.

You can well imagine how I, the civvies and everybody else in the guardroom reacted – with laughter, so much so that it hurt and tears were streaming down our faces. It was hilarious to see this lad being chased around the Ops room with the officer holding up his trousers. Poor lad was never allowed to forget it. Thank goodness it wasn't me!

I still laugh when I think of it today. The poor lad was never allowed to forget the incident; whenever the officers or senior NCOs got the chance, they all had a laugh at it, even after we'd returned to Catterick, ruddy hilarious.

P.O. Tut

We had with us a young pilot officer; he was newly out of training and like us was almost immediately sent on active service in N. Ireland. His name and rank was Pilot Officer Tut, I used to call him P.O. Tit. Though not to his face. Whilst speaking to him one day, I forgot myself and I did call him P.O. Tit. I immediately corrected myself and apologised. He looked shocked and amazed but didn't seem too perturbed and smiled, thought nothing of it, probably used to it since school.

Laughing too much

However, after he'd gone, I thought back to what I'd said and had a chuckle at it, then I burst out laughing, the more I thought of it, the more I laughed.

Then the other blokes wanted to know what the joke was, I told them when I got my breath back, this had the effect of making me laugh again. P.O. Tut fortunately took it well, in the end he told me to shut up, but that had the effect of making me laugh all the more.

He tried everything he could think of to stop me, like dropping stepladders on me, throwing water over me, the more he tried, the more I laughed. He then started to get really annoyed and still I laughed. I have never before (or since) ever laughed so much and at something so comparatively unfunny; don't ask me why or how – it was just one of those unexplained things, probably something to do with the present situation. I couldn't even sleep for laughing, everybody else was getting really fed up with me, but even thinking about that, I would start off again, I laughed non-stop about 3-4 hours.

So much so, I was beginning to hurt inside but could do nothing about it. It must have been nature's relief valve allowing me to let off steam. I admired P.O. Tit – whoops; there I go again! – I mean Tut. I did admire him; he showed he had a sense of humour. I did apologise to him for it the following day after I'd recovered.

Mac's girlfriends

One day, I volunteered to go and collect the mail as I was expecting some myself. F.O. 'Mac' McLennan, after opening his mail and reading the contents therein, said after a few minutes, "Look at this!" He threw photos of three very beautiful women on the desk and said, "Look at these, I wish they would leave me alone, I told them I'm not interested in them anymore but they insist on writing to me!"

I asked if he didn't want them, could I have them and start to write to them with a view to a relationship when I got back to UK. I said it in jest, knowing he would say no. I had two girlfriends at home waiting for me but that didn't bother me. But he said no with a smile; he knew what I was like and my reputation.

Mac had a reputation for being a lady killer so it used to be interesting as on occasions, both he and I would chat about our girlfriends and compare notes and methods of chatting them up, and more importantly – to get them to buy a round of drinks in the pub.

It was during our first detachment to N. Ireland that Mac got fixed up with a very rich doctor's daughter who was a nurse at a local hospital. Daddy offered to buy her a car. Thing was she couldn't make up her mind which one, should she have a red one with white upholstery or white with red upholstery; daddy bought her both!

To have heard Mac go on about her was an education. He told me about his 'latest flame'. "If you don't want me to finish with you, then you'll throw two parties, one for my men and the following week a party for my fellow officers c/w food, drink and women thrown in for good measure!" There were two parties thrown for his officer friends and the lads on his section. Great guy! I do hope he was successful in life! He's one who deserved it.

Army R.A.C. shot, taking up a collection

After finishing duty one day, we heard that one of the Army R.A.C. (Royal Armoured Corps) sergeants had been shot dead by an I.R.A. sniper. Some of his men were coming around the camp with a collecting tin. I wanted to give but had no money as it was the day before payday.

I promised this army man I would ask around the Sqn the next day after pay parade. I did just that, yet the thing that surprised me was those who I thought would give, wouldn't give at all, saying things like, "So what, he was not one of ours, he was a Squaddie!" This was the wrong attitude and I told them so. For example, if it wasn't for these army lads, it could have been us out there on the streets getting shot at.

Yet those I thought would have told me 'Foxtrot, Oscar' (F*** off) couldn't give me enough, especially Andy Rowe who gave about a fiver.

When everybody else was giving only 50p or £1, "I was amazed and very pleased"; respect to Andy.

This same sergeant who had been shot, I was told by one of his men after taking them the money, was looking outside his canopy of his armoured car and was hit in the head by the bullet and his head split open, so at least it was quick and clean and he wouldn't be like a cabbage for the rest of his life, as some were. Though when I heard about him, it saddened and upset me for several days. I was a bit subdued. This soldier said, "Not to worry though, we got the b*****d killer." Though the person concerned wasn't Irish, in fact he was not of these islands! (And that is all I can say!) He did tell me and at first I was shocked but not for long.

Whilst in N. Ireland, we had the use of choppers for training, which involved starting at ground level and debussing with full kit including full backpack, rifle, webbing and full fighting order.

Rope descent

We then took up A.R.D. (All Round defence). Then we did it again with the chopper hovering just above the ground, then to 2 feet (which made the aircraft platform floor you were standing on about 5-6 feet off the deck). Again, we jumped out of the aircraft and into action.

At about 9 feet, we then started to use ropes for the descent, with the chopper gradually working itself higher and higher till we were doing it at 20-30 feet, then at our maximum working height – 80 feet, with full kit.

By now I was getting a bit nervous as I had done this thing before but not as high as this. With about 150 pounds of kit, it had a tendency to pull you over backwards. I couldn't get used to using my feet as a brake on the rope. This other lad in the aircraft (thought he was a bit of a hard man) was told he didn't have to go as he was due for de-mob in a couple of weeks' time.

He kept saying he didn't want to start a new job with a broken leg, if he was lucky. He was taking the mick out of me because I was taking a long time to get the rope around me and trying to build up the courage to launch myself into space and make a grab for the rope. Which, on the winch, was just out of reach.

I seemed to be at the hatch for ages and eventually, I got the hang of how to position my feet for a brake. I then thought, "Well, it's now or never!" I pushed myself off, grabbed the rope and down and down I came at a fast rate of knots. Followed closely by this loud mouth, I'd shamed him into it.

Afterwards, he started telling his mates about the sprog who had been frightened to come down a short (80 feet) rope. I turned to have a go at him, but before I had a chance, a Cpl, who had overhead the conversation and had been in the chopper, turned on him and said, "He (me) had to be admired, as he conquered his fear and went through with it!" He then threw a quotation at loud mouth, "He who knows no fear is a fool, the man who knows fear and conquers it is a brave man!"

This shut up loud mouth for good.

Reality of active service

Another reason the situation out there brought home the reality of active service to me was one evening whilst watching TV news in the Naafi, they reported the first of three soldiers shot patrolling the border between N. Ireland and Ireland in one week. The next day I was just leaving the G.D.O.C. when an army convoy came in through the main gate. There were 5 Land Rovers two at the front, two at the back with an armed escort. In the middle was a Land Rover with a Union Jack-draped coffin of the soldier who had just been shot the day before, with his beret and belt on the coffin. I saluted with my rifle.

But seeing him being brought to camp (prior to flying home) upset me; we were not invulnerable, were we?

Before I finished with the N. Ireland tour, we heard that Halfway House that we used to frequent on our first visit had been bombed as the landlord had received several threats from the I.R.A. terrorists, concerning his allowing the forces to use his pub; in fact, it was bombed out a couple of times.

All in all, I enjoyed my tours of N. Ireland; they were hard, exiting times and I got on well with the people; they all seemed glad we were there to help keep the peace.

We then finished our tour. And it was a very happy and relieved Sqn that left for Catterick. We left behind one lad who volunteered to do another tour immediately afterwards, making 6 months in all. He had a mate on the Sqn that was relieving us and wanted to see him. Though none of us on the Sqn ever saw him alive again; he was killed out there while off duty.

He and a couple of mates had hired a car and going around a bend in the road near the airfield, the brakes failed (tampered with) and the car ploughed through the wooden stake fence and he got a wooden stake through the chest, very close to his heart. He was alive by the time the nearest medical unit got to him, the R.A.F. M.O. at Aldergrove, but the moment they tried to move him he died.

I vaguely recalled his face but with him not being in my Flt, I hadn't really known him nor had much to do with him.

Initiative test

After coming back from N. Ireland, we went for our two-week embarkation leave, in which we wound down and had it easy for a few weeks.

The officers thought it a good wheeze if they were to stop us getting bored and they devised a 'jolly', which was a forced march, initiative test, map reading and a physical fitness test all rolled into one and all at the same time.

On the Thursday, the day it was to start, we were paid only 50p for emergency phone calls back to Sqn office. And our wages were held for us till we returned – to try and eliminate cheating.

The money was given to us from the Sqn fund, which we had to pay back.

We then clambered aboard the four-tonners and set off. We didn't have a clue where we were going, only that it was a long, long way from camp and we didn't have the foggiest idea where we were, only that it was in the middle of nowhere.

One by one, the different teams were dropped off and eventually it was our turn, we were last. There were three of us in my team.

The first task was to find out where we were on the map in relation to our actual position on the ground. For this, we had two maps to cover the area between us and camp Catterick. Each map covered an area of about 40 miles.

Very quickly, we found out where we were on the map in about 5-10 minutes, then we looked how far camp was from our position, what we saw made our hears sink. We thought, "Oh no, it's bloody miles away. We'll never make it, it's too far!" (Had it been straightforward by following the main road all the way, it would have been about 25-30 miles.) But with detours and such, it was more by the time we'd finished. The officers had also given us a set time to finish it in and penalties if we took too long like extra duties, dirty jobs, etc. The winners got a barrel of beer, we were to soon find out that they had not only made it complicated but had added a few miles extra that we'd have to do such as we'd have to go several miles off the main road to answer a question they had set us, then back to the main road. Each team was the same and had about twenty questions to answer; the officers had cleverly interwoven a lot of the questions so that if you didn't bother going to a location to find the answer to a question, then you couldn't answer the next few as they were interwoven.

The winners would be the team back in the shortest possible time and with the most points – 2 points for each correct answer.

Phone up

We set off and straight away had to deviate off the main road for an answer, we began to hate these deviations. Then head back to the main route the same way, you couldn't even take a shortcut back to the main road, such were the roads on the map and the questions. After we'd done this 3-4 times, I said, "Bugger this, lads, there must be an easier way?" Then it came to me. I used my initiative, which was what it all was about, told the other two to look out for a phone booth; they asked why. I said, "Find me one and you'll find out!"

This we did, we found one about half an hour later. I walked into the call box and rang up the operator. I said, "We have a number of questions to answer, to save us miles going off course. Do you think you could maybe answer a few of the questions for us?" This she agreed to do and consequently she gave the answer to about two thirds of the questions for that area.

She saved us a lot of miles, the lads were chuffed about this and we did the same thing once we got to a different area.

Of all the answers we submitted at the end, only two were wrong. So we were very grateful.

Flagging down a bus

At one point, we flagged down a bus in the middle of the night, in the middle of the countryside, the driver looked a bit worried and scared as it was about 10:30 at night. He probably though at worst we were a bunch of terrorists about to hijack his bus. "Take me to Cuba!" as they always used to say.

We had with us our full packs and we were dressed in our combat gear too. He may have even thought we were an S.A.S. unit on exercise.

However, he seemed to relax a bit when we offered to pay our fare to our next destination, as far on that road as he was going. After all, who ever heard of a bunch of terrorists hijacking a bus and then paying the fare? It did happen in N. Ireland, some 'newly trained' terrorists doing exactly that a few years later.

We had been dropped off late afternoon and after we'd done 10 miles, our flight/section commander sergeant met us with the four-tonner and a hot cup of tea/soup. That went down very well.

The first few times, we found Sergeant (Tug) Wilson waiting for us. We walked all night and were so tired that I had to try and not only stay awake but try and keep the other two awake and out of trouble. At times without realising, we fell asleep while walking, we were that tired, we just kept on walking and then woke a few seconds later to find ourselves in the middle of the road or about to walk into a ditch and we only ever stopped to look at the map or answer nature's call.

On and on we walked, we watched the sun go down, the stars and we watched the sun come up on a new day.

Last R.V.

We got to our last R.V. (rendezvous) and Tug Wilson wasn't there; normally he would have been. We waited for an hour and still there was no sign, we thought, "Stuff him, we'll get our heads down for an hour and see if he turns up." This R.V. was in a farm yard and so we took out our ponchos, spread them out on a haystack and went to sleep for an hour or so. Only we slept for several hours longer, naturally under the circumstances.

Tug gets lost

We were soooo tired. We felt something running over us, we discussed it later and came to the conclusion that it had been rats, but we were all too tired to care or do anything about them and just turned over. When we woke, we rechecked our position and were still convinced we were correct. Still no sign of Tug! So one of the lads went to phone up the Sqn from the nearest phone box he could find, he was gone about an hour and it was while he was away that Tug finally arrived, going spare at us calling us all idiots under the sun for getting the map-grid reference wrong. He said he had been stuck at an X road for hours waiting for us.

He had been worried, thought we'd had an accident and had been run over or something. So we all sat down and worked out the grid ref we should have headed for from the last location.

The result was we were right and Sergeant Wilson was wrong, so wrong in fact that he had been sitting at this X road about 30-40 miles away. The reason? He had read the map upside down. We just couldn't believe it, and he also taught Boy Scouts in his spare time – map reading.

I didn't think it possible but that was what happened.

Setting off and arriving at camp
We set off walking for the Sqn on our last leg, completely revitalised after that sleep and knowing that the next stop was camp. We got to camp about 9-10 am. Camp had never looked as good and when we walked in through the main gates, we let out a cheer.

I had an early lunch and shower, reported to the Sqn, got paid and we found we were the second team in and the winners had only beaten us by half an hour, had it not been for that twit Tug Wilson, we'd have been first and won the beer.

I then thumbed a lift home and fell asleep in the passenger seats of the lorries and cars that I got a lift in. Good job I wasn't driving.

Cheats
Some of the lads had cheated and had taken more money than they should have and spent the night in a hotel, another who didn't live very far from camp or had a relation living nearby, I'm not sure which, cheated by phoning home and a relation picked them up in a car and drove around the different locations; they were both found out. Cheated? According to the officers! Pardon, but wasn't it an initiative test and they had just done that!

Before I left camp, we worked out how far we'd walked and were shocked to find we had walked the farthest distance of all – over 40-45 miles. In about 19 hours, further than anyone else! And that was with saving ourselves a lot of unnecessary miles.

Another chap who, by the purest luck, had an idea which direction he might go in the morning so the night before, he got one of his mates to follow him in his car and left his in a pub carpark. Once on the walk, he made a detour, picked up his car and drove around the route. The odds against that must have been tremendous that he would get that route. (Unless, of course, he bribed the senior NCO into giving him that route.) Was it pure luck or was it arranged? We didn't find out.

Whilst I'm on about cheating and skiving, that brings me to another incident. Some of the lads had been caught skiving at camp by Tug Wilson. During a conversation with him later, Sergeant Tug Wilson said no one could skive for more than an hour without him (Tug) catching them.

We called his bluff and one morning after muster parade, when there was nothing special on, we all disappeared into various parts of the camp, at a pre-arranged time, Tug set off to find us. There was only one stipulation, and that was we were not to go off camp.

Tug finds us hiding

So the entire Flt, about 30+ of us, disappeared. I hid myself in the education centre. I was found after about half an hour, which was very good. Within 45 minutes, he had found every one of us. The places some of them went to made me laugh. The barrack block, that was the first place he looked, in the wardrobes, cleaning/tool cupboard, laundrette, Naafi – that was pretty obvious as he found about 25 in the Naafi – the general office, pay office, museum, tent store, under the A/A guns. And about 5 of them just walking around camp. He never had anybody skive on him again as we had all given it up as a waste of time. As he said, he knew all the tricks as he had got up to the same when in our places years ago.

We had a West Indian lad on the Sqn whose surname was George but he was called George as a Christian name, I always wondered why! I eventually found out why, he confessed he hated his Christian name! It had biblical overtones. And some people in the past probably took the mick.

Other West Indian lads on the Sqn were nicknamed for obvious reasons – Snowy, 23:59 and Midnight. Depending on the hue of their skin, i.e., the lightest skinned was 'Snowy', the darkest 'Midnight'. Though they gave just as good back – 'White Honkies'! Especially when they caught us sunbathing. "Hey man, you take the p**s, but as soon as the sun comes out, you want to look like us!" Cue laughter.

Not very PC. (No such thing in those days.) But we meant no offence by it and none was taken. It was just banter and accepted as such. It was a man's job and environment, no room for the timid and weak. Couldn't get away with it these days.

One morning on parade, I was informed that two of the Sqn had been chosen to represent the Sqn at this year's Royal Tournament and I was one of them.

Royal tournament

I was chuffed as it was the fulfilment of another small ambition of mine – to take part in the Royal Tournament. I was at the R.T. in London for three weeks. I was billeted in Earl's court itself where the show was taking place. It was really interesting but very long hours, but it seemed like a very long 3 weeks in London, you got the sensation of feeling claustrophobic in the middle of the city. Well, I did. It was the longest time I had spent in London, never before or since have I felt so closed in.

R.N. guns

I was doing the job of usher, showing people to their seats, checking for bombs, explosive/inflammable devices. At the end of the three weeks, I was absolutely sick of the displays. I had to watch them three times a day, + two rehearsals. The Royal Navy used to wake us all at 5 every morning by having a run through their field gun display and finishing it off by firing their 25-pounder field guns 8 times a day! In all. And if you can imagine what two artillery guns sound like indoors where any sound echoed around the building, you have a good idea how we felt to be woken up by these dammed guns every morning. At the end of my stint, I was slowly but surely building up a hate relationship about the Royal Navy. The Navy lads were more sick of it than we were. Revalie was about 7 am. And 'dismiss' was after the show had finished and the building had been checked through, about 10:45 pm.

Beer

After a couple of shows, I and everybody else realised that we'd lost out, we couldn't even get a pint of beer before we went to bed. So, as it turned out most of the others and I on usher duties saw the last customer away from his area and then ran to catch the last 10 minutes before the bar that Naafi had set up closed for the night. I and some of the others didn't mind going back to our sections after to check everything out, but others didn't, it was all a calculated risk, but some of the lads were prepared to take it for the sake of a pint of beer.

Three girls

As far as I was concerned, the best part of the detachment was the three civvy girls who were working on my floor – Jane, Helen and Maria. They were part Italian and very pretty and friendly. As a matter of fact, I fancied the eldest, Jane; she was pretty, well dressed with expensive-looking clothes and had that something about her I could only sum up as 'class'. She wasn't even interested in me though she was very friendly. Their mother also was working there; what a quartet they made! Italian/Cockney Londoners from Shepherds Bush.

I tried my best to get her to come out with me on my one and only day off but she didn't return the advances I made. I was annoyed at this as I had only ever had one other girl refuse my advances before. I was beginning to wonder if there was something wrong with my method of chatting them up; it shouldn't fail as it had been tried, tested and proved over the years.

I had never thought that it might just be that she didn't fancy me, it was something else. Jane said that she had been engaged to a US sailor; I didn't believe her; I think it was her way of putting me off.

Soho

We had one evening off on a Saturday but had to attend the matinee performance in the afternoon. The chap who had come down from 37 Sqn with me wanted to go to Soho, well known as the sex centre of town, but also known as a very dirty rundown part of the city, not to mention people trying to take your money at every possible chance.

I had nothing better to do so I agreed to go with him. I found it was true, it was a rundown, dirty, filthy place. In fact, of all the so-called sex centres I'd been to since (Berlin, Hamburg and the brothels and sex clubs), Soho was the dirtiest, degrading and the most expensive!

As we were just about to leave Soho, we were looking up at the windows at the 'ladies of the night' plying their wares; it was interesting to see them leaning out of the windows/doors advertising their 'services' and showing what could be had if you had the money or the inclination.

Part-time hooker

We walked a bit further and I wasn't paying them much attention while my mate, Dave, looked behind him, stopped and said, "Hey look, John, doesn't that one look familiar? You know who she looks like, don't you?" I had to agree that the resemblance of the girl in the window advertising her wares did look very familiar, so much so that even to this day I have a strong suspicion it was her, but I'll never know for sure. The girl in that window advertising her wares looked remarkably like the girl I had fancied at the Royal Tournament, Jane, or was it a coincidence, a trick of the light or someone who just looked like her? If it was her, no wonder she didn't want to go out with me; she was too embarrassed to tell me. I was dreading that Dave would tell the Sqn, "Hey, John's girlfriend's on the game in Soho!" I thought, "Ruddy 'ell, if the chaps on the Sqn hear of this, I'll never live it down!" Fortunately, Dave kept quiet.

I hoped it wasn't her; I was dumbfounded, my dream image of her was shattered. Dave must have seen my jaw drop in shock and quipped, "Never mind; look at it this way, if it's her, she might let you have your end way for nothing and not charge you for it!" Now I knew why she couldn't come out with me on a Saturday night. If it was her, it was her best night for business and she wasn't going to lose money going out with an airman when she could be earning a lot of money, selling her 'you know what'! Why give it away for free when she could be making money on it? Dave kept saying, "Go on, go upstairs and get her alone and stripped off. Here is your chance, go on; what are you waiting for, she may even give you some discount!" But I wouldn't, as I told him, "If I have to pay for it, then I'm not interested, I'd rather go without; besides, you don't know what you will catch. I haven't paid for it yet! And I am not going to start now!"

I wanted to 'make it' with her on the strength of my character or because she wanted me to, or not at all, no money would change hands. Even if I did fancy her.

Funny though, from then on in, I wasn't bothered about her, I'd gone off her. It must have been her for as soon as both Dave and I looked at this girl at the window, she saw us, looked quite embarrassed and disappeared inside.

When I went back to work at the R.T. and saw Jane for the first time since Soho, she definitely acted a bit edgy, embarrassed and avoided Dave and myself. A coincidence?

After all, how many people on 37 Sqn could say, "My friend was a part-time hooker!"

Though Dave wasn't bothered, he was having fun with Jane's younger sister, and I think she was married – but not to Dave. While the cat's away and all that.

We walked around that part of London and eventually ended up in the Hammersmith Palais dance hall.

I.R.A. terrorist group supporter
We were in uniform and when we went to the underground to catch the tube, a civvie started to insult us, the uniform and singing pro-I.R.A. songs and saying things like, hoping the I.R.A. kill more British troops.

I was mad, I turned and ran towards him. I was going to beat him up but Dave grabbed me and pulled me away and wouldn't let me have a go at this 'traitor'. The civvies around I felt were behind me and wanted me to shut up this bum. (He looked a bit drunk/drugged.)

Guard of honour, H.M. Queen
Each day, there was a special 'guest of honour' about halfway through the planned number of shows. The Cpl in our section was moaning that he'd been picked to do a 'guard of honour and escort to the Queen' when she came to see the show. I said to him half-jokingly, "If you don't want to do it, I'll do it!" He promptly arranged for me to take his place.

Next thing I knew, I was standing at the edge of the red carpet along with representatives of all the branches of the forces. There were also several R.A.F. police dogs, who made a mess on the carpet just before the Queen arrived. On her departure, they left their 'calling card' from the other end and the Queen just graciously side-stepped both times without appearing to notice the 'deposits'. It was strongly rumoured that the dogs had been deliberately 'got at' ready for the Queen's arrival, how true that was I'll never know, but a strange thing to occur at that particular time! Before she came out, I and some others had a close look at her limousine. Inside and out.

Go looking for yobs
Despite the traditional inter-service rivalry, when it mattered and faced with a common enemy, we all stuck together. One such instance occurred at the R.T. Some army lads got beaten up and robbed when leaving a local

pub by some local 'yobs'. The word went around and after the evening show was over, 200 servicemen in uniform went looking for these 'brave heroes', Royal Navy, army, Royal Marines and R.A.F. Regiment. The military police stopped us when we were leaving and wanted to know where 200 servicemen were going armed with web belts and brasses, etc. When we told them, they passed the word to the off-duty policemen and they joined us in the search.

It was as well they were never found as one can only imagine what would have happened to them if they had been caught.

Hammersmith Palais

Another Saturday night, at Hammersmith Palais, Dave and I found an empty table at the side of the dance floor. After about half an hour, a gang of three or four Royal Navy sailors came in and asked if they could sit at our table, then shortly after, some army chaps came in. They too sat with us; this went on all night long and eventually, at our table there must have been about 40 or so servicemen, about 4-5 R.A.F., 6-7 army and far outnumbering us were the sailors and Royal Marines.

We took over the entire building, we were asking girls to dance with us who had their boyfriends with them and the first couple of times, the boyfriends wanted a fight so the sailor, soldier or airman just whistled and 39 other 'friends' got up, prepared to go to his assistance. There wasn't any trouble as the civvies backed off and the rest of the civvy men in the hall kept out of our way. We did as all servicemen did, we got very drunk, fooled about and took the mickey out of each other's branch of the service. And jointly, the civvies. Especially the civvies.

The girls with us would dance but nobody got anything that night, a) we were too drunk anyway, and b) the girls weren't interested.

We had a great time and I really enjoyed it.

Drink to 'Ark Royal'

At the end of the evening, the Navy lads took us all to their club, which had the bar still open long after all the civvy bars had shut. We were so drunk that we were past caring and were expected to drink the health of the R.N. aircraft carrier, 'Ark Royal', that was about to go to the breakers yard, and do it standing on the tables with our beer on top of our heads; some of the lads got wet through.

The Navy lads were in tears as they thought about the 'grand old lady'. "To think," they were blubbering, "that this time next week, she'll be reduced to razor blades and we'll be shaving with Ark Royal!" Cue more tears and sobbing.

How Dave and I got back to Earl's Court that morning I'll never know as we were drunk and just did not know where we were. It was a mystery.

The last couple of days we were there, I found out it was Jane's birthday. So I had a collection from the rest of the lads on the floor for a present for her. Then went round again for some money to buy drinks. I did cheat a little though, I put a little money aside to buy her a present but I told her that I'd bought it out of my own pocket. I was very sad to see the end of the Royal Tournament; I was going to miss those good times with the people.

During my time at Catterick, I went to a couple of Elvis Presley fan club conventions as I was a member at the time. The first of these was at Leicester. I went in uniform and had a great night; there were stars including my favourite, Anita Harris, and all for £1. I was stuck for a lift and so I asked the DJ to make an announcement and ask if anybody would give me a lift back to camp.

I waited outside and saw people leaving, all the teenagers, cults, Mods, rockers, beatniks, flower-power people, but no one offered me a lift. All these people were supposed to be sworn enemies and fought whenever they saw each other but this lot were getting on well together and no trouble. Here, they all had something in common, Elvis. I was unable to get a lift so I reported to the local police station. So they made me out a travel warrant for the train to get back to the nearest railway station at Darlington, then on to camp on the bus. The warrant was then paid by the R.A.F. to the police and I repaid the R.A.F. by paying them back weekly.

E.P. 'Do' at Redcar

The second one was a smaller one at Redcar. I met and chatted up a nice-looking girl who was there with her own stall selling Elvis souvenirs such as records, posters and rare magazines. She gave me a lift most of the way down the A1. (I had also taken a mate with me from camp.)

As I got out of the car, I thanked her for the lift in my own special way!

I gave my mate the nod to take a walk, which he did, then I turned my attention to this girl – I believe her name was Janet.

I, being the cheeky one, then made advances on her, she reciprocated, as I knew she would, we were still virtual strangers and here we were involved in things that her mother wouldn't want her 'little girl' doing until she got married. But whenever had I let a little thing like not knowing each other stop me before? Never!

Winter survival (mountain climbing), Scotland

Another detachment I did was for winter survival training in Scotland.

A farce as regards survival training. The notice went up on the noticeboard, "So you think you're hard, can you hack it, then prove it! Volunteer for winter survival training, place names below!"

I and only about 4-5 others did so. We had the use of a four-tonner and Lanky Benson. One other and me drove up there and took it in turns to travel in the back where it was cold, especially as we got further north towards Scotland.

It seemed that I spent the most time in the back on my own while the other bloke travelled in the cab with Lanky. I didn't mind that so much as when I did get in the front with Lanky, I felt sick, his body odour was too overpowering, it was an offence to the nostrils because of his lack of washing and use of drugs. The journey seemed to go on forever. I was beginning to think that it was never going to end.

Eventually, it did and we arrived too late to get a pint as all the pubs near the site were closed as it was about 11:30 at night.

This winter survival in reality was really mountain-climbing; it was great. I really enjoyed it and it was a challenge. It was also very, very tiring.

In our party of 12 including officers and P.T.I.s, there were some guys I nicknamed ruddy mountain goats. We would be climbing up the hill/ice cap at a steady pace and heading for a spot for a rest. And the 'mountain goats' would run, yes, run up that damn mountain while it took some of us all our time to put one foot in front of the other.

The set practice was that everybody in the team for safety sake had to stay together and travel at the pace of the slowest man (that was usually me). I was aching all over and I was struggling to get up that mountain but I had a 'never say die' attitude and I kept going regardless. And this occasion was no exception.

After about three hours of climbing, we would get to the R.V. and rest, have a drink, within five minutes, the mountain goats were impatient to get going again so off they would set at a gallop while we were trying to get our breaths back.

The mountain range was known as the 7 sisters, we climbed 6 of them during the detachment. They were the range of mountains near Shiel Bridge, only a few miles from Inverness.

Leaving me behind

Things went fine on all the mountains until we were on the 4th mountain. We had climbed the peak and were on our way down, about halfway down and still on the snow/ice cap, everybody shot off ahead and I was left alone on a big empty mountain; it was starting to get dark by the time I'd cleared the ice cap, thank goodness but I still had about half the mountain to negotiate. I got to the bottom without injury, which was remarkable considering all rocks, holes and traps there on that bleak hillside.

At the bottom, all I could see between me and the main road, the A87 was a very wide and fast-flowing river about 300 yards away and there was no way I was going to cross that river in the daytime, let alone at night. It was so frustrating; I could see all the traffic driving by quite unaware of my predicament.

Setting of distress signal

After about 30-45 minutes, I felt that I had no alternative but to sound out the distress signal – three blasts on a whistle. The sun had set and the night was now getting on and although I had come prepared for any emergency, I had supplies of spare warm clothing, sleeping bag, food, water, waterproof sheets and plastic bag (to keep my sleeping bag dry and prevent dampness being drawn in) but I was not prepared to spend it at the bottom of a cold damp mountain.

Once I blew my whistle and shone my torch, I saw cars start to stop, in a few short minutes, someone was shouting my name. It was the detachment's main H.G.V. driver whom I didn't know. He had seen that I wasn't with the rest of the party upon return to camp so had taken it on his own back to come out and search for me. Armed with a map, he was able to shout instructions to me and direct me to the nearest bridge.

Lad rollicks officer

I found my way to his vehicle, he asked what had happened and how come they had arrived at base without me. I told him and he went ballistic; he told me he had had a go at the officer in charge when he saw I wasn't there, and when he told them that he was taking the wagon out to try and find me, the officer had refused permission, so he had taken it on his own back.

Upon arriving at base camp – tents on a caravan site – he got out of the vehicle, found the officer in charge and in full view of all ranks, gave him such a dressing down as I have never heard any one rollicked before. He was saying, "Under no circumstances do you split the party up! You have to stick together and wait for the slowest man!"

He was, of course, quite right.

That was the first and most basic rule you must always stick by. The self-same officer had said as much the first day we were there and now he wasn't 'practising what he was preaching'! This driver was not even a junior NCO, only a plain ordinary S.A.C. like me. It was rather decent of the chap and I admired him for it. But that wasn't just an isolated rebellion. It was the start of something else. I had had nothing to do with this chap before – or since; in fact I hadn't even spoken to him before.

Mutiny

The following morning, he led a well-supported 'mutiny' on my behalf out of disgust at the previous night's debacle. We all, except the P.T.I.s and NCOs, refused to go climbing with this officer that morning due to lack of confidence, we even refused to get out of our sleeping bags when told to get out of bed by a senior NCO; we just said one by one, "Foxtrot, Oscar. I'm staying here". We were threatened with being charged, court-martialled!

But we were so disgusted, we all said was, "Try it, go on if you dare!" They didn't as the real reason for the mutiny would have been revealed. They were in the wrong! We were all united to a man, even the mountain goats, about taking this stance and it was spontaneous, not even discussed or arranged.

We just worked around the site that day, the officers/NCOs/P.T.I.s ignored us on their return to base camp but by the time we went to the pub in the evening for a drink or two or three or more, all had been forgiven.

Antlers

The following day, we continued mountain climbing; as far as the lads were concerned, the incident was forgotten and we had made our point and protested. During the climbing of the mountains, which I enjoyed immensely, I came across the skeletons of two stag deer with their antlers still intact.

I very much wanted one of these sets of antlers; they were very prestigious and also very expensive to buy – if you could get hold of a real set, that is.

Thing was, I just didn't have the heart to break off the deer's skull/ antlers from the rest of the body. I knew it was dead and all that. As much as I wanted those antlers lying on the hillside, I just couldn't bring myself to do it; though now years later if faced with the same choice, I would take it without fail.

Each day we would have about 10-12 hard hours of mountain climbing and burning up the calories like nobody's business, we must have lost a lot of weight, but we would come upon the nearest pub and put it all back on again in a matter of minutes and we would be drinking all night every night.

Dogs' flying lesson

During the detachment, there was one thing I and most of the blokes hated and that was these ruddy officers had to bring their bloody dogs along with them, they always had to, pain in the bum it was.

These two dogs were constantly getting in our way and I thought to myself, "If I am up on the mountain, those dogs better not get in my way – or else!" That day did arrive. I was on the ice cap near the summit and nervously edging my way along a very narrow ledge about 6-8" wide with a sheer wall on one side and a sharp drop down the mountain of rocks on the other.

I was gingerly making my way around a bend when I was confronted by my biggest dread; yes, it was one of those dammed officer's dogs.

I stood my ground and tried to stare it out; it looked at me, licked its lips and gave me a sideways look, the minutes ticked by and neither the dog nor I would give ground. And there wasn't room for both of us to pass on that ledge together and I couldn't go backwards. Then the dog made a move towards my legs and I thought, "This is it. I'm going to be knocked off the mountain by a bloody dog." The damn thing was in between my legs and I thought it's him or me. So I then made my move. I tried 'gently' to persuade it to go backwards with my foot. As my hands were otherwise occupied in hanging on for dear life, it slipped and missed its footing and went sailing off the edge of the cliff with a worried yelp. (Sorry, dog lovers.)

It disappeared from view. I thought, "That will teach it. It will not get in my way again, if it lives!" (It did, and was unharmed.)

It didn't fall far, only about 5-6 feet onto a narrow ledge. Later in the camp, the dog's owner asked me if I knew what had happened to his dog up there on the mountain.

"Yes Sir, I saw it walking on the ice and it missed his footing and he/she fell off the mountain – Sir!"

He accepted this story, but was a bit suspicious all the same; he probably didn't believe me but couldn't prove anything. I am sure he knew that I had something to do with his little precious taking impromptu 'flying lessons'. Nothing more was said but the officer did try hard to keep his dog out of my way from then on.

Visiting Inverness

Towards the end of our stay in Scotland, it was arranged for us to have a day's shopping in the nearest large city, Inverness. We went via the famous Loch Ness and no one saw the elusive monster unfortunately, as I expected it not to make an appearance when it knew of the presence of 37 Sqn rock-apes in the vicinity.

Inverness is a beautiful city and never before or since had I seen so many beautiful, pretty and gorgeous girls, the place was crawling with them. It must have been the bracing mountain air that must have agreed with their complexions.

The monster legend I believe is all a publicity stunt. Every place you went into a shop or pub, there were Loch Ness monster souvenirs and plenty of shops selling things with a monster's picture on, and one thing I remember was a tea towel saying, 'We've got a monster in our Loch' with a cartoon drawing of the 'monster' smiling below.

R.A.F. board of enquiry, dentist in NI

Upon returning to camp, I was told to report to the station dentist for an examination and then to the board of enquiry being held in the general office. I wondered at first what it could be for but then I figured correctly that it was to do with the incident with the so-called Irish dentist who had messed about with my teeth while on detachment.

At the enquiry, I was asked what the dentist at Catterick had done before leaving for N. Ireland. The Irish dentist was claiming about £200 for me alone. As I told the board, it hadn't been that much work.

The R.A.F. didn't pay him as far as I know, neither did they pay him for the other claims too, all because he had become greedy. Serves him right; had the R.A.F. paid him, he would have made about £1200 for an afternoon's work, a substantial amount of money in those days.

Princess Anne visits Catterick

Shortly after the death of the Duke of Windsor, we were paid a visit by H.R.H. Princess Anne. She was dressed, as expected on such occasions, in black.

Prior to her visit, the proverbial saying came into effect during the panic to get things ready for the inspection – if it moves, salute it; if it doesn't, paint it. Even the faded patches of grass got a coat of green paint. The kerb stones were painted black/white and yellow and black.

We had been practising a fancy drill movement, men lining up on both sides of the road and on the command, 'fire', the first man fired, then a split second later the next man fired, then the next and so on, giving a rippling effect down one side of the road and back up the other, very impressive I must admit. Even just to see the men taking part in the drill, standing with one foot forward and rifles on the shoulder. Princess Anne halted in her open Land Rover at the end of the squad and we went through the drill, then as she drove forwards and got about halfway along our lines, the order was given to 'fire'; it was very impressive and H.R.H. looked a bit shocked but then smiled in admiration and waved to us.

I took careful note of what she looked like close up, my verdict was that she was far more pretty then she appeared on TV and not so 'hard' looking.

Some demos were laid on for H.R.H. There was a mock attack by some phantoms and the tiger cats. A/A missiles of 48 Sqn were ordered into action. The Bofors of 16 Sqn also engaged the aircraft. (No live missiles or live rounds were actually fired though.) 37 Sqn's effort consisted of a mock-up of a terrorist camp setup on the airfield. We then laid explosive/incendiary charges all around the camp and wired them up to a control box. As a couple of aircraft came in low and fast to bomb the camp, the officer in charge on the ground waited till the aircraft got to a position and detonated the charges one by one – giving the effect of the aircraft having bombed and shot up the camp, leaving it destroyed and burning.

We had used old equipment that got written off, such as tents and the like. After the aircraft had gone, the R.A.F. Regiment fire services came in to give a demo on how quickly they could put out the fire.

Before Princess Anne's arrival, the R.A.F. had flown 5 S.A.R. anti-sub-marine warfare Shackletons (8 counter-rotating propellers) and about 8-9 men all the way to Catterick from Hong Kong. The R.A.F. fire service had already burnt two during practice prior to Princess Anne's visit. During which one of the firemen went inside the blazing aircraft whereupon a vacuum had sucked off his protective helmet and he had been severely burnt.

We on our A/A guns had been talking to him only about 10 minutes before the accident. Princess Anne was driven onto the airfield and watched as the fire service set fire to two of the remaining three aircraft as if there had been an accident. They then set about putting it out in record time. Princess Anne was, I believe, quite unaware of the accident the day before.

It was reported that the officers were trying to get Princess Anne to the officers' mess for lunch, when she saw a building and asked what it was. "The sergeants' mess!" came the reply. To which she was believed to have said, "I'll have my lunch in the Sgts mess." Much to the consternation of the officers who still tried to get her to the officers' mess. Afterwards, the officers asked her to come to their mess for after-dinner drinks; she refused and asked, "Where do the airmen have their lunch? I would like to see them!" The officers were having kittens by now.

We had just put our weapons away and were having lunch when in walked Princess Anne; she sat down and started talking to some of the guys from the Sqns. She had the reputation as being a bit snooty and unapproachable, but not after that visit, she left with a lot more admirers and respect.

Giving demo at Be-dale school

A selected few on the Sqn were chosen to go around local schools and give a demo to the school kids. I was one of those chosen; there was Ben Holingson plus an H.G.V. driver, the location was Beadle school. I talked through the basic-issue rifle and firing positions and so on. One of the kids, as kids will, asked, "Did you shoot and kill anyone?" when I'd been to N. Ireland. Of course, the school teacher told this lad off but I gave a non-committal answer such as "We don't know, the sympathisers always rush away with the bodies before we can recover the target!"

The two lads with me were taking the mick because they thought me daft to go through the various positions such as the prone position – lying on the floor. Later, I snarled at them and said, "And what do you think we are here for? This is to show the kids what we do!"

They still thought it wrong of me and put it around the Sqn but no one took much notice of them as they agreed with me that that was the reason we were sent to the school in the first place.

Given my own room

After being at 37 Sqn for about 2½ years, I was given my own room being the senior man in my room. (On condition that if a Cpl was to move into the block, he had to have priority for the room.) I was also told that there would be snap inspections and if the room was ever found to be dirty, then I would lose my room.

So I made sure that they would not be able to throw me out. I gave myself an extra bull night each week to shuffle along on a couple of pads of soft cloth; this had the effect of bulling the floor. I didn't want to walk on the floor to save work; this room was where I stayed till I was posted.

Dirty W.E. in Cpl's room, talcum powder

In the next room to mine was a Welsh Cpl; he was asked by his mate one Thursday if he could have the loan of his room for the weekend as he wanted to bring a girl back to the block for weekend sex!

This was agreed providing the room was left clean and tidy ready for his return on Sunday night. Upon his return on Sunday night, he opened the door to his room and found it a mess with bedcovers scattered everywhere!

And talcum powder thick, deep and everywhere. What had ensued was as follows:

When his mate had had his fill of sex with this girl for the weekend, he had hired out the girl to the guys left in the block. At £5 a time, splitting the money with the girl.

His mates queued up waiting their turn to go and 'have some fun' with this 'very friendly' girl. Afterwards, the men used the talcum powder available. When the Cpl came back, he went mad. This mate of his had to clean up the mess immediately.

Though it was my long weekend off and I had gone home, I still had plenty of opportunity other weekends to see girls in the block as everyone in the block had more than one invitation and opportunity take their turn and participate. One was expected to keep 'One's end up' and 'Take one for the team', 'show you're one of the lads'!

I was able to get out of it, thank goodness. I didn't really want to 'Boldly go where many men had gone before!' Sorry Capt. Kirk!

It got to such a stage that the fully dressed or half-naked girls getting washed in our washrooms/showers became commonplace (still forbidden in R.A.F. regulations) and neither the girls nor the serviceman would bat an eyelid; we would just greet each other with a smile and a 'Good morning'!

Freedom of Richmond

We were given the rare honour at Catterick of being granted the freedom of Richmond, Yorkshire (a local town nearby).

This was the first time it had been granted to the R.A.F. Regiment, and as you can imagine, we started rehearsals weeks and weeks before and when we got to about two weeks before the parade, rehearsals intensified until we were so sick of rehearsals that the standard started to drop, as was the usual case. We were doing it as if we were programmed robots; we were going through the parade and not even thinking about what came next, it became automatic. By the time the big day arrived, we marched on to the Parade Square in the grounds of Richmond castle; it was quite impressive. It was a bright sunny day and the local populace were out in their thousands to see us.

There was a flypast of sorts. A Wessex helicopter flew over low and slow draping below the fuselage the standards of the R.A.F. and the town.

The parade was 100%; we didn't have the benefit of the free beer that the publicans had offered for the servicemen as we had to return to camp immediately after the parade in buses. Yes, buses and not four-tonners this time. Some of us, including me, got changed and went back into town to sample the 'free beer'; trouble was that it was no longer free as although we were in No 2 uniform, the barmen didn't know who had/hadn't been on the parade that afternoon. What a con, so they must have made a tidy little profit. And we didn't get any free beer.

Booking for USA; Told we were going to British Honduras

I had booked for a holiday in USA with the Elvis fan club in England for a number of weeks. It had been granted by the C.O. but I heard coming back from a detachment that the Sqn was being put on 'stand by Sqn'. The Sqn was told to prepare to go to reinforce the British garrison in the British Honduras, Central America, as the Guatemalan army were poised on the border ready to invade and the stand by Sqn who happened to be 16 Sqn were rushed out there to Central America to deter and be prepared to fight and help defend the R.A.F. airfield against attack with their Bofor guns.

I checked on it and found out that it was true and asked how it would affect my holiday. I was asked by the Flt Commander, "If asked to make a choice, which would I choose? Go to Belize or go on the holiday?" I asked when was the detachment due to fly out R.T.U. UK and I found that there was a gap of about two weeks between returning from the Sqn detachment. Half the Sqn was to go out for three months, then they were to be relieved by the second half of the Sqn.

I told the Flt Commander that I didn't want to miss the chance of going to Central America on possible active service, neither did I want to miss the opportunity of going to USA. (The main reason for the visit to USA was to see Elvis Presley. But I didn't tell the officer that.)

I requested if it was at all possible for me to go on the first detachment to Honduras. Then go on my holiday. As there was a gap of two weeks afterwards, I would have returned before flying out to America.

He said he would see what he could do for me when he saw the C.O. of the Sqn, but he didn't hold out much hope. As it turned out, I couldn't do both but had to choose which one I preferred on the grounds that if something happened (shots were actually fired and it became a shooting war or the aircraft broke down on the way home), I wouldn't make my holiday. I told the Flt Commander I didn't mind, I was quite prepared to risk it so I could do both. But it was not to be, and having had to choose, I chose USA on the promise from the Flt Commander that they would send me to Honduras as soon as the opportunity arose; however, I was told to leave my address of where I'll be at any one time so that if worse came to worst, and the fighting started, I could be recalled immediately by the Sqn and report to the nearest US military base and the US forces would fly me out immediately to Honduras to join the Sqn. (I was not called out.) Regrettably, I had to accept it.

American Interlude: Summer 1972

Insight to the holiday

The original date for the holiday to commence had been put back about three weeks once they had found out Elvis would be in Las Vegas (on one of our stopovers); this would be the first month he had returned to live shows after finishing his film commitments.

I visited several places – Main, Nashville, Memphis, Tupelo (birthplace of Elvis), Los Angeles, Hollywood, Las Vegas, Disneyland and Tijuana in Mexico.

In the holiday, there were about 12 single men, 4-5 married couples and the rest about 160-180 single girls aged about 17 to 26-27 and a great time was had by all the single men.

Girls from all over the world

There were girls from all over: England, Scotland, Wales, N. Ireland, Southern Ireland, France, Germany, Holland, Greece, Norway, Denmark and a white South African girl. We got three flights (all served with champagne), all the transport to and from, food, accommodation in four-star hotels, tips and taxes paid for; in fact, everything was paid for in the price of £190 for two weeks. This was before the oil crisis that was to hit a little while later.

How the club secretary did it on the money I'll never know, it was a single man's – stud's paradise!

Given list to enable us to make friends before we left UK

Before the holiday, the fan club had sent a list to each person travelling on the trip with the names and addresses of each passenger going so you could contact each other and strike up a friendship before you set off, thereby doing away with breaking the ice. Here are some examples:

1) I met a girl who lived in London while there with the Royal Tournament; we went for a walk along the serpentine and through the parks. I nearly walked her off her feet. I thought she was alright but when I saw all the other girls on the trip, I couldn't be bothered with her; besides, she wasn't that friendly when I saw her on the trip probably because she had a friend with her and really wanted two guys.

2) I got writing to two girls – one from Norway and one from Denmark. The

main one I was writing to was Agatha Magnus from near Copenhagen; she was a well-built girl as I had hoped for and seemed a nice girl with a 38:28:39 figure. "I'll be all right here," I thought. "She's bound to be a 'goer' from Copenhagen, they are all 'free with it'!"

So I tried it on a bit and was politely told, "No! I'm not that sort of girl!" "Damn," I thought, "just my luck, she's probably the only virgin in Denmark! And I found her!" That was the last time I paid any attention to her. She was chatted and picked up by another chap.

3) The other was Mandy Gregson. Her father was a farmer but had five cars and my present one wasn't very reliable and her father said I could use one of his and take it to Catterick with me. Damn decent of the chap. "Take your pick!" I couldn't believe it, especially if he knew my intentions towards his daughter were far from honourable! (She was horse-mad.)

I'll never forget the first date. I couldn't believe what she told me. We set off for Doncaster about 15 miles away and as we had nicely set off on our way along a country road on a lovely warm summer's evening, she said, "Stop and pull in here, will you?" (She was about 18 years old.) "Now," she said, "let's get one thing straight, I'm a virgin and I wish to stay that way! Unless after we've known each other for about 6 months or we both mutually decide otherwise!" I was dumbfounded, but not for long though. I agreed with everything she said; meanwhile, going through my mind was, "Never had a girl ever before been as upfront as per sex, before anything happens." My mind started thinking of her statement; I might be able to turn it to my advantage! At the dance, we had some drinks and my mind was churning over doing overtime. I thought, "Let's see what happens if I put my plan into effect!"

"You know," I said, "I respect the decision you have made but if ever you change your mind, I will be gentle with you, the perfect gentleman in fact!" (While I busied myself taking her virginity.) "And I won't be rough either, not only that, but I'm not the sort that will tell his mates what I have been up to and with whom!" I was really having a job to keep my face straight and not laugh! "Wait till my mates heard about this!" I thought. "She'll go mad if she finds out!" A few moments later, she surprised me again with the reply, "What you said just now, did you mean it?"

"Of course," said I. "I wouldn't say it if I didn't mean it." (This was said whilst I was biting my cheeks to stop myself from laughing.)

"Then," said Mandy, "let's go home – the long way!"

"Have you changed your mind about losing your virginity in 6 months' time then?" said I with my fingers crossed. "Yes!" she said with a large naughty smile.

"Right then, let's get our coats and we'll head for your house!" It took us about two hours to travel the 15 miles home. Whenever I wanted to stop at a likely dark part of the woods, she said, "No, go a bit further. I'll show you where!" Eventually, when we got to the place she had pointed out, I killed the lights and backed off the road into the wooded clearing. I turned towards her and thought, "This is it; this is my lucky night, this is where she gets to 'the point of no return'." I leant over – she was fast 'asleep'? Typical of my luck! I finally got a chance with a virgin and she fell asleep on me. So frustrating, at first she clearly was ready to 'go all the way' and give me the honour of being her 'first' but chickened out at the last minute.

Should I have woken her and reminded her of her promise?

She never suggested after that another place, another time. But "Wait till we get to America". If what I'd heard from other guys on how they behaved, i.e., never leave you alone? Then I was probably well out of it. She might have ruined my chances of 'playing the field' whilst in the States.

As for Mike Barley, my roommate, he didn't take the hint when I wanted to be alone with Mandy, knocking on my door and standing there all vulnerable.

She was telling me before we left home that she was looking forward to going abroad. I couldn't be bothered with her now as I had my eyes on two or three other girls a bit older than she and more mature.

Day 1: Gatwick airport

We were seated in the departure lounge of Gatwick airport. There were people wearing Elvis scarves, badges, hats, tee-shirts, people could see that it was an E.P. outing.

Due to industrial action, most flights to US were cancelled, but we were OK as we were called forward. Tony Prince, the Radio Luxembourg DJ announced over the tannoy about the British E.P. Fan Club leaving for a two-week holiday culminating in seeing Elvis live!

When he made the announcement about the British E.P outing, a great cheer went up from us all.

I overheard an ageing American woman as I was going past, "Oh gawd, damn wish I was going with them!"

Poor woman, she and several dozen other Americans were stranded due to this disruptive action.

Flight out, arrival at Main and Nashville

During the 6-hour flight to Main to refuel, we were shown 2 Elvis films – 'The Elvis special'. We listened to his records all during the flight; if, on the 'Elvis special', you happened to get bored with all these records and films, then you were in trouble. Of course, no one could get to sleep as everyone else was singing along and cheering when their hero beat up the baddies and wry comments when E.P. was playing a love scene; there were suggestive comments coming from the few male members of the tour. This of course upset some of the female fans on the plane. Meanwhile, I was eating a steak lunch and sipping champagne.

After landing in Main, we went through the passport/entry formalities. After half an hour or so, we took off again for Nashville. There was nothing to see or do in the arrival lounge at Main as there was a sign all over as the place was upside down being rebuilt. Upon our arrival at Nashville, Tennessee, we got our first view and taste of life out in the south in the former 'colonies'. Todd Slaughter and Tony Prince along with Dave Wade, the Fan Club travel consultant, all suggested that we take a couple of hours looking around the city first as we were not allowed into the hotel because they hadn't had a chance to book us in yet.

The billboard outside our hotel said 'Welcome, E.P. fans!' so we were rather chuffed about that. While we were waiting, I and most others went on an organised sightseeing tour to the city. Some went to drive around the houses of the stars while the rest of us settled for the most interesting one of all. The tour of the city culminating in a visit to the famous 'country music hall of fame' and the 'Grand Ole Opry', very interesting.

Grand Ole Opry & Country Music Hall of Fame

The Grand Ole Opry was originally a church and situated in a dark and dismal part of town. At the Hall of Fame, we were shown around and it started with a film on the history, start and origins of country music; problem was while the film was on, most of us, including me, were fast asleep as we were tired from the flight, call it jet lag if you wish but it was the first and only time I have had jet lag as I have travelled thousands of miles since and not suffered from it.

In the evening, it had been arranged for the fan club to visit the local TV studios to have a look around and see how things were done and as guests of the TV company to sit in as the invited guests at the recording of a country and western show, which was being filmed prior to going out on the national network and to be sent to American troops in Vietnam.

Dolly Parton on Porter Wagner's show

The show was 'The Porter Wagner Show' staring Porter Wagner and his wife. Also an unknown and 'slightly built' Dolly Parton who wasn't as big as she is now, if you get my drift? Rest assured, I would have noticed if she had been. She was a relatively unknown at that time in UK.

I keep wondering what has happened to her body since seeing her then to now, she's suddenly grown several inches in the right places! Both of them.

Tony Prince was making a big fuss of Dolly Parton and invited her to visit him and his radio station if ever she was in Europe. She seemed to make a lot of friends amongst the fans as she came over quite shy, modest and approachable.

The guest star was Burl Ives.

The TV company made a big fuss of us because the British Elvis Fan Club had graced their studios with a visit. We also had a look at the studios where the C & W stars recorded their records.

The following morning, we set off in coaches for our next destination on the itinerary, the home of the King himself – Memphis!

Day 2: Memphis Hotel c/w ducks

The American coaches were the most comfortable I'd been in, very roomy, air-conditioned and even a toilet and a bar that served drinks, fantastic. Memphis confirmed my first impressions of the States – what a massive place it is, the streets are so wide and the distances sometimes between buildings was huge and the people are so very friendly, especially when they heard the British accent.

We checked in at our hotel, the Sheraton Peabody, famous for its resident pets, some Mallard ducks reportedly brought back from Vietnam by a 'son of Memphis' in the US army upon his return to US; they used the hotel fountain.

As soon as we were checked in and I saw that my suitcase was in my room, I went out for a look around the city.

Day 3: Tupelo

Another six coaches arrived and they took the entire Fan Club in convoy to Tupelo. The birthplace of Elvis.

The trip took about three hours, we stopped off en route by the roadside to have a close look at the main crop grown in that part of the States, 'cotton' very interesting. The further south and the nearer we got to Tupelo, the more nervous our African American drivers got as even today, things in the deep south are not all they could be.

Police escort

On the outskirts of the town, we were stopped and escorted into the town by half the local police force. There were 2-3 cars and about six motorcycle outriders to escort us in with lights flashing and sirens sounding.

The drivers weren't very keen and kept an eye on the white Tupelo policemen. Todd 'S' and Tony 'P' had to reassure the drivers that they would be OK and there are 200 Elvis fans to look after them.

We had Elvis records played for us on the bus ride down there (as we did every time we used an aircraft or coach) and even I was getting fed up of the same records over and over again. Gawd knows what a non-Elvis fan felt like, though there were only about two or three of them and they had been 'converted' by the end of the holiday. They even piped the music into the 'john', as the Americans so quaintly call the loo.

Elvis's birthplace

With the quiet country air being shattered by the noise of the police sirens, we entered Tupelo in triumph – the honoured guests of the mayor who was outside Elvis's birthplace to greet us.

The birthplace was about as meagre as you could get, it was a small – and

I do mean small – two-roomed wooden shack, the entire fan club stood and gasped in shock as we saw it for the first time. We knew that his family hadn't been very well off and we had seen photos of the shack before on TV. But we weren't quite ready for what most of us would consider downright poor – on the bread line! We thought all those hard-up stories floating about had been part of the publicity machine, how wrong we were.

We were addressed by the mayor who welcomed us and told us something about Elvis and his days in Tupelo before making it big and how proud they were of him, etc. We'd heard it all before and weren't (I wasn't at least) convinced of his sincerity. I bet he didn't even know Elvis before he had made it big.

Tupelo: Police Officer who handed over his side arm for me to check over.

Police motorcycle cop

We spent several hours looking around buying souvenirs and chatting to the locals.

I got chatting to a motorcycle cop who had escorted us about different things like law enforcement in the States and UK. About drawing his weapon on duty, he said he never has in about 20 years on the force. The only time he ever took it out of the holster was to fire it at the police shooting range for his annual shoot. He laughed when I told him all the American 'cop' shows shown on British TV. That showed all policemen from detective down to patrolman in regular shootouts with the villains. As he said, it probably happened – and then only very rarely, in the big cities such as New York, L.A., Chicago, certainly not in the average small American town/city.

So maybe USA wasn't as gun happy as we would believe. (Since this writing, I have had to eat my words.)

One thing shocked and surprised me; while we were talking about weapons, he took out and offered me his side arm, fully loaded, to look at and handle, which would never have happened in England.

He asked if it was true that the average 'English cop' walked the streets unarmed and I told him officially yes! But!

Dinner, Ladies' Guild

On the way out of town, again we were escorted by the police. They led our convoy into a motel, where we were told by the mayor to go inside as a surprise awaited us. The billboard had on it 'Welcome! Elvis Presley fans from England!'

This port of call was even a surprise to the organisers, Todd 'S' and Dave Wade, who knew nothing about it. It had been organised by the Ladies' Guild of Tupelo. Inside, it was festooned with Elvis posters, record charts pictures, badges and so on. We were greeted with speeches by the guild and invited to join them for lunch – a 7-course affair. As we were leaving, we were given all manner of souvenirs, pictures, badges.

In the building, there was a shop run by the 'Natchez' Indian tribe. I spent more money there than I had so far as I always feel sorry for them, the way Hollywood always made them out the villains of western films. But who had more right to live their life unmolested than the Indians? They were selling native crafts; most people bought something from them. After a slap-up meal, we returned to Memphis.

Memphis: Riverboat paddle steamer

During the evening of our third day in Memphis, I and a few others went for a sunset cruise on a traditional Mississippi paddle steamer riverboat based in Memphis, and went down the famous river.

I bought a confederate flag and got chatting to a pleasant African-American girl. She asked if we had many racial problems and riots in England and I was proud to tell her no! She told me that there was hardly any in the States and those there were nearly always made out by the media to be ten times worse. Most people, regardless of race, religion, creed and colour, got on well with each other.

Graceland: meeting Elvis's uncle Vester

Our biggest priority whilst there was, of course, the pilgrimage to Elvis's home in Memphis, 'Graceland'. We travelled along Elvis Presley Boulevard, so named after him.

We pulled up in front of those world-famous gates with the image of Elvis and his guitar and music notes. We, and I was no exception, began to feel nervous and apprehensive as we neared the mansion, daft wasn't it? As only an Elvis fan would understand. The gates opened to allow the British Fan Club up the drive to look at the house from the outside, close up, and to walk in the grounds; we were rather excited.

It was a very large house but looking closer, it confirmed my suspicions that though the Americans had large lovely houses, they were mostly made of wood. We had photos taken and I helped myself to some samples from the grounds, such as pebbles of the drive and cuttings from the hedge. (I tried to grow them at home in UK but to no avail. Been too long without moisture.)

I saw some of the staff walking in the grounds and got talking to Elvis's uncle Vester. That was a most interesting chat with several of the fans looking on in envy.

Memphis: outside the home of Elvis Presley – Graceland and those famous gates.

Las Vegas

After four days in Memphis, it was time to pack up once more and set off to our next stopover – the gambling capital of the world, Las Vegas!

We were warned about Las Vegas beforehand that it could be very, very expensive but in my case, it turned out to be about the cheapest place I had visited, simply because I took advantage of all the free offers there, and there were quite a few.

As was popularly shown on TV and films, the moment you got off the plane in Vegas, you were surrounded by dozens and dozens of one-arm bandits. The place was festooned with them.

We left the airport and drove the few miles to the city through the scorching Nevada desert. As we got nearer to the famous 'Strip', there were large roadside billboards advertising the shows on in Vegas! Then I saw it first and said to all the others, "Look what show they're advertising!" It was Elvis himself. A great cheer went up!

Everybody on the trip felt nervous and excited that now we were actually in the same city as our hero, less than 5 miles away; we couldn't believe it! After all these years of being fans, we were at last going to see him 'live'. Though I must have been a fan for a very short period of time in comparison to some there who had followed his exploits from his first years in rock and roll.

Circus Circus messes up bookings

We proceeded to our hotel, The Circus Circus, which – as seen in the James Bond film, *Diamonds Are Forever* – was a casino/circus/fairground all rolled into one.

Here, we had our one and only hitch in the entire well-organised holiday. The Circus Circus had failed to book our party into the hotel as arranged. So Todd 'S', Dave Wade and Tony 'P' were looking very worried and told us to wait and they would try and sort something out for us, not to worry. I wasn't worried, I was enjoying it, though some of the girls were definitely worried.

Booked into the smallest motel at a moment's notice (the entire F.C.)

About 15 minutes later, the guys came back and said they had approached the nearest motel and they had agreed to take in our entire party, all 200 of us. We were told that it was the smallest Motel in Vegas, with over 1,000 beds and 5 triple swimming pools, one main, one therapeutic and one children's pool. Making in all 15, yes, 15 pools! Such is Las Vegas!

Our motel, The Westwood Ho! had all the usual mod cons that we had come to expect, i.e. air conditioning, maid service for each room and an ice-making machine at the end of each hallway. All rooms came out onto a large veranda. I found that the chap who was allocated to share my room with me in Nashville was to be my regular roommate for the rest of the holiday.

The rooms, as always, were quite big and had two separate beds. I suggested to him from the first day that it be best if we had an arrangement in case either of us wanted to bring a girl back to the room 'for obvious purposes' and that was that the other would go for a walk for an hour or two to allow his roommate time alone with the girl of the moment. He agreed to this arrangement. He was from Manchester and his name was Mike Barley.

Mary Stickler

Within an hour of arriving in Las Vegas, some of the real dedicated Elvis nuts were heading for the Hilton where Elvis was appearing to try to get a ticket for the evening's show.

About 5-6 of them went to the show and the first I knew about it was late in the evening when I was having a bite to eat in the café and talking to Tony Prince and Todd Slaughter; we were talking about this and that when the most famous, or should I say – the one who 'peed' everybody off as she was so obsessed with Elvis it was weird – even in the fan club circles, Mary Stickler came rushing in, interrupting our conversation with tales of the Elvis show she had just seen. We were a bit peeved with her as we were busy talking so Tony 'P' told her, "Mary, just piss off, we're having a conversation here! And we're not interested!" She wasn't having any of it; as far as she was concerned, we all had to hear about the show.

She went on and on so we just ignored her as if she wasn't there, too thick to take a hint. Some of the real dedicated 'nuts' saw every single Elvis Presley show there was in the four days we were there – about 9 shows in all.

As much as I was a fan, I thought, and so did most others, that when in the famous Las Vegas there was so much going on, it would be a shame not to see it all and I saw about 3-4 shows myself starring Elvis.

Circus Circus
The Circus Circus was the most amazing place. While you played the machines and tables, there were circus acts going on above your head. Upstairs, they had a fairground with all the amusements, such as a full-size Ferris wheel and a shooting gallery with 88 life-sized stuffed African/Indian animals.

The most amazing thing was that each animal had a red spot on its forehead and if you shot it and hit it on that spot, the animal came to life and roared as it charged at you. The first I knew of it was when I fired at a gorilla. I hit it and it roared and charged at me through the under-growth, stopping only about three feet from me. I was rooted to the spot because never before had my target 'come alive' and charged at me when not expecting it. Usually, when I hit a target, it stayed down, just somehow didn't relish the thought of the other animals charging me like the elephant, hippo, rhinoceros and giraffe.

When playing the machines/tables, waitresses would come around and offer coffee, doughnuts and other delicacies for free. Whenever you wanted to eat, you just went outside and took a leaflet from the rack and cashed it in for a free breakfast, free mid-morning meal, free lunch, free coffee, free dollars (sometimes money and sometimes discs) to play on the one-armed bandits' tables, though only certain games and free gifts.

The amount they gave you depended upon the hotel concerned but it usually ranged from $2 to $5. This was the way I lived in Las Vegas and it didn't cost me hardly anything though the vast majority of the people didn't do this and of course, Las Vegas cost them a lot more than it needed to.

Las Vegas breakfast
I only spent about $5 of my own money on gambling but using the free cards valued in all about 7-8 dollars, I came away about 2-3 dollars up. Not many people could leave Las Vegas at a profit. One thing I didn't like was

the Las Vegas style breakfast, which usually consisted of chocolate dough-nuts and waffles dripping in syrup, ugh!

Elvis at the Hilton

I went to the Hilton to book a ticket/seat to see Elvis live. I was told to arrive ready to queue up at least two hours before the start of the show. I wondered why but I was soon to find out. Although you had booked a seat, you still had to queue up with everybody else because with the star of the show able to pack them in like Elvis, you had to wait behind everybody else who wanted to get in.

The long snake-like queue wound its way round and round the gaming machines (the management didn't miss a trick) and if you got bored while waiting, and most people did, then you were tempted to play the machines, poker, blackjack tables or have a spin at the roulette wheel.

Your names were checked at the door against the bookings and when confirmed, you were taken to your seat. By now I was getting very excited and still couldn't believe that in a few short minutes, we would set eyes on our hero, the guy who was directly/indirectly responsible for modern music and for most of sexual and near sexual adventures with members of the opposite gender.

You sat down for about 45 minutes, had dinner, which was steak with all the trimmings with a small bottle of champagne or three beers, the show lasted about 2½ hours, all for $17 dollars, very good value. After dinner, the plates and such were cleared away and the show started.

The lights slowly dimmed, the giant chandeliers were raised up in the ceiling and the orchestra tuned up, the curtains swung aside and a great cheer went up from all the Elvis fans. We expected Elvis to be on stage straight away but we were disappointed; you could literally hear the sighs of disappointment as the first of the artists walked on stage. We were to be very disappointed as the so-called comedian of the show came on. He was greeted throughout by a wall of silence as 99% Elvis fans and most of the others didn't find his typical American humour funny, least of all the British fans.

He finished his act – not before time. Three years later when the Fan Club went again to Las Vegas, they said that the same comedian was telling the same jokes. He walked off stage with the majority of the audience glad to see the back of him.

Again the excitement began to build up in the pit of our stomachs and we were thinking, "Now he is surely coming on!" but no.

The lights dimmed once more and all fell silent. And on stage walked a three-girl singing group, they were the Elvis female vocal backing group, the 'Sweet Inspirations', three coloured girls and quite good. One of them looked quite attractive and I gave her the eye. In fact, on the third show I saw (the second was a block booking for every member of the Fan Club), I kept making gestures and signs at her; she was attractive and returned my smile, so much so that she missed her cue and was embarrassed. After the girls had finished their 40 minutes or so, they left the stage. One of the sweet inspirations had a small daughter by the name of Whitney Houston! By now, we thought this a good dream gone bad and we weren't going to see Elvis at all. A few moments later, again the lights dimmed and the chandeliers were raised to the roof. We detected the faint strains of the orchestra tuning up, a minute or so of silence, then a familiar tune, quietly and gradually getting louder and louder, then it was loud enough to distinguish quite plainly that it was the theme from *2001: A Space Odyssey*! Elvis's theme tune culminating in the large kettle drum, then the orchestra started playing, again for a few moments nothing, just the orchestra and the backing singers, the girl group and a male vocal group.

The excitement and atmosphere was unbelievable! We were hardly able to contain ourselves, very soon would be the moment we had all dreamed of for years and years, about to be fulfilled – Elvis Presley – live on stage right in front of our eyes.

One verse and the orchestra played into the song, but still no Elvis, we were beginning to feel let down and disappointed. The orchestra progressed into what sounded like the second verse, and suddenly! He walked on stage, arms and sequinned cloak held aloft, accepting the cheers, there he stood grinning, his hands on his hips – that impish smile that was famous all over the world. 'The King' Elvis Presley was on stage accepting the adulation of his subjects, and none cheered or shouted louder than the handful of fans from England. And I cheered the loudest of all, he took the standing ovation and all the years rolled back.

He stood on stage in full command and surveyed the audience while he took the bows, he stood tall, slim and more handsome and young-looking than all those millions of photographs taken of him over the years.

The female members of the audience were having hysterical fits because of the excitement and this was before he had done or said anything. It had been a rapturous and deafening welcome – as expected. I can't begin to explain the atmosphere in that room at that moment, it defied words to describe.

He waited for the noise to die down, then raised the microphone to his mouth and uttered a couple of words trying to thank the audience for the welcome, he laughed at the reaction and said something to his group who were behind him and they all laughed.

Eventually, when the audience allowed him to start the show and singing, he did the usual opening song with *Johnny 'B' Goode*; he did another and then paused and introduced himself. "Good evening, ladies and gentlemen, I hope you enjoy the show tonight, my name is on the hoardings outside!" This was greeted with a great tumultuous cheer and his famous curled lip smile. "I believe there are some people in the audience tonight from (he then consulted a piece of paper) England! Who have come all that way to see me, thank you very much, I really do hope you enjoy the show tonight and I'll do my very best for you!" The 8-12 people in the audience from the Fan Club let out a whoop of joy so Elvis would know where we were.

He smiled and went into his next song. Of all the songs he did, the one I and everybody in the Fan Club liked the most was about the only one he hadn't recorded at that time, he apologised for reading the words off a piece of paper and said he had only just learned it, though after the second verse, he threw the paper down and did the rest by memory. It received the best applause. *You Gave Me a Mountain!*, which if one or two words were changed sounded just like his life story. Elvis sounded better live than he does on record, which was a pleasant surprise to me as nearly always an artist was never quite as good live as he/she was on record. Up to that point, I hadn't been awfully keen on his 'live' albums but now I was converted.

It was a marvellous show and Elvis was on stage a lot longer than I thought he would be, about an hour and a half. Eventually, he sang a song made famous by Frank Sinatra, *My Way*, which when he got to the part that says, 'And now the end is near and so I face the final curtain', the audience sighed in disappointment thinking this was his last song but it wasn't; he went on for another ¼ hour and finished off with his now familiar way, *Can't Help Falling in Love with You!* He took the applause to standing ovation looking resplendent in his very colourful blue jumpsuit and glittering cloak held aloft.

He took a few bows and was gone with everybody clamouring for more; we sat there stunned. It was not to be but that was the way to leave an audience – wanting more as they would come back and see you again, as we did.

It was the best produced and directed (directed by Elvis) show I had ever seen and the most professional production. And I am not just saying that because I am a fan but because it was. It also had the non-Elvis fans in the audience won over and clapping and cheering as loud as any fan. He was superb, the only criticism I had was the seat; though it gave you a good view of the whole stage, it wasn't near enough for my liking. I was determined to do better next time.

I was to find out later that if you didn't tip the waiters, that was about the best you could expect. Any nearer and those seats consisted of people who had bribed the waiters and 'special guests'.

Elvis: the second show

The second show I saw was the block booking by the fan club.

We were all queued up with most of the fans (not me) with Elvis badges, scarves, tee shirts. Some were even singing Elvis songs, the yanks in the queue thought the British a little mad (not without just cause).

We were seated about halfway back in the auditorium, which was what I had expected, it was further back than the one I had the day before. A few minutes before the show started, we had a surprise. Tony Prince walked on stage and the spotlight picked him out. He introduced himself to the

American audience and explained who we were and what we were doing in USA.

He was of course greeted by the British Fan Club with loud cheers and at first the Americans didn't know who he was; when he'd finished his speech, he was cheered loudly by both the British F.C. members and the Americans.

On a table behind us, there were two couples; the women were dripping diamonds and mink stoles. One of the chaps leaned over and asked me and my roommate Mike Barley if we were British and part of the Fan Club that Tony Prince had just mentioned. I proudly replied that we were.

We were then promptly invited to join them at their table and help them finish these bottles of champagne they had on the table, which I duly did.

This show, Elvis acknowledged our presence in the audience and promised an extra special show just for us and thanked us for our support. Everything he said and did was greeted by loud cheers by the British element; he kept laughing at this, each song was cheered louder by us than anyone and he certainly knew of our presence.

It had transpired that before the show, Todd Slaughter and Tony Prince had taken a few people backstage to meet and interview the great man. Todd Slaughter had told everyone that whatever they did, not to mention his wife (they had just divorced) or more importantly not to ask if or why he hadn't been to England yet, but guess who did so? Yes, Mary Stickler did just that! She said, "Why haven't you been to England yet, and do you ever intend to come? You're being unfair on your British fans that have stood by you all these years!" Todd didn't know where to put himself.

I had noticed that people who had taken photos of Elvis were having their cameras confiscated and the films removed. Something to do with copyright. Though when Elvis saw someone raise their camera to snap him, he posed for them and gave them a smile.

I had come determined to go home with some self-taken photos myself so after getting the lay of the land on the first show, I took my small insta-matic camera with me for the second show but I deliberately left off the flash to reduce the chance of being caught; it worked and I took about 12 pictures and two came out very well.

Another show, I got very near and Elvis saw I was about to snap him and he paused, looked my way and gave me one of his famous lopsided grins. I was able to sell these photos upon my return to UK (more about them later). On returning to the hotel, nobody wanted to sleep and I'll give you one guess what the topic of conversation was!

Elvis: third show – Bribing waiter for a good seat

The next show, I thought I would try a little experiment and see if the stories about US were true, about 'money talks'. That next night, Mike Barley, the South African girl and I went to the show; I told them to follow my lead. The South African girl was trying to convince us that she wasn't a fan of Elvis but had come over just for the holiday.

I hadn't booked the day before deliberately to see what would happen.

At the door, I gave the manager a name and he said, "I am sorry, sir, I don't see your name on the list; are you sure you have booked?" I told him I had (though I hadn't) and he said he couldn't let us in because we hadn't booked.

So, I started to kick up a bit at this, that he was saying he couldn't let me through, in the best possible posh English accent I could muster. "It was disgusting that I'd come all this way and this girl from South Africa had travelled even further to see Elvis and we were not allowed in due to the hotel's incompetence!" The manager saw that I was going to make a scene and thought it better to give me a seat to keep me quiet so he beckoned to a waiter to show us to some seats; we three smiled at each other and followed the waiter.

He showed us to seats right at the back of the hall and I told him I wasn't going to have them. So he took us further down and again I told him they weren't good enough; we tried a third one about halfway down, and he said that was the best he could do for us so I said (taking out a $20 bill and putting it in his top pocket), "Are you sure you can't do better?"

"Please follow me, sir!" he said. He took us right alongside the stage. "That will do fine!" I said with a smile; the other two gave me their share as previously arranged. We were so close I was able to put my beer on the edge of the stage.

It was at this table that I took my best photos of the star of the show.

It was also at this table that I fulfilled another small ambition. Elvis was walking from one end of the stage to the other and kissing all the girls (well, at least those he fancied) and on the spur of the moment, I jumped up and stood next to the stage when he got to me. Elvis was so used to bending over and kissing the girls that when he got to me, he was a bit surprised so I shook hands with him and noticed that his fingers were covered in rings, large and small.

I shook hands with him and was carried away and said, "You're the greatest, Elvis, the King!" Did I say that? How embarrassing!

He smiled and said quietly, "Thank you very much, sir, you're very kind!"

I said, "When are you coming to England?" He said something that I missed due to some girls screaming; now I shall never know.

Before the show started, the South African girl started to get very excited, probably wetting herself as the tension built up, by the time he came on stage, she was near hysterical, almost tearing her hair out and screaming. I was watching her and having a good laugh but she didn't notice me laughing at her.

This was the girl, if you remember, who wasn't a fan and didn't like him. I asked her during a break in the singing, "I thought you weren't a fan and didn't like him?"

She replied, "Now I am, and now I do!"

Elvis had another convert and had won her over with just a song or two, such was his sheer magic, and she wasn't the only one to fall under his spell this way, it happened to others in the party too.

I have only ever met two people who have a magical something about them – an aura, charisma if you like, and that is Elvis and Margaret Thatcher.

On stage, Elvis would be singing and would put up his hand to stop the music and fool about. He would then pick up a pair of female underwear that some over-enthusiastic girl had thrown on stage after quickly removing them.

He would pick them up and feeling that they were still warm, say, "Hi honey, are these yours?" Cue screams and shrieks from the girl concerned and others around her. "Say, they are still warm!" The whole audience reacted to this. "You just taken them off?" More screams and a large beaming smile from Elvis. "Keep it warm, baby, I'll see you after the show!" And this was done several times, with several pairs of knickers lying on the stage. This very nearly gave the girl/s in question a heart attack! And got the audience rocking in their chairs with laughter. Now you know where Tom Jones got the idea from – from Elvis himself.

Other times, some girls threw their hotel keys on stage.

Elvis, asking whom they belonged to, said, "I would like to get to know the owner!" (More screams.)

He would do some more songs and stop to pick up another set of hotel keys, asking whose they were, about a dozen girls screamed out that it was theirs; he read out the hotel and room number and said, "I'll see you later, honey, keep it warm for me!" sending this girl too into a whirl and frenzy. And didn't Elvis love baiting the girls! Yes, he did! He carried on and picked up more keys – the same approach, only this time he said, "I'll see you after I've finished at the Mint!" (This was the name of the hotel/ casino.) Eventually, after doing this to three to four girls, he picked up another. "I-I-I would sure like to oblige you, honey, but I guess by this time I'll have no energy left!" More screams, shouts and cheers than before and this comment nearly brought the house down; of course, Elvis loved every minute of teasing these girls, smiling that impish, devilish grin of his.

We were told that Elvis's manager had told Todd Slaughter that the entire Fan Club en masse would be invited upstairs in the hotel to see Elvis' dressing room and have some free samples (Elvis' management team). Only a few chosen ones there were invited to meet the great man in person backstage. As it turned out, I was chosen to lead one of the 6 groups; we'd been split into teams. Upstairs, when we got out of the lift, we were directed to a hallway with photos of Elvis. There were dozens of large soft stuffed cuddly type toy dogs about 4 feet tall (made In honour of one of Elvis early hits, *Hound Dog*).

I bought one only to sell it later when I realised I might have a problem getting it home. I didn't know how all the others managed. An even larger one was specially made for and presented to Todd Slaughter – the Fan Club and on behalf of Elvis.

We were directed into a small room whereupon we saw all these 'goodies', all these 'free' goodies as he called them, which weren't free at all but cost $20, a downright fiddle. Just before the fan club was called to his dressing room, Todd Slaughter approached me, a little embarrassed at the time but I didn't give it a second thought, he said that it was only a small dressing room and it wasn't enough room for everyone so did I mind not going in. (I don't remember if it was just me or my group.)

I was gutted, of course; I wasn't going to see 'The King' up close or have my photo taken with him, but hey ho! I'd spoken to him and shaken hands with him so all wasn't lost. It wasn't until sometime later that the idea came to me that there might have been some other reason for this! Was it because Elvis's management might have overheard me saying to one of the girls that I thought he was 'not entirely honest'?

Elvis's management team kept going on about 'The great loyal British fans'. But they were still quite happy to make money out of us if they could.

Goodies cheaper downstairs

Downstairs, I had noticed on the way up that some items cost only $16, upstairs they were $20. Others were $20 downstairs – $30 upstairs. Upon calling at the kiosk on the way back down, they had now been reduced to $12 as I suspected they might have been. I was not going to be conned so easily as the others had been and regretted it when they found out they had been 'had'.

I had never liked or trusted this certain person on Elvis' management team. I'd always known he was out for himself – a quick buck here, an easy dollar there. My meeting with him on that hot summer's day in the middle of the Nevada desert confirmed the suspicions I always had of him – and a lot of others including officials of the 'Official Elvis Presley' fan club. I always said that if anything ever happened to Elvis, he would eventually be found out to be the person he really was. I was proved right for after the death of the King, he was taken to court by Elvis' ex-wife for just that!

Kiosk girl offers to pay so much towards a bag

At the souvenir kiosk, there was an attractive girl I'd been friendly with. I was looking around and contemplating buying this bag of Elvis goodies that Elvis' management had tried to sell me upstairs. I was telling this young girl about what I thought of him, she of course tried to sell me the water colour painting of the star of the show, which was the most expensive item on sale at $35. I didn't want it as a) couldn't afford it and b) couldn't manage to get it home undamaged due to the sheer size and bulk.

She asked how much had I got. I told her only $15 and to this she replied, "If you can find $20, I will give you some discount and put the rest in myself!" I thought what a very nice gesture; nobody in England would do that for you in a shop. Was it because she fancied me that she had made the offer? Or did she feel sorry for me? Either way, I declined her very kind offer. Instead, I bought a hard photograph of the same pose and was given a $5 discount and a smaller b/w picture.

Elvis: fourth show – Debbie offers me a free ticket

On the fourth show I saw, I managed to get a seat right next to the stage again and shook hands with Elvis again. I shook hands with Elvis a total of 3-4 times in Las Vegas. I then started chatting up this beautiful American girl, Debbie Humphries. She was my vision of an American beauty with beautiful red hair. She told me that I could have her ticket she had bought for the show tomorrow as she had to leave for L.A. She would give me a ring at my motel and leave it there for me, at no cost to myself. Of course, I didn't believe her as it seemed too good to be true that a strange girl would give me her ticket for nothing. She had to go home early she said and this was the reason. We arranged to see each other in Los Angeles, my next stop. Though I took her with a pinch of salt.

When I awoke the following morning in my motel, there was a call from Reception that this girl, Debbie Humphries, had indeed left me a ticket for the Elvis show that night. Just as she had promised! And a letter. I couldn't believe it, but it was true. This ticket allowed me to see the special that had just been arranged, an extra show starting when all the other shows in Vegas had finished for the season. This gave the stars of other shows the chance to see him and in the audience were Shirley Bassey, Tom Jones who looked very scruffy in jeans/tee shirt and as he stood up, so did his bodyguards as they looked around for signs of any one about to have a go at their charge, that was the unsavoury side of America. There was Shirley Maclaine; as she stood up, she was booed and jeered as left wingers were not liked in the States. There were other people in the audience who were home-grown talent and we didn't know in UK.

As I mentioned, other stars were appearing in Las Vegas at the same time as Elvis; 'The Rat pack' Sinatra, Dean Martin, Sammy Davis Jr, and my biggest regret of all, 'The Rock 'n' Roll show' featuring the greats who were still alive – Bill Hayley, Jerry Lee Lewis, Little Richard, Chuck Berry and so on. I have regretted not seeing that show to this day.

Riding in the Nevada desert

One day, Tony Prince, one other chap, myself and three girls (two of whom I'd been chatting up since we'd arrived in US) went out riding. The one I had fancied was called Priscilla and her friend.

I had tried to get somewhere with Priscilla in Nashville as I had with other girls but it looked like the word had gone through the female grapevine about me, 'Watch him, he's only out for one thing!' Which was true about all us lads there, only I didn't go beating about the bush and pretending I wasn't even if the others did. I let it be known about my intentions straight away with a girl and if she was interested, fine; if not, I didn't want to waste valuable time chatting up a lost cause.

I would move on to someone I thought I stood a better chance with; however, one time while I was in the bedroom of Priscilla, she went into the bathroom to wash and left me alone with her roommate.

I got a bit bored waiting for Priscilla so I turned and made a play for her friend, who stopped me saying, "Wait a minute. I thought it was Priscilla you were going out with?" So I said, "Who's counting? Anyway, if you don't tell, her I won't, and how else is she going to know, she'll be half an hour yet!" Her friend agreed not to say anything! Ah, those were the days!

Studs' paradise!

Anyway, back to the riding now. Tony 'P' and Dave Wade had hired a large American car for the day. I asked him when there was just him, me and three other men around, "What is the thing that sticks out the most about this holiday?"

"Well, of course, it's seeing Elvis, and for the single chaps – all these available single girls, it's a stud's paradise, isn't it?" I had to agree with him. "If they don't get their end away over the next two weeks, they never will!" How true that was. "Even the ugliest, thickest bloke ought to be able to have two or three women before we go back."

We got to this stable where we hired horses for all. I was asked by the ranch hand if I could ride. "Of course I can," I said, "Been riding for years!" It was only a partial lie. I had ridden before, but not for a long time. I was just dreading getting a horse that might bolt but it so happened that I got an awkward one. It was untied from the hitching rail and just wouldn't move. I was given a second one, which only went about 30 yards away from the ranch and promptly turned around and galloped back to be with its friends. I felt such a ruddy fool. Eventually, I was given a third horse by the name of 'Strawberry', which was very reluctant at first to do anything apart from walk. By this time, I had wasted about half an hour of the time; the others were a long, long way away. So I thought I'd better try and go at a gallop to catch them up, this was fine and I was able to catch them up, only problem was it dawned on me, I'd never actually galloped on a horse before. "How the hell do you stop this thing when it's in full flight?"

Fortunately, I was able to bring it under control and stop it without too much trouble as this horse wanted to be with the others and near stopped itself once we'd got there.

The other chap who came with us was making a play for Priscilla by making out he could ride and was showing her how to, I was initially a bit annoyed about this. "The cheeky so and so, trying to pick her up! But then I got to thinking, Oh well, I can't be bothered with her after all, she's so full of herself and stuck up, and thinks she's the 'Bees knees'." (I was proved to be right eventually.) There had been a couple of girls I had had my eye on since arriving stateside so now was as good a time as any to try my luck! So I let this bloke chat her up. I got the distinct impression from this chap that he was holding back at first to see what my reaction was, in case I wanted to fight over her. Not bloody likely, she wasn't worth the trouble; besides, I had always made a point of not fighting over women, they were not worth it, especially if I didn't fancy them anymore. As it turned out, she didn't fancy him anyway.

On the way back from the ranch, I must say I liked the American wild west style saddles compared to the English, they were far more comfortable and easy to stay on with. We broke down so we went for a drink in a little café in the middle of Boulder City, where they had once found gold and this was what had started the Nevada gold rush. I asked, "What is this sarsaparilla that we keep hearing about?" So the girl behind the counter offered me a large glass full, free! It was OK but I didn't have any more. After our four-day stay in the bright lights of Las Vegas, we left for our next stop on the itinerary.

Los Angeles: the 'Strip'

Most of us were a bit sad to leave the city though and there were a couple who wanted to stay for another day or two and join us later in L.A. It was still sinking in about seeing Elvis live and most of us still couldn't believe we'd seen him.

We stayed at another 4-star hotel, this time in the very heart of the famous 'Sunset strip'; we were staying at the large and magnificent 'Hollywood Roosevelt'. To get to the very large swimming pool, you had to walk through a tropical forest surrounded on all sides by tropical flowers and orchids. I saw the sights in downtown Los Angeles starting outside the hotel and looking at the gold stars set in the pavement with all the names engraved of the famous film and TV stars.

Grauman's Chinese Theatre

The equally famous 'Grumman's Chinese Theatre', where all the film stars put hands/feet and anything else they fancied into the wet cement, was opposite our hotel. A couple of things stuck out in my mind about this place: how small the stars were as opposed to the image they portrayed on screen. John Wayne, for example, was not that big, but one of the tricks of Hollywood was to surround the star with small people or have them stand in a ditch. To put over the impression that one was larger than they really were. Humphrey Bogart was another small man but unlike the others, had not just left his imprint in the cement but also written a message to his good friend and director, saying that 'He's going to come back from the grave to haunt him and to kill him!'

Marilyn Monroe wouldn't be outdone; she started a new fashion for the female stars that were suitably well endowed, by putting her hands, feet and breasts into the wet cement. I must have stood out as a typical tourist as I walked up one end of the strip and down the other side, head bowed, reading all the names on the gold stars.

Hotel has own TV station: news flash!

The hotel had its own TV station and broadcasting unit. The first evening in the hotel as I was waiting for dinner, I switched on the TV. There was a news flash! The hotel cameras had 'just happened' to be in the area. It showed a police patrol car that had been ambushed by a sniper and the police had opened fire on the gunman. Even before reinforcements had arrived, the police had opened the boot of their car and it revealed a veritable mobile armoury, including a machine gun, and had trained a 'bazooka' on the house.

Dinner with Debbie's folks

At L.A., this girl whom I'd met in Vegas, Debbie Humphries, met me as promised and took me in Daddy's open convertible for dinner at her place with her family. As I said before, the Americans were very friendly towards the English people.

The Seven Seas

While in L.A., my favourite activity was going to this bar, 'The Seven Seas Hawaiian club', where there were girls dancing the Hawaiian dances in traditional dress. It was great; I always loved anything Hawaiian.

They had a large alcoholic orange-tasting drink in a large brandy balloon, which by state law you were allowed to purchase one in any 24-hour period, and was drunk through a straw.

Some of the people on the trip were refused to be served in the bars as they appeared to be less than 21 years old and no one under that age was allowed alcohol. Some of the chaps, who were very annoyed, ran back to the hotel (about 200 yards away) and brought their passports and showed them to the barman who was then obliged to serve them.

Yobs with knives

I felt a little nervous on the way back to the hotel day and night as there was always a gang of 5-6 menacing-looking yobs with flick knives at the ready, cleaning their fingernails.

I was determined not to appear bothered, I thought, "Bugger them, I'm British; they are not going to give me any trouble. I'll sort them out if they do!" The last bit was a bit of bravado on my part.

They never gave me any trouble but they did upset some of the girls with us; when they told us, it united every man in the Fan Club. The word went around the hotel and when we were all together, we set off to look for these yobs but they weren't to be found.

The first full day in Los Angeles, I took advantage of the extra trip that was on offer to the California-based Disneyland.

Disneyland

After a short trip of a couple of hours on the coaches, we arrived at Disneyland and it turned out very cheap as the entrance fee was in the form of one of three different books with free tickets to have a go on some of the amusements.

As we got in, I was still on friendly terms with Priscilla and her friend, though I'd dropped Cilla at this point. But straight away, they decided to have a meal and a drink in the café. I thought this a complete waste of time as we only had a few short hours there, far too few to waste on eating and drinking so I told them I was going on my own as I wasn't going to wait for them. They asked me to stay and go around with them, to look after them. But I thought, "Why on earth should I? I'm going to see as much as possible while I can."

The first thing I saw was a tropical hut near some Hawaiian dancers so I went inside and took my seat on a wooden chair grouped in a circle. I began to wonder where the show was going to take part as we were all sat facing one another.

Parrots

The MC came out and started giving us an introduction to the show then the first 'artist' started to sing. We looked around and saw no one but then looked up in the roof and saw a spotlight on an artificial stuffed parrot, the roof had dozens of every conceivable type of coloured bird you could think of singing and dancing, some singularly, some in groups, once we'd gotten used to them, I quite enjoyed it. It was quite clever and well produced. The audience applauded the stuffed birds after each song. I just laughed to myself and shook my head in disbelief. Typical yanks, they'll applaud anything.

'It's a small world'

Another place I went to in the same area was 'It's a small world!' Here, you boarded a small boat and went into a cavern. Throughout, you rode through sections made out to look like different parts of the world and in each was a dozen or so dolls dressed in national costume and singing the songs one would always associate with that country, such as in England's section, *'God save the Queen, rule Britannia and land of hope and glory'*.

Submarines

There was a large lake full of 'pleasure craft', only these were different from what you would normally expect. They were small fully working submarines, several people went on board at a time, the submarine went around on the surface a couple of times, then without warning it suddenly submerged, or gave the impression of submerging. And looking out the port holes, you could see sea monsters, mermaids and such, quite an experience.

Inner space

There was a building nearby with the slogan 'Come inside for the experience of a lifetime' (I was already having that since arriving in the States.) 'and travel through inner space!'

So I, game for anything, went inside and the amusement was based on the film, *Fantastic Voyage*, in which you were made to feel that you, like the heroes of the film, had been shrunk to microscopic size and were travelling through the human body via the bloodstream. It was a marvellous thing to behold and very clever how they had done it.

Davy Crockett Land: paddling own canoe

Davy Crockett Land: For this experience, you paid your money/handed over your ticket and were nominated as part of a five-man crew and were expected to pull your weight by pulling on an oar, yes, you had to 'paddle your own canoe'.

Everybody on the staff was dressed up as Davy Crockett and we at one point had to chase an old-style riverboat (the girl allowed to steer it at that particular moment, unbeknownst to me, was a girl from the Fan Club, Jan Meer).

We went around a bend in the river and as we did, we heard what sounded very much like an Indian attack. We saw what was supposed to be a settlement in flames and the settlers all lying dead with arrows/spears in them. Further on, we came across the Indian lodges and the 'Braves' and squaws all doing a war dance, only they weren't real but very realistic robots, so realistic you had to take another look to make sure they weren't real and finally, as you have sailed past, they are attacked by the cavalry.

Swiss Family Robinson

We saw the tree house as used in the Disney film, *Swiss Family Robinson*; quite clever how they had rigged it out as a complete home.

Captain Hook's ship; Mickey Mouse

Then there was the ship that was built as a model for Captain Hook in the film, *Peter Pan*. I went on board as a matter of curiosity to see what they had done to it and discovered several tropical/marine fish aquariums. Also a bar selling drinks at which I participated. It was in this specific area that most of the Disney characters were to be found walking the streets – Donald Duck, Pluto and, of course, one can't go to Disneyland without running into the most famous character of them all, Mickey Mouse.

Adventure Land: The great white hunter'

Adventure Land: Not knowing quite what to expect here, I was intrigued to find out that I had entered another path to yet another boat. This one thankfully was a little larger and you didn't have to paddle it yourself; here, I met some of the lads from the Fan Club and quietly we went on board.

The guide was all dressed out in his best 'Great White Hunter' getup, he then surprised us all by trying to put on a posh British accent, which made him seem absolutely ridiculous. He thought he would be a typical British 'Soldier of fortune/hunter'. We set off down the river and it was set up to give you an idea of the adventure you would encounter in the jungle/on safari.

Rhinoceros; hyenas

We heard what sounded like wild animals and frightened humans and saw around the bend several natives trying to climb a tree being 'got at' by an angry rhinoceros with several hungry-looking hyenas licking their lips at the thought of 'dinner'. Again, robots.

African bull elephants; hippopotamus

When all was quiet for a while, we were suddenly surprised by several large African bull elephants charging at us from the river bank and into the water after us, stopping a matter of four or five feet from us. Three hippopotamuses suddenly surfaced and threatened to overturn the boat; all the time the guide was trying to be 'so British' about it all and casually fired blanks into all these expensive robots, not even pretending to take aim.

Poor British accent, 'old chap'

The adventure finished, my friends and I disembarked and I said to the guide, "Quite interesting, old chap, but I don't go much on your British accent, you need a lot more work on it! Cheerio, goodbye, old bean!"

I left him standing there, quite gob-smacked, for the first time with his mouth agog.

New Orleans

The last part I went to was built to represent various parts of the traditional part of the States. I visited the New Orleans section, which was built to represent Orleans as it had been about the time jazz had come into fashion, and of course there were plenty of jazz bands in the street.

I left Disneyland dazed, amazed and happy, and this was the effect they set out to create and it worked wonders.

American hamburger

It was at Disneyland that I tried my first American hamburger; what a surprise I was in for, though I should have guessed the Americans didn't do things by halves.

The burger itself was about three times the size of one in UK and not forgetting the garnish – lettuce, tomatoes, radish, cucumber, onions – in short, there was everything inside the hamburger you would find in a normal English summer salad. All for $1.50.

Universal Film Studios

The following day, I had the choice of going around the stars' homes in Hollywood or visiting the film studios; this appealed to me more. So that is what I chose, I caught a bus – one thing about American buses was that if one goes by full or you miss one, there is always another one just behind; in fact, you see it before the other was out of sight.

Glam tram

You paid your entrance fee and set off in a 'Glam tram', a gaudy decorated tram, with a guide to point out the sights on the way. First stop, we pulled up beside a lake for no apparent reason.

Torpedo

I looked out to the middle of the lake and there appeared to be a submarine coming to the surface and slowly towards us, about halfway to shore, a large ripple was seen coming fast towards shore.

I quickly realised that it was supposed to be a torpedo; nobody on the bus had seen what was happening so I chuckled to myself and waited for the fun to begin, a few seconds before it struck, a few others happened to see what was about to happen. There were several screams followed by some of us, including me, laughing as it struck and exploded.

This was to set the seal of the tour – full of surprises.

Along the road, we came across a permanently burning building used in the Alfred Hitchcock film, *Psycho*.

Land of the Giants

We stopped for coffee; I insisted on tea, we British have a reputation to keep up. The restaurant we used was next to the store area for some props used in films mostly from the then popular *Land of the Giants*. We tourists were allowed to handle the props. I had my photo taken holding aloft two giant boulders nearly as big as myself – made out of polystyrene and quite light.

We were shown around a storeroom where they kept the scale models they used to give the impression that they were real and full size, including a Mississippi riverboat, the aircraft from *Airport*, etc.

Tree washed away

We came to stop down a hill in a 'Mexican village' and were told to watch the main street and this particular tree. I heard a low rumbling noise getting louder and louder and then we saw that a log dam had given way and a torrent of water was rushing down the main street, it came at us and it looked as if we were about to be swept away but just in front of us, this tree was swept aside by the water and then righted itself; amazing really, c/w the sound of breaking roots/branches.

Then water then disappeared, some women on the 'Glam tram' screamed when the water had rushed towards us but laughed afterwards. Even the houses rebuilt themselves, it had all been an act for our benefit.

Gorilla
Further on, we stopped outside a large bungalow with a swimming pool where suddenly, a Gorilla swung down at us from the trees with a great roar; quite a shock! Yep, I was in Hollywood all right.

Dressing rooms of the stars
We saw the dressing rooms of the stars, the principle being the bigger the name, the bigger the dressing room and facilities.

This meant people on a production could get changed in anything from a luxury bungalow to going behind the bushes to change. We went inside the dressing room of Lucille Ball, very luxurious it was too.

Starsky and Hutch
We saw the props used in the film, Ben Hur, and also the set of the then popular *The Virginian*. We drove through the permanent town, 'Medicine Bow'. We also saw 2-3 TV series being filmed. One in particular that stuck in mind was a brand new one yet to be seen in UK called *Starsky and Hutch*!

Wild West train
We got out of the tram and watched an old Wild West train puff its way into the station from around the bend. I recognised the station from many Western films and TV series; they just added a bit here and there or removed parts depending on the effect wanted in a particular shot. The train then puffed its way out of the station the way it had come and as a matter of curiosity, I walked down the tracks and followed it.

Around the bend, I could see the train parked up along another and that was all there was of the track, it abruptly stopped there so the whole thing was only about 150 yards from start to finish, though when seeing it in the films, you would never have believed it as it would be authentically covered in 'trail dust' from its trip across the vast plains of the untamed west!

I enjoyed seeing how all the films were made and how, for example, most of the inside/close ups were done on a sound stage in a large hangar-type building. The set could be rigged up to be either the open plain or some luxury apartment.

Wagons
In the close-up of the wagon scene, you would only see the top half of the wagon, because there was only half a wagon, what you didn't see were the stage hands out of camera range effecting the movement of the wagon moving across the plains by rocking it backwards and forwards.

Further on the ride, we stopped and were told to look over at the hill in the distance and see if it looked familiar; it did, for in countless westerns, we had seen thousands of American Indians about to charge down on some poor unsuspecting homesteader or about to sweep down on the US cavalry or a wagon train.

On the other side of that hill, we were told, was the main interstate highway from L.A. to Las Vegas! We were taken to the top of that hill and shown the main road, all 8 lanes, 'one way' of it.

Indians

From that day on, a Western with Indians was never as exciting again, for I couldn't help thinking of what that girl had told us. Not forgetting that when the extras and Indians arrived first thing in the morning for filming, they all drove into the studios in their big open convertibles. Then got changed for their roles.

Buildings built small and incomplete

Most buildings had only three walls and half a roof, just enough to give the impression of a complete building. The doors of the building were so made according to the effect the studios wanted to give, such as the star was bigger (height-wise) than he really was, not forgetting surrounding the star with lots of small people. Overall, what an enjoyable day out, and educational also.

'Yobs' outside ask me for drugs

As I had just left the studio to catch the bus back to the hotel, I noticed a police patrol car go by and at the same time, a gang of four menacing-looking local yobs with the by-now familiar flick knives approached me. I immediately went on my guard trying to figure out who I would drop first in the event of any trouble.

One of them walked towards me and I was ready, though not ready for what he was to ask me. "Hey Mac, you got any grass (drugs) you can lend me (give)!" I quickly came back at him and quipped sarcastically, checking my pockets and laying on the accent good and thick, "I am very sorry, old Bean, I appear to have run out, sorry about that, old chap!"

The poor chap looked at me strangely and walked away muttering under his breath something about 'bloody silly limeys'.

Tijuana, Mexico

Another extra trip we could indulge in, which I did, was to Tijuana, Mexico; what a dump and a disappointment that place turned out to be. It was a waste of time and money…

Children begging

All we saw as we crossed the border was dirt, smells and squalor; there were enough people from the Fan Club to get two buses laid on for us. We crossed the border and walked a short distance away and almost immediately, we were set upon by about a dozen children begging, some of the girls almost straight away were going to give them some money as they felt sorry for them. I warned them not to; if they did, they would not get rid of them. A couple of girls did and I was proved right, though most of them held out as long as they could.

Once we had got to the main part of town, we split into three main groups but we stayed mostly together. At the head of each group, there were two or three men making the decisions where to go and the female populace were definitely a little nervous and not wanting to be left on their own.

Funny thing was that they were more scared at what may happen in Tijuana as opposed to Los Angeles. Yet they were probably at more risk in L.A.

A young West German chap and I assumed control of our group. As we turned each corner, we seemed to be looking down the same street we had just left, everywhere looked the same, nothing but hundreds of earthenware pots and only about three different designs.

These kids begging were hanging on in the hope of getting something; they were in for a long wait if they thought they would get anything from us. They were trying everything they could; crying, looking pitiful, dressed in rags, holding their hand out. The overwhelming thing I noticed was how well they looked remarkably fit and healthy, not starving at all.

With everywhere looking the same, it finished up that each time we came to a crossroads, we tossed a coin to see where we were to go. 'Heads we go left, tails we go right.'

A familiar name outside a shop

Eventually, we came across a newish building whose name looked somehow familiar, 'Woolworth's de Mexico'. I suggested that this would be the best place for souvenirs, not so much for price but for quality.

I had a hamburger and Coca Cola, so did most others. At first, we were trying to order various different things in English and the poor young girl couldn't understand what we were trying to say. So to prevent 'Spanish tummy', which we had been warned about, we settled on the hamburger and coke. I placed the order, which even this young girl would understand. "57 cokes, 14 hot dogs (that caused problems) and 43 hamburgers please!" The girl looked at me strangely as if they were all for me.

It was a bit difficult getting her to understand that we wished to pay for them separately. Those who didn't listen to us and had other foods got Spanish tummy (served them right) and they were ill for two days.

We went for another walk around and the kids swarmed around us again. The girls were really weakening now and I saw some give the kids some money. I tried to warn them again but they didn't listen, as they felt so sorry for the kids.

I shrugged my shoulders and said, "So be it but don't come crying to me when you can't get rid of the dozens of kids around you!" Within about another 30-50 yards, there were about 40 kids running in and out of our legs. I was right again, I have had experience of these things; the girls weren't very happy with me when I told them I wasn't interested. "Get rid of them yourself! But you did ask for it; you wouldn't listen!" Two kids tried it on me and the German and we told them to 'go away' in strong terms. We were the only ones who remained strong-willed and in the end, the girls were begging us to get rid of these kids.

The next stop was at an 'off licence'. I thought while in Mexico I have got to buy some tequila. The young girl in the shop allowed me to try some before buying; that was a good way to get a free drink.

I bought only one bottle and I later wished I'd bought more. Most people had bought the familiar Mexican hats and knitted over vest of the type that Clint Eastwood always wore in those spaghetti westerns. Then there was me with my one bottle of tequila.

Strong repugnant smell: mule s**t on the coaches

On the bus back to L.A., there was a terrible smell, like burning horse manure. Todd 'S' and Tony 'P' showed us what was responsible, they had bought some cigarettes by the name of 'mule sh*t'. I could not believe my eyes but it was true. It even had a picture of a mule's rear end with its tail in the air – passing the said 'mule sh*t'! It said on the packet, "The real thing, made with real genuine mule sh*t! Will clear a room in two minutes or less!" This was the proud boast on the packet. We had no doubt that the claim to 'clear a room in two minutes' was justified. Problem was we had to endure it for another three hours more on the trip back to Los Angeles. The lads thought this a great ruse as they saw everybody moving nearer and nearer the front of the bus to get away from the smell. Though after a while, I saw the funny side of it too. We were told that Todd Slaughter and Tony Prince had bought several packets to take back with them to UK to give away as presents to people they didn't like. What a dirty trick! Ha, ha, ha, they did eventually listen to us and we eventually persuaded them not to smoke anymore. My advice to anyone contemplating going to Tijuana, Mexico, is don't! Save your money; it's not worth it.

Pub crawl

The last but one evening in L.A., all the men agreed to go on a pub crawl together as there was something planned for the last night for the entire Fan Club.

It was arranged that we would all have dinner and later meet in the hotel bar where we would have a few drinks before we set out on the real drinking session. I was a little late getting down, about half an hour later than planned. I half expected they would have all disappeared by then, but no!

Bought drinks by ex US soldier who likes the British

It transpired that an ex-US army vet from World War II was buying everyone drinks and the lads were all in a happy mood by now. I sat next to him and got chatting away to him, I cheekily asked why was he buying us all drinks and not allowing us to buy him some in return. He explained that during the war, he had been in the US army and based in England – Liverpool to be exact.

Contrary to popular belief, the US army were not that well paid and couldn't afford to go out every night as much as they wanted to. He had been alone in a foreign land and feeling homesick. The British would invite him out for drinks and have dinner at their homes and generally try to make him feel at home. He had been shown that much hospitality and had never had a chance to repay it. Tonight was the first time he could repay the hospitality shown towards him and he flatly refused to let me buy him a drink and was buying everybody else's drink.

We tried to explain that we had all arranged to go out that evening but he wouldn't let us go till we were all drunk or at least merry. I happened to tell him that I was in the Forces, and he was the first to say that the American soldier was not as good as they were cracked up to be. But in his honest opinion, the ordinary British Squaddie was undoubtedly the best in the world! He had proved it. As history had proved umpteen times before.

We eventually made our excuses and left him to go on our pub crawl, he seemed upset at our leaving and wanted us to stop a bit longer but there was something far stronger calling us – beer and females! Irresistible combination.

Seven Seas again

We proceeded to our first port of call but that was where we stayed for the rest of the night. We went to the 'Seven Seas' Hawaiian club! This was rapidly turning out to be my favourite after-sundown haunt.

Picking up dancer – Dragged on stage

As expected, we all got drunk that night and I and one or two others got chatting up the girl dancers dressed in all their best finery as grass-skirt 'natives'. When talking to one of them and asking from where she hailed, "Honolulu sir!" I didn't believe her for a minute.

She looked and sounded like a local downtown L.A. girl to me. During the latter part of the evening, when we were all three sheets to the wind, there came a point where I was expected to be dragged on stage and give a demo as part of a competition to find the best 'Hawaiian' dancer in the audience. I was dragged on the stage by this girl I'd been chatting up. (The other girls also picked a couple of guys.) As it turned out, there were four men on stage, three British and one American, the American won. I was too drunk to dance and instead of doing Hawaiian, I did my own 'thing', which was not what was wanted.

I had everybody laughing at my efforts but was so far gone I was past caring. As I finished, I gave her a kiss – I was the only one to do so from us all. This was greeted by a loud cheer and rude remarks from the British in the audience.

When we left that night, I vaguely recalled seeing those same yobs on the street corner and it looked as though they were going to try something but when they saw there were about a dozen of us, albeit drunk, they thought better of it. That was the last I remembered of the evening due to this potent 'Hawaiian punch' I'd been drinking. What happened next I had to find out from the other lads next morning.

Passing out in hotel lift; put to bed

I had staggered into the hotel and had headed for the lift. Hoping to somehow get to bed, I had approached the lift and as I arrived at the lift, it had opened and out stepped Tony Prince, who upon seeing the state I was in burst out laughing and when he found out what floor my room was on he put me in the lift, pressed the appropriate button for my floor and sent me on my way.

At my floor, the lift doors opened and I was found by a Welsh couple on the floor of the lift in a heap, asleep. This chap whose name was John found my key in my pocket and carried me to my room whereupon he opened the door and put me on the bed, fully clothed, and left me there.

Looking and feeling rough

This was the position I found myself in next morning still dressed but needing a shave and shower. I went downstairs and had breakfast, still feeling drunk. I made my way to the lift and my room to get smartened up.

I felt and looked rough, unshaven, shirt and trousers crumpled and needing a press. I saw from a distance Todd and Tony talking to some newsmen c/w camera team; they were being interviewed and filmed.

I knew what they thought! And figured if they got the chance, they would try to get me on TV, knowing I was not ready so I decided there and then not to get involved and tried to sneak past without being seen but to no avail.

T.S. and T.P. get me on TV in my state

I had just turned to disappear and heard Tony Prince say to the interviewer, "Here, why don't you ask this chap about Elvis, he is a big fan!" I couldn't get away and was surrounded by the news team. "Excuse me sir!" said the interviewer. I was trapped. I couldn't get out of it and there were Tony and Todd laughing their heads off behind the camera at having got me cornered. I was mad with them and gave them a black look and said, "Wait till I get hold of you two!" They laughed all the more at that. 'Excuse me sir, what did you think of Elvis in Las Vegas?"

I was immediately carried away. "Great, bloody great, well worth every penny I've spent to get out here to see him and he is far better live than on record!" Once I started, the interviewer had a job to shut me up and get in on the conversation.

Before we left, I saw myself on TV and cringed when I saw and heard myself.

Farewell party

The last night in L.A., the F.C. held a farewell party for us all and it was funded, we were told, largely by the $1,000 donation given to the Fan Club by Elvis's manager on behalf of himself and Elvis.

There was a group hired and the hotel laid on the food.

After a little while, Tony Prince went around the room getting as many people as possible to partake in small competitions and the winners won some souvenirs obtained from Elvis by the F.C.

One such competition involved him as he went around the tables asking people to sing an Elvis song. And I knew, as sure as eggs were eggs, I would be collared, he made out he was about to walk past our table, I breathed a sigh of relief, then he turned back on his heels, shoved the microphone in my face and with a grin from ear to ear, he said, "Sing John, everyone else has!" I tried my very best to get out of it but to no avail as Tony had an answer ready for each excuse.

Finally, I said, "OK but I don't know any song well enough all the way through!" He said, "I don't believe you, as everyone here knows some Elvis songs all the way through – no more excuses!" Knowing I was beaten, I had to sing *Can't Help Falling in Love!* There was a big cheer for me when I had finished but I felt so embarrassed.

African American pianist playing in the cupboard

There was an African American employee in the hotel who agreed to play the piano for us on the condition that he did it behind closed doors in a broom cupboard and Tony had to pass the microphone through to him. Really funny, the whole F.C was trying their best not to laugh in case he was offended. He thought he was another Stevie Wonder. The waitresses sang together as a group and Tony Prince called them, tongue-in-cheek, 'the new Supremes'!

Jan

There was one lovely girl on this trip who I had spotted right from the beginning, I had noticed how feminine she was and quite fancied her but the trouble was, on this trip, you were spoilt for choice and you had to decide just in what order you were to chat up the different women.

I had meant to chat this one up for some time but had never got around to it. Once I saw that the festivities were about over at this party, most people wanted to leave to go elsewhere for their last night in USA.

Seven Seas yet again

I went over to this girl to chat her up and to my surprise and delight, she agreed to come out with me for the last night. Jan Wilson was her name and we went to 'Seven Seas'. She said she didn't want me to spend my money on her as it was unfair on me. So we agreed to go dutch, 50/50. She bought one of those special drinks and I did too but she was unable to finish it, so I had it as well as my own.

Taking Jan back to the hotel

At the end of the evening, I escorted Jan to the hotel; she was drunk and as soon as the fresh air hit her, she was a goner.

We were going to stay in my room for the night but Mike Barley was there and wouldn't leave. At the lift in the hotel, I offered to see her to her room but she said not (she didn't want me in her room as she must have, 1) heard what I was like with the other girls on the trip, or 2) she was just shy, or 3) could be she didn't trust me alone in her bedroom whilst she was drunk – I might take advantage of her! As if I would do such a thing!

I, however, insisted by reminding her we were in L.A. and it was quite possible to discover that someone had been in your room so I convinced her it was best all round for me to come with her and check out the room first, she agreed to this.

Getting carried away; interrupted by friend

I unlocked her room for her and went in and checked out the room, it was OK. She entered and I insisted on saying goodnight my way. She instantly responded and we got carried away, oblivious to all around us; after a little while, we heard knocking on her room door but we both ignored it, the knocking got louder and more intense and eventually, the door was opened by her roommate who walked in, not saying a word and proceeded to go to the bathroom to wash and undress for bed. Without a word, she got into her own bed and went to sleep.

We meanwhile were so far gone and carried away and completely ignored what her friend was doing. Although quite aware of it, we didn't want to be disturbed from the exertions we were presently engaged in.

When I look back now, I think how I could have had the nerve to do that, even me! I shall put it down to the Hawaiian punch we had that was so potent, the girl, the time – altogether having a magical effect on us both.

Having a go at Mike Barley

After we had made ourselves respectable, I went back to my room, whereupon I gave Mike Barley a piece of my mind, reminding him of our agreement and that he had let me down each time. And the ruddy cheeky bar-steward had the audacity to say, "What agreement?" I felt like dropping him there and then though I didn't.

The following morning I got out of bed just in time to catch the Fan

Club bus to the international airport at Los Angeles. The convoy of buses left our hotel on the first leg of our return trip back to UK and not a single person spoke on the entire ride to the airport. Everyone was so sad to be leaving the States and going back home. What a wonderful two-week holiday that had been; I bet few people have had such a good, enjoyable holiday of a lifetime!

Collecting names and addresses

Before we all said goodbye, I just had to get the name and address of Jan. I realised then I couldn't bear to let her walk out of my life and not see her again, so I made sure I got it. I felt that she was special, we had something going. I got the names and addresses of other girls too, though this was on a business basis. I had promised to sell them any photos of Elvis that came out.

I arranged to meet Jan again back in UK and did several times. It was a very sad and down-in-the-dumps fan club that got off the plane at Gatwick and all went our ways home at the end of a fantastic unbelievable holiday.

37 Squadron R.A.F. Regiment (continued)

SWO

Not long after my return to the Sqn from the holiday in USA, the S.W.O. arranged for me to do a bit of wine waiting at the C.O.'s house one evening when he was having guests in. The S.W.O. said, "Lad, I am not letting you do it for less than £5, if the C.O. offers you less, tell me and I'll sort him out!" I then marched into his office for the briefing and was offered only £3 for the night. I told the S.W.O., he stormed into the C.O.'s office and came out smiling. "You've now got a minimum of £5 for the night, lad!"

C.O. tells his guests about who I saw on holiday

All the C.O.'s female guests were coming up to me and saying, "Is it true you have just seen Elvis live in Las Vegas? Is he good? What was he like?" The C.O. had proudly been telling all his guests about my holiday.

Going out with six girls, giving excuses

Things started to get back to normal for me soon after the USA trip. I used to like keeping several girls going at the same time. Once, and for a while, I had managed to do something I had always wanted to do and that was to have three or more girls on the go at once; it was great fun while it lasted – but expensive. But I was not successful with all of them.

It was inevitable, as my mother once said, "You will be found out one day!" "True," I told her, "but I'll enjoy it while I can!"

Girl 1 was Jan Wilson. I liked her best of all, and after meeting her in USA, still kept in touch with her and went to her place or she came to mine quite often, though not every weekend.

Girl 2 was Karen from my hometown, she had a round, curvy figure, she seemed quite the girl-next-door type but sexy. After de-mob, I was later to work with her brother, a little disconcerting to say the least! I was always a little bothered about how much he knew of our antics.

Girl 3 was Natalie, a school teacher, and she had the opposite figure to Karen; she was slim, too slim really, but she had one thing going for her, she was well off financially. She also had a car. I didn't have one at the time. And she used to run me anywhere I wanted to go in her car. She proved very convenient. I'd jump in her car, have a few drinks and off we'd go.

Girl 4: Though I forget her name, she was a Catholic and lived only a matter of 100 yards from girl 2. This girl was no virgin! She didn't need any effort from me to get her interested.

Girls 5 and 6: We were not much more than pen pals and I saw them only occasionally.

My usual procedure was to go out with, say Karen one weekend and say, "Sorry can't see you next week, I'm on guard duty, then on exercise, I'll give you a ring a day or two before I come home!" That weekend, I would go out with the other girl. This worked on most of them, but occasionally, I would change my excuse. "Sorry, I haven't been able to see you for a week or two as planned but as you know, I'm on standby at 12 hours' notice (not quite true) and we have to fly out to put down a riot/civil disobedience somewhere in one of our colonies. I'm sorry I can't tell you where it is as it is supposed to be hush-hush!" The daft thing was – they all fell for this line.

No 4 was useful in that through her, I was introduced to another girl – her friend.

Girl 7: One of the most beautiful, sexiest girls I had met, with an hour-glass figure, a perfect specimen of womanhood. Her name was Samantha and she lived in a small village near where I lived, Broughton, and to give you an idea what she was like, she had long natural golden-blonde hair and her job was a physical training instructor at a physical training college. And I didn't half fancy her, but I was pally with about 4 girls who were the best of friends and we would to go out together as a gang.

Dilemma! How do I make a play for Samantha without the others knowing? If she turned me down and told the others, I'd finish up with none of them. What a quandary to be in. But nevertheless, I was willing to risk it and did indeed make a play for Samantha and we started going out without letting on to the others.

I was going out one Friday night with No 4 and she suddenly said to me, "You're going out with another girl, aren't you?" I was caught unawares by this so automatically switched on 'defence' mode.

"Me, I wouldn't do such a thing!" I replied. "You're the only one!"

"No, I'm not! Don't deny it; you were seen out with another girl!"

"OK, OK, she was my cousin."

"Try again!"

"My sister?" Half-heartedly.

"You DON'T HAVE a sister!" she said tersely.

"Oh, all right, you're right! There are others!"

Her reply was totally unexpected and completely floored me. "Don't get me wrong, I don't mind, it's just that I don't like being led along!" I was shocked; I couldn't believe what I was hearing, I'd finally been found out, just as my mother had said I would be. So I carried on seeing both girls! Including Samantha who was incidentally part of the same band of friends and best pals. Had Samantha confessed to girl 4 that I was seeing her as well? Probably, what a girl, what a time I had!

Asking for ex posting

After about 2½-3 years at Catterick, I felt I'd had enough and wanted a posting away to another camp, so I kept my eyes on the notice board and my ears open.

Now, in the R.A.F. at that time, if an airman of equal rank/marital status and education qualifications wished to have an exchange posting with each other, they could do so. For example, someone from Scotland posted down south could exchange with some Englishman already based at one of the Scottish bases.

One day, I heard rumours going around the Sqn that one of the corporals had been posted to a helicopter Sqn, but didn't want to go. I approached him and asked him right out, "Is it right that you are posted and don't want to go?" He told me it was true. I asked him why. (None of my business really.) "Well, my wife has nicely settled in and more importantly, the kids are settled in school and I don't want to move them anymore if I can help it!"

I came to an instant decision and half-jokingly said, "I will do an exchange posting with you if you like so that you can stay here and I'll go in your place!" He was pleased at my offer and we went into the orderly room to see the S.W.O and started the ball rolling. I had never expected my application to get anywhere being a different rank and no qualifying points, i.e., married/kids.

I had forgotten clean about it as I had never thought I would hear anymore. He, like me, thought with him being a married man and a higher rank, nothing would come of it.

Tug makes my mind up for me

On the Friday about 3-4 days later, I was called aside by Tug Wilson and he said to me, "Rowbottom, as of five weeks hence, you are now posted to 33 Sqn at R.A.F. Odiham down south!" I had mixed emotions. I didn't know whether to be pleased or not as I had never expected the request to come through. I replied, "I haven't said that I wanted a posting for definite, only made enquiries!"

He snapped back, "You either want the posting or you don't, make up your fecking mind – and now!"

So I thought, "Stuff you and your dammed arrogant attitude, bollocks to you! I will have the posting and I'll be well rid of you and your kind!"

Decision I never regretted

It was to be the most important decision I had yet taken since I decided to join up in the first place and one that was to change my whole life forever.

It was to be at R.A.F. Odiham that I was to have the happiest times in my entire R.A.F. service and most importantly, meet someone who was to change me from this 'girl chasing, beer swilling, devil may care person' I had become.

R.A.F. Odiham: 1972 to 1974

Taken while at Odiham, 1973

33 Squadron

From the time I said I would leave 37 Sqn for Odiham, I had been a bit worried if I had done the right thing or not. I needn't have worried as it turned out to be the best posting that I'd ever had whilst in the R.A.F., for not only was the station run with a family atmosphere and easy-going, it was here that I was destined to meet my 'soulmate'.

Easy-going camp

The first notable memory I had of Odiham was how easy-going and friendly everybody was, there was no one running after you telling you to get your hair cut, boots bulled or any silly military things like that.

It was run as the R.A.F. and the rest of the services should be run – discipline with a relaxed atmosphere. Things were done just as efficiently, if not more so, and most people would put that little bit more effort in and seemed happy and relaxed.

Cpl's wife makes newcomers 'welcome'

Once I joined 33 'Puma' helicopter Sqn, I asked around what the entertainment was like and what the local women were like as I always did and what were the chances of a bit of 'nookie' from the local girls.

I was told that if I definitely wanted my leg over, there was a Cpl on A.M.Q.'s whose wife would oblige me. She liked to 'welcome newcomers' to camp – and anyone else for that matter. This was with the full blessing of the husband, money was not turned down if offered, but you did not have to lay money out if you didn't want to. I couldn't believe it (it was true). I had seen this said Cpl around camp before and remembered thinking that he looked a bit of a weird one and this was before I was told about his wife.

I never bothered indulging. I wasn't THAT desperate! Inevitably, about 2-3 years later at my next posting, I read in the Sunday papers that he had been caught. That meant he'd been at it for at least 4-5 years before being found out.

There had also been caught at the time four airmen of different ranks at the house from L.A.C. up to chief technician and a senior NCO. They too were done along with the Cpl.

The Cpl was court-martialled and thrown out, after serving 5-6 years military prison on the charges, bringing the R.A.F. name into disrepute – living off immoral earnings – activities encouraging his wife into prostitution and about 2-3 other charges as well.

This was, of course, what the R.A.F. did to him, thing was as soon as he came out of the 'glass house', the civvy police would be waiting for him and would charge him with much the same charges, where he would probably serve time in the civvy nick as well.

I should think once he'd gotten back to civvy street, he would carry on where he had left off because he would not get a job after being dishonourably discharged, but even if his wife remained faithful, they wouldn't make very much money as she would be about 10 years older and less attractive.

Hearing about the famous Odiham discos and the girls that dwelled within

The next thing that I noticed about this camp was the great Thursday night dances that were held in the Naafi. These dances were frequented mainly by drunken airmen, as per norm, a few of the families from M.Q.s and mainly by nurses from the three large hospitals in the vicinity; mostly they (the girls) came from the very large hospital complex at Basingstoke.

They even laid buses on to bring the girls to/from the dances. These girls came from all over the world – all corners of the British Isles, Jamaica, Barbados, Africa, India, Malay Chinese, but mostly from the Philippines.

Meeting Viola for the first time

It was at the second/third dance I'd been to that I saw...met a gorgeous, attractive girl that I really fancied, so much so that I then decided for the first time ever to break my one golden rule, 'not to try to take anybody's girl off them or fight over a girl.'

Going out with Daisy Misonia, my first Filipino

I fancied that girl. Viola was her name. I saw Viola about 3-4 times then she didn't come any more. I did wonder that had happened to her. Meanwhile, I'd gotten off with another Filipino by the name of Daisy Misonia.

She was a bit peculiar as I wasn't allowed to even hold her hand or kiss her, let alone be allowed to do my 'thing' with her. "Don't touch me, I don't like it, I'm not that sort of girl!" The Philippinos were all a bit reserved and uncomfortable about touching and public shows of affection. But once you got to know them, they all almost seemed to be 'all for it', some more than others. Typical of nurses in my experience.

So after a little while, I dropped this Daisy Misonia. And she didn't know why. This was eventually blamed on Viola. 'For taking my man away' and she harboured a grudge. If she felt that way, why wasn't she more responsive? She didn't have to drop her knickers if she didn't want, only be a bit more responsive and friendly.

I intended to have Viola for myself. Even if it meant that once I had her, I might get bored with her and dump her like I had done with so many others before.

Thing was she was going out with a fitter I knew on 72 Sqn (Wessex helicopters). I wasn't going to let a small thing like that worry me though. It was her personality that struck me at first, and then her looks! She seemed so nice and genuine, sincere. I got chatting to her and this chap, Des, her boyfriend; though to be truthful, I was more interested in drinking at the time.

It was years later that I found out that Viola hadn't liked me at first, though I liked her. I must have grown on her, as she certainly grew on me.

The infamous 'Pigs bar'; Dobby Donald

There was a sort of 'public bar' in the Naafi that had the minimum of décor and wooden furniture where the drunkards and alcoholics hung out, known usually by its nickname quite appropriately – 'The Pigs bar'. It was frequented mainly by drunken alcoholic rock-apes such as 'Dobby' Donald and his pals. Very few rock-apes (or non-rock-apes) had either courage or dare to enter this hallowed drinking den.

The 'Pigs' looked down on you even if you were a fellow rock if you didn't drink with them, especially on a dance night. You were expected as always to be 'one of the lads' and not be into this 'Nancy-poncy' game of dancing and chatting up the girls. They didn't seem to have many friends, only rock-apes. I thought it worthwhile risking their displeasure to do my own thing.

Regiment tough nuts

Being R.A.F. Regiment, we still had a reputation, on most R.A.F. camps such as Odiham, of being tough nuts, psychos, animals and not to be trifled or messed with. We were generally disliked by the tradesmen and we used to dislike them. They called us 'rock-apes' and we generally called them 'shineys' – clerks. Snowdrops were R.A.F. police and the main nickname was Penguins or 'guins'.

On other camps, the Regiment men usually spent their off-duty hours beating up the others if we were bored or they as much as looked at us the wrong way. Heaven help them if they had done the dirty on a 'rock'; the poor penguin then had the whole Sqn/Regiment personnel on camp to deal with.

Fortunately, Odiham made us mellow and easy-going and it was even known for a 'rock' to get quite pally with the opposition, such was the effect Odiham had on us all. But we weren't liked because the non-alcoholic Regiment personnel were very well known for taking the 'guins' and other rock-apes girls off them or telling the girl made up stories to try and get her to finish with him, just for a laugh! As what had happened to me with this farmer's daughter when on 37 Sqn, as you will recall.

Telling chap to finish with Viola

So to keep up the reputation of the Regiment – and for my own needs – I approached Des one day in the barrack block early one evening and said to him, "Des, are you thinking of packing up with Viola in the very near future? I hope so because I want her, and what I want – I get! Even if we have to fight over her!" (I still didn't want to fight over a girl, but this one I was quite prepared to make an exception for.) "I will win anyway, so you'd better pack her in – NOW!"

He replied, "You'll have to join the queue as there are my three mates who fancy her as well!"

I said, "No way, I'm not joining any queue, I want her and I get what I want!" A week or two later, he did finish with her, unbeknownst to me. Surprise surprise!

The first ever Sqn exercise I went on was a pleasant surprise. Some of the regiment chaps took the Sqn vehicles whilst I flew in the John Strong, the Sqn C.O.'s helicopter, to the exercise site. Upon landing, I and the regiment personnel patrolled the site singly and in pairs to check it was all clear.

Upon my return, I saw a sight to behold, a sight I never thought I would see with the R.A.F. Regiment on exercise: the officers air/ground crew putting up their own tents! I got talking to the C.O. and approached him (trust me), "Sir, is this normal for the officers to put up their own tents?"

The C.O. said, "Yes, you see, there won't always be R/Regt personnel available to put up the officers' tents up for them, especially if in a wartime environment and if the aircraft comes down behind enemy lines so they have to learn how to do it themselves!"

I explained that it just wasn't heard of in a Regiment Sqn, not that I was complaining, and I told him how we had to do everything for officers on a Regiment Sqn, like putting their tents before ours, erecting their toilets, etc.

He agreed that it was very wrong to expect the men to do this, especially before getting their own tents up! What a gentleman.

C.O.: "Besides, as far as I am concerned, the Regiment has far more important jobs to do and that is to clear and defend the site/aircraft, after all, that is their job and that's what they're paid to do!"

Once most of the erecting and unloading had been done, the C.O. gave instructions to the officer i/c ground crew, including engineering person-nel, the engineering officer to get hold of SNCO (chief technician) to come and see me, as I was in charge of the ground defence of the site. I had as a backup one young L.A.C. Regiment lad. I told the SNCO what had to be done and where I wanted people stationed during 'stand to'. They then relayed my instructions to the mechanics who knew nothing about ground defence! (The Regiment Sgt and Cpls were on the other site with the other half of the Sqn and were to act as an enemy.)

My position at 'stand to' was with a lad who had been allocated the G.P.M.G. gun. He hadn't a clue! Not only hadn't he been trained on one before (only the Regiment was trained on that weapon) but he hadn't even seen one before.

He was panicking, dreading any attack that may come; it was inevitable that there was to be an attack. I had been told there would be! He didn't know what to do first. When the attack came, I must have given an air of confident calm, I remained cool 'under fire'. The enemy had blanks and thunder flashes; we had none. So 'cool hand' me had a cigarette in my mouth, tapping the gun with a stick and saying, "Bang-bang-bang-bang!" (A long drag of my cigarette) "Bang-bang-bang-bang!" In rapid succession interspersed with a bored sigh or two! I think the lad was impressed at the cool rock-ape.

Meanwhile, as the blanks and thunder flashes were going off all over the site, he was panicking more than ever. I was trying to reassure him with things like, "Fecking sprog, damned idiot! Get a fecking grip," and one or two other fruity sayings.

When some of the aircrew were stood down for a few hours during the day, they took to the nearest hills and were flying radio-controlled model aircraft.

Even during off-duty hours, they were still thinking about flying. I got in some sunbathing. Most evenings were spent in a nearby country pub, which we all enjoyed. We would go for a couple of hours and then return to camp and others would go. With this young lad and I being the only regiment representatives, there we got collared with guard duty for the aircraft, trust us to get this duty!

I thought it unfair to pick on the two of us plus one technician to look after three aircraft. I will never forget how I came to find out how it was done on 33 Sqn. I had been spotted by one of the SNCOs walking around the aircraft with my weapon at the ready; I was approached and asked, "What the feck are you doing?"

"I am on guard, of course!"

"Don't be fecking daft, lad, we don't do things like that here on this Sqn, you're not with the Regiment now! You're on flying Sqn. Things are run a bit different here. When you're on guard on this Sqn in the field, you get your sleeping bag out, put it on the aircraft and get your head down, and you don't walk around all night!"

What an unexpected surprise and pleasure that was. This was what you call organisation. I was in for another pleasant surprise; I was told I could lay in till about half an hour before the aircraft needed to be 'scrambled', which would be about 08:30 hrs.

As soon as the aircraft fitters started work in the morning, they saw I was asleep and tried not to wake me until about 10 minutes before take-off; this was about 10:30 by then.

Another surprise. I had been given the day off to recover from the 'hard night on guard'. (Some of those Regiment SNCOs on my old regiment Sqn would have had a seizure if they could see just how soft the rock-ape's life had become!

This was the day I spent sunbathing!

The first night though I didn't get much sleep as I was cold and shivering. I didn't realise that once the aviation fuel in the tanks cooled down, it got very cold and I was forever waking up and shivering; the next and subsequent nights, I made sure that from there on in, I put under my camp bed a spare camouflage net, which gave a 'cushion' of about two feet thick on which I put my bed, then sleeping bag. It did the trick.

The first Saturday on site, we were allowed out to the local town for a night on the ale. I changed into my second clean combat kit and had a good wash down.

I tried several pubs and was quite bored. I found myself finishing up at the local branch of the British Legion. Normally, members only but upon production of my ID card (as were the rules), I was allowed in. There happened to be a dance on that night, all dressed up to the nines in evening gowns, bowties, the lot.

As soon as I walked in, some of the old ex-servicemen and their wives approached me and all wanted to buy me a drink and ask about the service life now as opposed to when they were in, and they were making a big fuss of me.

After a few minutes, the manager approached me and wanted to know what I was doing, especially in combat kit.

"Didn't you know there was a social 'do' going on? And it's evening wear only!"

The manager then said, "You are causing a disturbance and you are offending these people" The ones who were buying me drinks and making a fuss over me! "So when you've finished your beer, please leave!"

The members around me talking to me went barmy at this! As they said, this was an organisation for looking after past 'and present' members of H.M. Forces. Some members told me in front of the manager, "Stay where you are, you're not leaving. You're welcome to stay as long as you like! The manager has not the right to throw you out, as you are behaving yourself!" They were going mad with the manager and a blazing row had now erupted between the members and this 'little man'. Everyone in the room was now watching as more and more ex-servicemen and their wives came to join in the argument! As things unfolded, these people whom he said I was offending were the ones making a big fuss of me and standing up for me against this bum of a manager. I told them it was all right, I would leave as I didn't want to cause trouble.

The manager was told in no uncertain terms that he was not only going to be reported to the Committee but a lot of the members were going to resign over this and membership would suffer. I finished my drink and reluctantly left.

In all the ex-service clubs I'd been to, I had never been made to feel more welcome – or not! Than I was that night.

Though when I considered joining the Legion since that episode, I always remembered that stuck-up twit. I lost all inclination and interest in joining the British Legion from that day. It was not every day that a serving serviceman got thrown out of the British Legion club, in uniform. I must be one of the very few that it has happened to! I still wonder today what happened to this manager – was he kicked out? Forced to resign? Not a claim to be proud of.

Land Rover and H.G.V. course at St Athan

Not long after getting to Odiham, my name was put forward for an H.G.V III driving course. It was to be held at R.A.F. St Athan (east camp) in South Wales.

When I arrived ready for the course to start, I was told I would have to learn to drive Land Rovers first. I was very annoyed as I informed them that not only did I drive Land Rovers for the R.A.F. every day at Odiham, I have had a full driving (civilian) licence for about four years. They said they weren't interested, as far as they were concerned, they had no record of me ever taking my driving test there, so officially I couldn't drive! You can well imagine how mad I was at this. (You will note this was the opposite way of the Army R.C.T. Houndstone camp.) Had the army done this, I would have probably stayed in the army and my life would have taken a different path.

Crazy instructor

Unfortunately, I knew I couldn't win so I resigned myself to the fact that I was going to have to learn to drive in a Land Rover all over again. I was assigned to a Cpl driving instructor; I was quite pleased to see him, though not for long.

He was a nutcase! When I made a mistake, he screamed and shouted on the top of his voice at me, then of course I made more mistakes, the more he screamed. He said I couldn't drive and how on earth I'd ever passed my test.

Another thing I didn't like about him, which was more important, was when driving down the high street, if an old woman or child or anybody for that matter was crossing the road, I would automatically slow down and be prepared to stop. In his eyes this was wrong, I would get my knuckles rapped for this, he used to scream, "Go on, go on! What the f**k are you slowing down for? Put your foot down; she'll/they will get out of the way and if they don't, f*****g tough!" Time and time again, he would say this and it frightened the hell out of me; he wasn't teaching me to drive, he was teaching me how to kill with a new weapon.

This was his driving attitude; it was a wonder any of his pupils ever passed their test and more amazing still were the very low casualties (pedestrians) on his route. Eventually, I had enough of him and told him to shut his mouth or else I would shut it for him. As far as I was concerned, I was a good driver and had proved it on each R.A.F. camp where you had to have a test before being allowed to drive that station's vehicles. I had been complimented at Odiham by the SNCO i/c M.T. and the station's driving instructor so that was good enough for me. This stupid Cpl kept threatening to have me put in for a pre-test test. "If you fail, you would not be allowed to go on for your H.G.V. III course but R.T.U.'d in disgrace and embarrassment!" So he said.

Bringing in the chief driving instructor

Eventually, I had had enough of his mouthing, so I called his bluff and told him to do it and shut up! He did. Come the morning of the test with the chief driver training instructor. I was aware what the consequences were but was confident I would come out of it all right.

So when we set off with the chief driving Instructor in the front and the Cpl instructor in the back, I wasn't at all nervous, I was confident. I had the attitude of, "Just watch me, you raving nutter, I'll show you up!"

Upon the return to camp, the CDTI stopped me and said, "Well, I just can't see what the problem is, you can drive and drive pretty well, in fact it was a perfect drive, no major or minor mistakes. If you drove like that on a test, you would pass with flying colours. As a matter of fact, I'll put you down for a test the day after tomorrow, if that is OK with you?" (It certainly was.) "Cpl. Why on earth have you bothered to bring this to my attention and waste my time? I have more important things to deal with, and I'll see you in my office immediately!"

He got an almighty rollicking for that and was removed as my instructor. I passed the test as expected though I never before or since have driven as well as I did for the CDTI that day.

The following day, I started my so long awaited H.G.V. III course. For the rest of my stay, I noticed the Cpl instructor would be glaring daggers at me when he thought I wasn't looking. I allowed myself a smile and a chuckle, I could afford to. When our paths crossed again, he would be rather aggressive in his tone of voice to me so being the sort of person I am, I would give him back as good as he gave me.

He was the sort of person that whenever he walked into the bank to do business, the alarms and bells would go off and he once told me they did!

Nice H.G.V instructor

The H.G.V instructor on the other hand was a nice chap, again a Cpl but a different kettle of fish to the other barmy instructor of mine.

I was unable to pass my H.G.V test. I was suffering far too much with nerves and they let me down, maybe also this nutter I had before was playing in the back of my brain. Though thankfully, the instructor thought me good enough to be put in for my test. This time there was a shortage of vehicles in relation to the amount of people wanting to drive, although it was the main R.A.F. driving school.

We also had with us army lads from various regiments, sailors, Royal Marine commandos. I got the impression that rightly, or wrongly, the army R.C.T must only train their own people.

'Hoss'

My co-driver was nicknamed Hoss after a well-known character on the old TV show, *Bonanza*. He had the same sort of build – tall and stocky. He too was R/Regiment. And when he got behind the steering wheel, was mad as a ruddy Hatter. He must have had the nutter Cpl instructor I previously had.

Years later on reflection, he would have made a good Filipino driver. (Brake, what brake? I only know the accelerator!) When it was his turn to drive, he got behind the wheel of that big four-tonner and to him it was a weapon and the name of the game was to knock down as many civilians as he could. He didn't like civvies, so much so when driving down the high street, he would go looking for old ladies or invalids, then aim the four-tonner straight for them. When the instructor told him off, his reply was, "If they don't get out of the way, fecking tough! Foot down hard!" Where had I heard that before? The instructor was slowly going round the twist, he got so fed up of telling off Hoss that he gave up and would look at me in desperation as if to say 'God help us'!

He just prayed that the old people with their sticks and Zimmer frames were still agile enough to get out of the way in time; fortunately, they did. Being as reckless as he was, it was inevitable that he would cause damage to somebody's vehicle and ours. Once, he damaged someone's car door, another time he caught the canopy of the wagon on a low bridge; actually, I was guilty of this also. Though I only tore the tarpaulin; he bent the frame.

Jocks dressing up in the Naafi

The evenings were livened up by the 'Jocks' who were with us and used to go to the Naafi and the discos dressed up as women, poofs, etc.

Unfortunately, the local female populace didn't like us or give us a chance, they didn't trust us – why ever not? They must have thought us all a bit crazy, even though the rest of us dressed and acted normally and didn't try to put an act on.

We were all branded weirdos yet it was the local populace who seemed to be a bit weird. Though I must say that not all the girls were 'prim and proper' little virgins!

Unbelievable sight outside the Naafi

One evening, I had been to a local pub for a pint or two and thought I would came back early and catch the last couple of hours of the disco at the Naafi. I turned the corner and my headlights picked out the front of the Naafi. The lights also picked out something else. My headlights had focussed on an unbelievable sight! There on the grass, in front of the Naafi, was a local girl, naked from the waist down and she was being given a good 'seeing to' by one of the servicemen there on a driving course. There she was, half-naked and her partner on top, his bare bum going 20 to the dozen. They were completely oblivious to all that was going on around them; they were enjoying themselves too much for that.

This was in front of the glare of very bright sodium light. I just didn't know how they had the nerve. Once people had seen what was going on, they walked past and paid them no heed as if it were quite normal and an everyday occurrence.

Once past them, you still saw their dancing shadows lit up by the sodium lights on the walls of the Naafi; it was an act that deserved a medal, above and beyond the call of duty.

No brakes

I had gone to St Athan in my car with no brakes! A garage near the camp at Odiham was supposed to have fixed them but after about three or four days, they were just as bad. How I never had an accident on the way down there, I'll never know, even more so when you consider that for 90% of the way, I was travelling on motorways – the M3 and M4.

I drove nearly 200+ miles on my gear box alone at an average speed of 60+ mph. As it turned out, it was to be very good practice for me as in the R.A.F. method of H.G.V. training, you were not allowed to use the brakes except in an emergency. One weekend, I drove all the way to Basingstoke and back with no brakes in an emergency.

Substandard mess

On St Athan east camp where we were training, the food and mess were disgraceful, hygiene was non-existent. There were birds flying about in the food hall, leaving their droppings on the floor and table, no attempt was made to clean the tables. Rat droppings on floor and table, remnants of food from the previous meals still there and on the floor, civvy cooks with long hair (which constantly fell into the food) and no hair nets. Wiping their noses on their already dirty cook's whites, of approximately 250 cups available (I took time to count them once), only about three or four were clean and not broken or chipped, all the cutlery was dirty and had not been washed from one meal to the next and still greasy.

We used to dread mealtimes. Never before or since has this happened. Everybody was complaining! As I said to my fellow regiment lads on our table (all units/regiments/trades would sit together), "If I ever get the chance, I shall complain bitterly!" They all said they would too, though I never believed them for a minute as through experience, I found most of these sort of guys were all talk. I was later to be proved right several times.

One lunch-time, we saw several high-ranking officers walking around and asking the men in the dining room if they had any complaints They had been around most sections of the hall but had not approached the R/Regt table. I think the Regiment was branded as trouble-makers, as we usually were by the other trades and officers, and so best avoided. Some of the lads kept muttering under their breaths that if they were to be asked, they would 'tell it like it is'. I allowed myself a wry smile, then the officers came around to our table and a high-ranking air officer – an A.O.C! – along with the catering officer asked if everything was all right. Of course, the big mouths said, "Yes Sir, everything's OK!" I gave them such a glare and a lot of stick after the officer had gone, calling them all hypocrites, cowards, all talk and such.

Approaching the A.O.C.

One lad said, "If you feel that strongly, why don't you say something!" I made some excuses then took another mouthful of that horrible food. It was so awful I thought, "That's it, enough!" A guy had even hurt his tooth trying to bite into a pea, producing blood. I had had enough. I literally threw down my cutlery in utter disgust, much to the annoyance of the others on the table, I quietly got up and started to walk towards the group of officers; one of the lads asked where was I going. I told him, "I have had enough and if you are too frightened to speak up, I'm not!"

As I approached the officers, a sudden very noticeable silence fell over the mess. As I was walking towards them, I thought, "Blow it. I'll not see the catering officer; he'll only make some feeble excuse to get rid of me. No, if anything is to be done, I'll have to see the senior rank, the A.O.C." (Air Vice Marshall).

You could feel the fear in the air – someone was actually going to complain! I approached the A.O.C. and he saw me approaching and smiled. I smiled back. "Yes son, is there anything the matter? Do you have a complaint to make?"

"Yes sir, that's putting it mildly! I do have one or two things to say." The catering officer then tried to pull me aside, saying to the A.O.C., "Leave this to me, sir, I'll deal with it!" Facing me, he said through gritted teeth, "You are not to bother the A.O.C! Go and sit down!"

I said, firmly shaking his hand from my arm, "Sir, if you don't mind, the A.O.C. would like to know what I've got to say! And I would like to tell him!" The silence in the mess was deafening, you could cut it with a knife, I could actually feel the fear from those watching and those too frightened to watch. The A.O.C. then interrupted and said to the catering officer, "Yes, let this chap speak, if he has got something he wants to say then let him say it! Now what's your problem, Son?" I cast a sideways glance at the catering officer; he was glaring at me with clenched teeth as if to say, 'Don't you dare say anything to the A.O.C. about my mess! Don't you dare complain.'

And with that, I began my story:

"Sir, I feel so strongly about the disgusting, unhygienic state of the mess that I can keep quiet no longer, some of the other lads were going to raise this matter to you but chickened out so it's up to me." I cast a glance towards my table and the guys were so embarrassed they looked really uneasy in their chairs; I had put them on the spot. It was so quiet you could hear a pin drop and there were about 200+ people in the mess at the time.

"One of them has just hurt his teeth trying to eat a pea, another has cut his gums and the blood has flowed, the chips (French fries) are like pieces of wood, inedible, but I shall tell you in more detail just what is wrong and what needs to be done to improve things here, Sir!" I then told him all the things aforementioned. The birds, rats, dirty/chipped crockery, dirty cutlery, cooks' hair in the 'food', dirty tables/floor, and so on.

I must admit that once I got started, I got carried away while telling him of my complaints. Throughout, the catering officer tried to make feeble excuses but was completely ignored by the A.O.C. and me. Afterwards, the A.O.C. looked very worried and said to me, "Nothing could be done about the birds, mice, rats and cockroaches!"

Not only didn't I believe him, I told him, "Let the Regiment in, Sir, I can guarantee that we'll get rid of them, what we can't shoot, we'll gas with the gas canisters at our disposal!" Talk about overkill.

"If all you say is true, then I shall get something done about it!" I thanked him for his attention and care.

As I turned away to go back to the table, the catering officer was still trying to excuse the state of the mess. The A.O.C. wasn't very happy with him, firstly went to check the cutlery/crockery and went straight back into the kitchens and started to go through it like a typhoon. We could hear from our table the cooks getting it in the neck for their dirty turnout and long hair. As I approached my table, I was cheered by everyone in the mess for what I had done; it was a nice feeling. But they thought it was on their behalf. It wasn't, it was for me and me alone! The lads on my table cheered and congratulated me, patting me on the back, and I turned on them and told them, "Go away, hypocrites." Actually, the language was much stronger than that! Why didn't they go themselves, they were all talk – chicken.

A week later, the mess had closed down to be fumigated, de-animalised, de-loused, redecorated and reorganised. We ate in the WRAF's mess, a world of difference between the two; upon the return to our mess, we were pleasantly surprised to see the difference and the overall drastic improvement. But there was still a lot to be done. Even the civvy cooks had been made to tidy themselves up, fresh, clean whites were worn when serving, they had been made to wear hats/hair nets, cutlery was washed, all the old cups were thrown out.

After I'd returned to Odiham, I heard that the standards had dropped again and were now as bad as before. Funny it should happen as soon as I leave. But still a lot of people preferred to buy meals from the civvy caravans that used to park near the Guard room.

Back at Odiham; no fire piquet

The Regiment personnel were excused from fire piquet duty or guards on the barrier. It was our job to mount a mobile back-up patrol for the R.A.F. police, answerable only to the duty R/Regiment SNCO or duty officer.

There was only a few of us on the camp allocated to the flying Sqns and the station personnel in the Regiment section, probably no more than 25 altogether. We were our own bosses with just a Sgt i/c in the guardroom or officer on call, but usually an SNCO. Not even the O/Sgt could tell us what to do. In the event of an incident, we were the experts in our own particular field and were expected to use our own initiative as the O/Sergeant was a tradesman and knew nothing of how the Regiment was trained to react.

All their instructions were, in the event of an incident, call out the O/Officer and the R.A.F. Regiment SNCO and they would take it from there! Before the arrival of our SNCO or the orderly officer, we were to take orders from the duty R.A.F. policeman only if they outranked the Regiment personnel.

Bomb dump incident

One early evening, I was with another Regiment lad in my Land Rover and we checked out the bomb dump and other areas that were not under us, but the responsibility of the duty R.A.F. policeman. I discovered to my horror that the compound surrounding the bomb dump had been breached; the wire fence had been torn down with a concrete post as if a lorry had driven into it.

I reported it over the radio that 'Bravo Delta' had been broken into (the service phonetic alphabet) but the trouble was the SNCO who was O/ Sergeant didn't understand a word; all he knew about was aircraft. I just couldn't get him to understand what I meant by Bravo Delta. The thicko didn't even know what part of camp we were in and couldn't understand our meaning, stupid man. So as risky as it was, I had to leave the area without checking it thoroughly and sped to the guardroom to give him a rollicking (and did). And I, only an S.A.C., heavily outranked by him; the proverbial 'manure hit the fan'.

He then had the common sense to call out the duty R.A.F. policeman, who in turn called out everyone else including the Regiment SNCO, orderly officer, who called out the duty officer who then called out the station commander himself – who in turn called in the S.I.B. branch of the R.A.F. police from London and the local police.

There was hell to pay; why hadn't the alarm gone off? Why hadn't the R.A.F. police or the Regiment patrols spotted it by now? The (previous) mobile Regiment patrols were getting it in the neck, as if it were their fault. As I said, it wasn't our area of patrol. 'Pass the buck' sprang to mind. After a while, we found out. The fence had been brought down weeks ago by a R.A.F. police patrol vehicle but they had been frightened to report it. It had remained unfound until I had the idea to check out that area and finally stumbled upon it.

I was congratulated on my alertness for discovering it.

Ordering Elvis L.P.

Once I got back from USA, I ordered an Elvis L.P. from the local branch of W. H. Smith, *Aloha from Hawaii – Live!* at the store, this girl said to me, "I'm afraid I can't find the album in the catalogue, do you know the number, Sir?" "No, the record hasn't been released yet!" The look on her face was a treat.

"There is nothing I can do until it's released, if it's released!"

"Oh, it will be released all right!" said I. "Would you like a little bet on it?" We did.

A pleasant surprise awaited me a few weeks later at St Athan. I received a letter with a card in it informing me that my record, *Aloha from Hawaii – Live* was now ready for collection. Also in the letter was a £5 note, my winnings from the bet I'd completely forgotten about, that was rather decent of the lass.

Had I not been going out with Viola, I would have taken her out as a thank you.

Priscilla

Before meeting Viola, I saw that just down the road from camp there, lived the attractive but stuck-up Priscilla whom I had originally met on our destination USA trip. She was, I remember thinking at first, one of the few well-off and sophisticated girls, for that was the impression she tried to give. Though I liked her, I could sense that it was just an act, she was I suspected, just a stuck-up snob who thought she was something special. She, like most, had invited me to 'drop in anytime if I'm in the area'. She thought this a pretty safe bet, I was (and she knew) based at Catterick over a couple of hundred miles away and was unlikely to knock on her door and surprise her. But I decided I would take her up on her offer, as she only lived about 5 miles from Odiham. I thought, "Why not? I'll drop in and see her reaction; besides, I might find out just what's she really like and whether she's putting on an act or not." I thought as long as I was on her doorstep, I might as well try my luck; if I got the chance of a 'bit of other', then all well and good.

Girl from 'Destination USA' in curlers

That evening when I knocked on her door, at first I couldn't tell if it was her that had answered the door or not. I barely recognised her. She had no makeup on, hair in curlers and a dressing gown, and she looked rough. I suddenly lost all interest in her!

And it turned out she was busy that night and for that week. I could take a hint. But my turning up like that was totally unexpected. Surprise, surprise! And yes! My first impressions of her were right; she did come over 'stuck-up'! And her house was nothing out of the ordinary, a three-bed semi. Just an act all along.

A.T.C. civvy

Another evening we were on guard as usual in the Land Rover, in the early hours of the morning we saw a civvy acting suspiciously and coming out of the air traffic control building

I was with our Sqn Regiment Cpl, Phil Lewis, and he told me I'd best check that civvy out. I challenged the man as to what was he doing here at this time of morning and tried to establish his identity. I was told to go away and not to bother him. He was rude and ignorant. I reported back to Phil. Phil said that he would challenge him and if I saw him 'arresting the civvy', I was to get the Regiment SNCO called out.

He is taught a lesson

Phil approached this chap. I sat watching from the Land Rover, though I couldn't hear what was being said. I saw them both arguing with each other. He did attempt to arrest this intruder who was resisting arrest so I called the Orderly Sgt who called out the Regiment SNCO. By then, Phil had grabbed the bloke and was dragging him towards me and the Land Rover; the civvy didn't want to be arrested but Phil was having none of it and our Phil was a bit of a hard man, not one to be crossed if you got on the wrong side of him. So I leapt out of the wagon and helped bundle him in the back of the Land Rover whereupon we sped to the guardroom.

We stripped him, searched him and then threw him in a cell to cool off. After a couple of minutes or so, the duty R/Regiment SNCO arrived and if Phil had a reputation as a hard man, then this sergeant (whom I didn't know) was the undisputed 'king' of Odiham's Regiment hard men. At times he seemed O.T.T. And unfortunately for the civvy, this was one of those times; he had not liked to be pulled out of bed before his time, least of all by a civvy.

When he arrived, he was raging mad and kicked open the guardroom door and shouted over to Phil, "Where is this f***ing civvy that's got me out of my bed!" Phil filled him in with the details on how he'd tried to give Phil and I a hard time, how he had insulted the Regiment and resisted arrest.

Our sergeant bellowed over to the orderly sergeant who was quietly cowering in a corner, hoping no one would see him, poor man, he wasn't used to seeing the rock-apes in full aggressive mode. "Oy you, Orderly Sergeant, get off your f***ing arse and get your f***ing self over here and open this f***ing cell door, I want to have words with this f***ing civvy who resisted arrest and gave my lads a hard time, I want to interrogate the bar-stad!" I felt sorry for the orderly sergeant; he was very timid, not used to this sort of attitude and seemed scared of the duty Regiment SNCO. The cell door was unlocked and the Regiment SNCO kicked it open. The orderly sergeant ran back to his corner; he hadn't reckoned on this, he had thought he was in for a quiet night. Some hope!

The Regt SNCO waded into the cell and Phil shut the door behind him. We left our Regiment SNCO to interrogate the suspect while we resumed our patrol. Just before we knocked off, we went back to the guardroom and all we could hear was this civvy shouting from the cell, things like, "I'll sue the lot of you for damages, wrongful arrest, R.A.F. Regiment brutality!" What had our Regt SNCO done to him, I wonder? "I'll have the book thrown at you; I'll get you all court-martialled and thrown out in disgrace!"

The Regt SNCO had interrogated him! But there wasn't a mark on him. We were about to knock off when the station commander walked in. The orderly sergeant looked worried, what had he let himself in for, was this nightmare ever going to end? How was he going to tell his wife he had just done a duty and was going to be court-martialled into the bargain?

The station commander asked Phil what was this incident all about. Phil told him. The station commander went into the cell to talk to this civvy and it transpired that he had every right to be in the A.T.C. building as he worked as a MET officer, prior to flying.

He was told, however, that if in future when asked to cooperate with us and produce proof of his identity, it would be a lot easier to cooperate than to resist, as he now knew to his cost.

The threats of a court martial all around and charges in a civvy court were dropped; the station commander had instructed him that it would be very unwise to argue when he was in the wrong. The orderly sergeant seemed to breathe a little sigh of relief at that.

Had the civvy cooperated in the first instance and shown his ID card, we would not have had all this hassle. One thing was for sure, neither we nor anyone else ever had any trouble from him again; he'd learned his lesson the hard way, funny that, wasn't it?

Getting out of patrolling

Another time on patrol, my partner and I felt tired and didn't feel like running around the airfield all night so with his agreement, I said I would get us out of it. So we decided as it was Thursday and Naafi dance night, we would go and have a few beers (while we were on duty). Only at Odiham!

Going to a dance whilst on duty and in uniform

So we would take it in turns, I would drink and dance for an hour (in uniform) and my partner would sit in the Land Rover and listen to the radio in case of a call out, then we'd swap over and he would drink, this would go on until the dance had finished for the night. No one ever questioned or challenged us; all there must have known we were on duty. The 'Odiham factor!' Great fun, now that was what I called guard duty, it beat being stuck in a depressing guardroom or on a cold draughty barrier all night (we never got caught).

Though we were a bit obvious, dancing in full combat kit with our large boots on. Now and then, the chap that was on standby would go for a run on his own in the Land Rover just to pass the time.

Another night doing this duty with a different 'oppo', we didn't feel like staying awake till 8 am so I hatched a plan to get us out of the duty.

I then drove to the farthest part of the airfield and called the guardroom up on the net. I put our Sqn hangar between us and the receiving set, retuned just slightly off the channel we were using and called them up.

Making a call, I spoke very low and quiet as I knew the reception wasn't what it should be, it was in fact very poor. The orderly sergeant kept saying over the air that he could barely hear me and couldn't make out what I was saying so I'd better return to his location to try and see what could be done. Though to be perfectly honest, we could hear him quite clearly.

The orderly sergeant tried to make out he was a clever so and so, and suggested all sorts of things to remedy the fault in the communications (none of his ideas would have worked in a real situation).

So he said, "Go back on the airfield and try and call me up from different locations to see if that has cured the problem!" We knew it wouldn't – we made sure it wouldn't! "If it doesn't get any better, then you'd better come back in and get your heads down for the night!"

We tried to communicate though; just to be sure that things wouldn't work. I had another idea; as I was speaking over the air, I would crumple a crisp packet as I spoke very quietly, to signify static – it worked! We were told that it was a waste of time trying to establish comms and that we might as well pack it in for the night; I still tried to make out that we couldn't hear him.

So we came in on the pretext of seeing what else could be done but the orderly sergeant said, "Don't bother, lads, you might as well get your heads down but remain dressed in case I have cause to call you out in the night!" That suited us just fine, my little plan had worked, funny he didn't smell the beer on our breaths.

All that remained to do was get up in the morning and hand in the Land Rover to the M.T. yard and have the rest of the day off.

Smashing a Land Rover drive shaft

On one occasion, on guard on my own and travelling over rough ground hard and fast, the wagon wouldn't move so I had to put it into four-wheel drive low ratio for the rest of the duty. I found out later that a drive shaft had been broken, though the M.T. yard didn't really blame me as they said that it would have gone at any time. I kept quiet for once, though I reckon it was my fault. I wasn't going to argue. 'The Odiham factor' again.

New Sqn C.O.

Not long after I had arrived on the Sqn and settled in, we had a new C.O. posted – a Wing Commander, John Strong. He was a real officer and a gentleman and approachable by all ranks.

The very first thing he did when he took over was get everybody in the Sqn Ops room regardless of rank or status for an introduction session. He introduced himself thus, "Good afternoon, gentlemen, my name is Wing Commander John Strong, I am as of now your new C.O.. It is my job to keep as many of our aircraft in the air and serviceable. Other matters go by the board to enable us to keep as many aircraft in a serviceable state and as safe as possible at any one time. When there are visitors or other officers, especially the station commander or the A.O.C on the Sqn, you will address me by the correct appointment as 'Sir' or Wing Commander. But for normal day-to-day running of the Sqn, you may address me by my name John!" I couldn't believe my ears, especially after the strict discipline of the R.A.F. Regiment Sqn. We all said afterwards, "This sounds like a good chap to work for!" And indeed he was.

When he was answering questions from my Regiment Sergeant Alex Goddard, another gent (still in touch with him today) about haircuts, bulled boots/shoes, etc., his reply astounded us, "I am not bothered how long the hair of the head is kept, or whether you have razor-sharp creases in your uniform trousers, or even about boots being bulled up all the time. All I ask is that each and every member of the Sqn doesn't walk around dirty or scruffy, you're all trained airmen, it is up to you to use a bit of common sense about your appearance.

"However, if I ever hear about a member of my Sqn being picked up by the station warrant officer or the Stn commander or any officer around camp, I'll have an almighty purge, one you will all regret, so all I say is you know what is expected of you, keep it up, use your common sense and don't let your standards drop – or else! Then my officers won't be on your backs over trivial things like dress and uniforms, keep my aircraft flying and safe and you won't be bothered, that's all I ask!"

He had the knack and was the only person I have worked for to get each and every man working hard for him, even the well-known skivers. He made a point of learning the names of all the members of the Sqn, their wives, girlfriends and their children's names. And when talking to anyone on the Sqn, he would always ask by name how the wife/girlfriend/children were keeping. He had a genuine interest in our welfare.

Wom and Ella

Two of my best friends I had at Odiham were 'Wom' Powell, a West Indian lad (short for his nickname Wombat) and Ella, his wife, a lovely Filipino girl who was working as a nurse at one of the hospitals in Aldershot. A lovely lady she was. Wom was only an aircraftman (lowest rank) working as a general duties helping out in the airmen's mess.

Ella pregnant

Though he was a coloured lad, he would be one of the first to make fun of his colour. I was going out with Daisy Misonia at the time, another Filipino. Wom confessed to me one day that he was worried about Ella as she was heavily pregnant and was told she had to be out of the nurses' home by the end of the month, she was due to give birth a week or so later and they had nowhere to go and once she'd given birth, where to next, he asked! I asked about an M.Q., he said he wasn't entitled to one as he hadn't enough points; the usual waiting time was depending on your personal circumstances and availability of quarters. Usually about 2-3 years; of course, that was no good. I suggested for him to go and see the Padre or the doctor, even the families officer, after all, that was what they were for – to help you out in an emergency. He said he couldn't as it wouldn't do any good. "What can they do!" he asked. I kept telling him that was his best bet, take it or leave it. He said he was a bit embarrassed as I said to him, "What's more important – being embarrassed or Ella and her unborn child?"

I constantly kept asking Wom if he'd been to see anyone yet when I saw him, and he always replied no! Too embarrassed to ask. So by one Friday, nothing had been done and she was to vacate the nurses' home the following Friday.

I said, "Right Wom, I'll give you till lunch time Monday to do something, if you don't, I will, but not for your sake, it will be for Ella's!"

Fixing them up with M.Q.'s

The Monday came and as suspected, nothing had been done so I told him, "Right, I am now going to take matters in my own hands if you haven't the guts to do it yourself!" I immediately went to the medical centre. I booked an appointment to see one of the MOs on Tuesday at 08:30 hrs, reported for 'sick parade'! I walked into the M.O.'s office/surgery and he smiled and asked what the problem with me was.

"Nothing is the matter with me, Sir!" I told him. His smile disappeared and said, "Then why on earth are you here?" I explained Ella's predicament and the M.O. then said, "What are you doing here about it then, why doesn't the husband come and see me himself?" I explained it to the M.O. He was embarrassed. He seemed a bit annoyed with me and Wom. "All right, leave it with me, lad, I'll see what I can do!" I then reported to the Sqn ready for work, this was now 9 am.

At the tea meal in the mess, when Wom saw me, he went mad; he was so excited and couldn't thank me enough. He told me that the M.O./families officer had come to see him in the morning about Ella and somewhere to live.

He explained what the situation was and then the R.A.F. started to move – and move fast! By 10:30 that same morning, he was in a R.A.F.-sponsored quarter (a hiring) and was signing for his inventory from the families officer.

Ella was then instructed by the M.O. to move in immediately and come to the medical centre the following day for a thorough examination by the M.O. He and Ella were over the moon and couldn't thank me enough.

I felt mighty proud of the R.A.F. for the speed at which they moved. It just goes to show just what they can do when they make their minds up to do it. A couple of days later, when they had settled in, I took them to the Naafi dance as they had no transport. When I got there, I dropped them off and told them I would pick them up to take them home later, as I was having a night in the block; in reality, I couldn't really afford to go to the dance.

Later, Wom came to the block and insisted that I come to the dance; they were paying, so how could I refuse! At the time, I was still officially courting Daisy Misonia, though by that time I was rapidly going off her.

This was the first night I set eyes on Viola, which was to change my whole life! But I wasn't going out with her at this point.

Trying and fixing me up with Santo

Ella had a friend who visited her at home regularly, Santo, a really attractive girl. She was about 40% Indian, 40% Malay and about 20% Chinese; she was a ravishing beauty. I no longer had any interest in Daisy. Wom and Ella tried to fix me up with Santo but it was to no avail. I don't think she fancied me, though I was smitten.

Tall R.A.F. cook, constantly tired

A friend of mine and Wom's was a very tall cook who was supposed to be the 'airmen's mess stud'; he was always seen with a girl or two on his arms and then got off with a big, tall and adequately proportioned girl from Jamaica (a nurse) who was, we assured, very randy and couldn't get enough of 'it'. Our mutual friend, the cook, did try his best to keep his 'end up'! He was slowly being worn down and devoid of energy but always had a smile on his face!

At times, he could hardly keep his eyes open and staggered instead of walking.

Meeting and chatting up Viola

That evening, as I had promised, I took some of his cook friends and others to the dance that was being held in the medical/education centre at Basingstoke Hospital. At first, it looked like it was going to be just the usual run-of-the-mill great dances that I had been used to at Odiham (how very wrong I was).

After a few minutes of drinking and dancing and enjoying myself with more than the usual number of girls/nurses that come to R.A.F. dances, there were obviously more nurses this time as it was on their own territory.

I noticed out of the corner of my eye a familiar face: it was Viola, without her boyfriend in tow. I watched and observed and after a few minutes went up to her and said hello, we got chatting and we had a dance, I immediately noticed that she was in the very rare state of being drunk.

She was, I discovered, without Des, her boyfriend, whom I'd warned off; she was now free! She was, however, with another – not a boyfriend but someone who had escorted her to the dance, a very tall lanky civvy whom I looked at and thought, "Huh, he's no threat. If I can scare a serviceman off, leaving the field open for me." I realised that this was probably my only chance to win her over as she was so popular that no doubt the next time I saw her, someone else would be taking her out, and I wasn't going to have that, no siree!

So, it was a case of move in now all guns blazing while I had the opportunity so then I put into action my carefully worked out and practiced plan and made my move on her.

At the end of the evening, I offered to see her back to the nurses' accommodation, she told me that someone was supposed to be escorting her that night. I looked and saw this great lanky civvy waiting for me to go away and then to 'escort her'. So in my usual dominant/cheeky way, I started to lead her out of the building towards the accommodation, followed closely behind by this civvy and his brother and wife. Several times, I looked behind me ready for the usual fight that ensued when something of a similar nature occurred, but this time nothing!

I didn't then realise the importance of that meeting at that dance and how it was destined to change my whole life till a few weeks after. As we were leaving, I was approached by the three lads I had given a lift to who asked if I was going to give them a lift back to camp as promised. I told them no, not if I'm not back in 10 minutes. I knew full well that I wouldn't be, and so they cursed me for letting them down. (Not the sort of thing I did if I could help it.) I thought, "Bugger them, I'm not giving up this opportunity, I've waited too long for it and it may not come again."

We went to Viola's room (all five of us) and sat talking, drinking coffee. The hour by now was getting late and the first to offer to make a move at about 1-1:30 am was the couple, who left leaving 'lanky civvy' and I with Viola. It became very obvious to all of us what was now ensuing, but nothing was said. He was determined not to leave first on principle; I do believe he didn't trust me with Viola. However, I was having none of it, and if he wanted to try and wait me out then he was welcome to try. Viola was in the middle of this battle of wills and wanted to get some sleep. What he didn't know was that under no circumstances was I going to give in first. But also to my advantage was the fact that I was used to staying awake and alert all night on 24-hour duties due to my job and training, but he wasn't! After another hour or so, he gave up and unhappily left. I thought, "Fair enough, I'll just stay long enough to make sure he doesn't come back, and then I'll leave to let the poor girl get some sleep." We got chatting about this and that and when I looked at my watch to see if it was time to go, it was about 5 am. Poor old Viola, I made my excuses and left promising to ring that evening though unbeknownst to me, Viola wasn't really bothered if I did not as wasn't very keen on me, I later found out.

I did ring as promised but Viola kept giving me different excuses to try and put me off. So one night, I thought, "Bugger this! "I got in the car and drove to the nurses' home, knocked on the door and asked to see Viola, when she came down, I asked her out. She had no excuses now, I thought; we then went out together. I never at any time thought that she might not like me, it never entered my head and even if it had, I would have still tried to get her to come out and win her over! Such was my determination if I fancied someone as much as I fancied Viola.

Viola and I went out on a few dates and what surprised and delighted me was that she was the first girl I'd come across with whom I could hold an intelligent conversation on equal terms. Apart from Linda Masters. This was just not possible with all her predecessors, and that drew me closer to her once I had gotten to know her a bit better. I dropped Daisy Misonia whom I'd been going out with like a hot potato. Viola's brain, personality and kind heart put her and the others to shame. Though to be perfectly honest, I had already decided to give Daisy Misonia the push just before I went to that dance at the education centre.

Of course, knowing how bitchy girls can be, Viola was blamed by Misonia for breaking us up and taking me from her. 'Man stealer' was among the more polite names she was called. Of course, the more we went out together, the better we got to know each other, and of course, the other Filipinos were very jealous and there was a lot of backstabbing going on. The Filipino girls, through their R.A.F. boyfriends, knew of my reputation with members of the opposite gender; they then started to spread venomous lies, which now we look back on was the one thing that made us draw even closer together. Then the gossips and the lies really started to get nasty.

Exercise in the Orkney Islands

The Sqn flew off early one morning in Sqn formation for a tactical 'Escape and Evasion' exercise. I had told my mother and father to watch out for the Sqn as the flight path took us parallel to Scotter Road and only about 150 yards from my house.

I invited the C.O. and other aircrew in for a cup of tea but it wasn't really wise to leave a military helicopter on the ground, rotors turning and unannounced or unattended. Still I invited them, just in case they took me up on my offer.

The moment we flew over Scunthorpe, there was low cloud and we couldn't see my house and my folks couldn't see the Sqn, though we were heard going overhead. There were only four of us Regiment men attached to 33 and 72 Sqns (Wessex helicopters) taking part. We were assigned to a company of local T.A. soldiers and we were all taking the part of the enemy! That included Phil, the Cpl from my Sqn, and Andy Rowe of 72 Sqn (formerly with me on Regiment basics and 37 Sqn).

The purpose I found later on was that Phil had to give a report about Andy on his return to Odiham. As always in the Forces, rumour control was working overtime and we never found out the real reason. Various rumours were flying about such as he was being tested to ensure he knew his job or would have to go for retraining, though I found that hard to believe.

Maybe even Andy had reapplied for the S.A.S. and they were considering putting his application through dependant on how he performed during this detachment. He was keen to apply when on 37 Sqn. We never found out. Maybe even for another reason we knew nothing about?

Half the Sqn helicopters were attached to the 'friendly forces' and the other half were with us based with the local 'militia' who were supposed to have revolted against the government and a task force of Royal Navy Destroyers, Commando Carriers, Royal Marines and Royal Green Jackets had been sent to deal with us. Throughout, we did try to be as tactical as possible but it was near impossible as there was no tree cover, only rolling hills and sheep – lots of sheep. And when we found what we thought was a good concealment position, our presence was always given away by some Sauk's sea birds, telling the enemy just where we were by 'dive bombing' us continuously (we must have been near their nesting sites). It was very difficult to lie still and not be seen as you had to fight the birds off as they kept attacking our heads.

One day, we were instructed to leave our kit on one island while we flew off to 'fight' on another. We didn't see our kit for several days and I was getting a bit worried as it would prove very expensive to replace, so I thought I would cover myself and ask the T.A. officer to give me something in writing so that if the kit was lost and not returned, then I would be able to produce the note to that effect and not have to pay for its replacement. It did eventually turn up with a few items missing. Someone must have lost their kit and decided to make it up out of my backpack and others'. This was about 4-5 days later; fortunately, when I got back to Odiham, the kit (on production of the note) was written off as 'exercise loss' though I must admit, I used the opportunity to recover some of my other missing kit ready for the next kit inspection, whenever it should happen. I was promptly issued with fresh new kit.

Start of battle

Just before the start of the first battle, I and several others were in a defensive position awaiting the landing, and what I saw was very impressive. I now know exactly what the Argentinians felt like as they must have seen our battle fleet sail into a cove and start to bombard the shore prior to the landing; there was an old aircraft carrier converted to be used as a helicopter/commando carrier, two purpose-built commando/helicopter carriers, about six destroyers/cruisers. (The former three were taken out of mothballs and used in the Falklands campaign against the Argentinians.)

Meanwhile, the Royal Navy and Royal Marines and army helicopters had spotted our positions by hovering around us.

Once the landing craft and helicopters had made dozens of journeys ferrying the assault troops ashore, the officer with us changed our location in formation ready for the enemy when they showed themselves, the helicopters were still hovering around us and supposedly reporting our positions, it was frustrating as we wanted to shoot the helicopters down but couldn't because of the assumption that if they hadn't spotted us, then we would be giving our position away – what a dilemma.

I volunteered a young T.A. lad and myself to employ delaying tactics against the 'enemy', giving time for the rest of them to get away and set a trap for the enemy forces. This was quite a formidable task as the two of us faced the combined strength of the Royal Green jackets, Green Howards and Royal Marines support helicopters. It was a near impossible task but we did it. We held them off long enough for the others to get away. I positioned myself on the old abandoned air traffic control tower of a deserted airfield while the lad hid nearby.

Nervously we waited, then waited some more; eventually, they did turn up. When they got within range so that we couldn't miss in a real situation and with live ammunition, I opened fire with a couple of shots. To my complete and utter amazement, they walked on not hearing a thing, that was at three hundred yards. I fired again, nothing, four dead to me. I fired two more shots – 6 dead to me excluding how many the lad had 'knocked off' by now. I was completely astounded that no one had heard a thing, two more shots rang out from my rifle, surprise! A couple of the army lads heard my shots (after I had shot him and several of his mates), they must have thought they were hearing things; after all, who would want to shoot at them! Still further on, they were only about 50-75 yards away, two more shots from me – 10 dead to me but now they stood looking all around, realising someone was shooting at them and a) they didn't know from where, b) nobody took cover and got their heads down and c) nobody returned fire. Their JNCOs were screaming their heads off in abuse at the soldiers as to why they were not trying to find out where the sniper was and get to cover (the first instinct of survival). Funny thing was there was nothing around for hundreds of yards, no cover – nothing. Where an enemy sniper could be hiding, except my air traffic control tower, which was the only cover. Still they never thought of looking there, typical pongoes.

I'd had enough of this, it was rapidly approaching the time of our pre-arranged signal to beat a hasty retreat, leapfrogging and giving covering fire to each other. I opened up on them, finishing my magazine and putting another on, I continued to give rapid fire. I couldn't believe it, I had just fired about 30-35 rounds at them and still they didn't know where I was, except the JNCOs. They had spotted me and were screaming at their men to "Take him out in the control tower", but the 'soldiers' were still running around in a panic not knowing where I was or what to do, like the proverbial chickens with their heads cut off. I thought it about time to make a rapid exit from there as the booby trap that men of the Royal Engineers had set was about to go off.

So I emptied my magazine into them and reloaded, that made about 40 rounds I had fired and only now some of the more observant ones among them spotted me and were approaching rapidly, so I gave them something they could share among themselves. I threw four thunder flashes amongst them saying, "Share that among yourselves!" reminiscent of a line from an American war film.

So I leapt down those stairs three at a time and at the pre-arranged place and time met up with the lad who was with me and told him to run about a hundred then continue to do this until clear of enemy lines. Then cover me.

The first couple of times were OK and to plan but on the third, I gave him the signal to start running and would join him later.

To my horror, he just kept on running without stopping – unbeknownst to me as I was still engaging the enemy. I cursed him to high heaven then I thought the enemy were getting just a bit too close so I turned to run myself when from nowhere, I was surrounded by 4-6 of the enemy who had done a classic flanking movement and I had been unable to see them over the high bank I was hiding and engaging the enemy coming up the road.

The 'prisoner'

The T.A. lad had been in a similar position and could see over my bank and I over his hence my instructions to watch over my shoulder where I couldn't see and I'll watch over yours. But I hadn't reckoned on his nerve giving out. He had seen them coming towards me and panicked, not telling me I was about to get caught. I was disarmed, blindfolded and led back to their lines.

Just before being taken prisoner, I had the satisfaction though of watching my former hiding place, the control tower, blow up. Just as there were soldiers swarming all over it and had it been for real, it would have meant that the whole control tower would have blown up killing quite a few of the enemy, so I allowed myself a wry smile as I was marched away.

I thought while under guard, "If anybody was to be taken prisoner – pound to a pinch of dogsh*t – it'll be me!" I usually have the misfortune to be 'the one' as, like this incident, I leave it too late to make my getaway. My blindfold was removed and I was surprised to see that they had caught the lad who had run for it, and as you may well guess, I gave him such a rollicking.

'Prisoner' interrogation

It was not long before my interrogation began. A Cpl from Royal Green Jackets had been tasked to interrogate me and seemed rather nervous, definitely not used to it.

"What's your number, rank and name?" I told him.

"What's your unit?" No reply.

"What's your officer's name?"

"I don't know!" (And that was the truth; I didn't know the T.A. officer's name.)

"Are you not going to answer my questions?"

"No!"

"Oh, OK then."

With that, he went away; end of interrogation! I just couldn't believe it.

A few minutes later, one of their officers came in to tell us that was the end of our interrogation. And we would shortly be sent back to rejoin our unit.

He left and my interrogator and I got chatting; he said, "I see you're R.A.F., there isn't many of you on this exercise, is there?" I thought, "A lot less than you think, mate!"

He asked if I was directly involved with the helicopters and what my job was in the R.A.F. so graciously accepting one of his offered cigarettes, I told him R.A.F. Regiment. "Cor, I didn't know there was any of you lads taking part. Bloody hell, we're going to struggle against you chaps!" He must have thought I'd said S.A.S., not R.A.F. Regiment.

We were then released and sent back to our lines.

The war hero

I had been telling Phil our Cpl about the lack of discipline and expertise in the enemy camp.

So, on the spur of the moment, we decided to 'attack' the enemy, deep in the heart of their camp. No real plan was thought out, we just sort of played it by ear. We four Regt chaps just walked towards their lines up to their sentry post with our rifles slung over our shoulders, we didn't even make an attempt to remove our cap badges. We walked up to the sentry and Phil said, "Hello mate, not much longer before you're relieved."

Sentry: "No, thank goodness!"

Phil: "Is tea ready yet, mate?"

Sentry: "Yes, you know where the mess tent is, don't you?"

Phil: "No, where it is now?" So he told us, finishing off with "It's next to G.H.Q!"

We took our mess tins out and walked in the general direction of the mess tent and G.H.Q. We got there, hid in a building and hatched a plan, it wasn't much of a plan as such, but it achieved the desired effect.

Phil had borrowed a rifle as his S.M.G. didn't have blanks issued for it. I had my rifle, Andy had 'doctored' his rifle so it fired on automatic and the other lad had a general-purpose machine gun with about a thousand belted blank rounds.

When Phil said, "NOW", we came out guns blazing on single-shot and automatic. We shot up the entire area and all the enemy were so shocked they didn't return fire, we also had about 30 thunder flashes with us and we tossed them at the enemy and into buildings as we ran, it was great fun.

We thought we'd call in at the enemy HQ, the same building where I was 'interrogated', while we were there and pay them a visit; we sprayed it and other buildings with automatic, semi-automatic fire and tossed a few simulated grenades in for good measure.

We then 'borrowed' an enemy Land Rover and drove throughout the camp backwards and forwards, spraying them with machine gun fire, S.A.S. style. Then we got to the sentry we had walked past before and left him the vehicle and 'thanked him' for the loan. The sentry stood open-mouthed, speechless.

It must have looked impressive with us going in with guns blazing, just like a scene from a war film. After we got out of the Land Rover, we just quietly walked away and disappeared. The umpires who were attached to see fair play 'wiped out' the enemy HQ for 24 hours to try and give a bit of realism. We felt rather pleased with ourselves and so was the officer.

Night phase

Another time during a night phase, all our units were positioned along both sides of a valley with a power Stn at the one end. We were told the enemy would make a recce patrol or several during the night, so keep alert and awake!

So for the first time ever, I promptly fell asleep over my G.P.M.G.; that was very rare for me but I was so shattered I couldn't stay awake. The enemy could have sneaked right past me (and one other with me) and I wouldn't have been any the wiser! We saw some enemy caught.

Lighthouse

Another memorable engagement I was involved in centred on a disused lighthouse; we had to draw the enemy into the lighthouse for some reason.

We were waiting for them to come and ambush them and of course, they knew we were there waiting for them because of the damn birds dive bombing us relentlessly. They came nevertheless and we kept retreating and drawing them to us.

Finally, at the lighthouse, we had to surrender as we'd used up our ammunition and were surrounded; that is, all of us except Andy Rowe; we'd forgotten Andy, who had somehow managed to slip away from the rest of us, get up and into the lighthouse, although there were no stairs from the ground floor to the first.

The enemy had just disarmed us, relaxed and were having a smoke and a chat amongst themselves, not even paying us prisoners much attention. Suddenly, one or two stones started to fall about, and then on us, we thought some idiot was bored and throwing them. We then suddenly realised Andy was missing and looked up and it was Andy 'John Wayne' Rowe, looking down from a window in the lighthouse. We distracted the enemy and even they thought they had everyone as they had sat down for a cigarette to unwind. Suddenly, Andy started to shout insults to some of them, they thought it was us and told us to shut up, this got us laughing. A few more insults came forth, again the enemy told us to shut up, we were having a right old laugh by now.

Andy got fed up of them ignoring him so he dropped a couple of thunder flashes amongst them and then opened up with his doctored rifle on automatic, he had 'borrowed' a few light machine gun magazines as they were bigger and could hold more rounds. He stood there looking down and blazing away at them and throwing a few swear words in for good measure.

The enemy were running around like the proverbial chickens minus their heads. Running in circles and into each other, not knowing what to do next, not knowing from where the fire and thunder flashes were coming from.

We laughed some more, we thought this great fun.

Eventually, an officer told his men, "He's in the lighthouse, you fools, go and get him down!"

They came back presently, saying, "He's not there, sir, we've looked and can't find him!" We laughed louder.

Again, they had to go back and look and again, they couldn't see him. Cue more automatic gunfire and explosions raining down on them.

The officer was going daft. "He's in there, I tell you, are you all f***ing blind as well as stupid?" More laughter from us.

In the end, the officer had to take them and show them where he meant.

All this time, Andy was raining bullets (blanks) and thunder flashes down on them and swearing. Once they realised that he must have somehow climbed up without the aid of steps, they tried the same thing, but Andy was ready for them and came to the opening of what once had been the stairwell and opened fire + thunder flashes. The enemy were frightened off and retreated.

In the end, some of them were injured as Andy, getting carried away, fired at them at point blank range and they got burnt by the packing used in blank ammo (which can punch a hole in a tin); they had to have first aid treatment. It took the enemy about 45 minutes to get him down, only after he'd expended all his ammo. When Andy finally did come down, he was greeted by a great spontaneous cheer from all of us downstairs and he smiled that smug smile of his. Job well done!

I think Cpl Phil gave him a good report upon our return to camp.

Summing up

One other event sticks to the front of my mind and that is lying in wait of the enemy, seeing them coming over the hill in large fancy formation and opening up on them. They didn't try to find cover or find where the shooting was coming from so as to return fire, just stood looking gormless, and the umpires watching the proceedings, instead of saying to individuals, "You're dead, and you, and you!" stood by me and were saying – as they shook their heads. "One platoon, and another, wiped out." We were wiping out something like 30-40 men at a time.

An amusing part of the two weeks was the enemy flying low with the helicopters and dropping propaganda leaflets trying to persuade us to 'go over to them'! We also were supposed to have our own propaganda to help morale, extolling the virtues of our being 'martyrs to the cause of freedom' and all that.

Some of the things they came out with had us in stitches. 'Comrade Fred Blogs' was a good soldier and we will miss him, how unfortunate of him to fall under his plough and get ploughed into the ground!' and so on; it was hilarious at times though supposed to be serious.

The end of the proceedings were supposed to traditionally culminate with the now usual 'A' bomb! Which signalled the end of the exercise. Naturally, they didn't explode a real one for obvious reasons but the Royal Engineers simulated it by the use of a 45 Gall drum of oil and soap flakes – very realistic.

The Orkney's, although off the mainland of Scotland, have several deep water harbours, and it was there where we kept the large 'home fleet', at Scapa Flow and where the Germans scuttled their battleships upon surrendering at the end of the first world war. And today, you can still see where they were taken into shallow water and sunk. Parts of the superstructure still appear above the surface.

There are some men who have the contract to cut them up for scrap, it is a lifetime's work – and beyond. Enough for the next generation to earn a living off the battleships.

Pre-H.G.V. training (moving house)

Not long after my return from the Orkney Islands, I was to go to St Athan for another bash at getting my H.G.V. III licence.

So it was normal for Cpl Phil to give me some extra pre-course training prior to going to St Athan's. The training, however, was very little and limited and I doubt of any real use to me. It was helping a Regiment man move his family and possessions on discharge from his private quarters to the railway stn.

I was reminded of this incident not long back when I had managed to contact our Regiment Sgt, Alex Goddard. He reminded me that this Regiment man had refused to move out of his M.Q.s for several months, I don't know the reason for this as I was never told. However, when the time came to move him out, he left the Quarters in such a filthy state, it was uninhabitable with excrement and dirty nappies everywhere.

When you moved out of an M.Q., you were expected to leave it immaculate so when the new tenants moved in and unpacked, they could relax – no cleaning, even the cooker had to be left like brand new. Not this place, it was so bad we couldn't breathe; the chance of catching some dreaded disease was overwhelming. The only way we could manage it was with overalls and wearing our N.B.C. respirators. Not a pleasant job.

No brakes, reporting garage to the A.A.

My never-ending problem with my brakes had still not been sorted out so I thought that I had been lucky before not to have an accident but I couldn't go on chancing it as at some time or another, my luck would run out and I could get killed, at best seriously injured, not to mention knocking some pedestrian over and killing them.

So remembering my experience of taking the car to a local garage (prior to my first visit to St Athan's) and wasting my money £45+. Not to mention my copy of the workshop manual went missing. I was a member of the AA at the time and so annoyed with them that I wrote to the AA telling them that I felt I had been 'done'.

Spanner symbols

The said garage sported the sign of three AA spanners, the symbol of a good reliable garage. I received a reply that they were investigating the matter and would contact me later. This they did a few weeks later when I got back from St Athan.

The letter stated that after an investigation, they recommend taking the garage to court and would I like to help by giving evidence and they would see that things would be OK. I didn't fancy a court case as I didn't know how the R.A.F. would react, so I wrote to the AA telling them of my predicament and just asked that the garage be punished and not allowed to get away with it. They assured me they wouldn't!

(Overcharged) complaint

What also annoyed me was their sheer arrogance; when I complained to them in person, all they said was that they had done their best and if I didn't like it and if I wanted to make something of it then why didn't I take them to court!

They knew, of course, on a serviceman's wages, I couldn't afford it so they must have thought they were on a pretty safe bet! (They obviously didn't know me and had misjudged me.)

R.A.F. M.T. fitter has a go at fixing brakes

Left with no alternative, I went to see one of the M.T. fitters I knew well enough to chat and asked him if he would try and fix my car for me prior to going to St Athan. To my surprise, he agreed and when I asked him how much he wanted for the bits and pieces, he said not to bother.

The problem seemed cured now although whilst at St Athan, it re-occurred.

And I again tried another garage. They hadn't cured it.

People messing with my food

I have never been the sort to get into a fight over someone drinking/stealing or messing about with my beer. I have, however, felt very strongly about anyone messing about with my food and even though I used to bend over backwards to avoid fighting over trivial things like beer, women or the like, I have never been so inclined as far as food was concerned.

In fact, I always used to joke wherever I was posted, "Take my money, my girlfriends, you can even take my beer, but touch my food – and you're a DEAD MAN!"

Some of those that felt brave enough (not many) always threatened, but never tried it on. But just on the very rare and odd occasion one or two thought they would call my bluff – they lived to regret it! The one incident that really sticks in mind happened at St Athan because it was there that I carried out my threat, with a vengeance.

It started no different from any other normal mealtime. Some of the

Regiment chaps were fooling about by taking food off their mate's plate. One of the chaps took a chip off my plate when I wasn't looking, he then did it again and this time I did see it and I quietly warned him by telling him my favourite saying, "Take my women, take my beer, but touch my food and you're a 'DEAD MAN'!" He just laughed at me in front of his mates. And made an effort to take some food off my plate. I grabbed his hand and stopped him, looked him in the eyes and said, "Try that again and I'll make you very sorry you ever crossed me!"

He must have fancied his chances or couldn't be seen to back down in front of his mates and thought that he was a bit of a hard man and I, all talk!

Then he made a grave error, he DID try it again, so as his hand was over my plate, I brought my eating fork down as hard and as fast as I could and stuck it into his hand. He let out a scream as he rapidly withdrew his hand and saw my fork stuck in his hand and blood flowing freely. I said, "I did warn you!" and carried on eating. He swore at me and threatened to kill me, but then some of the other lads on the table from his Sqn told him, "You're being unfair to threaten John, after all, he did warn you beforehand!"

This chap then had to leave the mess to get his hand seen to; meanwhile, I said nothing and carried on eating. By the evening meal, it had gone right through the grapevine and I was the 'man of the moment'; some thought I was a crazy nutter, others thought I'd done the right thing. This wasn't the first time I'd done this but I didn't have to do it again as my reputation proved that I could and would do it!

Drilling St Athan's personnel

At St Athan, the training personnel thought it a good idea to relieve the JNCOs and SNCOs of the mundane tasks such as marching the trainees back and forth from the mess-block and around camp. So it was decided that we were to be split up in two groups The R/Regiment being the single biggest trade group represented, we made up about half of the total trainees, the other half consisted of 'penguins', under training M.T. fitters, visiting units personnel such as Royal Navy, Royal Marines, army personnel, even R.C.T. chaps, Paras and Royal Artillery with a smattering of other unit corps made up the numbers.

So each day, one Regiment man and one other was chosen to drill their respective groups. The first day, the one chosen to lead us was an ex-para whose reputation preceded him. This Regiment chap had had more time in the Regiment than me, he did reasonably well; come the second day and it was my luck to be chosen. So being a bit nervous, I tried to put it off as much as possible. It was a nerve-wracking event, standing in front of about 80-90 men who knew just as much about drill as I. I did quite well considering that quite a few of the blokes would be waiting for you to make a mistake and make fun of you. By the end of the day, I was quite relieved to see the end of it.

The following day, everyone was grouped together and the chief driving/training officer addressed the whole intake, both Regiment and the other group. He asked, "Who was the R.A.F. Regiment chap that drilled the Regiment personnel yesterday?" I thought I must be in trouble so I kept quiet. Someone behind me pushed me forwards. I was then told in front of the entire intake (about 150) that I had done so well with my knowledge of drill and a good loud voice (First time I'd been complimented on that! Usually got me into trouble.), that from now on as long as I was here – unless they got an actual DI in – I was to drill and parade everyone including the penguins, R. Navy and R. Marines, not forgetting the paras; they weren't keen on this as they thought one of their own should have been nominated.

My mind drifted back to Houndstone camp and Sgt Dredge, I was thinking, "Bet you never foresaw this, Sarge, bet you're proud of me?"

The Regiment lads were quite pleased that I'd been picked and several told me so. I was a bit embarrassed but rather chuffed as you may well believe. So I drilled them everywhere for about a week, then unfortunately, they got a real DI in on a course so I had to go back in the ranks instead of facing them out front.

Of course, when I drilled the large squad, I gave priority to the Regiment lads. Near the mess, I would give the order, "Regiment personnel only, on the march-fall-out!" The penguins I would bring them to the halt, left/right/turn fall out so that the delay would get the Regiment chaps in front of the queue.

'Battle of Britain' air display

Training was halted for a week while at St Athan's for the Annual 'Battle of Britain' air display. Preparations were made for the display with all personnel doing different jobs. Unlike my local display at R.A.F. Finningley, here there was a very good static display of WWII German aircraft. Some I hadn't seen before even in a museum. It was a long hard day and we were glad when it was finished. What annoyed us that we didn't even get a 'thank you for what you've done' from anybody.

During the weekend, I used to tempt fate by driving to see Viola at Basing-stoke in my car, along the M3/M4 motorways with no brakes. I used to take a heck of a chance. But I felt it worth it to see Viola (what a fool I must have been, or in love, which would explain it). I look back now and think that I would drive all the way through Barry, Cardiff, along the M3/4 motorway at high speeds with no brakes just to see Viola. I must have been mad!

Invited to a 'dirty week' with Jan

One week while I was at St Athan's, I received a letter from Jan Wilson, the girl I had met on my visit to USA who was a fellow member of British branch of the Elvis Presley Fan Club. I was being invited up for a 'dirty week', not weekend. But a whole week at her house as her parents were apparently away for the week and she was all alone in the house and she (as she put it) didn't want to be left alone in her large empty house for a whole week! I was very pleased to receive this letter as you can well imagine!

Considering that I'd taken months and months to get her in a position to get her 'down and dirty', the last time being in Los Angeles. She was at first behaving like an inexperienced frightened virgin, but not for long.

Back home in UK, I was able to get her worked up to a certain pitch usually before the point where most girls finally gave in and said OK. The trouble was with Jan, she was different. Once at that point of no return, she would suddenly freeze and switch off – most frustrating for me!

Once though I understood why, at her house one weekend she had just switched off and five Minutes later when we would have been deeply involved, in walked her 6'2" brother in his police uniform.

Once I had even paid a deposit for a room in a hotel in London for a dirty weekend thinking that once I got her away from her family, she might be keener for it and relax. Trouble was, although she had known full well my intentions, she chickened out at the last minute.

For this weekend, I was very tempted but I explained to her that I was on a course and couldn't put in for any leave at this moment in time, although I could come for a weekend, which she agreed to!

Nearer to the time it came for me to leave, I decided finally that it was not worth going all the way to Stockport, Manchester, with no brakes; it would be far too dangerous – suicidal, almost certainly! I didn't know the roads/hazards, and with no brakes, it just wasn't worth it, I had considered going by train but couldn't afford it.

I thought I'd rather see Viola. I think that now must have been the point at which I had become totally committed. That thing called love gets us all in the end. Now I think back a few years later, maybe it was fate that had destined my brakes not to work, for had it not been for those brakes, I would have gone up to Stockport, Manchester, for that 'dirty weekend' and maybe not have been drawn close to Viola. I would have eventually got married to Jan and I'd be living in Manchester now. Maybe someone had been watching me from up there and it had all been pre-destined all along?

So that weekend with Viola proved to be the definitive one in our relationship. And I finished with Jan over the phone in front of Viola. After all, if you turn down certain nookie just to see someone whom you didn't really know that well and had not often tried to get a bit of nookie from, then it must be love!

However, that weekend I had told Viola that I was 'on guard' and would be unable to see her. This, of course, wasn't true.

So I set off on Friday from South Wales for Basingstoke – again no brakes on the car. When I turned up that Friday night unannounced at Basingstoke Hospital Nurses' home, Viola was very surprised to see me.

I knocked on her door and she had a few of her nursing Filipino friends in, they all used to come to her for advice with their problems, as Filipinos still do today. We still laugh about it. Big momma – Mother Confessor! She must have a sympathetic ear. I saw her look of surprise and asked her to come outside with me a moment and told her to listen in while I rang up Jan who I had told I was coming up in my car for the weekend.

Viola kept saying, "I thought you weren't coming to see me this weekend!"

It wasn't entirely true and if she listened to me on the phone, she would understand. I then rang up Jan Wilson, who asked where I was and did I want her to come and meet me to guide me in to her house. (For house, read body!)

I explained that I was nowhere near her place; in fact, I was back at Basingstoke. Because I was spending the weekend with another and we may be getting married. Jan talked for a little while longer and seemed to be a sobbing a little, then a little more. I put the phone down and that was Jan and I finished.

Checking for V.D.

From the phone, we went back to Viola's room where she told all the other girls to leave and from then on, we knew we'd be going out together for a long time to come. It was while I was with Viola that weekend that she told me of the gossip and lies that had me riddled with V.D. Viola then asked me straight out if I would give her a true and honest answer. "Of course I will!" I replied, and she asked me, "Do you have the Pox, Gonorrhoea, Syphilis or any other sexually transmitted disease?" Talk about shocked! I laughed and told her no, I didn't. Nor have I ever had. I told Viola that we would shut up these liars and gossips once and for all! "I shall have a medical at camp to test for V.D. and I will get something in writing to prove it to you. Then as it will prove that I am clear, you can really lay into the gossips and bitches!" We both suspected the one to be behind these lies was none other than Daisy Misonia.

So it was when I went back to finish my course, I went to the medical centre at St Athan's for the test. I told the R.A.F. nurses that I'd be getting married soon and could I have a test for V.D. to put my girlfriend's mind at rest.

I will never forget the female R.A.F. nurse saying to me, "You're clear – no V.D. and you have never had any sexually transmitted disease, so you can tell your girlfriend. And tonight you can (quote) go at it like rabbits! And you can go at it all day and night if you wish!" (I should be so lucky!) This was done, telling her I mean! Viola even went as far as to put this on the nurses' noticeboard to the effect of: "To all those concerned, here is proof beyond all doubt that the lies and gossip being spread about by certain nurses about my boyfriend are all lies! And are totally untrue! Please read below a medical report!"

This had the desired effect! Of not only shutting up the bitches but the nice, decent people who knew both of us knew what sort of people they were dealing with. I had done something about quashing the V.D. rumour and it stopped the gossips dead! And from then on, we were as one and nothing could break us up. So in a way, we are glad the gossips had drawn us closer together sooner that normally might have been.

Getting brakes fixed at last

Eventually, I got fed up with dicing with death on the roads and during my last week at St Athan's, I took the car to the garage nearby and asked them to fix my brakes ready to go back to Odiham.

I had had two or three VERY close shaves with the car and I didn't dare chance it any longer. The night before leaving, I called them to ask if they were fixed. The garage owner said he hadn't had time to look at the car yet as he was so busy but he'll try and do it tomorrow. When I called in to pick up the car, he told me he had had a look at it and had managed to fix them, though by the tone of his voice, he thought I would consider that they were expensive. As it turned out, they only charged me £2.50. "Are you happy with the price?" he asked. I told him I was. As long as the problem was fixed. As it turned out, this chap had really and FINALLY fixed them. I told him of all the trouble I had had and all the money I had spent trying to get them sorted out. As it turned out, all that had been wrong was each wheel had two rubber seals on the brake cylinder and the rubber had perished so when the brake was applied, air got in and the brakes wouldn't work. Why was this not spotted before? But what the small garage had done was to cure the brake problem once and for all and I was very grateful for that.

WRAFs get 'high' and a good seeing to

At the end of our course, some of the WRAF girls said they had been so fed up and depressed at St Athan's that on our last night, they were going to get drunk and high and to hell with what happened after. (They were insinuating that if any of us chaps fancied to give them a good 'seeing-to' afterwards, they wouldn't mind.) I didn't fancy any of them as they were quite common and rough.

Most of them couldn't afford to get drunk come our last night there, so two of them confessed that they had heard of a way they could get drunk for next to nothing. So they had a couple of aspirins, a drink of Coca Cola and one or two beers, and they were definitely high or drunk, I didn't know which.

On the way back to camp, one of the couples were left behind and she DID get a good 'seeing to'!

Car burns

I was in Basingstoke nurses' home. I had decided to nip back to camp to pick up something I would need for the weekend. As I came off the motorway, I got stuck in a long traffic jam and when I eventually had reached the cause, I was surprised – and delighted to find out that there was a brand-new car on the side of the road – burnt out! (From the former AA-recommended garage who had overcharged me for my brakes and that I had reported to the AA.)

Driving past, I asked one of the mechanics what had happened, he told me that a customer had brought his brand-new car in for its first service and (surprise surprise) it suddenly burst into flames on its test run. I burst out laughing as I drove away and laughed all the way to camp, especially when I went past the said garage and saw for the first time that the AA had removed their spanner symbol. Just the thought that the garage would probably be sued for allowing the car to catch fire even if the owner was insured and that he would lose a lot of business through bad publicity, it made my day and I was rather chuffed. Though quite rightly felt more than a little sorry for the car owner.

"That will teach the bar-stewards," I thought and laughed all the way back down the motorway on the way to the hospital. I like to think that I was responsible for their demise, which will teach them to mess with me (and so with anyone).

Underslung loads

I was, for the first time since joining up, really looking to going back to work after a course; after all, the first and main reaction when told you were on a course was, 'Good, I'll get away from this place for a while'. Then at the end of the course, you would dread going to your main camp. Not so Odiham.

One of my main jobs was to prepare and execute underslung loads, strapping external loads (such as fuel, rations, weapons, ammunition or resupply a front line unit with anything they needed) to the underside of a helicopter, in this case an Anglo/French Puma.

This was work I really enjoyed as it was exciting and interesting and you were right at the sharp end by working directly with helicopters and 'those magnificent men in their flying machines'! The R.A.F. aircrew are without doubt the best in the world. Total professionals and real gentlemen.

First, you would prepare the load for lifting in the cargo net, then signal the helicopter hovering in the area that you were the 'load'; the helicopter then came in and hovered above you while the winch man guided the pilot in those last few feet. By this time, you were out of sight and the jockey, as we used to call the pilot, was guided on the spot by the other crew members, hence the good teamwork.

The aircraft would go into hover and then gently – ever so gently, he would come down and onto your 'eye' of the net in which you had the load. You would then hook on, give the signal and – no one told me to do this – run in front of the helicopter so the pilot could see me and then the moment the load was clear of the ground, give him the thumbs up signal and guide him safely out of the area; meanwhile, the winch man was also giving him instructions.

Though some of the winch men told you to stay and take up the tension on the strop before getting out. The first two or three times I did it, it was quite a scary thing to do! To see the helicopter hurtling towards you, hovering and then descending was quite unnerving at first. But you soon got used to it. Fear was replaced by excitement then you were quite relaxed and it didn't bother you anymore. But you still had to be switched on or else you put yourself at risk along with the aircraft and the crew.

Night flying

We also had to do night flying duties; so many that we were excused fire piquet or guard duties, this generally meant setting out the 'Bardic Tee', a means by which we were able to guide the pilot into the pick-up zone safely to be hooked up. There was never any shortage of volunteers as we certainly gained a lot out of it. Also with me being one of the few single men on the Sqn Regiment flight, I got most of these duties, which I enjoyed.

What used to happen was, at our Sqn Regiment room in the mornings, Alec, our sergeant i/c, would receive a call from the Ops room informing him of the intended night flying programme. Whoever volunteered for or was detailed for that duty was then told to take the rest of the day off and rest. Even if the call came through at 08:30 hours or at 15:00 hours.

Guards, time off

If the flying finished before 22:00 hours, we could have a lay in, report for work the next morning at 10:00-12:00 hours. If the flying finished after 22:00 hours, then you had all morning off. If later than 00:00 (midnight), then you had all the following day off.

If detailed for mobile patrol, then you were given the rest of the day off after the briefing by Alex or the orderly officer, then the whole of the next day off.

More than not, we even got chance to sleep in the guardroom after our patrols were finished. Unheard of in R/Regiment Sqn. 'The Odiham factor' again.

'Fire' in aircraft

One night when I was doing night flying on the airfield, the work was done and the winch man asked if I wanted to fly around the local area. On the odd occasion, we would do night flying out of camp; this would be interesting. I readily agreed. While I filled the centre seat in the cockpit (between the bulkhead), I was able to see very clearly in the cockpit, which fascinated me as the pilot flew low and fast over the airfield then climbed to safe height whilst flying over Basingstoke, Aldershot and surrounding villages.

The cockpit was aglow with different coloured lights, dials and switches. I was plugged into the intercom and listening to the conversation between the crew and air traffic control.

Suddenly, a red light started to flash in the control console; it had the word 'Fire' on it. Now I didn't need to learn to fly to know that we were in trouble! The pilot looked down at the flashing light and said – in the familiar type of R.A.F. pilots' cool unflappable voice that is now world famous! "I say, chaps, we appear to have a slight problem, one of our two engines is on fire!"

Then without further ado, he pressed a few buttons, pulled a few switches, the light went out and we carried on as if nothing had happened. The same thing happened very shortly after with the second engine: 'Fire' "We seem to have another fire, how dammed inconvenient!" More switches pulled and buttons pressed. To say I was sweating was an understatement, we landed outside the Sqn offices and as I got out, I stopped and kissed mother Earth.

Whilst airborne, I knew we would get down safely, I was in perfectly safe hands, how right I was! It hadn't put me off flying in the slightest.

I walked over to the pilot and congratulated him on a marvellous bit of flying. He said there was no need to say anything as there was 'no problem'. Rather modest, don't you think.

I pointed out, "No problem Sir? No problem? What about the fire warning signs?" "Oh that!" he said casually. "That was nothing, all that was, was my 6-monthly CAT test." (The test was carried out to ensure that the crew were still performing their jobs properly, including emergency procedure. They were never warned when it was going to happen; the C.O. decided when he would carry out the test.)

The C.O. had been the co-pilot this time and had decided that this was an ideal moment to carry out the test. He had 'fixed it' that that lights would come on.

The pilot passed the test and came through with flying colours.

'Squash the rock'

Once the aircrew knew that you were a new face or if they felt in a playful mood, they used to play, as I termed it, 'squash the rock-ape'.

What used to happen was we saw them approach from afar until they were just above you, about in the right position but just out of reach, you would have to stretch or jump to try and hook on and each time, they would back away just a bit more then come in and repeat; when they saw you were getting annoyed, they would hover for a while then when least expected, they would swoop down. "Good," you thought, "about time," but much to our annoyance, they would come down further and further making it more and more awkward for you. Eventually, the wheels would just be off the deck but head room would be about 3-4 feet. At times, you would be laying on your back (the best position) to hook on; meanwhile, the only thing you could see was the winch man talking to the jockey, telling him what was happening to you and near hurting himself laughing at you.

At first, before you got used to working with the helicopters, you didn't know if you were supposed to stay at your post hooking up or get the hell out of it. I felt that it may just be a test of nerves to see if you could 'take it' and to see if you would desert your post so I elected to stay there until the very last moment and see the job through and only to get out of it if it got dangerous. (If the engine ceased and it made a heavy landing, the aircrew would not be hurt nor would the helicopter be damaged as it would be only about three feet from the ground, though we underneath would have bought it.)

Losing their 'bottle'

'Squash the rock' wasn't much fun for us at the time though I look back now and laugh. Some of the other Regiment lads used to say, "Bugger that, I'm not hanging around to get killed!" This was a rock-ape talking, sounded like he'd lost his bottle. If the helicopter came too low, they would say to me, "Time I wasn't here!" and they would be out from under the helicopter like a shot.

It was very scary the first time but not only had I full confidence in the skills of the aircrew, I thought, "I'll teach them, I'll show I'm not scared." I stuck it out, the aircrew knew what they were doing and as usual, the winch man would be looking out of the underneath hatch/side door.

Mock anger

I knew they were playing games with me, as the lower they came, the more I cursed them; of course, the noise of the powerful Rolls Royce engines drowned out any semblance of conversation. But they could see that I was cursing them by watching my lips and seeing me shake my fist at them in mock anger (albeit with a smile on my face). This really amused them as I could see them having a good laugh and still they came lower. In the Regiment section, I was known as a) bloody stupid or b) bloody brave, whichever opinion they had of me depended on whether they liked me or not.

'Swinging' parties

The first few weeks since joining the Sqn (before meeting Viola), one of the 'penguins' from the Sqn approached me and asked if I'd like to come to a party he was having at his place that Friday evening, just bring a couple of pounds to pay for all the food and drink that I wanted that night, which I was assured would go on till the early hours of the morning. (He didn't realise what he was saying when he said, "All the food and drink I wanted!" For a couple of quid? "Bargain!" I thought.

Those days, I could out-eat and out-drink anyone! Even most rock-apes.

These 'dos' were every Friday to Saturday lunch time, and quite a friendly atmosphere! Especially if you were single and lonely, you weren't lonely for long, if you get my drift!

I didn't realise how friendly they could be until one Friday evening, I took Viola and three of her Filipino friends from Basingstoke Hospital.

About halfway through the evening, I was asked to take them home; she told me that things were getting out of hand! Viola said that she had been to the ladies room on three separate occasions that night and each time she had noticed that the bedroom doors were open and the 'hostess' was seen on those three separate occasions getting 'acquainted' in the most intimate way with three different men. Not that her husband was left out of the fun, he was no worse/better, whichever way you wanted to look at it, than his wife, he also was getting very intimate with other girls/wives. These 'swapping' parties used to finish up about lunchtime on Saturday morning after everyone that was left went for lunch to a restaurant for a slap-up steak meal.

I found out later that this went on most Friday nights. Though they were subtle as I wasn't aware of goings on. These parties progressed gradually until there were same-thinking friends and inevitably finished up as a full-blown orgy. Not that I was ever that involved or aware! Or even invited to the orgy before I met Viola. 'Swapping' wasn't my thing.

By then, however, I was courting Viola regularly and had been for a while.

It was heard around the Sqn a few weeks later that the C.O. Wing Commander John Strong had somehow got to hear of the goings on. This lad was on the carpet and given 'rock all'. I never heard what happened to him, as per military discipline, all we heard that the 'host and hostess' had got divorced! Not surprisingly.

One amusing thing I remember was he was mad on breeding gerbils of which I'd never heard of till then and apparently these desert rodents were always 'at it' and he had heck of a job to get rid of the resultant little ones.

Stag nights at the Naafi

One evening at the Naafi, during a strip show with a blue comedian and a drag queen, one of the girls, a West Indian girl, called this lad on stage. He had been saying all night what he would do to her given half a chance.

She called his bluff; of course, he backed down in front of his mates but to prevent too much loss of face, she asked him if he would help her with the next part of her act. All this look place while she was completely naked.

He agreed, so she put him on a chair on stage and stripped him as naked as herself. He was minus his front teeth and smiling a stupid toothless grin.

He was not even bothering to cover up his by now sodden and shrunken embarrassment. Not even the girl's antics with and without the fire could arouse or stir him into life, he just stood on the chair in the middle of the stage, baring all. What a sight to behold! And he wasn't even getting paid for it. Meanwhile, his mates were ridiculing him from the comfort of their chairs. This chap and his mates were from my Sqn; they were aircraft fitters.

The following morning, we, the whole Sqn were rather looking forward to 'taking the mick' out of him.

During roll call in the morning, the senior NCO called out the names and when it at came to this chap, no answer. The senior NCO called out his name 2-3 times and said, "Has anyone seen – – – – this morning?" This resulted in a chap in the back row calling out, "He's run off with the drag queen from the strip show!" That was greeted with guffaws of laughter from those present.

The senior NCO said, "Stop mucking about, lads, somebody must have seen him? Has anybody seen ----?" A voice shouted from the back, "I told you he ran off with the queer, the drag queen!" More laughter – and indeed he had! 'No names, no pack drill', as they say!

Neither his mates nor anybody had guessed he was a 'bit that way' right up to and including the show. We had wondered why the stripper couldn't arouse him, only the drag queen had been able too.

We never saw the chap again, we did hear that the S.I.B. had caught up with him and he was waiting for a court martial.

Motor club
Odiham, as most large stations, had a motor club where for a small fee you could join and use the station's facilities but just as important, you could get spare parts at very good savings, sometimes up to 60% on production of your membership card from local garages and motorist's discount shops.

Fixing clutch at work
I needed a new clutch for my Fiat 850. So I got 10% discount from this motor discount store + 50% in exchange for my old one, on production of my R.A.F. motor club card.

One of our Regiment Cpls (Phil) said to me, "If you can get the parts, I'll put it in for you; during normal working hours, bring the car to work one day outside the offices and I'll have done it for you by the time you finish work for the day!" And he was true to his word. That's all he did all day, fix my car. He was happy, I was happy.

Re-tax car, time off from work
I also needed the car re-taxing. I asked where I had to go to do it. I was told by Phil that it was few miles away so I asked if by any chance he had the address so that I could do it by post.

"You might as well have an early lunch and take a couple of days to sort it out!" I tried to tell them that all being well, I would be able to get it done that afternoon, but they insisted that I take my time and have a couple of days. Who was I to argue, so I did just that! It was only about 30-40 miles away; I was even back in time for tea. So I was able to relax the next two days, they said they didn't expect me back for that period of time even if I had gotten it squared up quickly.

This was what Odiham was all about.

M.T. services my car

We also had, or should I say I had, a bit of a side-line going here, I got my car serviced at the camp M.T. yard at little to no cost. There was an M.T. mechanic whom I knew to say 'hello' to around camp. I chatted to him about looking after my car; I would of course see he was all right, financially speaking. Not only did he service my car for me but he told me that he was able to do it during working hours in the M.T.S.S. yard.

He said he needed one or two parts so he had ordered them for my car through the official R.A.F. channels (Sgt Bilko would be proud of him!), claiming that it was a 'staff car'. How he got away with ordering parts for an old two-door Fiat 850cc banger, I'll never know! But he did. Whoever heard of a small Fiat 850 being used as a staff car? But nobody questioned it. 'Odiham factor' again.

He only charged me £5 for doing full service on the car as well. I offered more but he wouldn't take it.

Maths exam

While at Odiham, I tried again for my R.A.F. educational test Pt I, maths. I failed by four points (two questions) to get the required 80% pass mark. I was very disappointed, especially after all the education officer had done to help me.

I wasn't totally surprised as maths had never been my favourite or best subject.

I did try once more; this time, I failed by two points – one question.

Lift from M.T. to London

I wanted to go home one weekend but couldn't afford the train fare, so I chatted to a couple of chaps on M.T. and arranged for them to give me a lift as far as London and then I would get the train home from there.

On the way, we passed several Rolls-Royces with their rich owners in the back. Most of them were OK and some even gave us in our Land Rover a wave and a smile. We returned the compliment; others, however, were very snobbish and stuck up, they were clearly looking down their noses at us as they thought they were 'better than mere, common servicemen'. The driver told me, "If there is one thing I can't stand, that is fecking snobs." He proceeded to deliberately annoy and upset them by emphasising the things he thought they didn't like. He said "So, they think we're too rough for them, do they? I'll fecking show them how rough we can be!" When he was sure that they were watching, he proceeded to annoy them by picking his nose, looking at it and pretending to wipe it on the side window, pulling faces and making gestures. I just watched and we had good laugh at their reactions to his messing about. The worst culprit of all was some old biddy in a Rolls-Royce and fur coat so we really piled it on with her. Our behaviour I suppose wasn't what it should have been and they could have reported us (though they weren't to know what base or even what service we were from) and when one's wise with afterthought, we could have gone about bringing them down in a more subtle manner. Such was mad impetuous youth.

Singing in a pop group

A couple of lads on the Sqn, with some of their friends – all of whom played some musical instrument – started playing together as a pop group. It was known that I liked singing, especially Elvis, and I was invited to join them in their jam session; unfortunately though, the group didn't know too many Elvis songs. I couldn't figure out just why we weren't getting it together, I was singing at the right speed and at the right tempo but they were always that bit slow. I realised now that they were all playing at wrong key/cord and not together either, no wonder I had a struggle. I thought it was me at fault but it wasn't.

I took the hint that they didn't want me to sing in the group on their first public outing. They said they knew someone else who knew a more diverse range of songs; he would, they tried to tell me, be better for public shows.

A week or so later, when I enquired about their first engagement, their 'super singer' hadn't shown up. Must have gotten cold feet.

"Surprise, surprise," I told them. "Serves you right, I would have turned up!"

For the benefit of those who never tried singing into microphone, with an audience, however small, and who think it is dead easy, you're wrong, dead wrong. It must be one of the most difficult, nerve-wracking things in the world to do! Get up in front of an audience. I speak from experience.

I declined an offer to rejoin their jam sessions, I thought, "Bugger them, they've had their chance and they blew it!" However, it was not long after that I started to go out with Viola regularly; I had no more time for them, even if I had wanted to.

Free flight to Waddington

I had chance of a perk on the Sqn. I fancied going home for the weekend, but as usual I either couldn't afford it or didn't fancy the long drive home. I heard that one of the Sqn helicopters was going up north and was refuelling at R.A.F. Waddington about 40 miles from home. So I asked if I could have a lift up as far as Waddington, then when they landed to refuel, I would thumb a lift the rest of the way and catch the same chopper on the return refuelling stop from the display it was doing. It was all agreed but unfortunately, I overslept that day, I even remember hearing it circling the block I was in overhead.

Rags for shirts

Once after spending a fortnight's leave at home, I resumed work the following Monday morning. I went to pick up the Land Rover from the M.T yard before reporting to Sqn – as usual. I noticed M.T. lads near fighting over a box of rags in the yard. I asked what was up to cause such a commotion. I was told to take a look for myself! I saw lots of R.A.F. collar-attached shirts, they had been sent by stores to M.T. to be used as cleaning and general purpose rags; they were ripped up.

The ironic thing was and why everyone was going mad for them was the new collar-attached shirts, we hadn't been issued them as yet and all we had still at that time was the old-fashioned detachable collar type.

One of the lads said that he had taken these rags to the stores and exchanged what was left for good shirts, so I helped myself to what was left; there weren't many as most had been picked already. Nevertheless, I gave it a try. So into the stores I marched and called my friend aside, I smiled at him and said to him, "Hello, look, I've just arrived back on camp from leave (true) and I have discovered some rotten bar-steward has broken open my locker and ripped up all my shirts! (Blatant lie!) Any chance of changing them please?"

He gave me a knowing smile and said, "Don't give me that waffle and bullshit! I know where you got them from; you got them from a box in the M.T. yard, didn't you?" I had to tell him he was right, but he didn't blame me for trying to get some new shirts from them before the official issue. He smiled and called me a waffling bugger (and worse) but nevertheless, he did change them for me. I was most grateful. I tried not to overdo it and changed some each day over a week, the following week we were told officially to proceed to stores to change the old pattern for new.

In the space of about 10 days, I got myself about 20 new shirts (I am still using the last of them at this time). If the stories were true, it was still only half as many as everyone else got, due to my being on leave when they first arrived.

Cut wrist

One evening on the block, I was proceeding to the washroom whereupon I habitually put my hand forward to push open the door and this time clipped the side of the wooden frame on the glass partition and went straight through the pane of glass – slashing open my wrist. I stood there for a moment, looking at my hand through the smashed piece of glass and at the very deep gaping wound in the wrist. It was ironic that I should be injured in the block as I spent so little time there. I remember thinking, "That's strange; it's a deep cut!" I swore I could see the bone, yet it was not bleeding. Yet!

Then the blood started to flow, and quite fast, but fortunately, I had somehow missed cutting a vital vein or something of the like. I stood almost transfixed and then thought I'd better get myself down to the medical centre and get it treated. The blood started to flow a little faster – too fast for my comfort. So I started to run, not the brightest thing to do as the faster my heart pumped, the faster the blood would flow, but that did not seem to happen.

I must have been very fit to run and my heart not to pump too excessively.

The male nurse in attendance treated me by putting a couple of butterfly stitches over the wound; surprisingly, as deep as the wound was, it stopped the bleeding and allowed the wound to heal nicely.

The only night I was guaranteed to be found in the block was on bull nights! Once courting Viola, I would nearly always have tea, get washed and changed, then out of camp and up to Basingstoke to spend the evening with Viola. As much as I (in common with nearly everyone else) didn't like bull night, there was one thing that I would not allow to happen and that was to be thought of as 'not pulling my weight', so usually I would have tea, change and do my bit of bull night.

That was usually my night with the lads! I'd have a few pints and give Viola a miss that night, sometimes I would also go and see her after I'd cleaned up.

Filmed doing underslung loads

One morning when I reported for work at the Sqn, I found myself chosen to represent the Puma in the film to be made. The film was to be called *History of Aviation*, in which the important milestones in aviation history would be depicted. Also in the film, there was, of course, the Harrier – the world's first V./S.T.O.L. aircraft in Sqn service. I was to carry out underslung loads with the Puma, while also with us was one of 72 Sqn Wessex with Andy Rowe.

We flew up to R.A.F. Wittering one warm and sunny day, did the jobs and were filmed from a camera crew about 50 yards away. They did, however and inevitably, spend more time filming the amazing Harrier.

Proposing

It wasn't long before I took Viola home to meet my parents. After travelling over 200 miles to home, which was only two miles to go, Viola wanted to go back to Basingstoke; she was very nervous about meeting my parents for first time. But after travelling all that way and with only two miles to go, I sure as hell wasn't going to turn back. It was that weekend when I proposed to her.

Safari park

One of the places Viola and I visited was the safari park near Windsor.

This particular place was Longleat. There was Viola, my mother and myself. I wasn't keen on going into the lions' enclosure as my windows weren't working at all, just held up with bits of wood and string. I could quite easily visualise a great lion's paw clawing at my window, it collapsing and a big paw clawing at our faces. Although sweating and impatient, I couldn't get through that enclosure quick enough. Of course, we got through without a hitch, what a relief that was.

Engagement party 1974.

Viola's teeth

After a while, I found out that Viola had a problem with her teeth and that a civvy dentist had seriously messed them up. So I chatted to the R.A.F. dentist on camp. Being the gentleman that he was, he agreed to do something about it; of course, he didn't have to as R.A.F. didn't recognise fiancées, only legal wives. The next stage of repairing her teeth had to be carried out on my next posting.

Living in the nurses' home

I spent my time with Viola in the nurses' home most of the time, but the places I finished up in were like something out of situation comedy.

As you may well imagine, men weren't allowed in the nurses' home, let alone their room after 10:30 at night. I spent more than one night sleeping on the chair or settee in the TV room.

Another time when we thought we were about to be discovered in her room, I finished up in her wardrobe. But that is another story!

Comings and goings

Don't think I was the only guy to stay in the nurses' room all night. Oh no!

There were 8 rooms on Viola's floor and 7 of them had men virtually staying with them. The only exception was a nurse on her own who we all believed to be a lesbian. But she was to prove us all wrong, she finished

299

up 'living in' with a man, but the ironic part was that the man was thought also to be 'one of them' by his reputation around Basingstoke but it turned out neither of them were! So after a short time, all the girls had boyfriends/ lovers living in and trying to hide whenever the house warden came around.

As a matter of interest, a girl had about three men living with her in her room (though not all at the same time) but most only had one. Nina whose room was opposite Viola's, was a prime example, a lovely girl, natural redhead and only about 18-19 but was found to be 'at it' virtually non-stop. When I hear the term 'nymphomaniac', I will always think of Nina, for that is clearly what she was. She certainly liked her sex, though of course, she was on the pill; she had to be, she even liked to try the sex aids such as a vibrator while her boyfriend recovered, ready to 'go again'. I don't know how she found time to do any swotting for exams or even work at the hospital. She had 'others' waiting in the wings, so to speak, when she'd worn out one boyfriend, she wheeled in another to take his place, almost on a 'sexual' production line. One thing was for sure, all who left her room, Nina included, had the broadest of smiles. But barely able to walk.

What was it with these redheads? Those I met all seemed to be sex-mad. Poor lass, I felt sorry for her as she looked about thirty. No wonder, but she was enjoying herself! And there was no shortage of boyfriends only too willing and happy to oblige!

We even got a sergeant friend to mine from my Sqn fixed up with the last but one girl on the floor; she was Anglo-Indian! It used to be funny first thing in the morning at about 6:30-7 am to see airmen rock-apes and the odd civvy/soldier climbing out of the various windows or rushing down the stairs to prevent being caught in the nurses' home. They would all dive into their respective cars and at a racing start zoom out of the hospital grounds as fast as they could, very funny.

The carpark used to be like a military convoy at times as it would set off for camp. Nearly every window had a girl/girls looking out and sneaking a crafty last wave and look at their boyfriend as they sped away, giving their beaus a wave. I doubt if any of the girls still had their virtue intact – I doubt it very much.

Parade outside

For a laugh one morning, my sergeant friend, Tony Lane, a fitter on the Sqn, suggested we have an inspection and parade before we set off. So outside the block, we were mostly in uniform, it was great fun as Tony had us all lined up and inspecting us, saying things like, "What's up with you laddies this morning? Haven't you had time to get properly dressed this morning?"

"No, Sergeant."

"I bet you have been on the job all night, haven't you, laddie?"

"Yes Sergeant!"

"Dirty lucky bugger!"

"So what!" came the reply. "I bet you have as well, Sarge?"

"As a matter of fact, I have!" replied Sergeant Tony Lane. Everyone laughed.

"Anyone else get his leg over last night?" he asked. Everyone came back with a "YES!" as one!

When this happened, all girls bar none suddenly disappeared inside their rooms. Anybody would think they were shy or something.

Getting my own room in the nurses' home

Viola, in talking to the house warden one day, heard from her, "Most of the girls think I'm stupid, they think I don't know what is going on behind my back, and they think I don't know that they are letting their boyfriends stay the night with them in their rooms all night. I know it's going on, I won't say anything to the hospital authorities unless I have to, if there is any trouble!"

"Besides, if they have their boyfriends with them, there is less likelihood of them being attacked by a stranger breaking in at night!" Viola, then seizing the moment, said, "Being as its Christmas soon; can you get him a room of his own please over the Christmas period?" (Of all the cheek!)

It did, however, have the desired result: I did have my own room in the nurses' home. While Viola would be at work, I would while away the hours by making model sailing galleons.

Nurse looks for a doctor

An amusing thing happened one day. While waiting for Viola to finish work, I heard a knock on the door. Opening it, I saw a young nurse before me, wearing a short see-through nightdress and carrying medical books; she asked if I knew where a Dr so and so's room was. It was obvious she wasn't dressed for or going to do much studying, unless it was anatomy. I told her not only didn't I know, but I was in the R.A.F. I bet to this day she is still wondering why a R.A.F. man had a room in the nurses' home.

Two big mistakes

We had a Regiment chap who was normally working directly with the 'first line serving section' on the Sqn. He made two big mistakes for which the officers tried to charge him but he got away with it – lucky for him.

Incident 1: His job was 'refuelling Bowser driver'. This one day, he was re-fuelling a Puma. During a rotor turning refuel, instead of walking back with the hose to put it on the Bowser, he turned around and without think-ing threw the hose to the wagon. It was his lucky day for the down-wash threw the hose/nozzle down then sucked it up and sliced the nozzle clean off. There was aviation fuel gushing everywhere; how that aircraft and all the others on the pan didn't burst into flames or blow up killing all we will never know. Upon interrogation, the officer found out his excuse was that he couldn't concentrate due to thinking of his boy who had a hole in his heart! We then found out he had kept it to himself. He not only got away with it, but the R.A.F., to their credit, once they found out, sent him to see a heart specialist in Harley Street. Gave the best medical treatment possible including the best hospitals in the country with the best doctors/surgeons to be found with their practices on Harley Street, and you couldn't get any better or much more expensive medical help than that! Military or civil. And his boy had an operation and all was well thereafter.

Incident 2: He was towing an aircraft out of the hangar when he heard something metallic snap, so instinctively hit the brakes, as anyone would.

It was the wrong thing to do. The Puma, still in forward traction, crashed into the back of the Land Rover, damaging the flight control console with all the instrument panels. The aircraft was taken out of the line while all the instruments and flying controls were checked out. Then after a day or two, it had an air test prior to being declared serviceable again.

Again the officers tried to charge him but again he got away with it; he said, "How can I be charged for reacting instinctively, even though as they said I should have accelerated and not braked!" He got away with it, rightly so. (The metal he had heard had been a link pin in the towing arm snapping.)

My little episodes

I was again reminded of some 'little episodes' of mine and some memories of his by my Sgt Alex Goddard, which I had clean forgotten about.

"I remember you going to see Elvis in Las Vegas and taking some photos of Elvis on stage; you were selling them to those on the trip. You were accused by one of the people of taking a photo of a poster of Elvis and trying to pass it off as legit, and getting called everything under the sun!"

This was so, but the photo I had taken of Elvis on stage was genuine. It happened to be the same pose as the poster and Elvis wearing the same jumpsuit, still nobody else minded. It was only the stuck-up Priscilla who had complained.

He said, "The Sqn had been waiting for a part for an aircraft for six weeks to come, eventually it arrives and you go to the electronics department where they repair or send instruments away for repair. On the way back, you tripped, fell over, dropped it and broke the part into little pieces. So the Sqn had to put in another order in for another replacement!"

I received a 'telling off' from Alex, my only one. But that was the end of the matter; neither the C.O. nor servicing department of the Sqn ever said a word to me. That was 'Odiham' for you!

"As the aircraft was new and still being fully assessed as to their full capabilities, I remember having to test the G.P.M.G. on a door bracket on the aircraft. The L.M.G. was not as powerful as the G.P.M.G. When 'rapid fire' was selected, with the G.P.M.G., it made the Puma nearly stand on its nose with the power of the spread!"

Viola pulls over the nurses' home Christmas tree

During our first Christmas together, we went to a party organised for the nurses and held at the nursing education centre. I saw Viola drunk for only the second time that night. On the way out and going back to the nurses' block, she saw in the foyer a large, decorated Christmas tree. She said she fancied the fairy at the top for a souvenir! I laughed and told her not to be so ridiculous, but she insisted and when I refused to get it for her, she tried to get it herself.

Now this tree was about 12 feet tall and way out of her reach, but as she tried to get it, somehow the tree wobbled and fell over with a sickening crash! The lights were smashed, the decorations smashed, but we didn't wait to own up to it. I just grabbed her hand and we ran like hell so we wouldn't get caught.

I think after the tree fell over, the fairy in question was the only thing that remained unbroken, at least it appeared so as we ran past it and left it lying there. We never heard any more about it.

Dobby Donald: Army pal on the fiddle

S.A.C. 'Dobby' Donald, Odiham's answer to Sgt Bilko, was a real life version of the irrepressible 'Master Sergeant Ernest Bilko' of the *Phil Silvers Show* and believe it or not, some of the antics that soldiers got up to then are still in use today, though obviously updated. In a nutshell, getting one over on the officers and making a quick buck, skive.

Para smocks

The craze at Odiham amongst the rocks was that they all were wearing Para smocks; it was the in thing of the time. I asked Dobby how much they were but the profit margin he had was too great for me so I didn't bother. I told some of the others, "Why do you want to wear a Para smock? You haven't earned the right to wear it, just as you haven't earned the right to wear parachutists wings, wear your own combat jacket as you have earned the right to wear that, wear it with pride!" Not many listened to me.

Dobby shows himself up

'Dobby' Donald, when not busy making money from all and sundry, was a hard drinker and founder member of the 'Pigs bar'. He used to drink all lunchtime and evenings. On the odd occasion when he was hard up (not often), he would have a few drinks, fall asleep in the TV room in the Naafi and by the time he woke up, there would be no one anywhere near him, at the side or behind. He would wake, look around and wonder why he was on his own, then looking down at the floor, he would see a pool of water (urine), sit and look at for it for a while and try and figure out what it was, then the realisation would come to him and with a nervous cough, he would get up and go back to the block.

His mate was no better; he was a real animal and alcoholic.

Incident in the Naafi club

One night the manager shut the bar on time and this animal demanded the bar reopen; if not, he would burn the Naafi down, starting at the curtains and then the chairs. She wouldn't open the bar and he started to carry out his threat by setting some of the curtains on fire, he was stopped before he could do any further damage. It was rock-apes like these two that gave the rest of us a bad name, though fortunately, they were the exception, but that didn't help the rest of us.

Dobby meets a challenge

Dobby was on 72 Sqn, they had Wessex helicopters, and, as I have said, could get you anything you wanted for a price! If Dobby failed to get you what you wanted, then his army friend was contacted.

He had a contact in the army at Aldershot army base. Another Bilko character. This ultimately pushed up the price by another fiver or so. Dobby would even get the Sqn transport section to go to and collect his goods for him and if that failed, then he exercised his option to get someone in the stn M.T. yard to go.

He also, like his TV namesake, had a card school and other gambling pursuits on the go. He wasn't the sort to turn down any money-making schemes. (Sound familiar?)

He did surpass himself on one occasion though, and us fellow rocks were proud of him. From his office...yes, even as an S.A.C., he had his own office. Normally, only Sgts and above were entitled to this privilege, good-ness knows how he had managed it.

This incident that we were so proud of him for centred on a challenge and a bet! From the 'penguin's social organiser'.

The 'penguins' used to organise monthly dos for their lads, though the rocks did get an invitation to these heavy drinking sessions. With one or two women there for good measure. One day, this chief 'penguin' threw down a challenge to Dobby to beat that for organisation if you can!

Dobby was not one to shirk a challenge, especially with the Regiment's reputation at stake! Now Dobby monthly dos were pretty good as they were with plenty of drink (as much as you wanted for a fixed price) and girls (though not as many as at the other do). We didn't want anything to get in the way of our serious drinking, besides, we couldn't be thought of as paying too much attention to soppy girls, the other side would think we had gone soft.

The 'do' was organised and all the rocks were told to be at the Castle Club by 20:00 hours. Nobody had been told what was to go down, not even his close pals, such was the need for secrecy.

The cost was a mere £1 for all the food and beer you could wish for. (Normally, we would be charged between £3-5.) There was to be a raffle, disco but no girls. Someone went up to Dobby and complained, "We've got a disco, drink, food but no girls, what is the use of that!" "Be patient," says Dobby, "it's only 5 to 8!"

At eight 8 o'clock on the dot, we heard the sound of helicopters getting louder and nearer, no one paid much attention as being a helicopter base, night flying was a normal happening. The noise of the engines got even louder and nearer, we went outside to investigate, we couldn't believe our eyes.

One by one, 10 helicopters of 72 Sqn circled and landed on the carpark, one by one outside the mess and Naafi.

One by one, they discharged their cargo! Girls – lots of girls! We let out a spontaneous cheer, old Dobby had done it in style, who else would have been able to arrange for virtually an entire R.A.F. helicopter Sqn to be detoured to bring and take home about 50 girls, mostly nurses from all the local hospitals – Aldershot, Fareham, Basingstoke and others. Quite a feat in coordination and for them all to arrive together on time.

It was the choppers from Dobby's own Sqn. how he'd swung this one I cannot even guess. He must somehow have a very powerful influence over the C.O.

It was a heck of a good do, one of the best I'd been to. "Well done, Dobby!" The penguin organiser who had been invited along graciously accepted defeat. And paid up. There was no way he could top that.

Dobby has his downfall

Dobby 'Bilko' Donald inevitably was to have his downfall and it wasn't long in coming. He also dabbled in scrap metal, unbeknown to most. This was to be the start of his ultimate fall from power.

The incident in question started unobtrusively in N. Ireland where both his and my Sqns had regular detachments.

One of my Sqn choppers had crashed when landing, the rock-apes on duty were at the scene first and assisted in getting the aircrew out of the aircraft for which they were given a commendation.

It was reported that with the very high rate of rotation of the rotor blade, one of the helicopter rotor blades had passed through the wall of the kitchen at the back of the mess, missing the cooks by inches. (It was the same principle of blade of straw being blown by the wind at such a high speed that it embeds itself in a tree.) The wreckage was brought back to Odiham, where we heard no more about it (inquiry into the accident pending). I could not say what happened or part, or not at all, was true. But 'rumour control' usually got it right. Allegedly, Dobby had gotten involved.

We then heard that Dobby had been summoned to a court martial, I enquired and was told that not only was he up before a court martial, but civvy police were involved as well. What had happened was 'allegedly', Dobby had heard of the aircraft going down and contacted his army/civvy associates appertaining to making a deal and a bit of money here. What had come to pass was Dobby did his 'Bilko' thing and 'allegedly' sold part of the crashed helicopter to this civilian.

This might have been all right normally and nothing more heard, but then Dobby had a piece of bad luck; this customer who had paid for the exclusive purchase of part of the helicopter happened to have a friend who just happened to be a police officer who went to his friend's house for a barbecue one summer evening. He spied a most unusual children's garden swing. "That's an unusual garden swing," the off-duty policeman was supposed to have said. "Quite unlike anything I've seen before!" "No wonder," said Dobby's customer, "that's the armour plating from the pilot's seat from a helicopter that crashed!"

That was it, that was the start and when the policeman went back on duty, he started making enquires and investigations that led back to Dobby 'Bilko' Donald. Allegedly!

That, however, wasn't all Dobby's troubles. There was more to come! 'Rumour control' also claimed it was said, 'allegedly', that whilst waiting for his court martial, he was also caught 'messing about' (whatever that meant) in the Naafi. They kicked him out with dishonourable discharge. If this was not true, apologies to all concerned.

So Dobby Donald's reign as Odiham's 'King of the Black Marketeers' was finally over!

Viola studies for her finals

While Viola was studying for her final exams, I agreed I would leave her alone for a couple of weeks or so while she did her swotting, but what to do in the meantime? One night, I went to the cinema in Aldershot to see the latest Elvis Presley film, *Elvis, That's the Way It Is!* At one point in the film, I was about to nod off when I was stunned into wakefulness; on the film, I saw an amazing sight. There, in the middle of the fans was the girl I had met in Las Vegas on my holiday to USA, Debbie Humphries, who had given me that free ticket to see Elvis. I had been corresponding with her too, what a small world.

Aircrew on the range for their annual shoot

I once went with Alex Goddard who had been tasked to take the aircrew on their annual shoot on the ranges. After they had fired their annual allocation of rounds (9mm S.M.G.s, sidearm's ammo), they were given the rest to shoot off as they wished. Some strapped their guns/holsters to their hips 'gunfighter style' and fired their guns one-handed – western style. Of those who drew and fired from the hip, western style, most were good shots, but the chap who was the best was also the fastest draw. Wyatt Earp – eat your heart out! Quite a character he was too, typical R.A.F. aircrew, with a large bushy moustache. He'd draw his weapon, 'gunfighter' style, and hit the target every time, a natural shot.

Wedding day

Inevitably, it comes to us all. Eventually, my days of girl chasing and getting up to all sorts of escapades were over. As I was about to finally get married.

By the time the date of our wedding came around, I was beginning to believe that surely I couldn't be that lucky and right up to the day itself. I realised that this was it – the 'big one'. John the girl chaser was no more, officially retired! The females of UK were finally safe from me. I approached my wedding like a military operation.

I checked that all arrangements were made and all people were 'reminded' not to be late, even a rehearsal of ceremony and preparation of my kit. I got married in uniform and borrowed a fancy buckle and white belt from Queens Colour Sqn, who did all the fancy drill on displays around the world. This set the uniform off to a tee. And 'Yes', I had finally received my long-awaited uniform that had been three years in coming. Just in time for the wedding. It was a quiet, simple wedding; the only hitch was that the photographer didn't turn up till after the wedding so there were no photos of Viola and myself before entering the church. To say I was mad was an understatement, and then to cap it all, he took too many snaps outside the church, duplicating each shot, and only had two left for the reception.

Finally, the days of chasing girls and having fun were over!

Inviting C.O. to wedding

Once I decided to tie the knot, we invited the C.O. to the wedding, not just out of courtesy but because both Viola and I wanted him to attend. We both liked and greatly respected him. As I've said, Wing Commander John Strong was such a gentleman I felt we would be honoured for him to attend our wedding.

Alas, it was his turn to take a detachment out to N. Ireland so he couldn't attend. Just before our wedding, the C.O. called me to his office and told me to take his personal Land Rover to the hospital and pick up Viola and bring her back to meet him in his Sqn office as he would like to meet her. I was pleasantly surprised at this gesture, so I picked her up. And we walked through the Sqn hangar, where Viola saw the line mechanics working on the helicopters, to his office. She was very impressed. We had a very pleasant surprise, the C.O. John Strong and his wife had bought us a complete 36×3 drinking glass set for water, wine and sherry. And good quality, we still have them today. He apologised for not being able to attend the wedding. He, a high-ranking senior officer, made us feel completely at ease and relaxed. For that, we were and shall be eternally grateful; it was very good of him.

We didn't expect it, and it was a pleasant surprise, typical of the man.

Wedding day

Honeymoon with ABBA

The honeymoon was a few days in Gothenburg, Sweden. Not recommended! The place, not the honeymoon. We caught the ferry from Hull, Yorkshire, to Sweden. On board were winners of the previous night's 'Eurovision song contest' ABBA on their way back to Sweden. I hadn't noticed them at first but Viola had seen them loading their vehicles and equipment on board. At the ship's disco that night, it seemed they were playing *Waterloo* every few minutes. I was getting fed up with it and wondered why, then Viola pointed out to me that ABBA, the group themselves, were dancing to their record on the dance floor with everybody in the audience, and indeed they were! I don't think anyone could have foreseen the success they went on to achieve!

Hearing of next posting

I also previously had a feeling that once married, it would be just my luck to get posted to Germany, not to some warm exotic climes, which I much preferred. I knew Odiham wouldn't last forever. My next posting was to 1 Sqn R.A.F. Regiment, Germany. Odiham was a great camp, great people to work with and a lot of good friends and for me that was unusual as I was a bit of a loner. Rank was never pushed. I had received notice of my next posting a few weeks before getting married. The first time it was out of my hands; usually, it was I that instigated my next posting. After about a couple of weeks back at camp, it was time to prepare for my next posting. I had asked the C.O. to try and cancel it as I didn't want to go and wished to stay on 33 Sqn.

He tried but the most I got was a couple of weeks delay and then I had to go. I was very depressed at the thought that I was going to leave Odiham and all the friends I had made while there. Sgt Alex Goddard, Wom and Ella, but we managed to find each other through social media.

I returned to Odiham three years later just before finishing my time in the services and found out that Wing Commander John Strong had been promoted and posted not long after I had left. He had gone to M.O.D. in London, someone had obviously appreciated his good work and seen his potential. I am glad, he deserved it. Good luck to you, John Strong, wherever you are, you are a real gentleman and it was a real pleasure to serve under you!

Once in civvy street, I had the misfortune to work under another 'John Strong' but this one was nothing like my C.O., for every positive, the civilian version was 10 times the negative of this officer and true gent!

Applying for an M.Q.

Once Viola and I were married, I submitted an application for an M.Q. (Married Quarter), though I knew I didn't stand much of a chance as priority was usually given to those with the most rank, qualifications and children. Though I had an idea that I wouldn't do wrong by this, especially getting my name registered. Even for a private or hiring.

I had a month's notice and made enquiries about 'disturbance allowance' and to my disappointment found out that when I got to Germany, I would lose out on a substantial disturbance allowance. As this was the first move, I was determined that this should not happen, so with further enquiries, I found out that there was a way around this problem – if we were to live out in a private or hiring with the R.A.F.'s approval before my posting to Germany.

So we arranged to stay with some of Viola's friends from the hospital for the minimum amount of time needed to qualify – a month. This was classed as our first move. We stayed in the nurse's home as long as possible before moving to this house, then once in Germany, I would receive my disturbance allowance.

Going away party' on the Sqn

About two weeks before my posting, I offered to buy the traditional going-away barrel of beer. However, Taff of the R/Regt section on 33 Sqn had also been posted about two weeks after me and offered to go shares with me for the barrel of beer, making it cheaper for both of us; naturally, I agreed.

At our re-pat do, we were both presented with an engraved pewter tankard. Afterwards, I staggered drunkenly off to see Viola and thumbed a lift to Basingstoke. My two weeks embarkation leave was not spent relaxing; I worked in a warehouse for a bit of extra money before I left for Germany.

This was the first posting that I didn't want. And wasn't looking forward to; I was quite content to see my time out at Odiham as I only had approximately two and a half years left to do in the services.

The last of Dobby?

The last time I visited Odiham was on my resettlement course to be held at Aldershot.

I ended up at Aldershot railway station. It must have been fate; anyhow, I saw someone sweeping the platform that looked very familiar! It was, or someone who was, the spitting image of Dobby Donald! Be it him or not, he seemed to recognise me but was a little embarrassed to strike up a conversation

So had he finally been court-martialled? Or had he seen his time (contract) out?

I'll never know; I didn't bring myself to ask him, as whoever this person was, if it was Dobby, he looked a broken and dejected man. A former shadow of Dobby 'Sgt Bilko' Donald!

The best posting

Odiham had been a very happy posting for me, the best I had had in the R.A.F. Even if I hadn't met my future wife, it still would be! But meeting Viola was, as they say, the icing on the cake!

It was the only place I would wake up and look forward to going to work, such was the feel-good atmosphere on the Sqn and Odiham itself. 'The Odiham factor', as I call it. The whole camp was run as a happy, easy-going place to work where everybody would help each other out, regardless of you being a rock-ape or not.

All the regimental 'bull and discipline' was put aside for the safety of the aircraft and crew, which had top priority. All summed up nicely by our C.O. Wing Commander John Strong.

Bad feeling about the future

The posting to Germany was against my wishes, as I had the gut feeling of what was to come. One extreme to another – I was to be proved not only right in my fears but more so than I had anticipated – 'messed about' from morning to night but most of it was due to lack of planning, panic and sheer incompetence on behalf of those 'in charge'.

Prior to 1 Sqn, I had seriously been considering signing on for the full 22 years. That idea went straight out the window after only three days on the Sqn. If Viola hadn't joined me in Germany – she kept my sanity! There was no telling what I would have done.

1 Squadron, R.A.F. Laarbruch: July 1974 to Re-pat

Arriving at Laarbruch

The day finally arrived when I had to fly out to Germany on my new posting. I was not looking forward to it at all; I really wanted to stay at Odiham. My C.O. at 33 Sqn tried but was unable to get me a cancellation as I had not been posted abroad before so I was overdue an overseas posting. At the end of June 1974, I flew out to R.A.F. Wildenwrath about two hours from my new camp-to-be. Upon leaving customs, I saw several R.A.F. coaches to all the R.A.F. stations in the area. So I boarded one for Laarbruch, my camp. A couple of hours later, the coach pulled through the stn main gate for the first time with me on board.

I booked in and after being directed to some temporary accommodation, settled down for the night. Of course, I had to have a nightcap first and try the German beer once more.

Camp near Dutch border

Laarbruch is situated on the former 'Siegfried line'; it was reputed, I found out when on the Sqn, that during the building of the camp just after the war, several weapons were found such as German 'stick' hand grenades, ammunition and such a stemming from the time of the First World War.

It was also only 100 yards from the Dutch (Netherlands) border, in fact the border came up to within a few yards of the outer perimeter fence at the rear of the camp. I know this because several times during my time there, we crossed and recrossed when we were playing the 'enemy' and getting into position to infiltrate/attack. It took a couple of days to get everything sorted out, booked in and ready to report to the Sqn.

Cpl Geordie starts to pick on me

One of the NCOs in particular, I was to detest the very day I met him. I shall call him Cpl Geordie Weirdo. As he was passing, he would give me some stick as to why hadn't I gotten everything done and reported to the Sqn yet? This made me think, "Oh hell, it's going to be one of them camps!" Later, I was to discover that was an understatement, well and truly!

Deciding to finish in the R.A.F.

Before I left UK for Germany, I hadn't made up my mind as to whether I ought to sign on again or not; if so, I would then sign on for the full lot – 22 years and get a pension as it wouldn't be worth doing less. I would also treat myself to a new car. (They were very cheap in Germany.)

If I was to come out, I would have the advantage to being young enough to get a future employer interested enough to employ me and it would be a lot easier to settle down, as I was not set in my ways. (It wasn't.)

In the first letter to Viola dated 9/7/74, after about two or three days on the Sqn, I wrote: "Dear Viola, get a house, I'm coming out in 1976 at the end of my time. I'm not signing on again!" I had made up my mind and very quickly too. It was a decision I was not to regret.

Once I moved into the Sqn barracks, dominated mainly by single chaps and a few married men such as myself waiting for a married quarter to bring their families over. They guided me as to getting things sorted out, such as it was best to open a German bank account as it made things a bit easier; this I did at Gemease Sparkasse.

'Cocky' lad instils fear in the single lads

We had all sorts of weirdos in the block, as is the norm. One chap in particular I remember who thought he was God's gift to women. He was usually first out of bed and washed, but he had one annoying habit and that was whenever he woke up in a typical early morning male state – if you get my drift? He would promptly go around from bed to bed of the single men and start to wake the lads up by throwing back their bedclothes and brandishing his now erect member and saying to the lads, "If you don't get out of bed in the next two seconds, I'm going to fecking shove this in your earhole until you do get out of bed!" Needless to say, these poor scared lads were out of the bed in less than a millisecond! The army had a bugler to wake you up in the morning! How things have changed!

I was waiting for him to come to my bed ready with a large and very sharp sheath knife. "Let him try that on me if he dares!" I thought, "and I will cut the offending thing off," and I would have as well and gotten away with it! Fortunately, he never came to my bed in such a manner. He did wake me up in the morning occasionally but in a normal way, but the knife was under my pillow – just in case!

This chap gets his comeuppance

Several weeks later in the Sqn hangar, before and after the morning parade, I saw the single lads laughing with each other and sniggering behind the back of this chap. He had apparently gotten his comeuppance; one of my mates in the block had had enough of this and had decided to put an end to it once and for all.

That morning, as this cocky (pardon the pun) married man came around his bed space, my mate was waiting for him and had – unbeknownst to anyone in the room, gone to bed with a can of 'mildly antiseptic' aftershave under his pillow. As soon as the 'cocky' lad stood beside his bed with his member in hand, my mate whipped out his can of aftershave and sprayed a burst of several seconds onto the exposed end of this chap, who promptly let out a wail of anguish and ran screaming into the bathroom to try and wash it off as quickly as possible; the lads burst out laughing and have been laughing since. The good news was that it cured this chap for he never did it again.

Trick for sprogs
A trick used to be played on newcomers/sprogs – they would be enticed into the flight store on some pretext or another, one of the guys would distract him by chatting to him, another would sneak up behind him, tie a piece of string on the back of the unsuspecting sprog's belt, and tie the other end to a camouflage net, tent or something heavy, another wag would come in and shout, "Everybody on parade!" whilst the rest leapt to their feet and ran out of the store. The newcomer would jump up and run and bring half the store with him – great fun, though thankfully it didn't happen to me as I wasn't a sprog on the Regiment squadrons.

Coffee in the ear: abandon hope
This Flt Sgt Macduffy, a tale told me by my pal Geordie Hall who swears it was true. For one reason or another, I was walking across the square outside the hangar, closely watched by Macduffy and others, who had a cup of coffee in his hand and was watching me like a hawk. When he tried to take a sip, he moved his head to watch me but didn't move the cup as well, and for some reason promptly poured the coffee in his ear. Which resulted in laughter from all who were present. Of course, who did he blame? Me! And I didn't even see it happen. Why did he do this? Goodness knows, he was so intent on watching me and concentrating on giving me 'bad vibes', the word Karma comes to mind. Or was it a senior moment?

On the day my pal Geordie Hall arrived on the Sqn, the very first time on the back of a four-tonner (the Sqn and I was away on exercise with the Harriers), they disembarked at the Sqn hangar, only to find a rope tied to a tree in the shape of an old wild west style noose. Some of the guys left behind were banging on the steel doors of the Sqn offices, demanding the occupants come out and face them like a man. Truthfully, if I knew there was a noose tied to a tree waiting for me, I sure as hell wouldn't come out. Geordie told me he thought, "What the hell is going on, what have I let myself in for!" He asked what it was all about but the guy who had gone to pick him up said, "Don't ask, just —— don't ask, don't get involved. Just wait in the flight storeroom for a while!" He never did find out what it was all about. 'Welcome to 1 Sqn, Geordie, welcome to the mad house. Abandon hope, all ye who enter here!'

Alt Weeze

This was the first German pub I visited. On the first night in 'Singly' block, the lads invited me out for a 'jar or two'. At the 'Alt Weeze' in the local town whereupon I was taught the only German I needed to know:

'Ein Klein bier bitter' = One small beer please
'Ein Gross bier bitter' = One large beer please

Then as the night progressed, the next step: 'Drie or Fumpf (3or 4) Grosse (large) biers' = Beers bitter please. I was shown one of the favourite meals to be had by the lads, 'Jaeger Schnitzel und pom frits' (breaded pork Escalope in mushroom sauce, with chips, peas and tomatoes). This was to become my favourite meal. Many years later, I visited Germany on several occasions with the Territorial Army and on holiday and I always ask for the Jaeger Schnitzel. I have been back to Weeze several times since the camp closed and all servicemen returned to UK. The last time was 2015 for a regimental reunion and I always ask for it. However, during and after the meal, the local German pubs usually lay on or did, in those days, entertainment in the shape of XXX films – full, uncensored, pornographic films. Even in front of German families there with their children. The servicemen had a trick they showed to me, which consisted of the waiter marking your beer mat every time you had a drink or meal and at the end of the night, you would cash in your beer mat and pay for your drinks/meals just the one time.

But the lads would drink half the night and when they saw the waiter getting busy, these same beer mats would 'disappear' and the waiter would start a fresh one on a new beer mat. This worked a dream not once but all the time. All the time I was in Germany, never did the waiters ever twig on to this scam, no matter where you were in Germany! It would be taken even further, you would retain the mat with the meal price on as it was too obvious to try and get away with this, but all other mats collected during the night would disappear so all you paid for was the meal and a couple of drinks and the rest of the beer was free!

Back in 2014, I was there at the 'Alt Weeze' and there were only 5 locals and myself, very quiet to what it used to be like and no XXX films this time. Not even any music.

Looking for a flat

Once I'd unpacked and settled into a routine, within days of arriving I had to get my priorities right and start looking for a flat somewhere to live so I could get Viola over ASAP.

I was told by the chaps and the official channels that there was no chance. That wasn't going to put me off! I would go to the education centre (where the station interpreter worked) and family officer to obtain addresses of the places if any available for hire. Although there were very few good places available.

Of those addresses available to me, I'd walk around the local towns/villages to see what they were like. A typical example of my day was I would finish work and tea. If the village was nearby or straight out after finishing work if a bit further afield and walk around during the evening checking them out. Occasionally, if there was nothing on the Sqn, it would be a customary for a Sqn vehicle to be signed out and we'd have a run around the farther places on the list. Some days I would be walking around till midnight, looking, seven days a week.

I couldn't find anywhere so I went to the family officer and explained the situation but she was unable to help me as she explained married quarters were allocated on accumulation of points. I had no chance! Besides, she said there was a new R.A.F. Regiment Sqn being formed (58 Sqn) and all decent accommodation that was available was being held back for them as they would arrive *en masse*. I had to try and get one myself, which looked impossible. Or most likely I would have to wait till Jan-Feb next year, which would only give us about a year there, so I wasn't prepared to do that and this made me more determined than ever!

When my mother and Viola heard this, they thought I stood no chance at all and suggested that why didn't we not bother getting Viola out there, why didn't we let her stay in UK and I would stay in single men's accommodation.

I said, "No way, I want Viola out here, and I will get somewhere to live, mark my words! I'm not beaten that easily!" As my folks knew all too well from past experience. I also said, "Be sure she's ready to move as soon as she gets the callfam." (Call family forward)

Finding a flat in a callfam

On Saturday, 11 July, I looked over a flat in a town called Goch, on Sunday, we agreed on terms, on Monday, I took the completed forms into the family office for them to check over and that day I put in my callfam. Less than two weeks since I had arrived in Germany, considering the obstacles that were put in my way, I think I did pretty well.

On 13/7/74, I wrote to Viola to tell her the good news.

The flat cost 3,500 German marks per month but we only had to pay the same as we would for an A.M.Q. (Airmen's Married Quarter). The R.A.F. paid the rest. So my share was only about 200 German marks per month.

By 7 August, we had been separated for a month and I was really looking forward to getting Viola out here. It might help me keep sane in this madhouse. Not to mention that we were to be financially better off too. A matter of about £40:75 p.m. It was about £10 per week living out allowance. This was to make up for difference in the cost of living between UK and Germany.

Trouble with passport

Viola though, to my surprise, didn't want to come and join me as she'd been offered a good job at a new upmarket store in my hometown.

I said, "No way! I want you out here with me!" As it happened, one minute she was coming and then she wasn't; she didn't seem to be able to make her mind up. Consequently, I had to cancel the callfam a couple of times. This was also due to the fact that the Sqn was due to fly out to UK for an exercise very soon after my arrival in Germany. Another reason for having to cancel callfam was we had a lot of trouble with her passport; it was out of date. The hospital was supposed to have brought it up to date and told her that they had done so, but this was not to be. It came to pass that once they knew she was going to leave nursing, they couldn't be bothered with Viola's problem anymore. Also because she was now British by marriage and it was not yet on her passport, so for her to come on a R.A.F.-scheduled flight, there was a problem with her citizenship.

25/7/74: Unpacking crates

Just before I went back to UK, our first crates arrived and I got them taken to the flat and started unpacking. I unpacked and discovered three broken glasses (three spirits) but to my dismay discovered that we'd only packed two cups, but four dozen glasses. I also discovered that a brown leather bag from Spain we had sent via British Rail from Basingstoke, Scunthorpe, containing personal effects and clothes had never arrived; it went missing. We had rowed about sending it via the railway. I said it would go missing; Viola had insisted so the only way for her to learn was to send it – of course, we never saw it again.

Looking around flat area: trying local pub

In Goch, I discovered a Forces family clinic only a 7-minute-walk away from our flat. And a small Naafi shop inside the local German army camp, but most important there was a nice little German bar opposite the flat, which was the deciding factor in accepting the flat. Not the main reason.

Before Viola came, I spent many nights there. I used to sit there on my own in this little backstreet bar with a glass of beer in one hand and an English/German phrase book in the other, practising my "Sprechen Sie Deutsch?" on this typically blonde, busty German barmaid.

I don't think the locals liked the idea of a Brit in their midst, but when they saw me trying to make an effort to learn their language, I became more accepted, even to this old man who used to sit alone in the corner and was ignored by everyone, and the spitting image of 'Der Fuehrer' Hitler himself.

'Blau Engel'

Eventually, when I walked in the bar, this barmaid, Klara, would put on English-speaking records on the jukebox and ask if I would like to play with

316

her (who wouldn't); what she meant was playing some electronic games, such as the pinball machine (more's the pity). Upon the arrival of Viola, Klara persuaded (these Germans were famous for their "We haf vays of making you drink") Viola to have a local liquor drink, a 'Blau Engel' ('Blue Angel', shades of Marlene Dietrich).

She had to knock it back, not sip, she was sober as judge inside and she asked if she could have another but Klara refused, saying one was enough, as she would see! How right she was, as soon as we were outside and in the fresh air, the fresh air hit her and suddenly Viola was legless and could not control her involuntary movements, not to mention that she was also drunk! Boy, what an effect!

We were told – on good authority, that the town of Goch was the local HQ of the S.S. Hitler's personal bodyguard and elite army unit, they also provided guards for the P.O.W. and concentration camps. Certain places were out of bounds to us as any servicemen venturing into these places were usually given a good going over and beaten up by the locals.

Looking forward to going back to the UK

It wasn't long before we set off for the exercise in UK. Although in Germany only a few weeks, I was already looking forward to getting to England again and seeing Viola, though we hadn't been told we would be able to go home to see our families. I knew we would. Because had they not allowed it, there would have been a mutiny on the Sqn, not to mention that the papers might have got to hear about it. It was just the R.A.F. getting up to their old 'tried and tested' ways again.

Block insects

I was also looking forward to it because it would give me a respite from the thousands and thousands of black insects; the camp was built in the middle of a wood and they used to fly around and get everywhere, especially in the hair and face. The warm weather ensured that there was no shortage of the blighters; it was as if they would sit in the branches of the pine trees and wait for some poor unsuspecting human to walk underneath and they then suddenly descended on you from a great height. You had the most difficult of jobs to get rid of them, impossible. I was fed up of them in my ears, hair, up my nostrils, in clothes; I was looking forward to getting away from them albeit for a little while.

Callfam

My callfam had gone in and it looked as though Viola might arrive whilst I was in UK. So I wrote to her giving her instructions as to what to do if that happened, also arranged with one of the married men's wife to look after her if she was to come. This was the normal procedure for incoming wives.

Stand by for Cyprus

A week or two before we left, trouble flared in Cyprus where we had a couple of Sqns. The Turkish Army had invaded the North of Cyprus and were to take over half the island for the benefit of pro-Turkish Cypriots.

Our troops had been issued live ammunition to protect our installations/airfields/army garrisons, and ordered to open fire if being threatened or fired on by the Turkish Army or civvies trying to take over their installation.

We were put on 24 hours stand-by and told the exercise was now in doubt. I was rather hoping the exercise would be cancelled; I was looking forward to going to Cyprus, especially if we were going to fight. I thought that this might be my last chance of some action. Not to mention all that glorious sunshine during our off-duty hours. If we got any!

We were taken off stand-by after about 10 days, and a week later set off for UK. The exercise was from 1 August to 16 August; we flew out from Wildenwrath where I saw my first Harrier V./S.T.O.L (Vertical/Short Take-off and Landing) aircraft close up.

In UK, we moved up to my, and everyday else's, former camp, Catterick. Where we had all done our basic regiment training, but not all were based there after training. It was an overnight stop and it looked just as dark, dreary and dismal as before, just as I remembered it.

Exercise in Otterburn

Next day, we set off for our exercise area, Otterburn, near Newcastle. It was officially named 'The first tactical fighter meet', the purpose of which was to try out fighter aircraft (Harrier) against other planes and new tactics for all NATO countries. Though primarily, it was to evaluate the Harrier's weapons and tactics.

We borrowed 16 Sqn (Catterick) 40/70 A/A guns, generators and relevant equipment. 16 Sqn had been R.A.F. Catterick's stand-by Sqn and had been airlifted out to Cyprus straight away at the outbreak of the troubles.

We set our guns in A.R.D. (All round defence); our crew of eight were left alone to our own devices, but only about ¼ mile on either side of us were two or more guns in the ring of defence.

I had been allocated to Cpl Geordie Weirdo's gun. Though I didn't know that he was the squadron pervert/weirdo, this I found out during the next two weeks and subsequently while in Germany.

Paul Henderson and the 'Scull' joke

After about 7-8 days, we were getting bored, all we had to do was 'stand to' and track the odd intruder aircraft. We decided to relieve the boredom and thought we'd 'attack' one of the other gun emplacements. This we duly did by drenching them with water, mud, fire extinguishers, rotten vegetables from their own slop bins – great fun. And once other gun crews got to hear of it, they too attacked each other likewise.

Now I'm not the sort who likes or plays practical jokes, but we had a chap with us on the gun team who I was convinced needed bringing down a peg or two, and I did! We on our gun got to talking in general and Paul Henderson was bragging, "I'm not scared of anything, nothing scares me, nothing, natural or supernatural!" (Until I came along, that is!)

"No?" I thought. "We'll see!" This was a challenge to me. "Right," I thought, "what can I do?" Then almost straight away, I had a 'lightbulb' moment; our P.O.L. (Petrol Oil Lubricant) point was set back a little way from the tented area and was lit by a paraffin-fuelled Tilley lamp. That night, by coincidence and luckily for me, was very foggy and gloomy, quite reminiscent of a night in which Dracula films are set with the fog rolling over the dark moors and Dracula lurking unseen, waiting for some unsuspecting victim. The mood was just right, a clear night and it may not have been so effective. Tonight had to be the night. There was a lot of sheep on the moors where we were and I noticed a sheep's skull on the way to attack the other gun. So on the pretext of going for a 'Jimmy Riddle', I left the tent, found the skull and brought it back to our gun. I took it over to P.O.L. point, then placed it in front of the Tilley lamp and placed a candle inside it.

I stood back and surveyed my handiwork, the effect was quite staggering and it really looked ominous and scary. With bared teeth, eyes glowing in the dark swirling mist. If I hadn't set it up, I might have been scared out of my wits. As if the devil himself was staring at me and the swirling fog set it off a treat.

I walked back to the tent. Henderson, the object of this plot, told me it was my turn to fill the Tilley lamp in the tent.

I made some excuse and persuaded him to go outside and do it himself; I started to count 5-4-3-2-1-0... "Aargh! Oh no, no, no, please no!" We heard from outside. I burst out laughing, the others rushed outside to see what was happening, thinking he had a heart attack or something, and he very nearly did. One or two of them said they'd 'seen the devil' and ran back in the tent shaking, their faces white with shock, as if their rear end was on fire.

Eventually, they all came back into the tent, they tried their best to calm Henderson down. I think he was in a state of shock, I was still laughing. By now, I was in pain from laughing. Eventually, they figured out that I had something to do with it, and when I got my breath back, I told them what I had done. But they didn't believe that it was only a sheep skull. So I had to go outside and bring it inside to show them, two of the lads dived into their sleeping bags as if that was going to give them some protection.

Once everyone had been convinced as to the truth of my tale, they all (except Henderson) burst into fits of laughter. Henderson, shaking his fist at me, swore, "I'm going to kill you, I am going to f***ing kill you – you bar-steward and I'm going to get even!" He never did. Or else you wouldn't be reading about it.

It took several days to calm them down and convince them it wasn't real and only a joke; there was nothing to worry about. It was the best laugh I have had since 'Fly off Tit – Tut' in Northern Ireland.

Threatened about going home

We had been threatened so often about how we may or may not be able to visit our families before returning to Germany that some of the lads believed the officers but I didn't, not for a minute. As an old hand, I'd heard this same old line time and again, "If you don't do this, do that, finish this/ that job etc., you won't go home early to have a long weekend!"

After I finished basic training and had done a few months, I had caught on to this straight away; what surprised me was that most guys with years of service under their belts never tumbled on it or realised they were being had.

The times I had to tell people about this time and again and I was always laughed at, always condemned as a 'know it all', though every time I was proven right. The thing was some people did try to make you work harder and faster; the only time I have ever seen them cancel or not fulfil their promise, there was a near riot, but after that they found they couldn't use that ruse any more.

Exercise debrief

At the end of the exercise, we all had a debrief, the pilots ran the film shot on their camera gun, bombing and strafing runs, these films showed the first gun being 'zapped' by the first Harrier, the pilots were smiling all over their faces, as pleased as punch they were.

Then we surprised them. Unbeknownst to the pilots, we had rigged up breach cameras in the breach of the main four guns at vital points, though ours was not one of them.

As the trigger was pressed, the camera took a photo; both films were run and evaluated and compared. The result was that the first Harrier had knocked out the first gun. But after that, each and every aircraft that had started its attack run was knocked out before it could do much damage.

It knocked the smiles off the pilots' faces.

Asked by me which he would rather come up against – a gun or missile – one of the pilots replied, "Missiles, every time, at least with them I know what to expect but with guns, how do I know whether they are any good? Or whether they are on the ball or not? They might get lucky! When you're up against a gun crew, it's like coming up against several mini computers. 'Will they get it right and work as a team or work against each other?' You might only have a split second to make a decision, act on it and carry it out."

At the end of the exercise, we did finally get the chance of going home albeit on a 24-hour pass. So I rushed home to be with Viola for a few hours.

But reporting back to Catterick, we were kept hanging around for two days. We were all fuming and very annoyed; why couldn't we have had another day at home? After all, the Scots and the Welsh couldn't go home as they would have turned around and come straight back as they lived too far away.

Eventually, we arrived back on camp in Germany on the 16th.

Evening in flat

Most evenings, once back in Germany, I used to spend in the flat, unpacking, having a few beers in the local and sleeping in the flat. I used to quite enjoy it, probably because I sometimes preferred to be on my own. Shades of Greta Garbo – "I vant to be alone!" Once I had got back from the UK, I was ill for a couple of days, must have been the food/water. Once back into a routine, I eventually met the landlord, a Helmut Schultz, and his wife, Greta Schultz They were a nice couple and turned out to be more friends than landlord and landlady.

I wrote to the R.A.F. News with a report and photo of our wedding for publication, but the week that it should have been published, it wasn't; instead, the only weddings published were that of officers and an SNCO only. No sign of mine. R.H.I.P. = Rank has its privilege. A well-known service saying.

Letter from Jan Wilson (Destination USA)

I found, upon my arrival from England, a letter for me from Miss Jan Wilson, my former girlfriend I had met on destination USA. The second girl who had meant a lot to me, before Viola. She was asking how I was getting on and wishing Viola and I all the best for the future. I thought that was rather nice and decent of her, most ex-girlfriends wouldn't do that.

Ex-mine detector

We went on a short exercise on the pretence that it was primarily a map reading exercise but all it was really was an excuse to get off camp whilst a high-power inspection was going on. We also had route march or two thrown in, which I always used to enjoy even though I wasn't a front runner. I always used to enjoy the day out, fresh sights, fresh air, it was infinitely better than being cooped up in a draughty hangar or keeping out of the way in the storeroom.

This time, two chaps signed for a metal detector to take with us. Permission had to be sought and granted by the West German Government as it was intended to be used in a sensitive area.

In the site where we made base camp, there was an old German AA gun site from WW2 so three of us set off to see what we might find.

We were unlucky as we thought we might be, we were told not only had all sites of military interest been 'gone over and cleared' by official bodies and representatives after the war, there had also been nearly 40 years of souvenir hunters going over them and there was very little likelihood of finding anything. Though we heard a lot of 'pings', they didn't turn out to be anything, that was until it started to get dark, then we got a large-sounding ping, it was about 4-6 feet long, we started to dig and dig frantically, we got down to about 4-5 feet but we couldn't see anything, and it got a bit too dark to continue. We had to postpone our digging till the morning, so all night we speculated as to just what it might or might not be, though it was not to be as we had to leave it and return to camp. So near to being discovered and all the hard work half done, whatever it was we'll never know! But it was big.

Sprog and his girlfriend

One of the first amusing stories I heard there was about one of the young sprogs on the fight concerning his girlfriend, whom he knowingly obtained carnal knowledge from, knowing she was underage. To add to his problems, she wrote to him to tell him...yes, you guessed it! CHIP (come home, I'm pregnant), and her father was gunning for him. Her parents were prepared to let him off lightly if he would marry her immediately.

He wisely went to see a couple of officers, who on hearing of his problem, arranged for him to be conveniently posted.

We had been back at camp about two weeks when we were away again on another major exercise. This time, it was my first Harrier exercise. The first of about 7-8. This became the norm – major exercise, a couple of weeks on camp and away again on another major exercise.

Hackett: why/how he started to pick on me

One evening, I came back to the tented site and some mail was awaiting me. Amongst other items was a large brown envelope, contained within was the legal documents for my new house, Viola had sent the house documents to sign and return.

I asked the SNCO Flight Sergeant Houseman and Flying Officer Hackett (whom you will hear a lot more about) if they would look after the documents to keep them safe for me. They wouldn't, and didn't want to be responsible. Bar-stewards!

The officer let slip his private thoughts, "Huh, just an S.A.C. and he's got a wife, a mortgage and an M.Q." (Hiring, to be precise!) "And me an officer, and I can't even get an M.Q.!" I took this as an apparently innocent statement at the time.

Or was this the start of his campaign of hatred/jealousy of me? The beginning and the reason of all that was to follow? He was an Officer but no gentleman. He tried to put me down every chance he got. All I wanted was to be left alone in peace, to get on with the job I loved. He even tried to court-martial me four times – and failed!

Had my service not been due to finish and I had to stay there a bit longer, I just may have cracked and given him what he wanted – to hit him and beat him up.

Amount to live on

In Germany, we were paid fortnightly as opposed to weekly as in UK; hence, the need for a bank account. For some reason, we had to keep all money orders to the UK to £2.

Eventually, my money in hand was only £73 per fortnight to live on, as I still kept paying £80 per month to the building society. That was approximately 200-ish German marks per fortnight. I had to live on 6.25 German marks = £1.

A lot of the guys used to bring about 50-70 German marks per day (£10-£14) to work, they would also drink in the Naafi at lunch times and at night. I eventually allotted myself about 5 German marks, less than £1, per day and that was enough for a couple of sandwiches and a cup of tea in the morning on Naafi break, and a cup of tea at afternoon break. I was happy enough with that, though as you can well imagine some of the guys thought me a tight b*****d and used to try and take the mickey out of me, but I used to throw back at them, "Aye lad, I maybe a tight b*****d but I've got a nice new house to go back home to and to show for my sacrifice, what have you got to go back to: a rusty car, not even new!" It would always shut them up.

Considering the price of things in Germany were a lot dearer than in England, I think I did well. Before I came out to Germany, I had had the intention of taking advantage to get a new car as they were about 25% to one-third of the price of a new car in UK but as I told some chaps when they asked me why wasn't I interested in a new car, as everybody else was getting one (I was about one of only three on the whole Sqn who never got a car), "I shall be a civvy in a few short months, I don't know how long I shall be out of work, I consider somewhere to live the most important priority, as you can't live in the back of a car for long!"

I didn't have enough time to do in Germany to pay for one; besides, I only thought I was going out there for 2+ years.

Viola due to arrive

I had been back from UK about three or four weeks, when Viola was due to arrive. I had already made arrangements to be off from the Sqn as they would be away on exercise when she was due – again! Of course, Hackett told me I couldn't stay behind, I had to go on exercise and I would either have to make arrangements for someone to meet her or cancel the callfam. This time, I went mad and told him, "No fecking way!" No matter what he said or did to threaten me, nothing would stop me from meeting her at the airport myself! It had already been arranged!

Someone must have had a word in his ear enough to tell him this was the normal procedure for married men whose wives were joining them.

I didn't hear any more from him as to whether I could stay behind or not but come the morning for them to pull out, I wasn't with them, I was still in bed. I deliberately stayed away from the Sqn. I just reported to the Sqn location in the morning as normal and the dozen or so skeleton crew and myself got on with a few jobs around the area.

She was due to arrive at Wildenwrath, and whilst waiting for her, I felt nervous and knots in my stomach.

When I saw her step through the arrival lounge in her fur coat, I was so happy to see her. She'd never looked better, slim, sexy and top-notch.

"Good, now that she's here, Laarbruch might be a bit more bearable!" I thought.

Disturbance allowance

We received £63 disturbance allowance, about 394 marks, a lot of money to us then, so that idea of mine to stay with Viola's friends from the hospital was spot on for had we not done so, we wouldn't have gotten a penny. That money came in very useful, enabling us to buy a few vital items we needed for the kitchen.

Viola meets Helmut and Greta Muller

After a few days, I arranged for Viola to be introduced to Helmut and Greta, our landlords. We were to go to their house for the first time to meet their daughters, they had three daughters aged about 11, 13-14 and the eldest who was about 19.

Was there any wonder that Helmut, although quite young, was completely prematurely grey! The eldest – Sophia at 19, the next youngest was a girl called Mila aged 13-14, there was another about 11.

Eventually, we heard from Helmut & Greta, true or not, that Sophia had gone on the game. Thanks to one of her aunties, an up-market prostitute. Though goodness knows why: her parents were very hard-working and well off.

Helmut told us one time that he put his daughters on the (birth control) pill from the age of 12. Why, we asked, at such an early age? To this he replied, "Children at school in Germany are taught sex education at a very young age (from 5 onwards). I don't want my 12-year-old daughters coming home one day and telling me, 'Dad, I'm pregnant'!"

Later on, just before we left Germany, Helmut and Greta had adopted two baby girls (who had been mistreated). No wonder he was grey at 37.

Helmut's cellar

His cellar was a home-made wine cellar with all the cupboards full of wines with a lot of three-litre bottles of brandy. Not to mention all 200 packs of cigarettes. All courtesy of his previous tenants in his flats. The Naafi drinks and cigarettes were very cheap compared to the German shops; for a bottle of whiskey in the Naafi was say 7-9 marks. In the shops, it would be about 80 marks.

Why Helmut prefers British servicemen to local Germans

I asked him why he preferred British in his flats as opposed to his own countrymen.

"Easy," he said, "if I had Germans and they caused me problems, I would have a hard job on my hands sorting them out. I would have to go to the trouble and expense of getting a solicitor to throw them out, going to court, etc. But having the British, all I have to do is complain to the families officer and she will deal with them for me. If they lack self-discipline and have to be removed, I just arrange for some new couple to move in. And thirdly, my money is guaranteed each month, no hassle."

Eventually, he had three flats going in the same block @ 3,500 p.m. each, total of 10,500 German marks p.m.; a very healthy profit indeed.

They all lived in his mother-in-law's house given to them outside the town of Geldern. With a swimming pool and each year after Christmas, they planted their Christmas tree in the garden. Now they had a mini forest of about 15-20 feet high, so they must have escaped the bombing during the war.

Our three-storey block in Goch originally belonged to Helmut's father and was given the flats for an income on condition he stay in one of the flats.

Helmut worked as a computer operator/installer, his wife, Greta, did babysitting in the evenings for friends.

Brothel confession

One time upon returning to Laarbruch after an exercise, I was in the bath and confessed to the wife, "Love, I've got something to tell you. While we were away, we had a spot of R & R and I and a few of the lads visited a brothel. But I give you my word that I did not participate! I was there, just watching the films, while the others went and had a bit of fun. They asked me to look after their jackets and wallets so they wouldn't get screwed by the girls." (Wrong phrase, I think.)

Viola said, "That's all right as long as you're telling me the truth and didn't try those girls!"

I assured her that was the truth, and it was!

Early the following week, Viola got a call from someone – she didn't tell me whether it was male or female, telling her, "Did you know your husband went to a brothel on exercise?"

Viola: "Yes, I know all about it, why?"

Caller: "Oh, you know about it then?"

Viola: "Yes, what about it? And who are you?"

With that, the person put the phone down.

What if I hadn't told her? I would have had to explain and convince her I hadn't 'dabbled'. We never did find out who it was, some jealous rat or his wife, whoever was trying to cause trouble, it didn't work. Could it have been Hackett? A nasty piece of work, whoever it was!

Viola's teeth: visit to R.A.F. Wegberg

With Viola having trouble with her teeth back in UK, the R.A.F. dentist from Odiham was true to his word and had made arrangements for Viola to go to the local R.A.F. hospital (Wegberg) to have a minor operation to sort them out.

I took her and it was done in a day, and fortunately, it did the trick and she never had any trouble since.

Mess food

The food in the mess as a whole wasn't very good, the only thing that was all right was the steaks, they had a foreign food bar with Italian and Chinese food; it was horrible.

Viola takes oath

Not long after Viola had been in Germany, my father arranged for Viola to take her oath of allegiance to H.M. Queen ASAP. I arranged with M.T. for transport to Bonn – the capital.

As soon as I got the chance, I started to show Viola around the camp. I showed her the camp swimming pool, a large affair, where we had barbecues in the summer months, and of course, the old favourite – the camp cinema. At Laarbruch, there were bars, lots of bars; no other camp I had been to had so many, not even Scampton.

Freedom of Weeze

The station was awarded the honour of the freedom of Weeze, a small town 3 km from camp, as opposed to Goch, which was 11 km. Half the population was servicemen anyway due to insufficient M.Q.s on camp. This was the first time that this honour had been bestowed on a R.A.F. station in Germany. Rehearsals started weeks in advance although all we had to do was march on, come to attention, stand at ease and present arms a couple of times, and march off. It took 1 Sqn R/Regiment. Two months to rehearse it almost every day – exercises permitting.

By the end of the time, the inevitable happened, the chaps got up to their best standard, then they started to get bored, fed up so the standard started to drop, so the officers and SNCOs were panicking and making us do extra training; of course, we got worse and worse. They never learn. The best thing to do was get up to standard, have a break and then go again.

I had always told the chaps on my previous camps that this was what happened but no one believed me until they saw it happen, then only one or two would openly admit to me that I was right.

Q.C.S.

The Sqn Warrant Officer (SWO) had done time in the Q.C.S. who gave all these continuity drill displays and formed the guard of honour to visiting dignitaries. So our SWO thought he would create his own little Q.C.S.

display team on 1 Sqn. It was doomed from the start, as we were either away on exercises, shooting or just back from/getting ready to go away. He thought we could give continuity drill displays in between exercises. This continuity consisted of a series of drill movements. (One display was 160 movements without a word of command.) All they got was 'By the left, quick march!'

But knowing 1 Sqn, they had to go daft and go over the top, they didn't want any coloured lads, any one less than 5'6" tall and wearing glasses, in the squad as it spoilt the 'clean lines' and appearance. Eventually, he had to change his mind as someone informed him that he was leaving himself wide open if the papers ever got to hear of it; he also realised that these rules excluded about half of the Sqn personnel. So, he finally relented and just excluded those with glasses, I didn't need to wear glasses all the time but once I heard this rumour, I was never seen without them and I got off this stupid drill squad. Can you blame me?

The coloured lads were, however, pushed into the back row.

On the real Q.C.S., they never carried on like that, they had all three, coloured lads, people with glasses and those on the small side. On Q.C.S., if you volunteered or 'body snatched' as we say, for this special Sqn, then as far as they were concerned – if you could do it, then you were on the display. We only did a couple of displays and the whole idea was knocked on the head and the display team was disbanded.

German carnival

In Germany, in the early spring time, they had an annual carnival over a whole week, which included a procession of gaily decorated floats with an annual theme, the last float was by far the most popular; it was the bar float giving away free beer – as much as you wanted.

Old Frau's night

They had dances, parties, one of which known as 'Alt Frau's Nicht' (Old Wives night) was quite unique, in which married women may dress up in dark and dowdy clothes and wear a mask, they then picked out a man they fancy and dance with, and if they wished, go all the way!

They were not supposed to take off their masks till after midnight. From the men's point of view, this was great for them. Especially if you got picked up by a nice-looking girl/woman. It could be your lucky day; on the other hand, you could get some old biddy, which would be unfortunate because you were not allowed to refuse the attentions of any female – no matter how old or grotty.

Other interesting facts also presented themselves. If you recognised one of the participants as your wife/husband, picking or being picked up, there wasn't a thing you could do by law and if your wife happened to get pregnant, the child was looked after by the state until it was legally of age. You couldn't divorce solely because one of the partners had been responsible for having a child. Providing the child was conceived that night. Of course, if one of the parties finished up having an affair, then divorce was permitted. Very civilised, these Europeans.

I liked the Germans' idea of one legal night on the tiles for married couples; great in some cases as it may prevent one of the partners going off and having an affair. I was assured that it was true about being protected by the law, though I got the information from Helmut and Greta, as they said, anything was possible on old Frau's Night.

One of the chaps who was known as the Sqn hard man, but also the Sqn idiot – as you will see – was taken for a ride on Alt Frau's Nicht.

He was picked up by an old pro, she charged him 200 marks (nearly a week's wages) and all he got was a hand job, and was asked why he'd paid nearly £40 for it, hadn't he realised he wasn't going to get his leg over, not to mention that he had to buy her two bottles of champagne. He never lived it down.

Oil-fried central heating

Our flat was up three flights of stairs, and oil-fired central heating. It was quite expensive to run, two 45 gall drums per month. We used to get in from work and because in Germany floor and ceilings were all solid concrete, the flat was very cold so we had to put it on full blast – number 10 setting.

This was for most of the night, so one night I had the idea that maybe it might be better to leave it on 24 hours a day – low setting, it may work out cheaper. So eventually, we left it on number 2-3 setting. And the flat was nice and warm to come home to. Our consumption was then down to a little more than half a barrel per month, a very big saving considering that a barrel cost us from 200+ marks to a little over 50 marks p.m. Plus I only had to refill the boiler every other day instead of twice a day. And the flat stayed warm all day.

Helmut's father, ex-S.S. man

I introduced Viola to Helmut's father who was living in one of the flats. He asked me if I were a soldier, I said, "Well, yes, a sort of air-soldier!" (Translated: "Ah ya, Laarbruch airfield.")

"I vas a soldier vonce; look, I vill show you a photograph!" (Indeed he had been, a corporal in the German Waffen S.S.)

"Ve vere not all bad men!" said he. (Of course he would say this!) "Though some sections of the Regiment did give the rest of us a bad name, ve did not like to be associated vith them!"

Helmut didn't want me to talk to his father and always tried to prevent us meeting. And maybe was frightened of me finding out, not knowing how I would react. I think Helmut also didn't like the thought that his father had been part of the S.S.

Helmut's father was living with the wife of his deceased brother, as man and wife. There were evenings when this woman would be knocking on our door late at night, crying because the old man had beaten her up due to the influence of 'the devil's brew', they called it Schnapps; he was a quiet man until he started drinking.

No food, no exercise

On one of our station evaluation exercise, I was in an Observation Post for 24 hours without food or drink; we had been forgotten, I was so hungry I promised myself 'never again' so from the next exercise on, I always went prepared with tins of soup/stew, teabags, sugar, burners, matches, etc. I never went without again, I always had plenty to eat and drink, unlike the other chaps who never thought ahead.

Helga boobies

Viola had a German friend by the name of Helga and her boyfriend, who spoke very little if any English, he was tall, lanky and gormless. What she saw in him I didn't know. But one could guess!

This young woman wasn't a ravishing beauty, more of a girl-next-door type, with a great figure. Attractive, in her mid to late 20s and very pleasant with a good command of English. One day she was visiting us on her own, in our flat in Goch. Whilst Viola was in the kitchen getting something ready to eat, Helga and I were alone in the lounge chatting, and for some reason, I moved the conversation to complimenting her on her fantastic figure. Although she always wore pullovers, her great figure could not be hidden, especially her 'magnificent mammaries'. Unplanned, it just came out of my mouth and I started to joke that her boobs were very nice, so large and round they must be falsies, surprisingly she took no offence at this, but casually smiled back at me and assured me they were the real thing! Maybe because she didn't take offence or subconsciously I sensed something, I didn't know, but I expanded the conversation, initially meant as a half-hearted joke, and said to her, "Well, I only have your word for it, I still find it hard to believe they are real, I could only believe it if I had a closer look!"

Helga: "Maybe this will convince you they are real!" With that, she stood up and invited me to have a good feel. I couldn't believe what she was saying, I walked over to her nervously, my hands outstretched, not believing what I was about to do, but just in case Viola came out the kitchen and caught me having a good feel of another woman's boobs, I thought I'd better tell her. I shouted to her, "Vi, I'm just going to have a feel of Helga's tits!"

"OK love!"

Walking forward, and with a few moments' hesitation, Helga clearly didn't mind me examining her mammary glands (through her pullover). I felt all around, weighed each one individually and together, and said again as a joke, "Well, they appear OK but I can't really tell from just a quick exam through your pullover!"

Was I subconsciously trying to see how far I/she would go? With that, she promptly and seductively took off her pullover and stood before me in a sexy flesh-coloured silk bra and invited me to 'examine her again'! Again I thought I'd better let Viola know in case she caught me 'at it', this time in a more embarrassing position.

"Viola, I'm just going to feel Helga's tits again through her bra!" Again I got the OK from the kitchen.

Again, I felt, examined, her breasts through her silken bra, this was a bit nerve-wracking and I must confess, a turn on. (Had it not been, then there would be something wrong with me.)

Squeezing, caressing and weighing her breasts, I said jokingly, and nervously, "Well, they certainly seem real through the bra but I'm not thoroughly convinced, the only way is for me to examine them without the bra!"

Did I really say that? Yes I did, I couldn't believe it myself, even after all these years, and again I had said it jokingly, not thinking for a moment that she would even let me feel her through her pullover, let alone where we finished up. With that, and with no hesitation, save a bit of a sigh, she reached behind her back and unclipped her bra, letting it fall to the floor. I think my jaw dropped open on my chest upon viewing those magnificent globes of female flesh right in front of my eyes, as she stood in front of me semi-naked. I was surprised Viola didn't hear the sound of my jaw hitting the floor with shock, a very pleasant shock, may I add! And with a little trepidation and I think a little shaking, I called to Viola, "Viola, Helga has taken her bra off, I'm going to massage and feel her boobs!"

"OK love," came the reply from the kitchen. I was still expecting Viola to walk in and catch us 'at it' at any moment but she didn't.

Shaking a little, I once again proceeded to massage, knead, stroke and weigh each breast in turn and then together. Careful not to abuse my luck, I avoided her nipples.

"Yeah, they're real!" said I.

Helga: "I told you they were all along," with a wicked smile!

With that, she put her bra and pullover back on, just in time before Viola walked in the room. Upon reflection, and after some time, I couldn't believe I had said and done all this and more surprising, that she had been happy to oblige.

This once again showed that the Germans were not slow in coming forward when it came to matters of sex.

After Helga had gone home, I asked Viola if she thought I was joking and did she believe me when I said I was going to feel Helga's boobies?

"No!" she said. "I thought you were joking, but if I had caught you doing it, I would have left you and divorced you!"

That was me, always the honest one, always upfront. Phew, thank goodness she hadn't come out of the kitchen and caught us doing what happened later!

Could I have gone on and had an affair with Helga? Probably, I think she was up for it. If I was so inclined, but being newly married, I wasn't! The signs were favourable though. This was the 'last hurrah' for the old girl-chasing John, never again. Though I believe I had other opportunities afterwards, had I been interested but I wasn't, I never indulged.

First Christmas together

Our first Christmas as man and wife saw us playing host to some of the single lads from the Sqn, which they claimed was the normal procedure. I didn't really want to, but they would have looked down on me if I hadn't, I really wanted to spend the first Christmas together. But I was 'assigned' to have an Indian lad for Christmas Day, one other, the Sqn hard man had been assigned to go to Paul Henderson's house in a place called Pfalzdorf near Goch, he didn't want to go to Henderson's house as he didn't like him that much, not to mention his wife who both had the most unenviable reputation and they were also missing out in the looks department. He asked if he could come also to have his Christmas dinner at my flat, he would come after making some excuse to Henderson to leave.

Things were going fine until the Indian got drunk and started to act the goat and swear. After several warnings to shut up, the 'hard man' took him outside onto the landing and had a word with him to watch his mouth, the Indian didn't so the 'hard man' took him back outside and promptly 'beat the Indian lad up'; they thought it time to go back to camp. That was a rotten Christmas, but it gave Viola and I a bit of time on our own.

Moving from flat

Eventually, we decided we'd better move a bit nearer to camp for several reasons. We would have a little longer at home, nearer to camp, we might be able to shop in the Naafi, thereby making things a bit cheaper. We would get some more disturbance allowance.

With Viola mastering the German language course at camp, she had a part-time job translating for Helmut and Greta after September when the course started. I started the course with her but was only able to get in two lessons, I was away on exercise again!

Viola picked the language up very quickly, I was very proud of her.

Bad heart

We tried to get a nice young lad off the Sqn who wanted to bring his wife out from UK out to Germany. Viola did the translating for him. Although only in his early 20s, he had a bad heart that had somehow escaped the notice of the medical people when he first joined. The first we knew of this was when one of our officers took me aside and asked if I was the one dealing with one of his men in getting a flat. I told him I was, he then told me to tell the landlord that he wouldn't be requiring the flat any more as he'd had a mild heart attack, was in hospital, would be sent back to England for specialists to check him over and then a possible medical discharge. So we arranged with the family officer to have someone else move in.

We never saw this nice chap from Liverpool again.

Taking R.A.F. policeman drinking

The replacement we were fixed up with was a 'spoon/snowdrop' – our nickname for R.A.F. policemen. About a couple of days before we left, we arranged to have a party for the new couple who were to move into our flat. We were to show them how things worked in the flat and then to show them and introduce them to the locals in the bar and meet Klara. It was quite clear early on that the Snowdrop wasn't used to the German beer; he got very drunk very early on. He finished up being very ill, all over the road signs. His wife was very embarrassed. As for me, all I had to do was cross the road and climb three flights of stairs.

I have crossed the road

Just crossing the road took me nearly 45 minutes. The proverbial one step forward and two steps back in all took me well over an hour to get into the flat. Viola was worried sick, especially when I tried to crawl on all fours across the road.

Fortunately, there was nothing on the road at the time, had there been, I would have been in real trouble. Probably doing my impersonation of a flat hedgehog.

More problems were to come. After only two hours sleep, it was time to get up and get ready to catch the R.A.F. bus to Laarbruch.

Reporting to Sqn drunk

As you can imagine, I was still very drunk and beginning to dread what might happen when I got to the Sqn.

On parade that morning, I was decidedly unsteady on my feet, swaying from side to side in fact. For some reason that escapes me now and is lost in the mists of time, most of the Sqn weren't there; they must have been on exercise again! I think I must have been given permission to stay behind to hand over the flat.

As was normal, a few people stayed behind for a variety of reasons.

The SWO came around inspecting us and when he got to me, he stood back, smiled and shook his head, saying, "What's up with you, Rowbottom, you're pissed, aren't you?" "Yes Sir!" I couldn't very well deny it.

He told me to follow him to his office, which I duly did. I thought that he was going to read me the riot act, charge me, even court martial me for being drunk on parade. And you know what? At that moment in time I couldn't have cared less! That was how drunk I was.

Anyway, he gave me the key to the Sqn canteen and told me to lock myself away there and stay out of sight, and out of mischief. I locked myself in and fell asleep at the table and stayed there till lunchtime. Lunchtime saw me make my way to the mess, there I saw Viola waiting for me, she was worried sick how I'd managed in an alcoholic stupor.

After lunch, I again locked myself in the canteen and went to sleep to try and make myself sober enough to go home. I was just about sober when I got back to the flat. After something to eat, I went to bed for a long sleep, I was ready for it. However, one glass of water that night and I was drunk again.

The next morning, I was finally sober but feeling very rough.

It didn't put me off drinking altogether, but I did cut back my consumption to 5-6 bottles a day from the usual 7-8 per day! Not counting weekends when I had a 'proper' drink at the pub. Before I left Germany, I was on a lot more than that per night. And most of the guys were on more than me! At one point before I left 1 Sqn, I must have been somewhere between 40-45 half-litre bottles a week.

Viola learns the real language

Viola was lucky in learning the language, apart from the theory side, she worked with the locals. It was they who taught her the real language, not learned from a textbook. She also spoke Spanish so that made her popular with the Spanish working there. There were also the hot-blooded, excitable Italians.

Not to mention the Dutch and Malays, so she picked up quite a bit of their different languages. By the time we left, she spoke Tagalog (Filipino), English, Spanish and German fluently, quite a lot of Italian and a few words of Malay and Dutch.

Nursing and language comes in handy

Her fluent German and nursing knowledge came in handy on one occasion. It concerned one of the Germans she was working with, a poof/homosexual. When Viola asked him what the matter was, all he could do was smile and say, "A very good weekend and I'm paying for it now! I can hardly walk!"

Viola gave him some medical advice, "Go and see a doctor and stop doing it, I've no sympathy!" He didn't give it up.

Moving out of flat to Weeze

We eventually moved out of the flat but stayed friendly with our former landlord and landlady. We moved into a bungalow in Weeze near camp. We never did meet the landlord, but the landlady seemed nice, though we didn't have much to do with her.

One of the first things she told us was that she'd noticed how we kept the toilet window open at all times in all weather; she was pleased about that, though she told us that our predecessor – a chap from 1 Sqn who had just been posted back to England, had never opened it and the place stank.

Having parties

We had a couple of parties in the place, after first obtaining permission. We used to roll the carpet up to prevent it getting ruined. The single lads from the Sqn told me I was the only married man whose house they could go to where they could really let their hair down, and they appreciated it.

Sqn 'Mini Olympics'

During the summer, the Sqn thought they would have their own little mini 'Olympics' starting with swimming events. They said that all people who could swim would swim for the Sqn in the Swimming Gala. Now I could swim, but not very fast, my strength had always been distance and not speed. So I was determined I was not going to participate; after all, I knew that I would be last and I wasn't going to be laughed at.

Now, if they had a long distance/endurance race, I would gladly have taken part. So as far as they were concerned, I couldn't swim, no one had seen me swim yet. So, when the Flight/Sqn had swimming sessions, I stayed with the non-swimming group.

Won't swim

One day, I forgot momentarily and was spotted by an NCO, who said, "Hey, you're swimming. I thought you couldn't swim?"

"Oh (me trying to unsuccessfully look surprised), I'm swimming, I'm swimming, hey, I didn't realise it!" I don't think the NCO was totally convinced.

It was fortunately too late to include me in the Sqn swimming team, what a shame, ha, ha!

So I watched from the stands and there was just such a lad who was so slow that he was about one and a half lengths of the pool behind the last chap home, he was, of course, last; everyone was laughing at him once the race was over but when he was about ten yards or so from the end, people were screaming at him to go faster as if he were going in a real race and the outcome depended who won a gold medal. Though watching them, I think I would have come in about ¾ of the way down the order.

Playing alternative sports (tennis)

When we had sports periods once a week, football and rugby were usually fully booked up by the same old crowd each week so people like me couldn't get a game. So I usually preferred games that didn't appeal to the majority, for e.g., tennis. I have always liked playing tennis, so I quite enjoyed it, though I was not very good at it. We also had an advantage over the others in that we used to play our games on the officers' mess courts and the officer always used to treat us to a drink from the bar before we'd finished.

Of course, needless to say, this officer i/c tennis wasn't Flg Off Hackett. This one was a true officer and gentleman.

Playing hockey

The other game I played was men's hockey. "Hockey!" I said. "That's a bloody girl's game! I'm not playing that; I'll be branded as a nancy, or worse!" I had no choice, I had to play; we had to play some sort of sport on sports afternoon.

But the surprising thing was how hard and tough the game really was. In fact, I got to enjoy it so much that the next sports afternoon, I volunteered for hockey. I got quite good at it so eventually, when we had an inter-Sqn 'Olympic game', we went to another R.A.F. Stn, Gutterslough near the East German border. We were there to play a knock-out hockey competition.

I was in the Sqn First team along with my pal, Norman Geordie Hall; we got through to the final; we lost 3-2. I scored one goal.

Talking of mutiny – attempted suicide

The pressure was on everybody in the Sqn, not just me. And of all the Sqns/sections I'd been on, this one had discontent running so rife that there was very frequent talk of mutiny. And attempted suicides; one chap on our Flt was having a lot of trouble with his back and with nearly always being on exercise almost constantly in pain. He tried to commit suicide by driving his car at home full throttle straight at a brick wall; he survived. He was eventually posted back to UK for treatment. So we didn't find out what happened to him.

Mum and Dad come for a holiday

In the midsummer of 1976, my mother and father came for a holiday for a few months. They stayed with us in the bungalow. My father loved going out in the early morning for a walk around the local area and nearby town, or trying the fresh bread and coffee at the local shops next door.
He asked if we could take them to the local dance hall for a dance, such as waltz, foxtrot, etc. He couldn't – wouldn't – believe it when I told him there was none. "Rubbish, lad, there is one, I saw it in Goch! It's done out in red and black!"

"No dad, that's the local brothel!" But he wouldn't believe me, no matter how hard I tried. So I figured the only way to convince him was to take him there and show him.

"All right, Dad, you don't believe me? There's only one way to convince you and that is to show you! Let's go and knock on the door and see!"

So that's just what we did, we jumped on the first R.A.F. bus to Goch.

Knocking on the door

I knocked, no reply, and Dad went around the back to have a look. So there was I on the doorstep with my wife and mother behind, what a sight we must have been. The door was eventually opened by a tall, very well-groomed and sophisticated woman with a red velvet dress slit open at the front and trimmed with ermine; she saw me but not my mother and Viola. So she smiled and pulled me inside quickly. "Hi, welcome, come on in!" in perfect English. I did…well, I didn't have much choice as I had already been pulled inside. Closely followed by Viola, Mum and Dad!

She stood taken aback by shock as it were. "Yes, can I help you, Sirs, Madams?"

"Yes," said Dad, "do you have any dances here; you know, waltz, foxtrot and the like?"

"No," said she smiling and in perfect English, "I'm afraid it's not that kind of establishment!" No, and now I knew beyond a shadow of a doubt just what kind of establishment it really was.

We were looking around and there were 8 of the most beautiful, sophisticated and well-dressed women you had ever seen by the bar. The décor, lampshades, upholstery, curtains, etc. were done out in various shades of red. It confirmed what I'd always suspected it was! A high-class brothel and we were being chatted up by the 'Madam'; even my dad was now convinced. Madam: "But you're very welcome to come in and have a drink if you wish!" What a very nice gesture, we thought; regrettably, we had to decline her very kind offer.

I said before and I'll say again, very civilised these Europeans when it comes to pleasures of the flesh! And all the time, Viola was trying to pull me away and I was trying to stay. So we finally did leave with egg on our faces. Finally convinced, my father never asked again if there were any more dance halls in the area, and boy, did he get some stick from my mother and me. He never lived it down.

I told the chaps on the Sqn the morning after, "How many take their wife, mother and father to a brothel for a night out?" This was greeted with great hilarity.

My father had to go back to England to work but Mother stayed with us for a few more weeks.

Having to reform new AA gun Sqns

The word went around the Sqn and was confirmed by the C.O. that the Guatemalan government in Central America was massing on the border of Belize, British Honduras, again! They had laid claim to part of Belize and were getting ready to invade. There always have been British troops there to protect from any possible invasion threat, even today, now that they are independent.

Well, the story had it that invasion was imminent! And M.O.D. realised that there wasn't enough AA guns or AA Sqns available to reinforce the garrison so they started to panic. A new Sqn had to be formed, and fast! To go out there ready to fight if need be.

Most had or were in the process of converting to the Rapier missile system or the field role, such as ourselves. So all Regiment Sqns had to gather all the people with previous knowledge of the Bofor guns to form a new squadron; we were all interviewed by the C.O. and SWO to get up enough experienced men to form a flight or ideally, two. The numbers on the Sqn would then be made up by new replacements.

During the interview with the Sqn C.O., he said that although I was a prime candidate, I was going to be left out as I was due out any time. The new Sqn, when reformed, would be flying out to Belize in Central America.

New chap has accident

One day, I and others not on gun training were going about our business and we heard and saw a commotion on the other side of the hangar. Suddenly, people were running around in a great flap and panicking, in a huddle together, we heard there had been an accident. "Aw, somebody has trapped a finger or something," we thought. If only that had been the case. We didn't pay much attention at the time and got on with our jobs. We found out shortly after, whilst training on the gun, this chap from another Sqn nearby had been involved in an accident.

Now we know what had happened. A former 37 Sqn SNCO Tug Wilson who had been posted to us a few months ago was training the gun team when there had been an accident. We believe that it was because he was trying to make the team go faster before they had got sufficient knowledge or confidence and this lad had been injured. I saw from one side of the hangar a large pool of blood on the floor and I knew then that it was very serious indeed.

We believe one of two things could have had happened: the former S/Sgt I mentioned was trying to rush the drill movements before the team was really ready for it. As I told the guys later, and they agreed with me, that when you get the confidence – speed will come naturally.

The other thing, maybe the hydraulic pressure gave way, split a seal forcing the jacking handle to come from the horizontal to the vertical too fast for him to get out of the way in time. Whilst using the releasing valve for controlled movement, his head was trapped. He was seriously injured. Very fortunately, there were three visiting helicopters on the station at the time; we realised that the medical centre would not be able to cope with his injuries so he was airlifted out to the nearest service hospital – Wegberg.

We got a progress report every couple of hours but I knew myself that if he was to survive, which I doubted being a serious head injury, then he could finish up as a cabbage.

The next morning after parade, the whole Sqn were tasked to 'clean and tidy the stores', which meant shut yourselves inside and stay out of the way. After about half an hour, one of our NCOs, Geordie Weirdo came in and asked for everybody's attention, and looking sombre and subdued, he informed us that the lad who had been involved in that accident yesterday had died about 40 minutes ago.

Nobody spoke for about 10-15 minutes, we were all too shocked and upset, that was the only time I had seen any rock-apes shocked into silence, we had lost one of our own! Normally, someone was always fooling about or cracking gags, but not today. This mood lasted for about three days. It still saddens me today whenever I think about it.

Collection for dead man

I decided to get a collection going for a wreath but when I saw the SWO for permission, he told me that one other was already doing it for his flight so I thought I'd do it for mine; when the word got around that I was doing it, some of the lads from the other flights donated some money, so I had enough for two wreaths – one from the Sqn as a whole and one from 'C' Flt ourselves. My mother also donated to the collection on behalf of her and Father. A day or two later, I asked permission to address the Sqn and read out the message/sentiments on the card on the wreaths.

Geordie the Weirdo

'C' flight Cpl, as I mentioned, Geordie Weirdo really was a sick character. I didn't realise how much until I had seen it first-hand. Oh yes, I had been told stories by the others when I first arrived but I didn't take much notice until I had a chance to make up my own mind. He admitted in a quiet moment to me and one other that he needed the artificial stimulation of blue films/pornography to turn him on and get him in the mood, the same also went for his wife, and to help achieve this, he had a large collection of porn films, nearly enough to fill a suitcase!

He also admitted that some of his accessories included vibrators of varying sizes and a 10 feet bull whip; he used to brag about these. He also bragged that he was going to take them back to UK through customs.

His interest in blue films: 'Geordie specials'

He not only collected blue films, but he also specialised in the real hardcore/sick, kinky films. Well, all of us were used to seeing these XXX films, but not his type. After all, in most German bars when you went for a quiet meal or drink with friends, they would be showing this type of films, pornographic by our standards – quite accepted as normal by the broad-minded Germans.

Though Geordie's specials were very strong even for the run-of-the-mill German films.

Last new year in the forces

Whilst my mother was staying with us, Geordie invited Viola, myself and my mother to his house in Pfalzdorf. We had been invited up for New Year's Eve, 1976 – my last new year in the forces.

It was one of the worst new year I have had to endure. There were all his friends, mostly from the Sqn; everybody was sat in their own little cliques, not wanting to associate with anyone else. It was a terrible atmosphere, but we definitely got the feeling that no one wanted to know us. Was it because I was there? I knew I wasn't popular with the creeps as I let these people know I hated creeps, they were (and still are) as far as I was concerned the lowest of the low. I had never ever been a creeper in my life and I'll stand or fall by my decision. It seemed that all the creeps on the Sqn were there, unfortunately, none of the nice people. Or was it because I had taken my mother with me?

Meeting Alex (ex-33 Sqn)

As I previously mentioned, a new missile Sqn was formed, 58 Sqn. One afternoon, I got a very pleasant surprise. About two weeks after it had been formed, I saw someone who looked vaguely familiar, it was Sergeant Alex Goddard from 33 Sqn at Odiham, I was very pleased to see him again. Though I thought at the time that he didn't seem like the old Alex I had come to know and like, as if something was troubling him. He was always in a hurry and didn't seem very happy. He couldn't/wouldn't talk to me much. I found out later it wasn't the knowledge of learning about the missiles system that was too much, it was something else.

Alex telling me about 'Rapier' system

I did get some information out of him; they had to resign the official secrets act. I asked what the Rapier missile system was like, was it as good as it was cracked up to be. I think he was thinking I was trying to find out too much information but when I convinced him that I was only interested, he told me: "No missile system or anything mechanical/electrical can be 100% accurate or reliable but the Rapier system is 99.99% accurate and reliable, the best of its kind in the world. If there's an enemy aircraft within range, then you can guarantee that the system will not only spot it but will shoot it down. If there are four missiles on the launcher and five enemy aircraft, then not only will it knock out four of them but the fifth might be brought down by the flying debris of the other destroyed aircraft."

Trouble was that these lads on the Rapier Sqn thought they were 'It', the 'bee's knees'; they wouldn't associate with us much on 1 Sqn (who can blame them).

Hackett tries to cancel my leave

With the pressure I was under on 1 Sqn, I was quite naturally looking forward to my annual leave and Hackett must have realised that this was what kept me going so he always did his best to cancel my leave, whether it was for a couple of days or for two/three weeks.

Now I prided myself in the fact that I could take more pressure than most when all about me were losing their heads, but as I said, they almost got to me.

Sick with depression; Second leave

I had to report sick with depression but it just seemed to make them pick on me all that more. This just made me more determined than ever not to crack up and let him win.

On my second leave, when it was finally granted, we had a 'Paddy' on the Sqn who was going to see his brother in Doncaster and offered us a lift in his car. We were grateful as it saved us a lot of money. We bought a few petrol coupons, which car owners were entitled to and enabled you to buy petrol at UK prices and not at German prices, which were dearer. We paid our way; going by road to Belgium was a long boring trip and we thought we weren't going to make it. In fact, if one of the officials hadn't taken pity on us and delayed the removal of ramp for a few minutes to enable us to get aboard, we would have missed the ferry.

Sergeant talks to member of the ship's crew

On board, we settled down and had a drink; we also had one other man with us – a Sgt from the Sqn who Paddy was giving a lift to. He got drunk and got talking to a member of the ship's crew in uniform and was telling him, "Ah, these customs people are stupid, they can't tell if people are smuggling bottles of spirits, cigarettes, etc. I mean, they won't be able to tell I am carrying more than I should. Are you a member of the crew?" "No!" replied this chap. Then I knew what he was! At the other end in Felixstowe, there were only about 5-6 cars, all servicemen, the rest of the ship's load was lorries and were permitted to drive straight through but all the cars were stopped. We were directed to a customs official, he looked vaguely familiar.

Customs stop us

He was that so-called 'member of crew' that the drunken sergeant had been bragging to! "Oh heck," thought I, "we're in for it now!" I was right. They had us out and found spirits and cigarettes, more than the allowance. Unknown to Viola and not realising that we were limited to just so many! So I got done.

But so did this sergeant who had done the same but he knew he was over and declared he wasn't. He got done as well. Paddy, unbeknownst to any of us, had done the same, but he had hidden all his stuff in and around the car, which also included cameras. The customs had a field day.

The car behind us also happened to belong to a member of my Sqn and when buying a car abroad, you had to keep it there for so long before being able to bring it to England, tax- and duty-free. You may bring it sooner if you had the relevant paperwork available and if brought home for two weeks, then you had to add that extra two weeks on the end of that entitlement period. The poor lad didn't know that and the customs made him get out along with his friends, whom he was giving a lift home to, and told him that the car was to be left there and impounded, he couldn't bring it into the country as he hadn't the relevant paperwork with him. He could pick the car up on the way out to Germany again, just before his boat sailed.

He was so upset; his 'so-called' mates were cursing him, "How the feck do I get home now. We were relying on you; we can't afford to get the train!"

We had a lift to Doncaster railway station from where we got a train home to Scunthorpe. Needless to say, Viola had a lesson in what you could and couldn't bring in duty-free.

Coming across an unusual phenomenon (secret base)

On one small exercise, we were on an escape and evasion map reading exercise. We had been told to stick to the main roads at all times but me and one other chap thought we were off course; we weren't, but didn't realise it. So we thought we'd better take a shortcut; we went across a field and then we had to cross a wide stream.

Just before we jumped across, we heard a lot of noise and sensed something was happening behind us. I looked around and there, in what had been an empty field a few moments ago, was now a large complex c/w watchtowers, high fences, spotlights and guards with noisy, active guard dogs.

We think they sensed our presence, we thought we'd better get out of there ASAP. After a few minutes and after putting several hundred yards between us and that damn stream, which we both fell short of clearing and got a bit wet, we looked back and tried to see just what had given us a start, and a further surprise awaited us. That place, whatever it was, was no longer there!

Had it really existed or had it been a trick of our minds? Who knew but I was sure that there had been something there that we had accidentally stumbled on and were not supposed to see. If my life depended on it, I couldn't go now to the same place, I don't even know what area or district it was in, honestly! No wonder we were told not to venture off the main road!

Viola collapses at work

During the hot summer of 1975, I was part of the defensive force of Laarbruch against another Sqn. We were in a wood just outside camp when I got word that Viola had been rushed to the medical centre with what was thought to be heatstroke, of all things, and that was with Viola coming from a hot country. It turned out she was fine but has suffered from this several occasions since.

Ways we had to amuse ourselves

When we didn't have much to do, we would try to amuse ourselves whichever way we could. One way we were kept occupied was to sweep the hangar floor.

So I formed the 'five brooms display team' with absolutely no engagements to our credit at all.

Whilst engaged on the useless job of sweeping, and out of boredom, we would devise a series of fancy manoeuvres. With our brooms going in several different directions and formations.

Another time, we'd be by the vehicle ramps outside the hangar, we would put an old cigarette packet at the end of the ramp as 'stumps', with one chap defending it with a sliver of wood as a cricket bat, and the ball would be a stone and we would have ourselves a game of cricket, usually with snow knee-deep around.

Another leisure pastime when we had time on our hands was to play volleyball at a permanently erected net. On other occasions, after parade, we would be detailed to sort out the store (Sqn or flight stores); with about 30 of us mucking in, it was usually done within an hour so we spent the rest of the day, excluding parades, meal breaks and such, just sleeping on the tents/camouflage nets or chatting with our mates.

It seemed to be the general idea that it was better to let the chaps have an easy day rather than try to teach all the very basics of tactics or weapon training. Nothing was guaranteed to get the backs up of the chaps, and did! More than to be taught the rifle, again! And again, and again. After all, everybody passed their annual weapons test time and time again, the 'old hands' with several years of experience, and then young lads not a year out of their basic training. We all knew our jobs and resented the insinuation that we didn't. The words 'granny' and 'eggs' come to mind!

Granddad 'S' dies

Once after I'd returned from exercise, I was told to report to the general office. I was told that my grandfather on my mother's side had died and the funeral would be the following week.

I asked the Sqn for permission to go home for the funeral; they said I could go home. When I went to the general office, they said, "No!" Their official reply was, "Grandparents are not important enough to warrant compassionate leave," though acknowledged that the airman and grandfather were close!

That finished my love and respect for the R.A.F. as if through Hackett and 1 Sqn it hadn't already. I have thought since was Hackett behind it for spite? The sort of trick he would pull?

Rusty, new car

As I mentioned before, you could get a new car at a very good discount... well, most of the lads did take advantage of this offer. While I was there, we had a chap posted to us who in civvy street had been a car mechanic. He offered his services to anyone who was interested and he would check the car over for them to make sure that they hadn't been 'done'.

One of the chaps on my flight picked his car up over the weekend and brought it to the Sqn the following Monday morning. The ex-mechanic looked it over, after examining the new car, he got up and said to the new owner, "Well, you've been done, this is supposed to be a new car, and it's riddled with rust! Within a couple of months, it will come through and be seen by all." (He was right.) "If you take my advice, you'll take it back and complain, you shouldn't have a rusty car when supposed to be brand new, you can and should demand another car, after all, you've paid for a new one!" To which the owner replied, "I don't think I'll bother; after all, it'll rust eventually!" The ex-mechanic said, "Oh well, if you're that stupid, don't ask me to help again, I am finished with you!" and he walked away!

'Tac-e-Val', do my back in

On a Stn exercise, I was in my O.P., observation post, that I had built on my own, and was just finishing my morning constitution when over the radio I heard a 'contact' report, the enemy had attacked the station, so rushing towards my O.P., I bent down to get inside and my back went out.

I had to call up the sergeant on the flight who was a trained physio in boxing ailments. I asked him to bring a Land Rover and take me to the medical centre. It took me ages to convince those in the G.D.O.C. that this was genuine and not a lark, once they were convinced it was genuine, they then thought it funny! And were laughing at my misfortune except the ex-boxer, he obviously realised that it was easily done and what sort of pain I was in.

Pulling a fast one

Geordie Weirdo had come with him to see that I wasn't trying to get out of the job. At first he was laughing but straightaway realised I was in pain.

The guys on the Sqn thought too that I was trying to pull a fast one. I replied, "Pulling a fast one, am I? Well, when you're nice and warm and having a beer after your Christmas dinner, think of me, regardless of whether it's snowing or not, I shall have to report to the medical centre for heat ray treatment!" They didn't believe me, I was so hoping that somebody would see me either leaving or going to the medical centre, fortunately, one of the guys did see me and said to me, "What are you doing here, John? After all this talk I've heard, I thought you were having us on and you were trying to skive, I nor anybody else though you might be telling the truth!"

"That's the trouble with most people!" I said. "They would rather not believe I tell the truth, unlike them who tell lies all the time and don't even know they're doing it!"

Christmas in the medical centre

I had to go every day during the Christmas period for the treatment, but it didn't spoil my Christmas too much.

Viola drunk

The second time I had seen Viola drunk and in a worse state was during the pre-Christmas festivities in 1975. She had been invited to attend a pre-Christmas function with the women from work in a purely 'women only' function. I and most husbands had to wait in another bar till they were finished. Eventually, one of Viola's friends came through to see me, looking very worried, and told me that Viola was very drunk and wanted to go home.

I went through to the other bar and there was Viola being propped up by two large women; she was definitely unsteady on her feet.

"John," she said, not knowing what she was doing, "I want to go home!" "But love," I said, "I am just beginning to enjoy myself! And I've just bought another drink! I don't want to go just yet!"

"Call me a taxi; I want to go home NOW!" she said in her sternest 'she who must be obeyed' style voice. Well, we all – except Viola, burst out laughing. She stood there in her stockinged feet and pulled herself up to her full 5ft something. "Don't argue with me, I want to go home NOW."

We were all laughing so much who could argue. I think the women there felt a bit sorry for me.

As Viola and I were walking towards our bungalow down the gravel path, it started to spit with rain. "Whoops," said Viola, putting her hand to her mouth. "What's up?" I asked.

"I feel seasick. I am going to be sick!"

"Seasick in the middle of ruddy Germany?" I said, laughing.

Then putting her hand out, "Oh, it's bristling!"

"Bristling, what on earth is bristling?" I replied.

"Oh, you know, bristling, little rain!"

"Oh, you mean drizzling!"

"Yes, that's what I said!" I laughed for ages after that and of course she wasn't even in a fit state to get ready for bed.

Getting organised on exercise

On 26 Feb 1976, we had a winter survival course at Soltau, some of which involved running about in stripped-down Land Rovers, stripped to the waist, initially, operating in biting wind and 2-3 feet of snow. The exercise progressed to the guys only allowed to wear P.T. shorts and boots and not only driving around in that cold weather and snow but carrying out normal military manoeuvres, which included going tactical and throwing themselves down in the snow with just their shorts on.

Though I can't quite remember the reason (maybe I had reported sick) but I was quite lucky in that I only had the cold weather to put up with for two days and the rest of the time I was assigned to work in the officers' mess where I developed and became well known for my 'culinary expertise' (joke) as the officers' cook. But all I could do at lunchtime with the raw materials available was steak sandwiches with a liberal sprinkling of spices;

they became well known and sought after, and most officers came back for more than one with the exception of...yes, you've guessed it, Hackett. He never did have any from me. Why? Did he think I was going to poison him? Ha, ha. Now there's a thought! Unfortunately too late now! So did he get food from another source or did he go hungry for two weeks? I really can't recall him ever coming for lunch; I do believe he preferred to go hungry rather than eating my food (more fool him), as if I'd do anything that would harm him, tut-tut!

I do recall the SWO one day after another heavy snowfall giving the Sqn C.O. an almighty rollicking about making the lads work in this environment. He risked some of them going down with hypothermia – even some of them dying from the cold, what he was doing was bloody stupid and he (the C.O.) was told to inform the guys to get dressed and do the rest of the training fully clothed with cold weather gear on. If he didn't, the SWO would not be responsible for the action he would take against the officer. The proverbial would hit the fan! "Whoa," I thought, "something's got to give here. I wouldn't put any money on the C.O. though!" The C.O. held out another day before he relented and the guys were able to get dressed.

Best Harrier exercises

When on the Harrier exercise, we got organised, at first we were allowed two cans of beer, we weren't very happy, we all as one let the officers/ SNCOs know it; after all, we were supposed to be 'old hands' and if we hadn't learned to handle our ale by now, then we never would. Anyway, before the end of the exercise, we had as much as we wanted and as we said, nobody had so much that they made a fool of themselves.

For about six months, Hackett left the Sqn on a course or something. Flt/Sgt Houseman said, "Let's get organised, if we can show the C.O. we don't need an officer, we'll be far better off and can relax, just do your jobs and there won't be a problem!"

So instead of having every man out in our O.P. trenches, we just had one. On site, Houseman split us up, 20 of us went to prepare the trenches and the site defences, the other 20 started to get the campsite organised, concentrating mainly on getting the tents up; the following day we swapped and reversed jobs, finishing off.

Once we were ready, we were all split up into three sections – one section on duty in camp on standby, one on duty in trenches and the other section was on day off, in the pubs, shower runs, shops, etc. No other sect/ flight had ever done this, it certainly worked, the exercise became almost bearable.

We used to enjoy the shower runs as we sometimes took in a film if at a military camp but we always would stop for a 'schnelly' (Schnell Imbis = quick food), not to mention a drink or two at a bar on the way back, yes, it was rough on exercise!

In actual fact, we should have been on location in O.P.'s all the time. It was amusing, especially in the exercise during warm weather, we would have one four-tonner carrying the kit, and one with the men in, and another 'unofficially' carrying nothing but hundreds of cans of beer, ice, several large plastic dustbins to put both in, not forgetting the old 45 gall drum that was converted to a barbecue to grill burgers, steaks and sausages. Maybe the Americans roughed it with hamburgers and ice cream in the field, but the British got their act together properly. Mind you, the other flights were still stuck with the silly two cans a night. So towards the end of the exercise, we would invite them for a barbecue and a few beers, at a price of course! Well, we had to boost flight funds for ourselves and this was a good way of giving it a boost.

How we roughed it

One exercise I remember particularly well. It was one September whilst the days were still warm and the nights were decidedly chilly so true to my reputation, I was always prepared though the little Boy Scout I was not!

I used to take a bottle of brandy with me on cold nights; there was never a shortage of volunteers to share my trench when they found out. Until I was caught by Hackett, who made a surprise inspection of my O.P. and told me, "I strictly forbid you to bring any brandy again in the trench! Is that clear? After all, you are supposed to be on exercise!"

"Righto sir, I promise I won't!" True to my word, I didn't! Next time I took rum instead!

But to make sure I wasn't spotted, I left the large bottle in my tent with my kit and used to fill a well washed out brown sauce bottle, yep. I was never cold or fed up in my trench again. Though only once did I come back to the site worse the wear for drink, which happened to coincide with a very cold night.

When my mates saw me stagger into the site, they smiled and said, "Had a hard night's exercise, John, its rough on exercise, isn't it?" I smiled back at them.

But we had an early end to the proceedings; word came over the radio net that a couple of wild boars still living within Germany were running loose around the Harrier site and one had just slashed the tyre of a Harrier, so we had lots of volunteers to try and scare them away. You could hear the blanks and thunder flashes going off all over the shop.

I was tempted to go in, guns blazing but thought better of it as there was bound to be several Wallys making a fool of themselves; I was right, when they got back to the tented area, I heard that these boars had chased a couple of the lads up the tent poles, so to speak. They could be quite vicious. Good job I didn't go after all.

Sex club in clearing

We heard one night that the cooks had had a night off the previous evening at a great local strip club and one had even tried to participate until the girl involved had stopped him dead in his tracks. This was one place I was looking forward to seeing, sounded a good laugh. So a couple of days later, I and some of the lads had the evening off. So off we went looking for this club.

We were walking through the wood; it was thick and dense, so dense that you couldn't see anything. But eventually, we came upon a clearing where there were about five or six houses, and at the end of the cul-de-sac, there was this sex club.

Inside, there were only about four or five of us and four locals; the beer was very expensive. Though there was no entrance fee, they tried several tricks to get you to spend like free peanuts, constantly wiping the table and the moment you put your empty glass down, they pounced like the proverbial kite hawks.

Interesting show

Anyway, the star of the show came on, a very attractive blonde, dressed as a bride all in white, she pretended she was calling her husband-to-be on the phone, then she was 'supposedly' turned on by what he said so stripped off, but kept her veil on at all times through the proceedings.

She proceeded to examine herself with the aid of several inanimate objects around her. But most of all, she liked to use the telephone, but not in a way the British Telecom's adverts would show. At the end of her act, the handset did a 'vanishing act' and she walked about the stage holding the cradle with the cord still attached! I really wouldn't have believed it possible had I not seen it with my own eyes. It reminded me of the stories of the brothels in Libya with 'certain creatures' I had heard about. Not permitted in Europe. One minute it was there, then it was gone!

The second girl came on later, a well-built coloured girl in a topless ball gown, initially! When she saw us there and heard us talking, she started to talk to us, "Hey, are you all Brits?" "Whatever gives you that impression?" I said. "We don't have to wear this uniform, but we do because it's the 'in thing' to wear at the moment!" She thought this funny and carried on with her act, whilst talking to us, the locals didn't appear to like this.

It turned out that she was from Birmingham, and after her act came and sat with us and had a chat. She said that she didn't often get the chance to talk English, only on odd occasions when there was an exercise and that wasn't very often. And of course, the poor girl felt homesick now and then.

F/Sgt Houseman, SNCO i/c flight

The last few Harrier exercises were the best; Officer Hackett was away on a six-month course. We realised, of course, that this probably wasn't the only reason Flt Sgt Houseman didn't want officers around, there must have been at least a couple of other reasons, one of which he had an 'alleged' racket going and that he was a part-time insurance salesman for a company, and as a new chap was posted, he tried to persuade the newcomers to take out a policy with him. I can't say whether the policy was any good as I didn't want to know. I already had all the cover I needed when I had bought my house and taken out a mortgage. Very few dared to refuse him and those that did, if on our flight, usually got the tough and dirty jobs to do, or if there were any toilets to clean out during the exercise, he would gather his little squad of 'rebels' and give us some waffle of how much he appreciated our helping him out! Those who eventually relented and took out a policy never got caught for these dirty jobs or duties again, but there were two – Geordie Hall, my mate and I, stuck it out to the end. Maybe that's why he didn't fight very hard to look after my interests when Hackett put on me.

Who knows; I can only speculate. I did want to take out some more insurance on myself and Viola but I wouldn't be pushed or bullied into it. Instead, I made arrangements with my mother to get that side organised when next I came home on leave. The other reason was to show the OC/C.O. that he could manage quite well, which wouldn't do his promotion prospects any harm, in other words a 'creep'!

When we entered the major phase of the exercise, then, of course, we were on hand and in position.

R & R at Mohne dam

On one of our official R & Rs that we were given, we spent at the local tourist trap, the 'Mohne Dam' of 617 Sqn Dam-busters fame. We were briefed, "Whatever you do, lads, DON'T antagonise the situation, you all know the history of this place, thanks to 617 Sqn, so for God's sake, DON'T remind them or rub it in!"

I know, from past experience, the worst thing an officer could say to the 'other ranks' was, "Whatever you do, don't do this or that!" That was the last thing that he should have said, it would almost certainly mean that was just what they would do. To spite the officer or to be rebellious. So seeing the chaps looking at each other and smiling, I thought, "Oh dear, something's going to happen, what are they planning?"

Sure enough, we left the carpark and made our way to the walkway on top of the dam. Nine of the chaps in three 'waves' of three (just like the real raid on the dam) ran along the top of the dam. In full combat kit, arms outstretched as if they were 617 Sqn, singing the dam-busters' march, "Da-da, da, da, da, da, da, da, da, da, da, da, da, da, da, da da."

I was embarrassed and pretended they weren't with me, but the locals did not like it at all. I heard comments of "Damn Britishers!" But I'm sure the language was much stronger in their dialect. All there was to do was look around and buy some souvenirs and drink, though I stayed out in the fresh air as long as possible before drinking, but not most of the others.

Although now almost blending in with the original brickwork, you could clearly see the newly rebuilt part of the dam, and contrary to the films and photos, the new brickwork took up half to two-thirds of the centre section.

I noted that it was a difficult approach for 617 Sqn, there was a steep dive over and down the hills, and two doglegs to make, twisting, turning to get on the 'bombing run'. It looked like the bomb aimer only had a few seconds to line up and drop the bomb. Impressed, great respect!

Buying collapsible chair

One particular time when we stopped at a little German general store, the lads with me stuffed themselves with chocolates, cigarettes and the like, I bought a handy collapsible garden chair. They took the mick out of me for days but as I said to them, "By the end of the exercise, you'll have nothing to show. You'll have had the cigarettes, eaten the chocolate, but I'll still have my chair." (I still have it today.) It turned out very handy to use on the exercise.

Chap's young wife doesn't like him drinking

One of the newcomers, a Paddy, managed to get his young wife over pretty quick; they had a young child so it helped.

Though at first unbeknownst to us, she didn't like him to drink or get drunk. Let's face it, you were positively encouraged to drink in Germany as the drinks were so very cheap, and he used to like to drink as much and as often as the rest of us. If he could get away with it. If he came home drunk or the wife suspected him of drinking, she would always then proceed to beat him up.

Many a time, he came on parade with a black eye or two. He probably liked his drink too much to want to give it up and felt that a black eye or two was not too high a price to pay for it. It even happened when his wife and he left our bungalow, we had a party to which some of the married men had come with their wives and they were two of the guests.

As we were seeing them off up the drive after the 'do', the husband started to show signs of the alcohol taking effect, she told him to shut up and behave himself or else. He didn't and she, in full view of us all, stopped and took off her shoes and then started to hit him over the head several times with it!

What a laugh; on parade though, he would stand there with his black eye and while we would be waiting to be inspected by an officer, one or two of the NCOs would approach him and say, "Good morning, Paddy, been drinking again, have we?" Then walk on with a smile on their face with the rest of us trying not to laugh.

Hearing automatic gunfire going past H.A.S.

Driving around the perimeter track one evening after work, we were passing a H.A.S. (Hardened Aircraft Shelter) when we heard automatic gunfire and we knew it wasn't blanks. We also heard a scream of pain and a dog barking, we thought, "Oh hell, I bet the R.A.F. policeman has fired at an intruder." We screeched to a halt in the Land Rover and ran towards the sound. We discovered to our amazement a R.A.F. policeman lying on the floor writhing in agony and clutching his leg, which was bleeding quite a bit by now.

We sent for an ambulance and asked him what had happened, apparently, he had heard a noise in the undergrowth and the dog had sensed something, so he had cocked his weapon. The police carried live ammunition when guarding the aircraft and potential target buildings, even in peacetime.

Once the weapon was cocked, the dog had got itself tangled around his legs and bolted for the undergrowth, pulling the policeman over, and with his finger being on the trigger, of course, caused him to shoot himself in his leg with three or four rounds. When we heard this, we burst out laughing. I know we shouldn't have really with the poor man lying there but we couldn't help it, service humour and making light of a dark situation.

Police had a rat problem

It was arranged once that if some Regiment personnel had an afternoon to spare, we would go to the R.A.F. police HQ to help them get rid of some rats they had there. The said rats were living in a large pile of sandbags near the dog compound. There was plenty of them running everywhere, at first we thought we would not only have a bit of fun but also try to find out where the entrance/escape holes were, so we threw in a few thunder flashes to liven them up a bit, suddenly there seemed to be dozens and dozens of them. The thunder flash must have had the effect on them like a huge stun grenade going off next to a human being. In fact, there was so many that the dogs and we too must have sent ourselves dizzy trying to follow them; in the end we were so confused we didn't know which to chase first. But in the confusion, one of the rats bit a police dog and it ran off yelping, its tail between its legs; it had the effect of causing the dog to lose its nerve and eventually led to it being removed from the R.A.F. police dog section.

We didn't kill many rats in the end aboveground; all we had were spades and clubs but I think you can safely say we did finally finish them off in the end. Some clever rock-ape suggested, "Why don't we use gas warfare on them?" That was what we did in the end, we blocked off all the entrances we could find, then we drew some CS (anti-riot) gas from the armoury and gassed them in their hole. After about an hour, when we hadn't seen any running about above the surface, we decided that the job was finished and the police said they would dig the nest up tomorrow.

Reunion with Jack (John) Skuse

One day, a pleasant surprise awaited me when I reported to the Sqn. We had just got a new posting in from Cyprus, it was a Sgt (though only S.A.C. when I had known him) – Jack (John) Skuse. When he saw me, he seemed very pleased; in fact, more pleased to see me than I was. We had known each other on 37 Sqn, but weren't really mates. He had been on a different flight to me. He had his friends and I had mine, though we used to pass the time of day sometimes, we never really had much to do with each other. I think it was a case of he was glad to see a familiar face so that he could settle in quicker. Nevertheless, we became the best of friends from then on in. I invited him to meet Viola and he came for tea a few times. One evening I showed him my collection of German *Glossy Girlie* magazines, far stronger than the equivalent British magazine.

He asked if he could borrow them, he said he would hide them in his loft so they would be safe. I asked what he meant and he said, "Never mind." Eventually, I managed to get it out of him that his wife was a bit funny like that, she didn't like to see him looking at pictures of naked women, or especially watching blue films.

He also admired a sexy keyring that I had and Viola told him that she was due to get some more from Holland, when she did, he could have one.

Though when she did get one to give him, she had forgotten that the wife was not supposed to like it. She gave him one in front of his wife. Poor old Jack, she glared daggers at him and Viola. She didn't like Viola and didn't invite us to her quarter but it didn't change Jack's attitude, thank goodness, as he was the only one, including Geordie Hall, that I know about who really did stick up for me. And more than once.

Though I shan't forget the look on her face when Viola handed the keyring over, her jaw dropped, poor woman. If only she knew the half of it.

When I left Germany on my re-pat and left the service, that was the last I saw of Jack until 2017 in Thailand of all places, where Jack, Viola and I had a happy reunion.

Geordie makes me drive

One day on the Sqn, Cpl Geordie Weirdo (the kinky Cpl) approached me and said, "Ah John, you've got a R.A.F. driving licence, haven't you?"

"No, I took and passed it in civvy street," which was true. He came back later to me and angrily said to me, "I thought you told me that you hadn't been given a R.A.F. licence?"

"That's right, like I said I took the test in civvy street!"

"That's no excuse, did you or did you not attend a R.A.F. driving course!" By this time, he was screaming and going red in the face, I thought he was going to bust to gut.

"Yes."

"Right then, you will drive our vehicles!" (I didn't want to drive in Germany, and I didn't like driving on the right, that was also part of the reason why I didn't want to get a car.)

"Oh no, I'm not!"

Cpl Geordie: "You will or I'll charge you for disobeying a direct order!" They always threatened you with that, like overgrown school kids.

Deciding to get out of it

I don't like or tolerate someone telling me what I can or can't do with my driving licence that I paid a lot of money for, lost sleep, worry and hassle. But most of all, I resented the manner in which I was approached. If he had approached me in a pleasant manner such as, "You have a licence, don't you? We're very short of drivers and will you drive for the flight!" I would have considered it.

You see, the R.A.F. could only make you drive if they gave you the licence, if passed in civvy street, as I had, they couldn't make you. That was a fact! That was why I was so annoyed. So I had the usual R.A.F. famil-iarisation test around camp and local roads. I even tried my best to fail, normally I do my best, but still they passed me. I think that 1 Sqn must have pre-warned the M.T. that I might try to fail.

When I got back to the Sqn location, Cpl Geordie and some of the lads took the 'mick' out of me, but when I got talking to my friends I told them, "Mark my words, you and Geordie may be laughing at me now but I WILL have the last laugh, I cannot be forced to drive on a civvy licence so I shall tell you now, that within 72 hours, they will take me off driving!"

"How are you going to manage that, John?" they asked me. I told them, "Just watch and listen to what happens, and what is said!"

Even they didn't believe for a moment I could do it but I told them "That they all thought there was nothing I could do about it, we shall see, shan't we?" And tell those you can trust what I've said too!

I was full of determination but not so much on confidence. Or how I was going to do it. So from them on in, everyone, the lads and NCOs alike saw me walking around with a smile on my face and 'full of beans', so to speak, they definitely looked on edge, they weren't used to me smiling and must have figured that I was up to something, though they hadn't a clue what it was – frankly, neither did I! They still hadn't learned that I not only spoke my mind but when I was determined to do something, I did it.

We were told that all drivers should be prepared to be called out that night as a call out was expected for us to be acting enemy for R.A.F. Bruggen. When I got back to the bungalow in Weeze, I was more depressed than ever, so I had a beer, then another and another, and so on, until I was drunk!

Yes, we got the call out, one of the lads stood on my doorstep and said, "Bloody hell, John, you're drunk!"

"Yes, 10 out of 10 for observation!"

"But you shouldn't be, you're driving, you knew we were going to get a call out!"

"Ah, f*** 'em, I'm past caring about those b******s, anyway, you're wrong, we're not supposed to know about the call out really, are we?" He had to agree on that point.

"So I'm perfectly allowed to have a drink at home, am I not?"

Again he agreed with me. "But you can't drive in that condition!"

So I knew if they pushed it, I was covered.

I felt though I ought to cover myself, so when Geordie told me to prepare the Land Rover for moving out, I told him and made sure my mate was a witness that I had been drinking and I wasn't capable of driving and I might kill someone if I was made to drive.

He ranted and raved about knowing I might get called out so I told him that he must admit I am not supposed to know about the call out officially, but that was by the way, I was not in a fit state to drive.

He, then and there, in front of my witness, ordered me to drive the Land Rover so I said, "OK but if I have an accident or the German police stops me, on your head be it!" As we were about to leave to go to Bruggen, the chaps in my Land Rover said, "John, you can't drive; you're not in a fit state to!"

"Want to bet, I was told to drive so I'm going to fecking drive, they didn't say anything about having a drink, did they!" They looked definitely worried and were on edge the whole time on the road, sort of one leg in and one out of the vehicle. I was smiling from ear to ear.

On the way there, I gave several Germans the fright of their life (and me too); they must have been convinced that I was out to kill them. One poor chap on a push bike fell off as I came around the bend in the road much too fast and swerved to miss him. Later, when the officers/NCOs saw the state I was in, they asked why had I been allowed to drive in that state, of course, Geordie had to explain to them, I was left alone but watched carefully that night, fortunately, we weren't given live ammunition, only blanks.

I win

I was asked by officers at Bruggen that if I was drunk, why was I driving. I told the officer concerned that I had tried not to drive but had been ordered to! I had to tell him who ordered me to drive. On the return trip, someone else was directed to drive my Land Rover back to Laarbruch. So if that was the case, why was I forced to drive when not in a fit state to?

When I got home that night, I had another beer before going to bed, allowed myself to smile and said, "Here's to a successful phase 1. Though how I got there and back in one piece without an accident or killing someone, I shall never know.

Striking back (John Skuse)

The next day, I made sure I got a few complaints about my driving, but unfortunately, Jack Skuse blotted my copybook. He put my plan back considerably by telling the SNCOs that he knew the perfect replacement for the new O.C.'s driver – JR! I had been the C.O.'s driver on the chopper Sqn. (True!) I could have murdered him. He was telling them what a marvellous driver I was and I should be Hackett's new driver. Trouble was he didn't realise how much Hackett hated me.

Houseman must have agreed with him. So I took Hackett backwards and forwards from the Sqn hangar; he only lasted three trips.

One of these trips consisted of me taking Hackett and leading a convoy of three Land Rovers and two four-tonners, I pretended that I didn't know my way around M.Q.s and led them up a one-way street the wrong way, down roads just big enough for a car alone; the four-tonner drivers were cursing me something rotten.

Another time, Hackett was convinced I was trying to kill him, I was headed straight for a brick wall, and I was trying to kill the both of us, which was untrue; I had no intention of killing me!

Eventually, he got out saying, "You're bloody mad, Rowbottom, you're trying to kill me! Don't bother picking me up, I'll walk, it's safer!" I had a good laugh at this.

When Hackett came back to our location, he called me over and said, "Rowbottom, I don't know whether you're doing it deliberately or not, or you're just bloody useless, but I'm taking you off driving with immediate effect, before you really kill me!" Whatever gave him that idea?

"What a shame!" I said with a smile.

Cpl kinky Geordie said, "No sir, don't do it, he's just trying to get off driving, he really is a good driver, he used to be Flt Commander's driver at Catterick for three years." (It hadn't been for as long as that.)

I was taken off driving there and then. Less than the 72 hours I had promised.

My mates couldn't believe me at first but I convinced then eventually, and we all had a laugh. And especially at those blokes that didn't know that I had set out to get off. All along, they believed the stories from Hackett that I was taken off because I was useless and I was trying to kill him, and they even thought they would have a laugh at my expense, but if only they knew how I laughed at them. Most wouldn't believe that I could do what I set out to do but as I've said before, when I set my mind on something, I usually succeeded.

Moving to M.Q.

I had the chance of moving into M.Q.s while my mother was still with us; once I had heard, I cheekily knocked on the door of my new soon to be Qtr and asked to have a look around. The outgoing chap seemed taken aback but showed me around any way.

We had the advantage of being near to all facilities, such as the main Naafi shop, cinema, it was also handy for Viola to get to work and I had a short walk to catch the same transport as the single lads.

Not to mention that we would get some more disturbance allowance.

Meeting our new neighbours

The neighbour on one side was an SNCO who in all the time we were there never ever spoke to us once; he apparently didn't like rock-apes or army squaddies, who happened to be our neighbours on the other side.

Stan and Katie and daughter, Vicki, were our neighbours who we became real friendly with.

Noticing my neighbour's anatomy (or a certain part of it)

The first thing I noticed about Katie was that she was a very well-built young lady – up top! She also seemed to have a distinct dislike of bras, even during winter. What seemed to emphasise her bust more than ever was she had large protruding nipples, and with her skimpy, thin tee shirts, you couldn't very well miss them – not that I wanted to!

Her husband only seemed interested in drinking and seemed to neglect her, he used to go out drinking 6 nights a week, 5 nights of those were spent in the R.A.O.B. 'Buff's Lodge. Trouble was, though I didn't realise it, I couldn't take my eyes off her ample chest but it was noticed.

Stan mentioned it to me a couple of times. Apparently, he didn't like it, I wonder why! So I had to tell him, "Tough, you can trust me, but if you don't want me staring at your wife's chest then why doesn't she cover up?"

We fool about

When it was the glorious summer of 1976, I was taking advantage of a couple of hours off to catch up on a bit of sunbathing. Before I knew it, Katie had nipped over the fence and dropped ice down my chest and front. So letting out a scream of anguish, I leapt up and chased her back to her yard and promptly returned the favour and put ice down her front and rubbed it in. She was screaming and giggling with delight, but took it in the manner in which it was meant – just good fun.

Fortunately, her husband and Viola weren't there or they wouldn't have liked it. But somehow, Stan got to hear of it and tried to have another go at me so this time I told him to "Foxtrot Oscar. You have nothing to worry about!" Though with hindsight, I think maybe Katie might have been making a play for me and if I'd have shown any interest, I could well have finished up doing what Stan thought I was after doing.

Hypocrite

Ironically in civvy street after I'd come out, they both visited us at home and although working near Scunthorpe, never visited us. He and I were chatting in my garage, the girls were indoors. When pressed why he hadn't visited us, he finally confessed that he had his 'bit on the side' with him so it would have been awkward. This 'bit on the side' just also happened to be his next-door neighbour, the dammed hypocrite. After all he had said and carried on at me in Germany, and here he was doing exactly the thing that he thought I had been up to with his wife.

Of course, Katie eventually found out, and the last we heard she was not only suing him for divorce, but insisting that he pay maintenance for her two kids (she had had another baby just before we left Germany) + his mistress and her two kids as well. Didn't he get himself into a mess!

I think her trouble in Germany was that she was lonely, felt neglected and wanted a bit of company.

Streak

Inevitably, I got drunk a few times, so much so that according to Viola, one night I decided on a 'streak' around the garden; fortunately, with all the trees that were growing outside and in our garden, I was hidden from view. When Katie got to hear of this, she was so disappointed that she'd missed this unexpected treat.

We had her over in our house several times while her husband was out drinking at night. I could have done anything with her and gotten away with it, all in good fun. Though I didn't push it. Maybe she fancied me as her 'bit on the side'? Maybe not, whichever was the case, she certainly paid me a lot of attention. It seemed to me that he wasn't interested in her, just used her as a convenience for sex whenever he felt like it.

It was a real shame, she was a lovely girl, I do hope that one day we can meet up again. And that she has found a real nice guy. She deserves it.

By now, Laarbruch was really getting to me, so not only had my cigarette intake gone up from 7 per day to about 25-30 per day but I was drinking ½ a crate (10 beers) per week to over two crates (40+). With what I drank at home and what I drank in bars averaged about 8/9 x 1/2 litre bottles per day.

Viola plays the piano

One of Viola's friends at work persuaded her to come along to the camp's amateur dramatics society to help out, but once she got there, she saw a piano and plonked herself down on it and you couldn't get her off it.

She played for the rehearsals and was asked to play on the nights it was showing, but she declined the offer. There was far too much of "What rank is your husband/what job does he do?" Of course, their husbands were always higher-ranking that anybody else and in a better job too. Anyway, she got a mention in the programme, we didn't even go and see the show once it opened.

Stn Tac-e-Val

It wasn't long after we'd moved into M.Q.s when 1 Sqn was 'invited' to play enemy again during a Stn 'Tac-e-Val'.

We had at first to 'raid' in organised parties, then we split up into small groups. We (though not my group) attacked the main barrier post only a few yards from the M.Q.s. There were machine guns, pistols, rifles and thunder flashes going off all over the place.

Viola was terrified with explosions and gunfire going off all around. She didn't know what a Tac-e-Val meant; she thought that a real war had broken out.

I organised attacks on the station armoury, incredible as it may seem, no one had thought of it before I did. Then I had the guys attack a very important target – the mess! Where we all had a meal and a smoke before setting off into the fray again; meanwhile, the camp's defenders were looking everywhere for us but didn't think to look in the mess.

Yep, I got my priorities right.

I also decided to hit a H.A.S. We ambushed the sentry from about 50 yards away; there were two sentries, shot by us. The sentry looked around, searching from where the shots were coming.

Rock-ape loses his temper

"Lie down," shouted one of my men. "F***ing lie down when I shoot you, you bar-steward," he shouted. The tradesman ignored him. "I'll teach the f***ing bar-steward to lie down when I shoot him!" So up this rock-ape got and ran forward towards this 'penguin' sentry. We followed, and as we approached the scene, we heard the rock-ape say to him, "Hey you, **nt, why didn't you play dead when I f***ing shot you?" No reply. "I'll f***king teach you to play the game in future; next time I shoot, you will lie down." With that, he raised his rifle and hit the penguin sentry across the face with it. Whereupon he fell on the ground.

We all thought he had broken the chap's jaw. (Fortunately not.) We stood there momentarily stunned at the course of events; we didn't think it that important enough to warrant hitting him. No wonder the R.A.F. tradesmen were a bit wary of us. This rock-ape also wasn't the sort to usually lose his temper, or so we thought. Must have been the adrenaline rush.

As he stepped over his prostrate form on the ground, he said, "That'll teach the bar-steward to play the game in future!" He then walked away, leaving us all agog.

About halfway through the exercise, we had to report back to the Sqn location. On the way, we came to a roadblock, funnily enough next to this aforementioned H.A.S.

Swapping ID cards

At the roadblock, we were stopped in our Land Rover while wearing our N.B.C. gear c/w respirators. I was with a West Indian lad in the back and as we approached the roadblock, he leaned over towards me and said, "Here John, give me your ID card!" and he gave me his.

At first I didn't know what he was up to but it soon became apparent. We stopped and the sentry asked who we were and asked to look at our ID cards.

I couldn't believe he would do it but yes, he did, he looked at our ID cards (Remember, I still had this West Indian lad's card and respirators on), checked us all and waved us through. I shouted at him, "Hey, are you satisfied with our identities?" He said he was, so I leaned over and told kinky Cpl Geordie what had happened, he went mad, we screeched to a halt, reversed and gave this poor frightened 'penguin' the rollicking of his poor young life.

All this time, the West Indian lad was laughing hysterically, clutching his stomach as it was aching so much. He told all his compatriots later that he was a 'whitey' for five minutes; when asked what it had been like, he laughed and said, "Fecking hysterical!"

Fair enough, you can't see very much of a person's face through a respirator but you can see the little skin around the eyes, if he had been observant enough to have spotted the swap.

Longer to serve

I was told before leaving UK that I had only about 20-22 months to do in Germany and then back to UK for the last six months to get in my leave, resettlement course, etc. This, along with my financial position, was the main reason why I didn't get a car, because you generally got it over a three-year period, and I certainly couldn't afford to pay it over this short period. After about 18 months in Germany, I hadn't heard anything about going back so I went to the general office and made enquiries accordingly and found out, to my horror, that I had to stay there till about six weeks before my discharge date, my heart sank to its lowest ebb, though to be honest I had half expected this to happen even before I left England for Germany; this was another thing that helped depress me all the more.

Alan and Rosanna

One of Viola's friends at work was a Malayan woman, whose name was Rosanna; her husband, Alan, was an English chap. Alan worked in one of the servicing hangars and like Tony Love at Odiham, was an SNCO and was i/c auxiliary equipment; in this case, the battery room. He was about 6'2", nearly as broad; she was five foot nothing in her stockinged feet and... how shall I put it? Wouldn't win any beauty or personality contests! But the crux of the matter was that he was scared stiff of her! Nay, terrified, she barked and he jumped!

It was embarrassing to watch; I don't know how he had gotten himself in that position. I know through experience that if my wife ever tried to treat me like that, there would have been lots and lots of rows or a divorce. She was an ex-bar hostess in Malaysia. Alan, on one hand, claimed he met her serving tables in the local sergeants' mess in the Far East, but listening to their stories together, and separately, and with photographs, we think that they met in a bar downtown, right or wrong, that was the impression we formed.

This Rosanna, like most Orientals, believed in free enterprise and had a small business on the go, selling 'Curry Puffs'. She claimed it was a traditional Malayan dish. Bollocks! All they were, were small Cornish-style pasties with curry powder; she wasn't fooling anybody, though most people were too polite to tell her, not me though!

Laying a carpet

Initially, we became friends, Alan asked me if I would help him lay a carpet that he'd just exchanged for an old one, we did a fairly good job in laying it, at least we thought we had until the peace and quiet was shattered by Rosanna upon her return from work, she went mad and laid into Alan. He had made a fatal error – he asked her opinion! And what she thought of the carpet? She then really laid into him, calling him thick, stupid and more besides. He was very embarrassed and so was I. So I made my excuses and left with the sound of her voice tearing into him and not a murmur out of him. I was determined then and there not to get into such a terrible position as he had.

Alan was due to be posted back to UK to R.A.F. Coningsby near Grimsby, with the temporary rank of C/T (chief technician); they were having a house built for them near Grantham and he was due to come back on the ferry and see about the house. So he offered to give my mother (who had been staying with us since before Christmas) a lift home in the car.

Borrowing money

I was away on exercise when they left, when I got back from the exercise, I was in the bath and Rosanna came to ask if she could borrow 5,000 marks (£800). This was to be for their solicitor in the purchase of their new house in UK. When Viola asked me, I said no as we didn't have 5,000 and I wouldn't lend that much if I had it any way.

We had only saved about 2,500 (£400) so I agreed to lending her 1,000 marks only, about £160. Rosanna 'insisted' on having the whole 5,000 but I stayed firm, even though she still insisted! Bloody cheeky cow! I thought she was getting out of hand so I told her, through Viola, 1,000 – take it or leave it! And no more arguing. She didn't seem too pleased but had to accept it in the end, she promised to pay it back in three weeks, but after about five weeks, there was so sign of the money, so I said, "I hate to have to ask for it back but it looks as though we have to, they seem to have forgotten that they borrowed the money!"

Asking for it back

We went around one night to see them and the subject was not brought up until it was unavoidable. I figured I'd better bring it up so I asked for the money back and was told, "No!" When I asked why, all she said was 'revenge'. We couldn't understand what she said or meant.

John: "Is that your last word?"
Rosanna: "Yes!"

John: "Alan, what do you say, do you agree with Rosanna?"

Alan: "I am not getting involved!"

John: "You are involved, whether you like it or not! So if that's your last word!"

Alan: "It is!"

John: "Very well, Viola, put your coat on, we're leaving!"

As I stopped at the door, I looked over my shoulder and said, "If you think that this is the end of the matter then you're very much mistaken. It is our money, you have it and I 'will' get it back, that I can promise you!"

We walked out, Viola was sobbing and very upset and I think she had written the money off.

"Don't worry, love, we will get the money back, I promise you that!"

S.I.B. get involved

The following morning, I asked Sgt Jack Skuse if I could go down to see the S.I.B., the military C.I.D. He said yes! The Sgt thought I just wanted to skive, I told the S.I.B. what had happened, they brought him in and interrogated Alan in a side room and the interrogation lasted for a week off and on. They gave him the spotlight treatment several times a day for a week, the S.I.B. told me that there was no way we could prove he had the money unless – maybe, just maybe, hope above hope, we could prove it by being able to quote/check on the serial numbers of the said notes. I rang Viola at work and told her what the sergeant S.I.B. had said. "Yes," she said, she had made a note of the money that we had lent Rosanna.

So the S.I.B. had him in again, they said to me, "He still denies having the money under the conditions you stated. So we brought him in again, and when we told him we could prove it as we have the serial numbers of the notes, he gave a different answer, the S.I.B told him to go away and think about it overnight, and give his answer in the morning." They told me that they would tell him that they were going to charge him with theft. Which was only a bluff to try and get him to confess. The following morning they had him in the office and he told the S.I.B., "My wife has instructed me to admit that we took the money."

The S.I.B. told me that they listened to that in disbelief; they asked me, "Could that be true, what sort of wife has he got who could cause him to say that? It sounds as though he is 'under the thumb'!" "He is!" I told them, and told them what she was like.

They asked me if I wanted to prefer charges or would I be happy to have the money back. This I agreed to, I was just grateful to get the money back; I asked if I did prefer charges, would I have to come back for the court martial.

They said that yes I would have to come back. "Then in that case, I can't because I am due to finish in the R.A.F. and go back to UK on de-mob, and if I get a job I might not be able to get back!"

"Will he be allowed to get away with it?" I asked.

"No!" S.I.B. replied. "He has just been made up on trial to C.T., he will lose that and when he gets posted to Lincolnshire, we will tell our counterparts there and they will keep an eye on him."

Revenge

We eventually found out what Rosanna had meant by 'revenge'. I had helped her husband pack his car for home before taking my mother home and I had suggested some ways he could get more in the car. I must admit I was quite good at it, for some reason she took offence though no offence had been intended – nor taken by Alan, I hardly think that should have been cause to 'seek revenge'.

Offering to help Helmut alter his flat

Whilst living in Goch, I happened to mention to our then landlord, Helmut, that I used to be a plasterer and offered to help him when he carried out his planned conversion of flats. At a pre-arranged time/date, Helmut picked me up at our M.Q. on camp and we set off for his flat in Goch, ready to start to renovate it.

The first thing he did when we got there was to go to the pub across the road, my old local, and he bought a crate of 20 beers. "Oh no," I thought, "he isn't, is he?" Sure enough, we got to the flat and once he got his coat off, he opened a couple of bottles and said in a typical Germanic/Teutonic manner, "Here, John, drink!" Who was I to argue? "We drink and then we start work, you drink in England before you start work? Yes?" I explained that we had a cup of tea. "Ah, no wonder the English industries is in such a bad state here, have another beer!" The time by now was only about 9:15 am. And just as we got some screwdrivers and tools in our hands, he said, "Just a moment, let's have another beer while we are working!" I let out a groan, by lunchtime I was woozy to say the least; it was a sight to behold a screwdriver in one hand and a beer (permanently) in the other.

Start drinking

He insisted I drink with him but I could only drink about five during the morning, stopping for a break mid-morning, I had another and he another 6. Helmut had to finish the rest of the crate as I couldn't, he was still sober, he said, "I go and fetch lunch, yes?" I thought, "Good." Bratwurst mit pommes frites (sausage and chips); when he came back, my jaw dropped, he had brought another crate of beer. These he insisted had to be finished before we went home tonight!

The end of the day, we had finished between us about 35 half-litre bottles (just over a pint). I had about 7-8, he had the rest himself; this German beer was strong so driving me back to camp, he was beginning to feel the effects of all that beer but I was totally sozzled.

Opening the door to me upon my return, Viola said to me, "I thought you were supposed to be working today?" "I have, German style!" After something to eat, I had to get an early night to sleep it off.

Viola wanted to stay in Germany when I had finished with the R.A.F. but I wouldn't have it! Not only could I not speak the language, there was no way I could have stood the pace, I would have almost certainly been an alcoholic – or dead by the years out. It amazed me how the Germans got any work done if this was how they carried on; still, they must be used to it. Also, their wiring system looked dangerous to me; few, if any, safety measures integrated as in the British system.

Hitting Pleb

There was a 'pleb/hard man' on 1 Sqn…well, there is always one, isn't there? Just like Kitchson on 37 Sqn at Catterick, he was all mouth and no brains, he was fooling about one day on a deserted aircraft pan behind the Sqn location during a break in training, we then boarded a four-tonner ready to go to a new area to try things out.

This idiot was fooling about on the back of the truck and accidentally, fell on to me and my glasses fell off and broke. I looked at them, then at Pleb, then my broken glasses lying on the floor, suddenly something snapped and before I knew what I had done, I spun around and dropped him in one punch, and hit him again twice more as he was going down. All the lads in the wagon gasped and stepped back, Pleb cowered in the corner and from then on, he stayed clear of me. The word went around the Sqn and I think I was more surprised of my actions then they were.

New C.O. invitation

We had a new commanding officer take over the Sqn and he thought he would have a 'get to know you' do, the invitations went out to the Sqn personnel for a summer barbecue.

"Officers, bring their ladies, Sergeants, bring their wives and O.R.s (other ranks), bring your women!"

All ranks from SWO down were mad and insulted. And we all decided and agreed between ourselves that we would boycott the 'do', especially because of the last line – O.R.s, bring your women! With my experience in the officers' messes, I saw many officers' wives but few 'ladies'! So on the day, the only people who turned up were a few officers who had to attend as it was considered a duty, a couple of SNCOs and one or two O.R.s (creeps). But the rest of the Sqn boycotted the 'do'; I don't think this was lost on the new C.O.. It was a complete flop with only half a dozen or so people turning up; it seemed to do the trick and he was careful in what he said from then on, but whilst there, there was never another 'get together' of all ranks.

Hackett: how he hated me (John Skuse)

Flg Off Hackett was i/c 'C' Flt, my flight. I shall never – ever, forget that name and the hurt he caused me. Jack Skuse, my mate the Cpl Sgt, told me that when they had their morning briefings together, Hackett always kept bringing up my name and seemed to be obsessed in putting me down, and Jack did all he could to stand up for me. I believed him, he really was a decent chap and turned out to be a good friend.

One such example, if I can remember, I was 10 minutes late one morning on parade, he gave me 14 days 'Jankers' (restrictions), the normal for such an offence was only 7 days. Whilst there at the Guard Room, I got chatting to a chap doing 28 days.

I finished my 14 days on Sunday night. And on the Monday I had to go sick and didn't go to work. 'Sick parade' was classed just as that, a parade. But even I was surprised at the attitude of Hackett, he charged me for being AWOL. So within about three days of finishing my jankers, I was back at the guardroom and this chap laughed out loud as he couldn't believe it.

When I told my father in UK, he phoned up the station commander himself, a Group Captain, and told him of what had happened and the next thing I knew was under his instructions, I was taken off Jankers. I had to see him in his office and explain to him what had been going on, he apologised for me having to do another two weeks but he would have it struck from my record and apologised for the days that I had already done. He laid off for a while but then started again. After the morning parade/inspection, you could guarantee that within 20 minutes, Hackett would either have me in his office for a rollicking about something trivial or, failing that, I would be caught for a bad/dirty job. It became the in joke on the flight. "Hey John, has Hackett given you a bollocking yet this morning?" "No, not yet, give him a chance, it's early yet!" and we would laugh. Try as he may to make me crack, I would annoy him all the more by simply smiling broadly at whatever job he gave me to do. Now this used to get him really annoyed and angry and there was nothing more that annoyed him so I was relishing it.

Hackett about to hit me

It came to a head when being accused of (nothing new) doing something, I was alone in his office and he was tearing me off a strip verbally. Suddenly, he lost his temper, lunged at me from the other side of the room and grabbed me round the throat, clenched his fist, pulled it back ready to punch me in the face; I was delighted! I was surprised with myself how calm I was. He then threatened, "I'm going to f***ing kill you, you bastard!" I was delighted, slowly I removed my glasses and smiled and said to him, "Go on then, hit me, Sir!" (Sarcastically.)

"I won't hit you back! It's what I've been expecting, I'll leave here and report you to the Sqn, and *you* will be court-martialled! I'll have you court-martialled and thrown out of the R.A.F. in disgrace!"

He dropped his arm and unclenched his fist and said, "Get out of my office!" I walked out smiling. Oh, how I wished he had hit me, it would have been all over for him, there would have been no more victimisation on me, how different things might have turned out had I reported him. I just turned around and being the better man, let it drop. Oh, how I do wish he had hit me.

1Sqn Germany 1974/76: live firing. (Author is nearest camera – on the left.)

There was a declared 'state of war' between my Flt Commander, Hackett, and myself. He knew with his constant hounding of me I had lost interest in the job I loved. But the only thing left that I really enjoyed was live firing of the weapons.

Once, outside the hangar, Hackett in front of most of the flight told me, "You're gun shy, you're frightened to fire live ammunition!" My jaw dropped once I realised what he had said, I and the lads burst out laughing at him to his face, as they knew it was a load of old rot and they all knew I was a good shot. So did he! But in case he didn't know, I and the lads reminded him of the fact! He was embarrassed and walked away. Was he trying to get a reaction? He had succeeded – but not as he had hoped. (I still miss this side of the life.) I just wanted to be left alone and get on with my job and no hassle.

Told we will be seeing the carnival

We had missed the local German carnival as we had always been on exercise and we had always missed it most years. This, we had been very disappointed in as the carnival was really something to see.

So just before we were dismissed, after putting our kit away from yet another exercise; the C.O. told us all on parade that this was the last Friday before the German Carnival started next Monday for a week and we wouldn't be going on exercise so we could enjoy it. We had arrived on camp at about 5 pm Friday and by the time we got everything cleaned, packed up and put away, it was nearly 9 pm before we got home.

Called out

At lunchtime the following day, I was in my M.Q. having lunch when the call out siren went off and the station tannoy, "All 1 Sqn personnel, report to the Sqn hangar immediately!" I thought, "Oh hell, what's going on now, this must be serious because the C.O. said we won't be on another Harrier exercise for a few weeks yet."

Fortunately, Viola had already washed and ironed my kit so I repacked it and grumbling, set off for the Sqn hangar; had there been a major incident, a terrorist attack or worse?

'Am Ende der Welt' postcard: "It's the end of the world – the rock-apes are on the warpath!"

'A' Flt gets drunk

When the siren and the station tannoy went off, the single lads were mostly in the 'Malcolm bar' with a lot of the married men too. They were all drinking and trying to unwind from the last Harrier exercise, they were not very happy to say the least, but also drunk. And most of them hadn't had their kit washed yet, so they had to take their dirty kit with them. At the Sqn location, we found out, partially to our relief, it wasn't the Russians invading West Germany or the declaration of world war three, but they had brought forward a planned two-weeks range exercise, firing all the Sqn and personnel weapons we had been trained on. "Two weeks, but you told us – you promised us a couple of weeks off for the carnival!" some brave soul shouted out. The officers made some excuse and disappeared.

We clambered into the back of our four-tonners and the Sqn set off in convoy down the Autobahn; the whole Sqn was angry to be torn away from our families – and the bar! We were fuming and most of the guys who were on 'A' (animal) Flt – the troublemakers and misfits were still drunk. I always wondered why I hadn't been posted to 'A' flight, being the troublemaker Hackett made me out to be.

The Sqn were asking for trouble – and they got it in spades!

Argument with German police

The first we knew of anything being amiss was when a patrol car of the German police stopped the convoy on the Autobahn We all walked over to 'A' flight's packet and listened to the argument between the drunks, the flight commander, the C.O. and the German police. We soon found out why the German police had stopped the Sqn on the Autobahn. It had transpired that 'A' flight were so annoyed and angry with being kicked out of the bar when they thought they could unwind from a hectic exercise and for missing the carnival, that one of them (we didn't know who) had vented his anger and frustration by throwing some of the kit off the back of the wagon onto the Autobahn. So the others thought this a good idea and joined in, and eventually, piece by piece they had thrown all the military kit over the tailgate of the truck and onto the Autobahn. Some German motorists had been travelling along at high speed and had to swerve to miss the tent, tent poles and camouflage nets, cookers, etc.

The flight commander threatened to charge them all there and then, his bluff was called, so he did charge the lot of them on the side of the Autobahn, NCOs included, approximately 32 of them.

To this day, few people outside 'A' Flt knew who was responsible for prematurely unloading the kit on the Autobahn and over the tailgate of the four-tonner.

One of the ring leaders and founders of 'A' Flt's reputation was a certain Jimmy Buchan, a leading light when there was trouble. He didn't stand for no bull-manure nor did the rest of the Flt. He may have been the No 1 honcho responsible, the scourge of the 1 Sqn officers.

Even now, some 45 years later, this episode is brought up each time we have a reunion and is still good for a laugh; it has clearly gone down in the annals of 1 Sqn folklore.

As soon as we arrived at the camp that was to be home for two weeks, the entire personnel of 'A' Flt who had been charged were taken to the nearest NATO military nick, for as long as they could and only released them in time to fire their weapons and then back home. So most of the shoot, we were minus 'A' Flt.

Our camp for the two-week shoot was at a Belgium Marine camp at Vogelsang, the camp had become infamous during the war as it had been chosen by Hitler to 'encourage and create' the pure Arian blond-haired 'super race'. Our accommodation was the cells used for such. Very sparsely decorated, all rooms were exactly alike, still beat living under canvas for a change.

It was at this camp I got my first taste of Belgium beer and what a pleasant experience it was too.

I was looking forward to this shoot once I got there as I have always enjoyed shooting; we were to fire everything from 9mm pistols up to the 5-ton gun 40/7O AA Bofor's gun. We were then an AA Sqn but we were about to convert to the field role, hence the shoot to get us up to standard. It was still the only part of the job that I really enjoyed doing, all the enthusiasm for the rest of the job had been drained from me.

Most evenings were free and the Sqn rigged up its own bar in one of the huts.

Home-made film

One evening, we had some unannounced 'home-grown entertainment'; one of the lads had brought with him a projector and a home-made film he had made.

He had two hobbies, watching horror films and film-making, so he thought he would combine the two; we were looking forward to it as we all envisaged what it would be like – funny! After about 10 minutes, we were all, without exception, falling about in stitches. Our very own budding Alfred Hitchcock was most annoyed and kept shouting above the noise, "Shut up, shut up, don't laugh, stop laughing, you rotten bar-stewards, it's supposed to be serious!" Of course, this was the last thing he should have said as the only thing it made us do was laugh all the more.

The film showed a Frankenstein-type monster and the evil Doctor, both were characters on 'A' Flt and both well known to be old hands. What made it less believable was that the 'monster' was dressed in R.A.F. overalls, boots, cam scarf. The make-up was hardly noticeable, little to none. They were both recognisable as the chaps we knew that we couldn't think of them as anything else.

The 'monster' was 'created' in the kitchen of a R.A.F. M.Q. who supposedly strangled the 'mad' doctor, who in his dying moments ensured that he turned to face the camera so it showed his 'good side'. The Monster stumbled outside into the garden, past the two wives (in curlers) who were talking over the fence to each other. The two wives looked towards Frankie, started to laugh at him and then went back to their gossiping; we creased up in fits of laughter. Officers had been invited to this 'World Premiere' and they were laughing just as much as we were.

The monster was eventually killed by others on 'A' flight. It was so corny and amateurish and so unbelievable, it should have been relabelled as a comedy film. Poor old Laurel and Hardy would turn in their graves. It was the best laugh I had had since that time in the G.D.O.C. in N. Ireland. It was just what I needed to cheer me up from all my misfortunes.

Two weeks shooting

On this two-week shoot, we had to work with the '36 Mills' grenade, which I would think has been phased out by now. The day started as any day, about to throw these nasty little things, we got the usual safety lecture as to how dangerous they were, not only to the enemy on the receiving end but to the user as well if you were not careful, and could literally blow up in your face.

Grenade throwing

We started to prepare the grenades in the waiting area, this was the only time I noticed some of the guys seemed a little apprehensive and quiet, don't know whether this was the first time they had thrown them, but I had previously so I was relaxed and not bothered. I always felt confident and unfazed when handling live weapons/ammunition, guess I was just lucky. I prepped mine and waited my turn to be called out to throw. When my turn came, I walked briskly out to the throwing bay, where one of our SNCOs was waiting. I noticed out of the corner of my eye someone in the observation tower overlooking the range. I chatted to the SNCO who was very calm and quietly spoken, done to put the nervous ones at ease?

Hackett on the ranges

Just before I threw, I heard a familiar voice come out of the control tower, giving the SNCO permission to carry on. It was Hackett! Of all the ranges in Germany and he had to walk into mine!

Hackett shouted, "Rowbottom, don't you bloody well dare to have a blind (fail to explode), do you hear me, Rowbottom? Don't you bloody well dare or I'll have to go out and destroy it!"

I had a gut feeling that if anyone was to get a blind today, and it was pretty sure someone would, then it would be just my luck to be the one. And with Hackett officiating! I threw the first, 'Bang'! Good, threw the second, nothing! It was the inevitable 'blind', just my ruddy luck!

Hackett: "I knew it, I just f***ing well knew it! Of all the people I knew who would get a blind, it would have to be you, didn't it, you f***ing well did it deliberately? Didn't you, didn't you?"

John: "Me sir? No sir, of course I didn't, it's just one of those things, a coincidence!"

Hackett: "Yes, you did, you f***ing well did, you f***ing did it deliberately so I would have to go out and blow it up!"

Note: the danger comes when having to walk out, very slowly and carefully, to detonate the blind; it can explode at any given moment. Even the vibrations of walking towards it can set it off. They are so unpredictable.

John: "I'll go out with you, sir (I meant it), it's only right I do, it was my grenade after all!"

Hackett: "No! You know you're not f***ing allowed to. I am the one who has to walk out there and destroy it, you f***ing well know that! Now go to the post throwing bay!"

I must admit, on reflection, that I found the whole episode rather amusing, and not only in the post throwing hut, they had heard what had happened. Afterwards and for a few days, the guys kept asking, "Go on, you can tell us, you did do it deliberately, didn't you? You were hoping the blind would go off and kill Hackett, go on, you can tell us!" It was common knowledge 'C' Flt, and probably around the Sqn that Hackett and I didn't see eye to eye. No matter how often I told them it was a coincidence, they didn't believe me and convinced themselves I had tried to deliberately blow him up. And it would be just put down to a range accident.

Falling in the trench

Whilst there, we had to do a night shoot! In between my turn to fire at an illuminated target, I was assigned to be the 'radio man', equipped with the trusty old C41 radio man pack, which most guys hated but I quite enjoyed using. Working with the range officer, passing on messages between him and the Butts. Calling the next party forward to fire and giving the all clear to commence firing. I stood alongside the range officer all night behind a vacant, unused firing trench. Some of the exercises entailed firing with illumination and some without, in the darkness, hence very careful planning and movement to be as safe as possible to prevent someone being accidentally shot. "Where are you, Hackett?" Unfortunately, he wasn't there that night – drat!

Once the shooting was over for the night, the lights came on and the range officer told me to go to someone on the range with a message; in my enthusiasm, I leapt forward at the double, running and forgetting all about the trench I had been behind all evening, and promptly fell in! I was wedged in with the radio and struggled to get out with my feet suspended and not touching the floor of the trench. This was just what the guys needed to unwind from a stressful nervous time. Always happy to keep the lads' morale up, that's me! For a few minutes, they gathered around me, looked at me, paused and all, including the range officer, burst out laughing. Bar-stewards! Led by that 'stinker', Norman Geordie Hall. It took several minutes for them to dislodge and free me; they had no strength from laughing.

I, of course, for the next few days never lived it down, soooo embarrassing! I wished the ground would open up and swallow me, wait! It very nearly did! What they said was so funny was that I'd been in front of it all night, no problems until I had to run this message, why on earth didn't I go around the damn thing? I was always good for morale, never a dull or boring moment while JR was about!

I was lucky, no injury, but one of the guys in a similar scenario had hurt his back, just one of those job hazards we had to put up with. Expected to take it on the chin – literally!

My own back

I got my own back on Geordie for laughing, indirectly though, call it Karma or whatever you like. Geordie drove back to camp, in stages that is, because he pranged three Land Rovers on the way back and they didn't take him off driving. So unfair when I didn't want to drive but was made too. That'd teach him for laughing at me. 'Der Svinehund'!

I had just fired the G.P.M.G. machine gun and was now about to fire the rifle.

Range shoot

I had noticed that whenever there was live firing on the ranges, Hackett was usually notably conspicuous by his absence; coincidence or what? It was generally accepted that each Flt practice was overseen by their respective Flt Commander.

On this particular practice, we were on the 600-yard range. For once, Hackett was i/c the range. When it was my time to fire, I took up my position. Of the 24 firing points, I think I was about number 22 or 23 and listened to the instructions. I thought, "That voice sounds familiar." I looked towards the control booth, I saw Hackett, but he hadn't seen me at this point. "Oh no," I thought, "I know what's going to happen, he's going to give me a low score just for spite, I just know it!" Hackett looked towards me and I am sure his face dropped. I just smiled a big smile at him and gave him a wink, he seemed nervous. He saw me handling that weapon with confidence and believe it or not, he ducked out of sight, so I wouldn't shoot him? Did he think I might have an accidental discharge and accidentally shoot him? He disappeared and someone else took over.

After the shoot came the totting up of the scores. We moved forward to the Butts where the targets were operated from, Hackett started to count my score and said I had hardly hit the target and I had failed! The pleasure he got out of it was obvious (as expected); the SNCO appeared and started to count my hits, he told Hackett he was wrong, I had more than qualified and told Hackett his count was wrong, count again! There ensued an argument between them, by now some of the other chaps who had fired came up and those in the Butts also counted the hits so by now there were about 8-9 people telling Hackett he was wrong, so very reluctantly Hackett had to put down the correct score.

He skulked away, scowling and gritting his teeth and mumbling something under his breath. He was not a happy bunny, strike one for me, a good day for a change. I never saw him again until I got back to Laarbruch. That made my day, I had a damn good laugh to myself at this, going down the range on another practice, I was chuckling to myself, the lads told me later they thought I was mad.

'Battle Alley'

One practice we did was 'Battle Alley' – realistic country lane or village with houses, etc. Targets would pop up from behind trees, rocks, houses, windows for about 3-4 seconds and you had to come, aim and get off 2-3 shots; two of us walked side by side down a valley, ready and waiting for 'opportunity' targets.

This was quite realistic, just the sort of situation you could face in the real thing; we had an SNCO walking besides each of us and a safety Marshall behind, giving the signal to another to raise the targets. A target would pop up and we would fire two snap shots at it, on small fig; 12 targets, they were the small ones, small enough for you to miss them when surrounded by the local vegetation.

On another practice – I had never been very good at hitting the target at 600 yards, very few were as the target was coloured black and sandy against a sandy background. And I could barely see it. So through the rifle sights, it appeared no bigger than a small matchstick. So I didn't know what got into me that day; I decided to cheat for the first time ever in my life! If found out, I would claim I was 'using my initiative'.

We had the usual four exposures, two rounds at each exposure for four seconds = 8 rounds. I fired just two rounds at 600 yards, not to arouse suspicion, hoping they would still count up overall and not each range, 2 fired = 6 rounds spare, same at 500 yards, fired 2 = 6 spare, now 12 spare rounds.

I had to fire off these saved rounds before the end of the practice, so at 400 yards, I managed to get off 12 rounds. At 300, 12 again = 4, at 200, 12 again, which now brought me even. From then on, I just fired as normal, I wasn't found out. And the next time on the ranges, this was what I did. A positive note was to get off 12 rounds over a matter of 8 seconds and hit the target each time – pretty good, simulating the rate of fire in a real situation.

After the hits on all the targets had been counted up by the range officer, an SNCO complimented me on my shooting. 'The best of that packet' (24 positions). Knock me down with a feather!

One day after all flights had fired the rifle, I was approached by an officer as having an equal score to a chap of 'B' flight and we were the best shots from the whole Sqn. I felt chuffed and was congratulated by the lads on my 'C' flight. And there Hackett saying I was gun shy!

I don't know whether it was just from that one day's shoot or points amassed from the two week detachment. However, they decided the matter couldn't rest there, the Sqn had to know who the best shot was! They had a competition, a 'shoot out' to find the best shot, it came down to a 'shoot out' between this chap on 'B Flt and myself representing 'C' Flt. I was dreading starting at 600 yards. But to my relief and joy, the powers that be decided to start at 400 yards. We loaded up with 40 rounds each while the whole Sqn looked on. 400 yards back to 100 yards, 40 rounds each, we fired. All square! We went again another 40 rounds, again, all square.

It was decided to make it a little more interesting and to break the deadlock by then moving to the 'Battle Alley'; this practice was more realistic than what we were used to and less time to get off your rounds. We set off, 20 rounds, all square. Another 20 rounds = result! I lost by 2 points (one round). I felt rather chuffed with myself. Still quite an achievement from about 130 people. Had I not been determined to leave the forces, I think this chap and I would have gone on and done a sniper's course.

I never did hear what Hackett thought of my efforts, he must have been told by the Sqn C.O., not a word was said! Bloody disgusting. He should have been proud one of his men did so well – it certainly must have stuck in his craw.

New lad on Sqn borrowing money

We had a lad posted to the Sqn/Flt, a lad whose father was in the army and had married a German girl, they all lived in Cologne, he asked Geordie Weirdo Cpl if he could borrow some money as he had a problem to sort out with his girlfriend.

This Geordie did, which I thought at the time was a bit of a risk as he had only been on the Flt since Tuesday and now it was Friday, nobody knew the lad but this was what the forces were all about, looking after your mates.

On the Monday, we heard that this lad had gone AWOL with Geordie's money; of course, Geordie was worried that he might not get his money back.

Three weeks later, this lad was picked up and returned to the Sqn, he was on pills from the M.O. and not supposed to drink with it but of course, he did and it sent him 'loopy', he had been on a tram and with his girlfriend and seen a woman in a fur coat, in his dazed state thought it was a bear and attacked it. His girlfriend pulled him off and got an ambulance to a local hospital. So Geordie got his money back, eventually. On the first Friday after his return to the Sqn, he asked Geordie for another loan and the daft beggar did it again; some people never learn, do they?

Again he went AWOL, again, Geordie was worried, he had lent the lad 200 marks (£40). After a few weeks, he re-appeared with the borrowed money. The next Friday, we had a repeat performance and it went on for four or five times – each time money was borrowed and eventually paid back.

I told Geordie, "If you're annoyed about him going AWOL with your money, don't lend him any!" "But I feel sorry for him, and I want to help him!" he replied.

Told we were against the S.A.S.

We did a station exercise and during debrief, the C.O. said, "And now for the bad news, the next Harrier exercise, the enemy will be 22 Regiment Special Air Service (S.A.S.)!" A spontaneous loud groan went up from the whole Sqn. "Oh f***! F***ing hell, not the bloody S.A.S.! They'll f***ing kill us, and they are only supposed to be playing! Oh hell, no!"

The reason for this discontent was we were to be pitted against the roughest, toughest, hardest and the best soldiers this country has ever produced, nay, the best in the world; this was the reason for our groans.

Geordie the Cpl and my mate, Jack, said, "What are you worried about, lads, don't let their reputation unnerve you, this is your speciality and you're all very good at it, have confidence in yourselves, they're not ogres, they are only soldiers – well-trained, very well-trained admittedly, but still only human!" We felt a bit better after that pep talk.

Meeting the S.A.S.

When we got to the exercise site, everybody was quiet, subdued, dreading the moment when we might actually come face to face with 'them' (our heroes).

The first any of us saw them was when two of them came to our tent lines to give us a lecture and some training. One of them was telling us of an incident, there was a labour MP, caused a bit of an uproar about their training methods, he said certain training had to be stopped, the S.A.S. said no! A compromise was reached; the S.A.S. permitted a first aid kit to be carried by the trainees, thereby indirectly making the training that little bit tougher as even the smallest extra weight over long distances made a big difference. And any soldier could verify that.

Afterwards, we had a chance to have an off-the-record chat; what surprised all was the fact that they looked ordinary, just like us. In fact, though I had met these chaps before, even I was surprised at how young and ordinary this chap was. It was as if he had just left school but the thing that mattered was that he was harder and tougher than any of us, he had proved it by passing their training course.

Most of 'A' Flt didn't rate them. And didn't think they were as tough as their reputation. The rest of the Sqn didn't share that view though. We thought Jimmy Buchan and his little band of 'Merry Men' – or should that be the outlaws? Might get up to something and the rest of us would suffer. – and we were dreading coming into contact with them on exercise, we knew they wouldn't harm us but they might just teach us a lesson in soldiering, that was for sure. Our worst fears were realised,(I can't say what) – we were waiting for the repercussions. Thankfully, they never came.

Discovery on mobile patrol

I was on mobile patrol one day and we fell for one of the oldest tricks in the book, they made us feel such fools, they caught us, stripped us off our weapons, Cpl Jeff Fanshaw was with us and gave them some verbal abuse; we cringed every time he opened his mouth as we thought, "For feck's sake, Geoff, shut your fecking ruddy mouth, you're making it worse for us!" But he carried on. A very brave man indeed! (Since that day, he earned the nickname 'Fearless Fenny'.) They stripped us off our uniforms and clothes! We were allowed to keep our 'shreddies' (underpants) on. They threw our uniforms and clothes everywhere in the undergrowth but our Cpl 'Fearless', the S.A.S. made him walk back to our lines through the woods naked! In broad daylight. To fetch us fresh uniforms and a Land Rover to pick up the rest of us. With the real chance he would be spotted by the local Germans out walking their dogs. He managed to get back unseen. We were, meanwhile, keeping a low profile; the last thing that we wanted was to be seen by the locals, this would be right up the Germans' street to see several squaddies in various state of undress.

He told us that upon walking into his tented area, his officer had come out of his tent, took one look and said, "Don't tell me, you have just met the S.A.S.?" and laughed!

Another day again on mobile patrol, I suggested that we go through this particular leafy track, which we hadn't been down before. After fighting off the overhanging branches that tried to hit us in the face, we suddenly came out in a clearing. In this clearing was a tented area, after a few seconds, a large guy, a very large guy! Whom we'd just disturbed having a shave, came out with the towel in his hand, we turned around and drove out of the clearing, we had gone only a few yards down the track when I shouted, "Hey stop!" The driver did. "Do you realise just where we've been? We've just driven in and out of the enemy's base camp, the S.A.S. Quick, let's get back and attack them, they won't be expecting it and we can catch them off guard!" The reply I received was expected and I will try and clean it up a bit. "Attack them, attack them? Are you stark staring raving bonkers? They'll kill us! Are you blooming mad, have you gone completely off your rocker, we can't attack them, they'll kill us, I want to live, not die!"

"Don't be bloody stupid; they are supposed to be on our side in real life. Anyway, they won't harm us and they will probably admire and respect us for having a go, that's what we're here for, isn't it? If you're all too frightened to have a go, I'm not!" Once we got back to our lines, I reported what we'd seen and asked permission from Hackett to launch a raid on the 'enemy'; this request was denied. I was fuming. I called them all a load of 'gutless spineless cowards' and such, I suggested that if they were not prepared to have a go, could I get a party together and do it myself? I didn't mind taking responsibility for the mission. Hackett said I could only go if I could get a party of volunteers together. Amongst that spineless load of gutless cowards, I found only one volunteer, my buddy, Norman Geordie Hall. So they wouldn't let me go, they tried to give me lots of excuses like, "You haven't long to go before you are demobbed, and we don't want you injured, which will cause you to be delayed in going home, you don't want that, do you?" This coming from Hackett; what a dammed hypocrite! "It will be a waste of time; they will have moved location by now!" (I was prepared to agree with him on that point.) He came out with lots of excuses to prevent me 'having a go'. I stormed off, calling them a load of spineless, gutless cowards. As the final word and say so had to come from Hackett, I didn't hold out much hope; they all lacked the backbone.

Running around airfield

When the Sqn had nothing for us to do or we were at a loose end, we were 'encouraged' to go for a run, in full kit. "It keeps them out of trouble and helps keep them fit as well." They said from our hangar all the way around and finish at the hangar – roughly 7 miles. I have never been one for running but though never last, I would be nearer the last man rather than the first but I did complete it.

Another time, I thought I would try and see if I could get away with 'cheating' my way around. I wouldn't be the first nor would I be the last to do so. We set off and as soon as I saw a Land Rover or car coming along the perimeter track, I would stick out my thumb and half-heartedly thumb a lift. When one car stopped for me, I was committed, so as we were driving past the others, I had to slide down in the seat so I wasn't seen. I had several lifts around the airfield, but as I was getting out of one car…who was there to see me but Cpl Geordie weirdo himself. He went mad screaming and shouting and made me run around again, this time on my own when everybody had finished for the day so it was dark by the time I had finished but I kept a smile on my face and had a little chuckle to myself that I'd been caught. I wasn't going to let this incident put me off; I was still prepared to do it again if we had another run in the future.

Pay office mess my money up good and proper

When I got back from a Harrier exercise, Jack Skuse came out to me and told me that he had a phone call from the pay office and I had to report to the pay office immediately. I was worried, what on earth could they want with me, something crossed my mind and I thought of something: "Could it be?" But I was hoping it wasn't as it would mean a lot of trouble for me, financial trouble. However, when I got there, my worst fears were realised.

The pay office W.O. said, "Ah, Rowbottom, come on in, sit down!" Now I knew there was trouble when asked to sit down.

W.O.: "I am afraid I have some bad news for you!"

J: "I thought you might have, that's why you have me here, isn't it?"

W.O.: "Yes, I'm afraid you owe the Royal Air Force one thousand two hundred pounds (£1,200).

I laughed and said, "You mean German marks of course, oh well, that's not so bad!"

W.O.: "No, you heard me wrong. I said £1,200!" I was struck dumb, I couldn't believe it, and it transpired that once you moved onto camp from outside hiring, the R.A.F. was supposed to stop paying you living out allowance, only overseas allowance. I was only on £40 a week, so these extras made all the difference.

I knew this and I had noticed a year ago that I was still getting paid. I took my pay slips to the pay office to query it and the chap looking after the pay of people whose name began with 'R' told me that the pay slip was right and to stop worrying. I went several times; this chap was getting fed up of me going about the same thing, he said, "Look, you get on with your job and leave me to take care of your finances, that's what I'm paid to do!" I made sure that he signed the slips at the time and I had visions of exactly this nightmare happening. I showed the W.O. the said pay slip, he claimed he couldn't make out the signature, which I didn't believe for a moment and told him so.

One of my mates in the singles block was pally with the clerk who was dealing with my slip and I was told that as soon as the news broke of this 'carry on', this pay office clerk was mysteriously and suddenly posted within 24 hours – surprise surprise.

I was trying to sort this problem out over about two weeks but of course, whenever I tried to get down to the pay office to sort things out, the Sqn was convinced I was only going for a skive. (I wish that was all I had to do.)

I was told that I had to pay it back as I had the money, point taken, but if they had listened to me, I would have had only a few measly pounds to pay back so we had to figure out how I was to pay it back before I went to UK and I only had about two months in which to pay it back.

So this W.O. said, "Make out a list of your expenditures and we will work out how much we can deduct each week, including your wife's wages!"

"Now just you hang on a damn minute!" I said. "Throughout my time in the R.A.F. and especially here in Germany, you (R.A.F. in general) are always going on about that the wives and families are not important, and they are no concern of the R.A.F. at all. Now you want not only my money, but you want to take in to account my wife's wages too? No!"

We tried to work it out but to enable me to clear my debt, we had to take her wages into account, but I wasn't going to let them get away with it.

"Can I use your phone? Viola – John here, pack your job in now! I'll explain why tonight!"

She did as I said. I put the phone down, smiled and said, "Now you'll just have to work things out with my money, won't you!"

W.O.: "You won't be able to manage!"

J: "I'll just have to struggle through, won't I? And manage." We did, only just. I paid it back between 5 June and 12 August 1976. I gave them a list made out thus: food, rent, clothes, cigarettes, beer, etc. That wasn't good enough for him, he said he wanted each item properly itemised, item by item, by now I was getting a little peeved to say the least. I was struggling to hold my temper.

"I suppose you want to know things like how much my wife spends on soap, sanitary towels and such?"

W.O.: "Yes, every item!" I hit the roof.

"No fecking way, that's just too damn personal, and you can't make me either!"

W.O.: "Want to bet?" With that, he produced some file of R.A.F. regulations and he was right, he could make me do it. From that moment in time, I looked at the R.A.F. through different eyes. I became disillusioned, disappointed and downright angry at the R.A.F. to think they could sink to such levels. I know they own you mind, body and soul but I thought you'd have some personal/human rights, but no! Despite all that had gone on whilst in Germany, i.e., all the exercises, Hackett hounding me, had none of it taken place, this matter of messing my money up would have been the watershed and on that alone, I would have left! It was fortunate and just as well that I had willingly tried to survive before on as little as possible because it stood me in good stead when this disaster struck. I felt closer than I had ever done since all this trouble began on 1 Sqn to really cracking up and losing my temper so we rang my father from Germany; he was very annoyed just as we were.

He promptly rang up the station commander (again!) and told him what was going on. Back on the Sqn, I was told to report to the pay office W.O. and he didn't look very happy!

W.O.: "The station commander has been in touch and he has asked me not to push it any further, and in fact, would you (me) tell the station commander that you want the case dropped?"

I asked him, "Why on earth should I, after the way I have been treated!"

He very dejectedly said, "Do you realise what this means if you don't? It means that several people's careers would go out the window with their, or part of their, pensions!"

J: "Yes, I realise what it meant, that's why I'm retaliating the only way I can!"

W.O.: "People's livelihoods are at stake here." Now he looked really worried.

J: "Tough! They should have thought of that when the mistake was first made and condoned each week for a year when various NCOs of varying ranks each prepared to sign my documents but couldn't be bothered to take the time to check things out. They have to take their punishment just as I would have to, had it been me who had made the mistake. No, I won't withdraw it!"

Was he bluffing about people's careers going up the 'Swanny'? He definitely looked very worried, so he was probably referring to his career and the lad who had ignored me. If it happened, would I have any regrets? No. And I would have done the same today. Yes!

They started to deduct about 85% of each week's money for two months, we had a few hundred pounds saved up to bring back to UK with us, and so we had to pay most of it to the pay office to help bring down the repayments. What would have happened if I had been buying a car like most chaps out there? We definitely wouldn't have survived. I would have had to sign on for another year or two – with Hackett! I thought that dammed Laarbruch couldn't do any more harm to me than it already had. But Laarbruch being Laarbruch, they had yet another (but by no means the last) surprise in store for me. About 3-4 weeks before I left for home, the incompetent imbecile had me in the office, they had worked out the re-payment figure wrong and told me that I had to pay them more, £40 more. So again I rang Dad and he rang the station commander to give him an update; by then I was still owing £432. The station commander declared £50 to be written off and I would then at the end of the period be £10 in credit – some conciliation.

Sqn goes to Berlin

We heard that we were to be the guest regiment at the Queen's birthday parade in Berlin in a few weeks' time in June 1976. I was looking forward to this as Berlin was world famous, though with Hackett at me for something or another and for some reason that I didn't find out, he thought I didn't want to go to Berlin, but unbeknownst to him, I wasn't feeling too good and was worried that I might miss it; no, I didn't want to miss it for all the tea in China. Though when he started to have a go at me, I thought that I'd have a bit of fun at his expense, so for weeks I tried to give him – Hackett, the impression in words and deeds that there was no way he was going to get me to go to Berlin. Knowing full well the way that he thought, even if he had been thinking of not letting me go (which he wasn't), he would deliberately do all in his power to ensure that I would go. The day before we went, he started to gloat to me in front of the flight, "You thought you were going to get out of the Berlin detachment, didn't you? I'm on to you, you're not going to get out of this, you are going to Berlin tomorrow whether you like it or not!"

J: "Oh, but I do like it, I want to go, I wouldn't miss it for the world. Tut-tut, whatever gave you that idea?"

And I told Hackett that if he wanted me off the parade, then fair enough, but he was not going to make me miss watching the parade (which he later tried).

At this, he went bright red in the face, started to fume quietly and then stormed off, I was grinning from ear to ear. Though he did get his own back on me before the detachment was over, although I had made no secret of the fact that I was not going to sign on again and that I was ready to come out of the R.A.F., I still wanted to pass my R.A.F. maths exam, it was arranged by the education officer with the Sqn for me to take my exam whilst in Berlin.

Of course, Hackett made sure that I didn't get the chance to take the exam, just for spite. This was the last chance for me to take it and I was very annoyed, annoyed that I was to leave the R.A.F. without completing a personal test, even though I had passed every other test set before me.

Farce, outward-bound

We were to proceed to Berlin via Weeze railway station and the farce they had trying to get the Sqn standard onto the train, which at first proved near impossible, was a treat to behold. Whilst the officers were struggling to get on without breaking the staff, we, the rest of the Sqn, were on the station platform laughing at them beginning to panic whilst trying to get the standard on board. The locals thought it funny too, who said the Germans had no sense of fun! Eventually, they managed to get the standard on board, along with all the other kit; the whole Sqn to a man let out a big cheer and laughed at the officers. Some wag shouted out from the back, "At fecking last!" Cue more laughter, and no! It wasn't me. The train left about 10 minutes later than it should have done. At the last station in the west, the train was decoupled and attached to another, we set off on the next phase of the trip on a German train but British R.C.T. military carriages; these carriages had the inside of the doors wedged with a piece of wood save that East German citizens tried to get on board the British train and seek asylum.

We also were given some information on points of interest along the way. I noticed that wherever we went and if we stopped by a lot of locals, we were given a very warm reception, lots of waving, cheering, smiling and singing, especially when they saw the very large British Union Jack flag painted on our side.

Journey through a rail corridor

The first and overriding impression you got when you crossed the border was how dull and dreary everything seemed to be, no colour, nothing new, in short, it was just like going back through a time warp, back in time 30 years. It was as though nothing had been done to brighten the place up. No money spent on things such as paint or even new buildings. It had an immediate effect on one of instant depression, poor souls, and I felt sorry for those having to live under the communist regime.

We also had, I noticed, company in the shape of being followed at all times from the moment we crossed the border by either a fixed wing aircraft or a helicopter. On our list of 'interesting things to see' was first, prisons holding political prisoners, East German army camps and tank depots, though we did not see anything of this as whenever we stopped alongside any of these, surprise surprise, a train (steam trains, not like our modern diesels) would pull up alongside us with high-sided wagons preventing us seeing anything at all, though they did 'cock it up' at one point when we pulled up alongside an East German tank repair camp. The funny thing was when the tank repair crews saw us, they cheered and waved to us and used this as an excuse to stop work on their army 'Tiger' tanks; yes, that's what they appeared to be, WW2 German 'Tiger' tanks.

Wednesday, 2 May: West Berlin

The moment you crossed into West Berlin, the first thing you were aware of was colour, newness and people smiling and enjoying themselves. Once on R.A.F. Gatow, only a few hundred yards from Spandau prison (where they were holding Rudolph Hess, Hitler's deputy), we noticed that wherever we went in the open, we were being observed from the 'Goon towers' by East German border guards watching our every move through binoculars, at first it was a bit spooky being watched but after a few days, you got used to it and didn't notice it any more.

Rehearsals started with the Sqn at the old site of the 1936 Olympic Games, which Adolph Hitler had attended.

Not allowed on parade

Hackett wouldn't let me participate in the rehearsals as I was due out soon – that was really no excuse, it was just to be bloody-minded. I was there for the full detachment and had done the rehearsals in Laarbruch, which didn't mean I should have missed the parade; he knew I enjoyed these types of parades, so there was no reason whatsoever except that he was just trying to 'come it' and just being nasty again with me. So I was assigned to the sergeants' mess to help out for the duration, not that I was really bothered, if he was doing it to upset me then he had gotten it wrong, again! As much as I liked drill and parades, I was not really that bothered anymore, I had lost interest by now. A few days before the parade, the plans were changed and it was decided by the parade commander that he wanted people in the open-topped Land Rovers to sit motionless to give that extra effect; by now there was a very small pool of people to call on in reserve so I got called in at the last minute, only for the plans to change again and the Land Rover personnel to be cancelled, though the Land Rover display still went ahead without us in the back.

As our Chieftain tanks would fire a salute, there would be the sound of small arms gunfire coming from across the border in the east, it was as if they wouldn't be outdone, they had to have their say as well.

My mate with me when our tanks fired said, "Hey, that's loud!"

"No, it isn't," I said, "I've been on artillery guns and that is only charge one, and I'd like to bet you that on the day when they fire, it is a lot louder, probably charge 3." I was right! On the parade day when everybody was now used to the level of noise they had come to expect and didn't bother protecting their ears, I did and was glad to do so as just as I had predicted, the tanks had increased their charge and when they did open fire, they near shook the buildings and I heard women scream with the shock of it, I had a chuckle to myself that the Tankies had had the last laugh on the E. Germans.

Jack's blue-eyed blonde

Jack, my mate, told me the first morning we were there that he had been out to the red light area the first night we were there and had a young blue-eyed blonde from the local brothel; it had been his ambition to have one of these girls and he did, in fact the next night we went out for a drink or two and he took me to this same place where he had been and we were watching the girls on the street getting picked up and noticed a few facts, (a) it was always the youngest who were chosen, so much so that you could put money on it, and (b) if they were young and blonde, then they would be up and down all the time. We watched Jack's girl after he had pointed her out to me, she was not on the street for more than five/ten minutes before she was picked up by another 'trick' and taken away again.

So a young blonde aged between 17 and 25 would have, say 8-10 customers per night, compared to the older girls who had, say: 3-4 per night so it was obvious who was making the most money.

Taking advantage of our right to go to the east

During our stay at R.A.F. Gatow, we were given a day off to take advantage of our right under the four-power agreement signed in Berlin, which gave us, the British forces, the right to enter the East German/Russian sector, 'Checkpoint Charlie'.

We boarded a white R.A.F. bus c/w a large Union Jack on the side. Before we crossed over to the eastern side, we stopped by some crosses alongside the Berlin wall. This was the one factor that had the most effect on me; when we saw the crosses and graves of the unnamed youngsters buried alongside the Berlin wall, no name, just a thin metal cross tied to some wire. 'Youth, male aged approx. 20-25 unnamed shot in the back trying to escape to the west. The day they were shot. That got to me, more than the scenes on TV of starving Africans, which we have seen so often that most of us become a bit blasé about it. There was something about these crosses and these poor people buried with no names that got to me! Their families in the east probably didn't know that their son, brother, husband had been shot and buried. We were told by our liaison officer that just before we arrived, a young man was trying to escape over the wall; the East German guards opened fire and shot him in the back. Now there just happened to be a West German film crew there making a documentary. They realised he was still alive and ran forward and gave him first aid. The East German Border guards opened fire on the film crew with warning shots to keep away every time they tried to help this young man. So consequently, he was allowed to bleed to death. Once dead, they were allowed to remove his body.

And up to that point in time, I wasn't very much interested in politics but coupled with the way the Russians showed absolutely no respect to their war dead in comparison to the way we tended our war dead graves

– wherever they may be buried in the world, we always remembered them on the 11th hour, 11th day of the 11th month each year.

From then on in, when I was in civvy street and I heard some dammed 'lefties' at work spouting off about the 'poor old comrade worker' being put down by the 'right wing fascist' government in power in UK. I would, not so gently, tell them of what I had seen in Berlin and had they seen that, they wouldn't vote for the lefty politicians in the local/general elections; this made me enemies as they thought I was a right-wing extremist. Nothing I said could convince them otherwise. I spoke of what I saw!

Parachute Regt climbing over the Wall

This liaison officer also told us another couple or so incidents, stating they were true!

One story involved some members of the Parachute Regt who had recently just left Berlin, they got drunk (nothing new there). One of them told his mate that he bet him he could climb over the Berlin wall and back again without being shot. "The bar-stewards wouldn't dare fire at a NATO soldier; it would mean war!"

So despite his mate's protests, he climbed over the Berlin wall into the east, waved at the East German guards, who waved back to him, then started to climb back over the wall to the west whereupon the East German guards promptly opened fire, whether it was good fortune or they 'chickened out' at the last second before squeezing the trigger, they only succeeded in wounding him and he fell back to the eastern side of the wall, so this caused a diplomatic incident that was not put in the public domain. He was held prisoner by the East Germans and Russians for 3-4 days before his Regiment could convince the East Germans/Russians that there was no ulterior motive. I was certainly glad I wasn't in his shoes, one could only imagine the repercussions, he was probably court-martialled and kicked out.

Now in the western sector, there was a large park in a prominent position so that it was easily seen by anyone in the eastern sector; the West Germans erected and lit an eternal flame partly in remembrance of the war and those who died there but also as a beacon to the east. "This is the flame of freedom in the west!" or something like that. One evening, two drunken Scottish soldiers were walking/staggering along in the park when one of them spotted the flame and thinking it might be dangerous, promptly took out his 'personal weapon' and the drunken Scotsman peed on it, promptly putting out the flame. This flame had been lit since the end of the Second World War. Of course, the West Germans went absolutely ballistic!

The East Germans apparently admired our post office tower in London and wanted one for themselves. They engaged British engineers to build them one. Once they had left, the East Germans realised that no matter what the direction or how brightly/dimly the sun shone, there was a cross on the glass – pointing west!

No matter what they did, they couldn't remove it. It was the way the glass panes and frame were set and it was impossible/impracticable to change it. So that beacon of freedom that beckoned west was left in place, much to the annoyance of the East Berlin government and the Russians also.

We entered the iron curtain through the British sector, 'Checkpoint Charlie'. I noticed several things at the border: 1) The Berlin wall was being painted and there were two East German border guards with sub machine guns watching the painter in case he had any thoughts of jumping over the wall to the west, and freedom. Under instructions to shoot if they had to, but watching the guards watching the painter were two more guards, on the remote chance of the first guards letting the painter get away, then they would be shot by these other two guards; so much for 'workers' paradise'.

2) All the windows facing the west were secured with iron bars to prevent a repeat of an escape previously carried out by an East German citizen.

There were a lot of other escapes we were told about and how measures had been taken to prevent other similar escapes. If the west was so decadent and bad, then why were so many people prepared to risk their lives trying to escape to the west?

Before we set off, I had made my mind up that I wasn't going to spend any money in the communist east. One of the first things we were told as we crossed the border was that from this moment on, the nearest friendly country we would come to if we continued going east would be South Korea! Quite an unnerving thought.

Treptoe Park

We stopped at a large park (Treptoe Park) for a walk and the first thing that you could see was a large statue of a peasant woman (Mother Russia) stamping on a broken swastika, Germany. You walk through the park and alongside there were five mass graves on either side, each containing the bodies of five thousand Russian soldiers (50,000). The graves had been dug by East Germans after the war. At the end of the path, there was a large mound with a building on top, made up by the corpses of 5,000 Russian soldiers, piled on top of one another, covered in soil and grassed, with this monument on top. I thought what a way to show disrespect to their war dead. Not one dead soldier was named so if his family wished to visit the grave, they would not know where their loved one was buried.

Norman Geordie Hall and I climbed the steps to this monument and saw inside the communist idea of 'Utopia' – a mural depicting a peasant child born in Russia, growing up to be a good party member and finally achieving his ambition – becoming a member of the Russian Red army and fighting the decadent west. I paused for a photo on the steps on the way down and as I was about to continue my journey down the steps, I was startled to see walking past me two Russian soldiers in full dress uniform. I was surprised, I had never expected to see them, but without realising it,

I watched them go by, glaring at them until my mate Geordie caught my attention and we carried on walking.

The only new buildings in the east were police, army or secret police buildings; the rest of them seemed to be still in the state you would expect to see after the city had surrendered. There was a distinct aura of gloom and depression hanging over the city.

Tomb of unknown warrior

Another place we visited was the East German tomb of the unknown soldier with the guards doing a Nazi-style 'goose step' and though they were supposed to be East Germans, they were, I believe, really Russians; they had that sloe-eyed eastern look, which was unmistakable, or maybe Mongolian?

Almost a diplomatic incident

It was there when my mate Geordie Hall said something to me and my reply almost caused a diplomatic incident. I shall say no more other than that was the moment the liaison officer thought we had outstayed our welcome and we headed back to Checkpoint Charlie.

Once we were back in the western sector, some of the chaps asked me if I had been true to my word in not spending any money in the east and I replied proudly, "Yes, I didn't spend a penny, I told you I wouldn't support a communist regime!" They told me, 'We wish we hadn't spent any money now, their beer was awful!' Upon our crossing back into the western sector, it was as if a dark ominous cloud had been lifted; there was a noticeable sigh of relief in the coach as several others who obviously felt the same were also glad to get back into the free west. It made me realise what a lot we had to be grateful for, it changed my political ideals forever.

Berlin's night scene

After parade rehearsals had finished, Geordie Hall and I decided to go for a night out. We had an early tea, changed and went to Berlin city centre, where we started to drink at 5 pm, got drunk, sobered up, then drunk again. We started on small beers, eventually graduating to large and one-litre (1¾ pints) Steins, Schnapps, whiskey, brandy, even Sake when we went for a Japanese meal; we had asked what was traditional Japanese fare, they tried to convince us for a traditional Japanese meal. Chicken and chips! We weren't that drunk to be convinced. We finished up with sukiyaki.

During our night out and early morning stint, we went from bar to bar, to a Japanese restaurant, to a nightclub, to discos, to brothels – just looking! There weren't many places in West Berlin that we didn't frequent at some time.

During our 'recce', we came upon this particular bar entirely staffed by topless girls. Sadly, some of them were no longer in their prime and their boobies were 'heading south for the winter'. Even we were a bit embarrassed, ordering beer with a naked pair of boobies not two feet away; we didn't know whether to look or look away, it didn't seem to bother the girls, they were obviously used to men ogling them while they pulled their beer. Nevertheless, we found it a little unnerving.

In the bar there were a handful of locals and 6 of the lads from the Sqn. So we sat with them and had a few beers. Meanwhile, going on in the background was a series of porn films, perfectly normal for the Germans. We all to a man sort of did the same, we pretended to take part in the conversation, but our attention was on the films. But trying not to make it obvious. Suddenly, a different film came on and the conversation slowed down so it was obvious no one was listening to each other, we looked at it trying to figure out what was going on, no one could see any female body parts. No one said anything until suddenly it dawned on me.

"Bloody hell, lads, it's two queers doing it!"

"Na, you're wrong!" some said. "It can't be!"

Then suddenly it hit everyone at once.

"Fecking hell, you're right, it's two queers!"

And although we'd just got a round in, every man, not a word said, got up and walked out disgusted. Now you'll never see a serviceman walk out on a full glass of beer unless something very serious has happened, this was such an occasion.

As I was leaving, one of the topless girls asked me, "What's the matter, why are you leaving?" I paused, pointed to the film and said, "We're English, we don't like that sort of thing!"

Once outside, Geordie and I went off on our own again. Back on the Sqn the next day, when we met up with the chaps who were in the bar, not a word was said about it, we were all still embarrassed.

Nudist disco

One point in the evening, apparently – I don't recall, Norman Geordie Hall so subtly reminded me of it during our reunion, we stumbled upon a club/disco advertised that seemed somehow different! I was unable to read German, apart from the odd few words, so had no idea what this place was. As we went in, we rang the bell and an attractive woman answered the door, dressed in a housecoat. Strange! We couldn't understand her though she invited us in. Another woman overheard us who spoke English, she explained that we had to undress, but keep our socks on for fire regulations, before we were allowed in. It was a nudist disco where you not only checked in your hat and coat, but everything else as well! With the exception of your socks. Norman Hall said, "I suppose the twist is banned!" This Geordie sense of humour was wasted on this woman. The old saying, "An Englishman always keeps his socks on", had now traversed the North Sea and taken hold in Germany. Had I been single, I would have been in there like a ferret down a rabbit hole! We hastily made our excuses and made a 'tactical withdrawal' – pardon the pun! But this sort of thing was nothing to the Germans; they lived with nudity, the public swimming baths included. So they probably wouldn't be in the least embarrassed. Geordie Hall and I soon sobered up. We weren't that drunk or desperate and didn't bother going in.

Longest drinking session

As the evening progressed, Geordie fancied a local girl at a dance, so I tried to chat her up on behalf of Geordie with my limited German, all to no avail. Once we knew we had been 'blown out', we went to the loo, we were both in the gents watering the horses when I looked up to the window and saw daylight.

J: "Bloody 'ell! Geordie, its daylight!"

G: "Nah, it can't be!"

J: "I'm telling you it is, look outside!"

G: "Bloody 'ell! You're right, John!"

(Looking at my watch), "Bloody hell, Geordie, we've only got 50 minutes and we're supposed to be on parade!" The time was 06:40 approximately.

"Bloody hell!" we both exclaimed.

On parade in the nick of time

We must have broken the two-mile dash records from the centre of Berlin to camp, changed and on parade just in the nick of time. Unfortunately, we were found out; the fact was we ran over the golf course early in the morning, though at first no one believed that we'd been drinking since 5 pm the day before and only had our last drink less than an hour ago. Not until one of the officers singled us out in front of all the others and gave us a rollicking in front of the Sqn for running across 'their' golf course, then our mates did believe us.

We were on parade and at attention. Geordie and I were swaying and stumbling and having a laugh. 'Drunk as a newt', though I haven't seen any newts as drunk as we were that morning.

The SWO came over to us, gave us a right old rollicking in front of the squadron and kicked us off the parade, telling us to go to the block and 'sleep it off' – how lucky we were!

However, we should have done a right turn and marched off; Geordie Hall, my fellow drinking pal, did a left turn and of course, the whole Sqn fell about laughing. Poor lad, he had to do another hour's drill as punishment but as we were both drunk on parade in Berlin of all places, where the Russians/East Germans were watching every move, phew, we could have finished up charged and doing time in the 'glasshouse'; we didn't appreciate then how lucky we really were, had it been Hackett, this would have played right into his hands and I would probably...definitely have ended up being court-martialled. God was certainly watching over me that day.

Berlin was one of those places that stick in the mind unlike most modern cities, it was/is a place I shall never forget and has had a profound effect on me ever since that fateful June in 1976 and I always think of Berlin with both sorrow and affection; the only other city's that made a distinct impression on me a few years later was Manila, Philippines and Venice, Italy.

Getting free carpet

We managed to get a free carpet from the R.A.F.; we received a message that it was time for us to exchange one of our bedroom carpets, we were expected to be in when they came around but I rang them up explaining that there would be no one there due to us both being at work and they suggested leaving the old carpet outside. I pointed out it would be not on, as someone may pinch it, not to worry I was told, it was only going to be burnt.

The new one was delivered but they didn't collect the old one. I kept checking up with them and they said they would send someone to pick it up, but they never did, at the end of this carry on, I was told, "Well, you can either get rid of it yourself, leave it in the M.Q. when you move out or keep it yourself!" So we did the latter, which helped us in furnishing our house in UK.

Geordie pays my mortgage

My mate Geordie Hall and I were talking in general about life and he asked how was I going to pay the mortgage if I didn't get a job. I said I didn't know but I would find a way! So Geordie invited himself to tea one night and asked both Viola and I how much per month was our mortgage, which I thought was a bit cheeky, and told him so. But we told him and with that, he took out his cheque book, made out a cheque and handed it to me, saying, "Here John, here is the first six months mortgage; I'll give you another cheque before you leave for home." He did too. 10 months in all! That was a perfect example of what true comradeship is all about! Which civilians find hard to understand! So the first 10 months mortgage was paid for us. Though fortunately, I got a job pretty quickly when I got back home.

There was no telling if we were ever to meet again (though we did once, briefly) so there was no guarantee he would get his money back, though once settled in a full-time job at home, I started to send the money back to him but the cheques were returned to me.

Meeting Geordie again: the old stories

One day in 1978, there was a knock on our door at about 10:30 pm. To my surprise and delight, there stood Geordie with one of his mates, John Talk, from the Sqn. Though he tried to refuse repayment, I insisted he take some (as much as we could afford at the time) so I made him take a cheque before he left our house.

Once we'd returned to UK, it took me everything I could think of over many years to try and track him down. I'd just about given up hope. Finally, in 2015, success! We finally met up again! The years just fell away. Finally, I was able to pay him back financially what we owed him some 39 years later but not his loyalty as a true friend and brother! That can never be repaid.

When we met for the first time in some 39 years after many years trying to track him down, he came to our house and we had 'one or two drinks' as one does. After all, we had 39 years to catch up on. Geordie told me things he had kept from me all this time. Some things I knew, some I didn't, some I'd rather forget! Apparently, some of my adventures and antics had gone down in 1 Sqn folklore and history. Such as the time I let rip and peed over a Cpl who was asleep in bed, I had forgotten that. When on exercise and having to dig our defensive trenches, I always seemed to be mostly on my own whilst everybody else paired up, this was hard work on your own, digging a 4-foot+ trench, then having to scrounge and find overhead cover and 'cam' it up. When you went looking for some more and you got back, the last lot had disappeared. 9/10 times I was on my own. I didn't mind this once the trench was finished and I was settled down for the rest of the exercise as I sometimes preferred to be on my own. But Geordie told me that it was Hackett and the SNCO who deliberately made sure this would happen, to be on my own and without a 'buddy' to spell me off and enabling me to get my head down. I had to stay awake the whole time. Hackett told the SNCO, "Give him a hard time; ensure no one is with him in the trench!" This explains everything.

Norman 'Geordie' Hall

But the ultimate test of friendship occurred unbeknownst to me. The F/Sgt took Geordie aside one day and said to him, "You're mates with Rowbottom, aren't you?"

G: "Yes, I am!"

F/Sgt: "Well, I'm telling you from now on to have nothing to do with him, is that clear?"

G: "Why, he's my mate, I get on well with John and his wife, they have made me welcome in their home and John has helped me and guided me with his experience doing the job."

F/Sgt: "I'm telling you now, he's a troublemaker, you're not to have anything more to do with him again – is that clear?"

G: "No, he's my mate and his wife, why should I do what you are telling me!"

Sgt: "I don't think you understand what I'm telling you, you will have nothing more to do with him! You will avoid him at all times, if you don't, it may affect your career in the R.A.F. and your chances of promotion!"

Norman Hall ignored these threats; he must have done as his attitude and friendship towards me never changed. I would have noticed if it had. When he told me this some 40 odd years later, I was fuming and said, "Geordie, why didn't you tell me this at the time? You should have, I had a right to know!"

G: "And what would you have done at the time if I had told you?"

J: "I would have probably smacked him!"

G: "Exactly, and where would that have gotten you? Charged, court-mar-tialled? You'd have played right into the hands of Hackett! It was just what he was hoping for – to give him some reason to court martial you. It was best I didn't tell you as it happened."

That's what you call a true, true friend, who was prepared to forgo any chance of promotion and getting on in the R.A.F. because he wouldn't betray a friend. There's not many like Norman in this selfish world. This just sums him up as a great guy and a true friend and brother.

Geordie Hall, on our reunion, told me another story that the single lads had a room to themselves in the accommodation block. When I was there before, I had Viola fly out and there were 6 to a room, so some improve-ment, even then that was luxury to what I'd been used to all those years, starting from the R.C.T. with 24 to a draughty wooden hut.

But I digress, Geordie had a friend who was going back to UK who had a Budgie and asked Geordie to look after it for him. He was told its name but missed what was said; by the time this chap had left the room, Geordie had forgotten what he had said. So he remembered me and called the Budgie 'John' after me. Fame at last!

Cutting the wire

On exercise, I along with Weirdo Cpl Geordie, came across some Don 10 communications wire in the middle of nowhere, we didn't know whether it was ours or the enemy's, we tried to trace it but it didn't seem to lead anywhere, and after much deliberation we decided that we had best cut the wire as it was nowhere near our lines.

When we got back to our lines, we found that officers/SNCOs were running around in a blind panic; due to an unforeseen disaster, the lines of communications had gone dead. It had been thought that the 'enemy' had cut the lines, Geordie looked at me, and I him, and he looked decidedly sheepish. We thought discretion and keeping our mouths shut was the order of the day, and we kept quiet and kept a very low profile from then on, hoping that they wouldn't find out. Fortunately, they didn't.

Last Harrier ex: caught short

On my final Harrier exercise, we had a few beers in the evening before turning in with our 'Green Maggots' sleeping bags. In the tent, there were 8 of us. During the night, I had the urge to have a 'Jimmy Riddle' and unzipped my sleeping bag and made my way to the tent's entrance, it was very dark in the middle of a large pine forest and you literally couldn't see your hand in front of you. I had lost my torch on the exercise and the SNCOs wouldn't give me a replacement so I was fumbling for the flap purely by feel and estimation as to where the flaps were tied double. It was pitch back, after perhaps about five minutes, I couldn't find the flaps to the tent entrance and then I started to feel the urge to relieve myself. The more I couldn't find the flap, the more desperate I became, and greater the urge and pressure to go. Slowly, the pressure built. I felt an inner panic hoping I could get out in the woods in time. By now, I was getting very desperate with one hand looking for the flap and one holding myself. I didn't know how long I could hold back the tide, so to speak.

Still I couldn't find the flap and the pressure became so intense I could not wait or hold back any longer, so after what seemed an eternity, probably ten minutes or so, and in absolute desperation (I was hoping against hope that I was somewhere near the tent flap) decided if I peed here, hopefully it would have soaked away by morning and no one would be any the wiser.

So with a very relieved smile on my face, I let it flow and boy, did it flow! Like a dam it gushed forth. No force could stop it. It momentarily reminded me of another 'wall' being breached in Germany; there too the waters had gushed forth. Moments later, I heard a gurgling noise and sensed someone moving nearby, suddenly the quiet and still of the night was broken by: "What the f***! What's f***king going on? I'm all f***ing wet!" and with that a torch came on. "You, you f***ing bas*a*d, you're f***ing pissing all over me!"

Then another torch came on, and then another and another, voices in the dark said, "What the f*** is all the noise? You've f***ing woken us up, you bas*a*ds!"

"It's him!" screamed Cpl Boyd, pointing at me. "The f***ing bas*a*d's trying to drown me, he's f***ing pissing all over me!"

There was a brief silence as the rest of the lads looked at Cpl Boyd, looked at me still holding myself with a few last drops dripping onto Cpl Boyd, they looked at each other, then Boyd again and suddenly the six others in the tent burst out laughing so much they were rolling off their camp beds, in their sleeping bags, half out and clutching their stomachs as the laughter was hurting them.

"Shut up! F***ing shut up, you bas*a**s, it's not f***ing funny!" More hysterical laughter.

"It's not f***ing funny, this bas*a*d has pissed all over my sleeping bag and it's wet through, I can't use it anymore!" More laughter.

All this time, I was apologising to him and trying to explain what had happened. One has to think on reflection, most people, including me, would have gotten out of the bag and 'dropped' the offending wrongdoer, but he didn't. I wouldn't have blamed him if he had done. It just shows what a decent chap he was, not many would have taken it so well.

I had long forgotten this incident but was reminded of it 40 years on when I had a reunion with Geordie Hall from the Laarbruch times and apparently this went down in Sqn folklore history, to be talked about long after I had gone and de-mobbed (amongst other adventures of mine apparently). Trying to put a positive lean on it, I suppose we really are brothers now as he shares some of my DNA.

Living on my nerves; smoking and drinking

On one of the many Harrier exercises I did, maybe this 'incident' was on the last one? Anyway, by now hating every minute on 1 Sqn and having Hackett on my back daily, watching me to give him the chance of having me court-martialled. I was becoming more depressed and living on my nerves by the day. And it was turning me into a heavy smoker and drinker as I drank to cope.

Damage rifle

One day driving through the woods in a stripped-down Land Rover with Geordie Hall at the wheel, without thinking I laid my rifle against the side of the vehicle with the barrel protruding over the edge, as I was really peed off with everything. I was told by my DNA 'brother' Cpl Boyd to hold it and not lay it down, as I could damage it if it hit a tree. So I reluctantly picked it up and held it for a few minutes. Without realising it, after a few minutes I had laid it down again. When suddenly – bang! – what I'd been warned of happened! The Land Rover with Geordie Hall behind the wheel had driven close to a tree and the rifle barrel hit it and bent the barrel by some 35%. Had the Land Rover not been stripped down, the following would not have happened. My heart sank, I realised I was now really deep in the 'doo doo'. I felt the panic rise and duly got a rollicking for it. Of course, rock-apes being rock-apes, immediately saw the funny side. Sympathy for me? Nah, none of that sloppy sentimental stuff, here was a chance to have a real good piss take at my expense. And they were more than happy to do so. I had the 'mick' well and truly taken. At one point, before returning to base, we were doing a foot patrol in the woods in which the German civilians were walking and probably a few Russian agents also! Saw me with the bent barrel, they stood and stared, unsure they had seen what they thought they had seen. The mickey-taking continued.

"You'd better not let the Russians see it, John, they will think we have a new secret weapon – a rifle that can shoot around corners!" Cue laughter.

"Are Mein eyes deceiving me or ist diss a new secret veapon Der Englanders have invented?" More laughter.

"Probably at the end of the day, there will be an emergency meeting at the Kremlin as to what they were going to do with this new secret weapon the Englanders are testing!" The lads thought this hilarious – I didn't!

Probably the powers that be thought they could use this for propaganda purposes; let the Russians think we really did have a rifle that could shoot around corners. Maybe that was why I wasn't court-martialled? Though to this day, I don't know or remember how I got off with it so lightly. My fear was if Hackett got to hear of it, he wouldn't hesitate to have me court-martialled, it was a court martial offence. And I wouldn't be able to get away with it. I wouldn't have had a hope in hell to beat this rap. But luckily for me, he wasn't on this part of the exercise; as my father used to say: "The gods in Valhalla were smiling on me that day." Certainly, the 'big guy' upstairs was watching over me again.

I can't remember the punishment I received, so it can't have been severe. The outcome is lost in the mists of time.

Hackett was deprived of his victory that day!

According to Geordie, I was told to go into the tented area and hide myself away out of sight. After a while, I was bored with nothing to do so the Sgt told me to clean the rifle, whereupon I got the 'pull through' stuck in the barrel. It wouldn't budge. Something to do with the barrel being bent, I suppose! They wouldn't give me a rifle for the rest of the exercise; did they think I would bend that as well?

Helmut gets me drunk

The wife had a cousin married to a German, we found out that one of the exercises would take part not too far from his town, so they would find out where the exercise was taking place and come and visit me. This they did, whilst we were packing up at the end of the exercise, they came and saw the officer/NCO and I was allowed to go with them for the day back to their flat.

In the flat, Helmut offered me a beer. Taking it, I told him I could only drink one as I was driving back to camp, but he, as typical German, wouldn't/couldn't drink one beer so offered me another; I tried to refuse it but he was offended.

So not to cause bad 'Anglo-German' relations, I reluctantly accepted. Several more beers later, they drove me back to the campsite, by now I was well and truly sozzled. I was ordered to drive back to the Sqn, I tried to tell the officer I was not fit to drive, I was well over the limit, but he refused to listen.

"So on your head it is, if anything happens while I'm driving!" I told him and drive I did. After the previous debacle when they had tried to make me drive, had they not learned their lesson yet?

After we'd broken camp, my Land Rover was one of the last to leave the site; getting on the Autobahn, I took a wrong turning and was heading east towards Berlin! And not west as required. "Anyone ready to defect to the Russians?" I joked, "I am, I've bloody well had enough of 1 Sqn and I'm defecting. I'm going over the other side; I'm going to seek political asylum in Russia!" This immediately put the willy up the lads in the Land Rover, they actually thought I was serious and I had finally lost it! I had a little chuckle to myself, after all that I was put through by our officer Hackett and certain NCOs, the lads knew I was really pissed off with the R.A.F. and I was liable to do anything. "You're a bloody nutter," one called me, but then we all were a bit crazy.

The first chance I got, I came off the Autobahn and headed in the right direction, west, much to the unspoken relief of the chaps in the Land Rover. We passed the Sqn laid up in a lay-by and I could see the anger on the faces of the officers as I drove past. I cast him a nice smile and wave as if to say, "You didn't really think I was going to defect – did you?"

We got back to the Laarbruch unscathed but it seemed to me a very long drive and the guys in the back were nervous wrecks by the time we drove through the main gate. Back at camp, the officer tore a strip off me; he had actually thought I was going to defect. I think the lads told him I 'was' going to defect, but changed my mind at the last minute, typical thick 'Rupert'!

Weirdo's XXX collection

Just before I was sent back to UK on my re-pat, Cpl Geordie Weirdo had by now accumulated almost two suitcases of hard-core pornography and he had just been posted to Bruggen, Germany, where he would continue to add to his collection. I asked him what he was going to do with all these XXX films he had, he couldn't take them through customs; they'd throw the book at him for importing such things. "Oh, it's alright," he said. "I'll tell them they are for my own personal use!" We just laughed at him. He had told us before that he and his wife couldn't do anything unless they got in the mood by watching some films and he had used his 10-foot bullwhip on his wife.

Have to do a signal course

1 Sqn in all its infinite wisdom, or were they just coming it again? But I was at the point where I had less than three working weeks left to do on the Sqn before returning to UK on my re-pat do/resettlement course.

They told me one Friday, "John, by the way, you're on this signal course; the Sqn is starting on Monday!" I was flabbergasted, I went mad, I went to see various officers and NCOs about the stupidity of it, but it was to no avail, though as one NCO put it, "Don't worry about it; after all, if you're going to be demobbed then all you've got to do is pass the time on the course, you don't have to try to pass it, if as you say you're flying back four or five days later, just take it easy!" But that's not me, if I started something then regardless, I aimed to finish it, and this signal course was to be no different.

It was to be a two-week course, which we were told was the equivalent of the army's Royal Signal's six-week trade training course. When we finished the course, I was told by not only Geordie the Weirdo Cpl and the signal's officer that no one thought for a moment that I would take much interest and certainly not enough to pass, which I did, not only for my own satisfaction but to 'cock a snoot' at the Sqn who had written me off before I had started.

We only had one chap who failed, a coloured chap. As my mate said, "Well, now that you have passed this course, you can go for a job with B.T.'s forerunner. You can lay 'Don 10' cable, tune in a radio set and send Morse code!"

J: "Yeah, and who the hell uses them nowadays?"

Flt fund

During one's stay on 'C' Flt, we all contributed money each week to the Flt fund, this fund was being run by the Flt Sergeant Houseman, the guy who was trying to sell insurance policies to newcomers, he had been posted a few weeks before and when one of my mates happened to mention to Jack the tankard we had all saved up for was due to me as I was the next to leave, Jack checked and there was no trace of any money or books confirming the same. So Hackett delighted in saying, "Oh well, in that case, you won't be getting a tankard when you leave, Rowbottom!" This was said with undoubtedly much relish, sarcasm and joy, but I wasn't having any of it. After all this time, they still didn't know what kind of person they were dealing with; I never gave up without a fight! I told him, "I paid for one tankard and when I leave, I shall expect one tankard, whether you like it or not, sir!"

Almost getting done out of my Tankard

Hackett wouldn't give in and stormed off, Jack then said to me, "Don't worry, John, I'll get your tankard for you, you've paid for it, and because that Houseman seems to have gone and no one knows where the money went, it does not seem right that you should lose out. Funny, why is it you that has to suffer again and it's ironic that it is you who just happened to be leaving first!"

Jack told me when I met up with him many years later in Thailand that whenever there was a meeting/briefing between Hackett, the SNCOs and Jack, Hackett always brought my name up condemning me at every opportunity. Jack was true to his word and although it took him a week to work on Hackett, he did get some money out of him and the Sqn fund and I did get my tankard when I left.

I received my tankard during a presentation from Hackett, thanks to the efforts of my mate, Jack (John) Skuse the Sgt. It really must have hurt Hackett very much having to get up and give a speech in front of the whole flight, saying how sorry he would be to see me go and he thought I was a good worker (as was traditional). Hypocrite! And his speech was over in a matter of seconds and he was definitely embarrassed to have to present me my tankard. This was done in the Naafi during my re-pat do and I was supposed to pay for the drinks but because of this carry on with the pay office deducting my wages, Jack arranged to have Hackett pay for it from the flight funds.

When I had to get up and give my speech, I thanked the chaps for their friendship, and then I had a go at sarcastically insulting Hackett! He left soon after. Again, the chaps said to me straight after he'd gone, "Hey John, you said all along you were going to have a go at him and stick the knife in on your re-pat do, we never thought you'd do it!" Again, after two and a half years, had they not learned anything about me? When I said I was going to do something, I did it!

Last man standing

The tradition was making the leaver drink a pint of his favourite spirit – neat and in one – and see how long he could remain sober and awake before collapsing. I chose gin knowing that I was fine with that and drank it down in one, as required and yet not only did I remain on my feet and conscious, but at the end of the night was the only one to leave sober! I had to help the other married men home.

This was not supposed to be the case, I was supposed to collapse but won the admiration of everyone, Hackett including, so I heard, a bit late for that now – that I could take my drink.

Once I got home, I headed for the cellar where I had prepared my sleeping bag and bed just in case I was ill (I wasn't). But Viola had the hose ready to give me the once-over if I was worse the wear for drink. She had used it before on occasions.

Re-pat to De-mob: 12 August 1976

2 July 1976: Starting prep for home

I started preparations for going home due to instructions from the Cpl in general office who had told me, "You can leave for UK as soon as it's convenient and arranged." I reported to the Sqn what I had been told.

The standard procedure was to hand over the Qtr, go on leave, return to UK, embarkation leave, report to R.A.F. Innsworth to finalise and clear up the paperwork, hand in my ID card (paperwork and official discharge), start resettlement course and termination leave. I had put in the request six weeks before; I had to chase them up for an answer. Finally, they said yes two weeks before I was due to fly out. So I said to the Flt/Sergeant, "With your permission, I will book a date for marching out of my quarter." He said that would be fine. Then a few days before I was due to march out, he cancelled it saying that he didn't know anything about it. Hackett interfering!

I told them that I was going on leave! Cleared from the Sqn, then handed over my M.Q. and moved back to UK during my leave. This they denied saying that I had told them that only my wife was going home. I said to them, "Why on earth would I send my wife home before me!" Eventually, general office told me to pass a message on to the Sqn that it was arranged when I was to clear from the Sqn and fly out, but when it came down to it, they denied it. Of course, Hackett and his cronies thought that I was trying to put it on again, which of course I wasn't.

Hackett tries to dictate where we were to sleep

Then I lost my leave because it was claimed that I had filled in my leave application form wrong. Hackett kept saying, "I will not be dictated to by an S.A.C.!" I wasn't trying to dictate anything, just pass the message on and do what I should have done. Not to mention that I was constantly being called a liar and that angered me. When I was finally told that I could have my leave, I was told that I would not leave for UK until 12 August 1976, and that my effective date of posting was 15 August. I pointed this out to the general office that it posed problems and clashed with my leave. They hadn't noticed the problem and so a Cpl on 'movements section' phoned up Hackett and told him I had to clear a day earlier, and by all accounts he agreed (what a surprise). So the now agreed upon dates were as follows: march out on 11th and fly on 12th.

The Cpl said on the phone to Hackett, "In that case, where are he and his wife going to stay the last night in Germany as they will have handed their Qtr over already? Several friends have offered to put them up for the night!"

So not to be outdone or have the initiative taken from him, Hackett said, "No, They will not! I will fix them up somewhere, where they will stay that night!" I knew then that to rely on him would mean that he would either deliberately mess it up or forget about us deliberately! So we would be without anywhere to stay. As it happened, I wasn't going to have anybody, especially him, dictate to me where I and my wife could or could not sleep! So I ignored him and slept at Stan and Katie's as previously arranged.

2 July: Day off, Viola finished work.

6 July: Last charge in the R.A.F. or so I thought (charged for being sick), got it admonished at a later date.

7 July: Another station exercise – my last.

21 July: Finished on 1 Sqn.

28 July: Won my case about being charged.

Finally, once and for all, finished from 1 Sqn. Hooray and rejoice! This was without doubt the happiest day in my time whilst in Germany; I couldn't believe that this wonderful day had finally arrived. After all I'd been through, what made me mad was that Hackett had no jurisdiction over me as I was now off strength and on station strength. As far as I was concerned, nobody, no officer or otherwise would dictate to me where I could/could not sleep with my wife! I know the services, they own you mind, body and soul, but that was just taking it too far…

As it was, my wife, mother and father were very, very upset at the treatment I had received whilst on 1 Sqn, especially this last incident. I do believe that I was very near cracking and retaliating physically. Had I have been there a few more weeks, I would have!

1 Aug: Got in free to camp cinema because we were late, waiting for my mate, Geordie.

Pay accounts

6 Aug: Have to go to pay accounts, they said I still owed the R.A.F. £40. After ringing Dad at home in UK, he rang up the station commander who reduced it by £50 to be written off, which then put me £10 in credit for the first time in months.

Yet when I got back to the Sqn, the bar-stewards started accusing me of skiving.

Going to Goch

7 Aug: Going to Goch to have a last look around, had lunch there and on our return, started cleaning the M.Q. out.

9 Aug: Cleared from the Sqn completely (on paper), drew my last 10 marks from the bank.

Cleaning the M.Q.

11 Aug: Handed over M.Q. The families officer came in to inspect the Qtr and was wearing white gloves; she started by running her gloved hand over various surfaces, then examining her gloves and seeing no dust/dirt, smiled and removed her gloves and checked no more. And unlike most of the other chaps on the Sqn who marched out, we didn't have anything to pay in charges. You were allowed a set percentage in normal breakages per month such as the odd broken glass, cup and such, so my charges were well within these allowances.

We said our goodbyes to our friends in Germany, Helmut Schultz, our former landlord and friend, who gave us a crate of quality German wines.

When finally clearing from 1 Sqn, Sgt Smith saw me but didn't even say goodbye, I was disgusted. I had known him since 37 Sqn. Hackett's influence, no doubt!

Clearing out from the Sqn

In the C.O.'s office, the C.O. said – and I'll never forget it! "Well, Rowbottom, enjoy your terminal leave and we'll see you in the C.I.O. (Career's Information Office) in a month, then the Sqn a few weeks later!" Was he being sarcastic? Or was he under the impression I would want to put myself through all that hassle again?

I laughed and said, "No sir, I doubt that very much, very much indeed!"

C.O.: "Oh, I think we will!"

J (through gritted teeth): "Oh no, sir, you won't!" And with that I saluted, turned and marched out of his office.

Hackett's hate campaign

When I cleared from the flight office, Hackett had mysteriously disappeared and was not available to sign my papers as he should have been and to 'formally' say goodbye. I know he was around because I had seen him earlier; he stayed out of sight until I had left the Sqn for the last time, then he went back to his office. (This I was told by a friend on the Sqn later.) He did all he could to avoid having to shake me by the hand; he couldn't face me man to man! He knew I would say my piece and he wasn't prepared for it and couldn't handle the truth. Still, it suited me. I didn't want to see him again, but on reflection was he frightened or was it meant as a final insult? The former, I believe! No more Hackett, I couldn't believe my luck! Now I could start to live again.

How can I analyse why Hackett seemed hell-bent on bringing me down? Making it woefully obvious he had it in for me and his NCOs also. And not caring who saw or knew.

Later thoughts made me think of or compare him to an old grizzly lion, fearing his days as the Alpha male of the pride was in jeopardy, unsure or insecure of his position against the one he deemed a threat and he lashed out. Was that the case with me? What had he to fear from me?

Maybe it was because of my self-confidence, I knew my job and knew it well, unlike most of the chaps on the flight who were mostly younger than me and with a lot less service in, and maybe I had stood out! I was always ready to help others, give them advice when asked for it. And I knew how the system worked, i.e., the tried and trusted methods adopted.

All I wanted was to be left alone to get on with the job I loved and have a quiet life! Now with this harassment and aggravation, I couldn't wait to get out and be a civvy again.

Prior to the start of his virulent hate campaign against me, when I had arrived in Germany, I had considered signing on for the full term, 22 years. Now I felt it was like being in prison, I was counting the weeks/days to my release, after one's term/contract has come to an end, as in my case had.

All these years, I believed it was only me who had incurred his wrath! How wrong was I! For, many years later, I was to find out that my replacement, an S.A.C. Walk who was posted in shortly after I had left, was also subjected to Hackett's hate campaign. Part two! It appeared he carried on with Walk where he had left off with me. He became Hackett's new 'whipping boy'.

There must be clearly something wrong with this man. If he behaved in civvy street like he did on 1 Squadron, he wouldn't last 5 minutes. If I am ever in the position to look him in the eye in the future, I would like to ask him just one question, "Why?"

Flying out & reporting to Innsworth

12 Aug: Flying back to UK and reported to R.A.F. Innsworth, when I walked out of the gates at Innsworth, I realised that this was the last time I would be walking out of a R.A.F. camp, it was, I also realised, the end of an era, the end of a major part of my life, that would have a telling effect for the rest of my life. I was about embark on another, so despite some of the good and bad times, I was sad to finally 'cut the umbilical cord', but cut it I had to.

Resettlement course (Welding)

16 Aug: Started the resettlement course. I chose welding while in Germany as I figured that it would be handy in civvy street in case I were ever to go on the steel works, which I tried to avoid at all costs.

I stuck this welding course for one day, found out it was quite dangerous and that was just the storing of the cylinders. I decided that it wasn't really the course that I wanted to do, and it was due to get even more hazardous (such as the breathing of the fumes and the damage to the eyes with the intense light).

So I asked for another course that was on offer. I saw a good course that would prove very handy and that was 'home repairs and alternatives'. I noticed the lowest ranks on the course were R.A.F. Sqn leader, RN Admiral, Army-General, so I thought I'd get on that course, after all, the college principal had said at the start, "We're all one step away from being civilians and so to get us ready for civvy street, there will be no rank here, we're all the same!"

Officers' course (R.H.I.P.)

Bearing that in mind, I applied for the 'home repairs' course and as expected, permission was refused on the grounds that there were no vacancies. I didn't believe it for a minute and I, true to form, told them so and that it was a case of still R.H.I.P. (rank has its privileges). It was denied of course and was suggested to me to try for another course, this I had to do and finally settled for painting and decorating. This has proven of great use in looking after my house, so they (the powers that be) still tried to 'turn the screws'.

I started terminal leave on 19 August.

Declared a civilian

17 Oct: Officially declared a civilian, which felt strange and took some getting used to. I fixed myself up with a job by phone (plastering).

18 Oct: Started new job.

19 Nov: Bought my first car since returning home (Ford Cortina).

29 Nov: Started at the steel works (unfortunately); first pay £55:20.

My first complete wage was £76.80 (in R.A.F. about £40/45). After I had finally finished with the R.A.F., I said to Viola, "That's it, I'm finished with the military, and you won't get me in anything green again! Let alone a military uniform!" But I did try and join up again, but was told there were no vacancies, this I didn't believe! I am sure that Hackett and Houseman had put something on my records to prevent me rejoining. Little did I know that in less than three years, I was to be in uniform again, this time in the Territorial Army but as they say, "That is another story, and another book!"

*****

Finally

My first steps into civilian life were not as I had hoped. I was not popular with the other civilian 'workers'; I still adopted the 'muck in and help each other' attitude, but was viewed as something strange – they didn't know how to handle me. They were not used to straight talking and the truth terrified them. I soon became aware of what they felt comfortable with: stabbing people in the back, gossiping, creeping to management and tittle-tattling. All very strange and alien to me and against the very grain of what I had become used to in the forces. I had grown accustomed to people saying to your face if they had a problem – and not going behind your back. Though I doubt I was the first or the last ex-serviceman to be put through this treatment.

This I put down to them not understanding the military mind-set, which made it harder for veterans to 'blend in and adapt' on our discharge.

They didn't want to, or refused to, understand how going through hardships together, the good times and bad, standing by each other – no matter what! created a bond in which you trusted each other. True friendship.

Living for weeks in a cold, wet and muddy hole, going hungry, without sleep, your clothes getting soaking wet and drying out on your back. Unable to wash or change into clean clothes, giving your mate your last cigarette, because his need is greater than yours, standing him his beer all night because he was hard up and not expecting anything in return.

But those who served and swore allegiance to Her Majesty the Queen, those who wore the uniform – THEY WILL UNDERSTAND.

Some Service Terms

GENERAL ABBREVIATIONS

M.O.D.	Ministry of Defence.
R.U.C.	Royal Ulster Constabulary (of Northern Ireland).
W.R.A.C.	Women's Royal Army Corps (now disbanded: women are in with the men).
W.R.N.S. (Wrens)	Women's Royal Naval Service: same principle to the W.R.A.C. and the W.R.A.F.
W.R.A.F./W.A.A.F's	Women's Royal Air Force: as the previous two.
Square bashing	Basic Military Drill/marching.
U/S	Unserviceable – doesn't work.
M.T.	Motor Transport Section: maintains vehicles ready to issue to Departments/Sections/individuals.
M.T.S.S.	Motor Transport Servicing Section: where all the Stations Vehicles are serviced and repaired.
L/R's – Lannies	Land Rovers: general runabout transport {Similar principle to the American Jeep).
C.O.	Commanding Officer.
O.C.	Officer Commanding i.e. small unit of 3O+ men.
I/C	In command: – or in charge of smaller group.
O.O-Ord Off	Duty 'Orderly Officer'.
O/S-Ord/Sgt	Duty 'Orderly Sergeant'.
O/Cpl	Duty 'Orderly Corporal.
S.W.O.	Station Warrant Officer: usually only answerable to the Station Commander.
P.T.I.	Physical Training Instructor.
D.I.	Drill Instructor: OR Daily Inspection of vehicle i.e. fuel, oil, water, tyres.
M.O.	Medical Officer: (Military Doctor).

S.H.Q.	Station Head Quarters.
G.D.O.C.	Ground Defence Operational Cell: Generally in reference to R.A.F. regiment.
A.W.O.L.	Absence without leave.
Glass house	Generally in reference to Military prison but also local Guard room.
F.P.	Fire Piquet – Fire Piquet Duty: to watch for fires, report, and attempt to put out.
M.Q.'s	Officers Married Quarters.
A.M.Q.'s or M.Q.'s	Airmen's (and N.C.O. 's) Married Quarters.
N.A.A.F.I.	'Navy Army Air Force Institute': Provide shops, Bars, indoor sports, (i.e. Darts/Billiards/Snooker, canteen facilities live entertainment, Disco's etc.
Y.M.C.A.	Young Men's Christian Association: provide same as naafi but to a better standard and are usually preferred, also accommodation.
R.T.U.	Return to Unit: After exercise, leave, Course.
R&R	Rest and Recuperation/relaxation: usually after/ during a tour or on active service.
Comm's	Communications.
R.V.	Rendezvous: or meet up point.
Restrictions 'Jankers'	Restrictions of Privileges: If charged and you get 7/14/21 days 'Jankers' after the normal working day one has to report to the guard room at 18:00 hrs (6 p.m.) for two hours work then at 22:00 (10 p.m) in your best uniform/boots for inspection. If OK, that is the end for the night, if you fail the inspection you have to turn up hourly until you pass. And you are not allowed alcohol or to leave camp until dismissed.
Recce	Ground reconnaissance patrol or flight by Aircraft.
N.B.C.	Nuclear, Chemical and Biological: warfare /kit/ Training.
O.C.U.	Operational Conversion Unit: Usually for training aircrew on a new type of aircraft they have not used before.
A.T.C.	Air Traffic Control: OR: Air Training Corps, Boys-young men with an interest in flying/aircraft who hope one day to join the R.A.F.

L.F.O.	Light Fighting Order: minimum webbing/equipment required on 'Reece' patrol, i.e. ammunition pouches, water bottle, emergency rations, maps/compass.
A.A. Guns	Anti Aircraft Guns.
Jennie	Slang for Generator, used to power the A.A. guns.
L.L.A.D	Low Level Air Defence: Guns or Missiles.
Re-mustered	Change trades.
Erks	Low ranking Airmen.
Shineys	Non R.A.F. Regiment trades: usually clerks and office people.
Penguins/Guins	The general term used for non-regiment personnel trades.

RANK ABBREVIATIONS

Army

R.C.T.	Royal Corps of Transport (renamed from the W.W.2 Royal Service Corps).
Private/Driver.	
L/Cpl	Lance Corporal.
Cpl	Corporal.
Sgt	Sergeant.
S/Sgt	Staff Sergeant.
W.O. 2	Warrant Officer class 2.
W.O. 1	Warrant Officer Class 1 (More usually referred to as the R.S.M.).
R.S.M.	Regimental Sergeant Major.

Officers

2nd Lt	Second lieutenant.
Lt	Lieutenant.
Capt	Captain.

R.A.F.

A.C.	Aircraftman.
L.A.C.	Leading Aircraftsman.
S.A.C.	Senior Aircraftsman.
J.T.	Junior Technician (Tech Trades).
L/Cpl	Lance Corporal (R.A.F. Regiment only).
Cpl	Corporal.
Sgt	Sergeant.
F/Sgt	Flight Sergeant-non Tech trades.
F/Sgt	(Tech Trades).
C.T.	Chief Technician (Tech Trades).
S.W.O.2	Sqn Warrant Officer class 2 i.e. on Sqn / Department level.
S.W.O.1	Station Warrant Officer equivalent to Army R.S.M. Officers.
P.O.	Pilot Officer.
F.O.	Flying Officer.
F/Lt – Flt Lt	Flight Lieutenant.
S/Ldr – Sqn Ldr	Squadron Leader.
W.C. – Wg Cmdr	Wing Commander.
G.C. – Grp Cpt	Group Captain.
A.O.C.	Air Officer Commanding.

Note

Both in the Army and R.A.F., L/Cpls and Cpls are referred to as J.N.C.O.'s = Junior Non Commissioned Officers. Sgts up to W.O. ranks are referred to as S.N.C.O.'s =Senior Non Commissioned Officers.

NICKNAMES

'Zob'/'Rupert'	Derogatory terms for officers used in both the Army and R.A.F. by all other ranks (including N.C.O.'s), when they become frustrated at the officers' incompetence or arrogance. One example would be when officers have to read a map or use a compass, as they are traditionally useless at this and tend to rely on others to do it for them. Hence the term: "Ruddy typical Zob!".

WEAPONS

T.O.E.T.'s	'Tests of elementary training' on weapon handling. One must pass all tests to show you can handle the weapon/s safely and confidently. To fail, recruit/solder/airman will not be allowed to fire weapon/s until proved fit and able.
.303	Calibre, Lee Enfield Rifle used in W.W.2 (replaced by S.L.R.).
9m/m	Browning side arm pistol issued by certain ranks, or depending on operation/mission.
S.L.R.	Self Loading Rifle – General issue to Soldiers/Airmen.
L.M.G. /Bren	Magazine-fed 'Light Machine gun' derived from the W.W. 2 Bren, adapted to fire the N.A.T.O. issued 7.62 Ammunition from the .303.
G.P.M.G. (GYMPY)	General Purpose Machine Gun. or 'Gimpy' Replaced the L.M.G.: more power, greater range – belt-fed.
36 m/m Mill's	Hand Grenade. I would envisage it will be withdrawn from service by now.
Thunder Flash	Used for training purposes, simulates mortar fire and Hand Grenades.
P.I.A.T.	Platoon Infantry Anti Tank – Though a W.W. 2 weapon can be used to identify any Infantry anti-tank weapon.
INERGA	Rifle launched anti-Tank weapon – now withdrawn.
T.P.T.P.	'Target Practice Target Projectile' in Rifle type round for practising with the 84 m/m (Carl Gustav) H.e.a.t. rounds which are very expensive in comparison.
Carl Gustav 84 m/m	Affectionately known as the "Charlie 'G" anti-tank weapon.
'66'	66 m/m American made anti-Tank/Personnel/Bunker busting weapon.
H.E.	High Explosive/s.
H.E.A.T.	High Explosive Anti tank projectile/Round.

In Memoriam

Remembering two former girlfriends: Kara and Sara, thanks for the memories. Remembered with affection.

David Stubley. Passed away 1985. Thank you for your friendship and memories. I am sorry we never got the chance to meet up again. Or the chance to say a final goodbye.

Epitaph for Sgt 'Tug' Wilson

I came to hear on the 'Regiment' social media site that my former Sgt (eventually reaching the rank of F/Sgt) 'Tug' Wilson had just passed away. He was my 'C' Flt Sgt on 37 and 1 Sqn.

I was an 'old hand' in my mid 20s with several years' experience under my belt. So 'Tug' didn't have much to do with me, we barely spoke.

To finish on a positive note, It was 'Tug' who was indirectly responsible for me making up my mind for a posting to Odiham where I met my wife to be.

Rest in peace old soldier, duty done!